American and Chinese Perceptions and Belief Systems

A People's Republic of China–Taiwanese Comparison

COGNITION AND LANGUAGE

A Series in Psycholinguistics • Series Editor: R. W. RIEBER

A Continuation Order Plan is available for this series. A continuation order will bring delivery of each new volume immediately upon publication. Volumes are billed only upon actual shipment. For further information please contact the publisher.

American and Chinese Perceptions and Belief Systems

A People's Republic of China–Taiwanese Comparison

Lorand B. Szalay and
Jean B. Strohl
Institute of Comparative Social and Cultural Studies, Inc.
Chevy Chase, Maryland

Liu Fu
North East University
Shenyang, China

and

Pen-Shui Lao
Kaohsiung Normal University
Kaohsiung, Taiwan

Plenum Press • New York and London

Library of Congress Cataloging-in-Publication Data

On file

ISBN 0-306-44980-3

© 1994 Plenum Press, New York
A Division of Plenum Publishing Corporation
233 Spring Street, New York, N. Y. 10013

Printed in the United States of America

AMERICAN AND CHINESE PERCEPTIONS AND BELIEF SYSTEMS
A PRC-TAIWANESE COMPARISON

Preface

The findings presented here were drawn from an in-depth study of comparable college student samples (n = 100) tested in Shenyang (PRC), Taiwan, and Washington, D.C. The data were obtained through an analytic technique called the Associative Group Analysis (AGA) method. Unlike traditional surveys, views and beliefs are reconstructed from the distribution of hundreds of thousands of spontaneous reactions to strategically selected issues and themes as elicited from respondents in their native language. A computer-assisted analysis of this data base makes it possible to reconstruct people's belief systems and subjective representation of their world.

Based on a comparative analysis of Chinese and American student samples, this volume presents findings on the contemporary views and values developed in three different socio-political settings: (a) the post modern, industrial environment of the U.S.; (b) the planned and controlled socialistic environment of the PRC; and (c) the fast developing free market environment of Taiwan. The results reveal previously uncharted dimensions of cultural similarities and differences and show the effects of different economic and social systems on people's views of the self and world.

This volume, which is the second in a series to come out of research conducted in the late eighties, encompasses the domains of Family, National Images, Religion, Economy, and Education. The results are summarized in bar graphs showing the main components of American and Chinese perceptions and evaluations of the key issues studied. At a higher level the analysis shows trends of perceptions and value orientations observed across related themes. For example, results on specific themes such as family, mother, and father reveal some consistent trends applicable to the whole domain of family relations (e.g., an American focus on love based personal ties, on individual roles, on husband-wife relationship; and a Chinese emphasis on social qualities of kindness, affection, and respect, on the parent-child relationship, etc.)

The analysis shows overall similarities and differences between the American, PRC, and Taiwanese culture groups on specific issues, on particular domains, and across their frames of reference in general. The results offer new insights into the scope and nature of both cultural and ideological influences. This volume, along with the previous one based on comparisons of American, PRC, and Hong Kong students, provides rich resource material for integrating culture and language in education, intercultural communication, and language and area training.

ACKNOWLEDGMENTS

The authors wish to express their personal appreciation and gratitude to the Department of Education, Language and Area Studies Research Program and to our Project Monitor Jose Martinez for sponsoring this comparative study of American and Chinese perceptions and belief systems.

The research involved the cooperation of scholars representing various fields of social and behavioral sciences from the People's Republic of China, the Republic of Taiwan, Republic of China, Hong Kong, and the United States.

Dr. Andres Inn from the Chinese University of Hong Kong organized the data collection efforts in Hong Kong and China and developed software for this research effort. Dr. Irene Chow collected all Hong Kong data and assisted in the data collection efforts in Shenyang. Dr. Liu Fu, head of the Department of Management at the Northeast University of Technology, provided subjects for the research and Dr. Chow collected the data in Shenyang. Mr. Sun MingHe translated the Chinese ideographs to English and performed the initial data analyses by collapsing responses across subjects. Mr. Sun spent many months of full time effort to complete this phase for both the Hong Kong and Shenyang samples.

The data collection in Taipei was organized by Professor Carl P. Epstein from University of Soochow; he provided valuable help without accepting any remuneration. The data collection in Taipei was performed by Dr. Epstein in cooperation with Dr. Pen-Shui Liao, formerly of Soochow University (now at Kaohsiung Normal University), and Dr. Emery Zsoldosh from Fu Jen University. We also received help from Professor Der-heuy Yee from National Taiwan University. Most of the extensive data organization in Chinese and the translation of the extensive response material was performed by Ms. Ming Foung Hsu and Professor Liao at Soochow University. They performed this time-consuming task with high accuracy and with motivation.

In Washington, D.C., Jean Bryson Strohl completed the data analysis, presentation of results on the groups tested, and comparative interpretation of the results. Mr. John Dombrowski, Ms. Shelley Vilov, and Ms. Heather Bent also contributed to the analysis and interpretation of results. We appreciate the diligence and youthful energy of our student assistant Giovanni Galvez in finalizing the manuscript.

Dr. Lorand B. Szalay, the Principal Investigator and Director of the Institute of Comparative Social and Cultural Studies, organized and implemented the project through its main phases from development to completion.

The project was delayed in its completion due to the repeated medical problems of key participants. The authors want to express their sincere thanks for all the participants, identified and anonymous. They express their sincere gratitude to Mr. Jose Martinez for his help and understanding in coping with the various problems encountered.

The work upon which this publication is based was performed pursuant to Grant No. G00844054 with the U.S. Department of Education. However, the opinions expressed herein do not necessarily reflect the position or policy of the Department of Education, and no official endorsement by the Department of Education should be inferred.

CONTENTS

Chapter 1

PSYCHO-CULTURAL FACTORS IN COMMUNICATION

Americans accept cultural diversity in principle. They are also fully committed to the ideals of democratic pluralism. Practically, however, living these principles is hampered by the lack of information necessary to recognize the views and values of other cultures. Differing views and values are what result in different approaches to human problems, in a different common sense.

Although people with different cultural frames of reference frequently share some of the same concerns about common human problems such as health or education, they often approach them quite differently. No matter what a particular program targets -- whether it involves health care, primary education, drug counseling, or job training -- its success probably depends more on people's perceptions of the program than on the actual services it offers.

Foster (1969) emphasized the need to acquire deeper understanding of culture and its influence on human behavior in preparing Americans for overseas assignments. Far more significant than the obvious differences in dress, food, and forms of greeting are the more subtle and commonly shared attitudes, values, assumptions, and styles of thinking that become part of every person as he grows up in his social environment. Because they are so much a part of him, he has little reason to question them or to be conscious of how much they determine his behavior.

Research on the Relationship Between Culture and Behavior

Hall (1959) labelled culture the hidden dimension, which "hides most effectively from its own participants." Anthropologists study culture by living within them and observing their daily life over time. Psychologists such as Charles Osgood, George Miller, and Harry Triandis, study culture by developing methods which allow the reconstruction of their subjective meanings, their systems of subjective views or representation of the world. Political scientists study culture and the influence of political beliefs and ideologies by using methods designed to reconstruct people's political images and opinions.

The literature on foreign cultures is rich in conflicting views and observations. Most sources are descriptive, and it is difficult to separate what is valid and timely from the more subjective and speculative accounts. This is particularly true about information on the People's Republic of China because the PRC has not been accessible to field research for the past several decades.

The available foreign area information usually describes people and lands from the perspective of an outside observer. While this is useful in many ways, it reveals little about the actual frame of reference of a particular culture group. For example, it would be difficult to find answers to such questions as: To what extent do PRC Chinese think in Marxist terms or in Confucian terms about their past and future, about ancestors and education? The scarcity of such information is a serious problem for international education, culturally oriented foreign language instruction, and practically all dimensions of the cross-cultural training process.

The approach used in the present study of American and Chinese cultures is multidisciplinary and is founded on the assumption that differences in behavior derive from different reality constructs, different systems of views and beliefs embedded in the culture. The culturally characteristic system can be reconstructed faithfully and parsimoniously from the subjective meanings of the key ideas or themes which the people use to identify, understand, and deal with their social, economic, and interpersonal problems of life.

Margaret Mead (1951) placed the problem of culture into global perspectives when she said:

> *A primary task of mid-twentieth century is the increasing of understanding, understanding of our own culture and of that of other countries. On our capacity to develop new forms of such understanding may well depend the survival of our civilization, which has placed its faith in science and reason but has not yet succeeded in developing a science of human behavior which gives men a decent measure of control over their fate.*

Problems of Language and Culture in Communication

Effective rapport and communication with the native speaker of a particular language requires not only familiarity with the language but also familiarity with the native speaker's images and meanings which follow from his cultural frame of reference. The main practical problem with cultural images and meanings is that they are hidden and there is a strong natural tendency to overlook this dimension. As the first volume in this series has shown, the American-Chinese differences in cultural meanings are substantive. The Hong Kong-PRC Chinese differences were similarly great and reveal how different life conditions influence the students' views and ways of thinking. The Taiwan-PRC Chinese differences could also be expected. These differences reflect contemporary trends shaping people's cultural frame of reference.

The in-depth comparative study of Taiwanese, PRC Chinese, and U.S. American students was sponsored by the Language and Area Studies Research program of the U.S. Department of Education. The research pursued four major objectives:

1. Generate timely knowledge of Chinese cultural images, meanings, and frame of reference

2. Assess the scope and nature of psychocultural differences between American and Chinese population samples

2

3. Examine how the economic, social, and political systems of the three different Chinese populations affect their images, meanings, and cultural frame of reference

4. Develop educational resource material to supplement traditional instructional materials for use in foreign language instruction, TESOL, ESOL, bilingual-bicultural teacher education, and international studies.

This volume and the previous one present the views and values of American and Chinese culture groups and were designed to promote mutual understanding between these countries and populations. The communication lexicon is designed to serve as a tool of international education and intercultural communication by making the hidden psychological reality of culture accessible, identifiable, and teachable.

By showing how particular culture groups vary in their perceptions and evaluations of dominant themes and issues, the lexicon informs on the subjective perceptual and motivational trends which are characteristically evasive to empirical assessment. By identifying consistent perceptual and motivational trends across broad domains of perceptual-semantic representations, the lexicon informs about the culturally dominant psychological dispositions. It promotes the understanding of culture as a framework of psychological organization which predisposes what people see, how they see it, and what they are likely to do.

In this volume we present comparative findings on PRC Chinese, Taiwanese, and American student images, meanings, and broader perceptual and motivational dispositions which are likely to influence communication and other types of behavior as well as international relations and cooperation between the American and Chinese people.

The Chinese Setting

China has, for the past four millennia, had not only what is arguably the world's most successful continuous culture, but has also, in recent decades, experienced some of the most radical social experiments ever imposed on a large population. Continuity and change are perhaps the most dominant themes for the Chinese in the twentieth century. For the past four decades the history of the populations of the People's Republic on the mainland, on the island of Taiwan, and in the enclave of Hong Kong has gone in radically different directions, producing highly divergent subjective worlds. This gives scientists, philosophers, and others a remarkable opportunity to weigh the effects of factors such as a government-imposed ideology, a rapid rise in wealth, and the influence of foreign ideas, music, films, and TV programs in creating divergent values and outlooks in what was a fairly homogeneous culture only five decades ago.

In mainland China about four-fifth of the population lives near subsistence level in primitive villages located on unpaved roads, in crude houses without plumbing or other amenities of modern life. In rural areas men and women work ten to twelve hours a day at their job and women work an additional four to six hours in the home. In urban areas (from which virtually all of the college students come), there are scarcities of almost everything, by Western standards, but especially of jobs for young people and apartment space for everyone. Salaries are usually less than a hundred Yuan per month for the vast majority of the population. (A Yuan might purchase roughly as much as a dollar in terms of locally produced necessities.)

3

Urban life in Hong Kong and in Taiwan, in relation to material well-being, is very similar to that in prosperous urban areas in Western Europe and the U.S., the main difference being that the rise in living standards has, over the past four decades, been far more rapid in Hong Kong and Taiwan. Taiwan differs from Hong Kong mainly in having much more rural terrain, occupied by very efficient and prosperous small family farms (not greatly different technologically from those in Japan), and in being much more open to many Western influences. Hong Kong, on the other hand, places great stress on preserving Chinese customs and Confucian beliefs and observances.

According to various authors, all three Chinese societies are conservative, but in different respects. The Taiwanese have preserved Chinese art, literature, philosophy, music, and architecture, especially temples; and some folk customs, as for example those related to village marriages. The Hong Kong Chinese have placed a great stress on preserving Confucian norms of behavior, beliefs, ceremonies, and relationships, especially in the family. On the mainland, what has been preserved is basically the peasant farmers' time-honored defense mechanism in dealing with adversity by greater family cohesiveness and cooperation. This applies whether the adversity comes from the elements (floods, drought, earthquakes, famines, etc.) or from government policies and bureaucratic demands.

The present findings are based on samples of university students. These samples are genuine representatives of Chinese children - they are all typical students who were born and raised in their respective countries and who went through essentially the same experiences as their contemporaries. While the research method offers insights of depth, the small size of the samples (n = 100) and the circumstance that they represent a special population has to be considered before drawing broad generalizations.

The Study - Sampling and Data Collection

University students in the United States, Taiwan, and the People's Republic of China participated in the study between 1985 and 1989. The American students were tested in the Washington, D.C., metropolitan area at the University of Maryland and the American University; the PRC students were tested in Shenyang (PRC) at the Northeast Institute of Technology; and the Taiwanese students were tested in Taipei at Soochow University the National Taiwan University. In the selection of the samples, comparability was the single most important criterion. The samples each included 100 students and were comparable in regard to age and gender (equal split of males and females). The students all were at the undergraduate level in a variety of major fields of study.

There are naturally wide regional, social class, and ethnic variations both among people in the United States and among people in Taiwan and the People's Republic of China. One hundred students tested in the capital city cannot be considered statistically representative of the entire population when considering the distribution of attitudes. Our in-depth findings -- e.g., on the effects of the Communist system on religious thinking --are nonetheless new and conclusive. The focus here is on the views and values as shaped by common cultural background and life conditions. As our past studies show, the question of how much intrasocial and regional variations exist in cultural images and meanings within large countries is usually one to be systematically examined in a second phase of research, involving cooperation of a team of foreign scholars.

The data collection was organized in Taiwan by Dr. Carl Epstein and Professor Pen Shui Liao. In the Shenyang data collection Professor Liu Fu worked in cooperation with Dr. Andres Inn and Professor Sun Ming He. In the United States the work was organized by Lorand B. Szalay and performed by a team of researchers from the Institute of Comparative Social and Cultural Studies (ICS) in Washington, D.C.

The testing involved written spontaneous associations to 120 stimulus themes in the student's native language, using the Associative Group Analysis method described briefly here and in more detail in the appendix.

The Method: Associative Group Analysis

The AGA method relies on a series of continued time-limited association tasks which are administered in the native language of the group tested. In group sessions the respondents are asked to write down, in response to each selected stimulus word, as many words as they can think of in one minute (see Appendix, p. 2-3). The adaptation of the free association procedures to the comparative analysis of subjective cultures follows the theoretical rationale described in the article "Verbal Associations in the Study of Subjective Culture" (Szalay & Maday, 1973). The protocol for identification of culturally salient and representative stimulus words was followed in the first phase of this project. Problems with translation of key themes is discussed in the Appendix. The final instrument included 120 stimulus words and took two hours to complete.

The extensive verbal association material, estimated to involve over 300,000 responses in this study, were translated and entered into the computer using specially developed software. Initially, responses of individual subjects are tallied and group response lists are formed. These group response lists show highly group-specific frequency distributions and provide the primary data for the consecutive steps of analysis and evaluation. The main steps of data processing and methods of analysis are illustrated in the Appendix. Computer assisted analyses are used to produce the following categories of information.

Cultural Priorities. From a practical psychological angle there is an important difference between issues and subjects which are dominant in people's minds to such an extent that they are likely to influence their choices and actions on the one hand, and those issues and ideas which they do not really care about. In other words, it is important to know what has high priority and subjective importance to other people. Group priorities on single themes and broader areas of concerns (clusters of related themes) reveal the hierarchy of values and motive patterns for the groups studied. The dominance score developed for this purpose is a sensitive measure derived from Noble's (1952) meaningfulness measure, which reveals how important a particular theme or domain is for a particular group (see Appendix, p. 10).

Psycho-cultural Distance. Just how similar or different are the views of people of different cultural backgrounds? Since these views are highly subjective and private, they have been though to be immeasurable. The group response lists to specific themes (like Ancestors) offer an opportunity to assess the extent to which the Chinese and American groups agree or disagree in their subjective images. One measure useful in expressing the similarity of response distributions is the coefficient of psychocultural similarity or distance (see Appendix). This measure can be applied to single themes or broader semantic domains or to the entire cultural frame of reference by using a large number of systematically selected themes which include the dominant cultural priorities of the samples compared. The strategy has been described in articles in <u>Current Anthropology</u> and <u>American Anthropologist</u>.

The several hundred thousand associations to be produced by each sample offer a unique empirical data base to measure their "psycho-cultural distance" through a computerized comparative evaluation of the extensive response distributions. Of primary interest here are the distances measured between Americans and Chinese in various domains of life ranging from family to politics. At a practical level the psycho-cultural distance measure helps to identify areas of cultural differences which may hamper international communication and understanding in these domains of life. A more detailed analysis focused on specific themes can then be used to identify components on which the Chinese and American groups agree or disagree. An awareness of these differences and a capability to cope with them is naturally at the very core of communication competence from a psychological and cultural angle. The intracultural distances can also be measured between the Taiwanese and PRC Chinese groups included in this study. Further discussion of the psycho-cultural distance measure can be found in several publications (Szalay & Bryson, 1974; Szalay & Maday, 1983).

Cultural Meanings Through Salient Components. In the task of lexicon development, mapping cultural meanings through salient components is the main analytic method. It is based on the content analysis of the group's reactions to selected stimulus themes. The analysis is performed by independent analysts representing the groups. Beyond the extent of differences, that is, their level of agreement or disagreement, it shows how the two groups differ in the interpretations of a particular theme. An example of this analysis in application to the image of Ancestors as seen by the American and Chinese students is given in Appendix, page 5.

To convey the results of this analysis in simple visual form we have used bar graphs to show the differential salience of the main perceptual and evaluative components of the groups' subjective image. Each bar represents one main component. In some instances the salience of a particular component may appear to be about equal for the two groups being compared, but the detailed response lists reveal clear group differences within the component. The actual responses given by each group are included at the end of each chapter. In the analysis of the cultural frames of reference we focus on patterns and trends which emerge with consistency across related issues and themes.

The findings show cultural similarities and differences in their actual proportions and generate a natural curiosity for finding explanations. The lexicon is designed to serve this purpose in a concise form. There are two major sources of information available for providing authentic explanations and interpretations. The first is the extensive data obtained within the study itself. How Americans understand friendship, for instance, is neither accidental nor startling, and it becomes readily understandable if we study the consistent trends which emerge in the analysis of related themes such as the self, happiness, family, etc. A second important source is sociological and anthropological literature and area experts to place the findings in the context of the background, history, and contemporary life conditions of the people.

The previous Chinese-American Communication and Culture Guide presents data on five major domains: Family, Love and Marriage, Friends, Society, and Work, and is based on two Chinese samples (PRC and Hong Kong) and one U.S. sample. The present volume comparing students in the U.S., PRC, and Taiwan encompasses the domains of Family, National Images, Religion, Economy, and Education. Each domain is discussed on the basis of results obtained on clusters of representative themes.

The findings on selected themes show which themes are of high subjective importance to each group. The culturally dominant themes are described with respect to their characteristic cultural meanings, i.e., how they are understood by the native speaker of the language. Special attention is given to those components of meanings which cannot be anticipated on the basis of the U.S. American frame of reference because they represent substantial differences between the American and Chinese cultures.

As is illustrated by the lexica prepared on various foreign cultures, the in-depth analysis of systematically selected cultural themes offers a way to describe subjective culture. The themes of a domain appear as independent words with separate meanings of their own only in the perspective of linguistic analysis. In terms of their psychological meanings, themes are interrelated; they share some common components. For instance, many of the education related themes, such as education, school, teacher indicate an emphasis on moral character and formal behavior. Similar response trends observed in the context of related themes reveal characteristic dimensions of the cultural frame of reference.

Main Categories of Information Relevant to Intercultural Understanding and Effective Communication

This volume, like the previous one, has been organized to help Americans understand Chinese and to help Chinese understand Americans in the various contexts of their interactions. It provides information along three dimensions relevant to communication.

What is important. It needs little documentation that the attention a particular message receives will depend essentially on the communicator's ability to relate to the main interests and expectations of his audience. In other words, it is important to know what has high priority and subjective importance to other people. It is apparent form the findings of the present study that the Chinese do have concerns and expectations different from Americans. The themes having high subjective importance are identified by using a well established theme selection procedure described in Current Anthropology (Szalay & Maday, 1973). Independently from this procedure the dominance scores show the relative importance of selected themes to the groups compared (see Appendix). In the present context the dominance scores show the subjective importance given by the groups to the themes studied; they provide insights into subjective priorities which the group itself might not estimate correctly if directly questioned.

How is it understood. A second key to effective communication is the speaker's ability to relate to the dominant concerns of others in a way which makes good sense to them. when the communicator discusses a particular subject with such different groups of people as PRC Chinese and Americans, the effectiveness of his communication will depend critically on familiarity with his audience's subjective meanings and with his ability to adapt to those meanings. The information presented in the following chapters regarding selected key communication themes will help one to recognize the important ways in which the subjective meanings of Chinese and American people differ. Components which show higher salience for the Americans than for the Chinese would be given greater attention by Americans but less by people in the PRC. The potential of the communicator to promote mutual understanding depends on his ability to use the priorities and meanings of a particular group as the realistic point of departure.

Earlier studies (Szalay, Lysne, & Bryson, 1972) showed that associative data reflecting salient cultural perceptions and dispositions of a particular group can be used to produce effective and meaningful communication. The principle for using this information on culturally salient perceptual and attitudinal components is simple. The more we capitalize on components that are salient for that particular group, the greater is the chance of producing communications which are relevant to members of that group.

How is it integrated into people's frame of reference. The cultural data presented in the following chapters reveal broad general characteristics of the cultural frame of reference. These characteristics emerge from consistent trends observed across themes and reflect shared psycho-cultural dispositions frequently labelled culture traits. Such traits have particular importance in communications as well as in interpersonal relations. The consistency observed in the salience of certain perceptual and attitudinal components shows that cultural meanings are not discrete or independent. They are actually interrelated elements of representation shaped by shared experiences. They result in shared perspectives and priorities which create strong predispositions for coping with the external world. Once they have been incorporated into people's subjective views of the world, these perspectives exert continuous control over their choices and behavior without their conscious awareness.

Main Areas of Application

The Communication Lexicon and Culture Guide provides rich resource material for use in enhancing cross-cultural understanding and communication between Americans and Chinese. To use this volume effectively the reader must be aware of its potential as well as its natural limitations. Since the information is new, it is important to know in what ways it differs from conventional resources such as traditional bilingual dictionaries, foreign area guides and handbooks, and survey research.

A Teaching/Learning Tool. While standard English-Chinese and Chinese-English dictionaries abound, nothing exists which addresses the cultural "loadings" of words on this level. Normally, lexicographers look for words in one language to match with words in another. Where concepts appear to coincide, one-for-one translations are assumed. Where notions appear more complicated, a series of equivalents in one or the other language is given. However, much of the contemporary work on cognition and psycholinguistics makes clear that the apparently translation equivalent words carry different cultural meanings. Furthermore, the connotations or attitudes attached to apparently translation equivalent words can also vary greatly. Ignorance of these connotations often produces inappropriate usage and breakdown in communication. To cope with these communication problems our Communication Lexicons based on the AGA method offer a new and effective tool.

The most important distinction is that the communication lexicon describes different types of meanings. Conventional dictionaries focus on denotative meanings, while the communication lexicon focuses on subjective psychological meanings of the words we use to communicate. Communications which do not take subjective meanings into consideration have less chance of being understood.

8

The subjective meanings of the American and Chinese groups included in this volume are a rich resource for better understanding the deep foundation of cultural meanings, the culturally shared subjective perspectives which influence our views and priorities without our conscious awareness. By showing that words which are considered to be translation equivalent frequently have different subjective meanings, the communication lexicon introduces valuable new information into the field of language instruction.

Improving Communications. The shared meanings required for communication can be taken for granted, to a large extent, between people of the same background. The speaker can use his own frame of reference and still be listened to and understood. Communication between people of different background and different experiences, however, requires that the speaker take the priorities and meanings of the other culture into careful consideration. It requires a more carefully planned process, a careful shifting from the one's own priorities to the frequently different priorities and meanings of another culture (Szalay, 1981). Naturally, this is only possible if we know how our dominant priorities and meanings compare to those of the other culture. The communication lexica developed on the basis of the AGA method are designed to provide this knowledge.

Several methods of testing the practical implications of AGA based findings on cultural priorities and meanings have been employed (Szalay, Lysne, & Bryson, 1972). Experiments were conducted to test how the cogency of communications built on the Lexicon compare with communications and assertions available from other sources. Since "cultural experts" are considered as the best source presently available, assertions produced by two Korean cultural experts were compared with assertions generated on the basis of the Communication Lexicon. Korean students then were asked to chose the most cogent or meaningful from these three alternatives. The Lexicon based alternatives were chosen consistently more than the assertions of the cultural experts by a highly significant margin. AGA based findings on perceptions and attitudes have also been used for domestic applications. For instance, Headstart programs directed at low income Black and Hispanic American mothers used insights into their cultural meanings to promote less punitive parenting methods (Alvy, Harrison, Rosen, & Garza-Fuentes, 1982). In addition, AGA based data on the perceptions and attitudes of drug users and non-users are being used in counseling programs to help professionals to reach and communicate with drug users. These different applications illustrate the ways in which the information on subjective meanings can be used to adapt communications to the perceptions of selected populations.

Foreign area studies: New data on psycho-cultural population characteristics. Foreign area studies provide a detailed description of a particular country's climate, geography, history, religions, economic conditions, social stratification, and political organization, but there is little attention to the psycho-cultural characteristics of the population. What is available is often stereotypical and biased. As important as these dispositions can be, there is a tendency to avoid them, at least as long as the information available is predominantly speculative and unverifiable. There is commonly little or no solid timely information on the actual contemporary thinking and psychological dispositions. It is mostly a matter of speculation how people perceive their own situation, their country, what they perceive as their most pressing problems, what are their fears what are their dominant aspirations. The lacking of such insights creates fundamental difficulties to understand people of foreign cultures. It hampers our capability to know what people with frames of reference different from ours are likely to do, respectively what they essentially incapable to do. This limitation applies similarly to every domain of life, political, economic, social as well as in the field of international relations.

The information offered by our Communication Lexica opens new opportunities to change this situation in several important ways. They show that particular culture groups have their dominant dispositions to see certain realities and to overlook others. They show that these dispositions have a high degree of consistency, that they form a system of subjective representation that influences how people perceive and cope with their environment. The findings show, for example, that the Mainland students, who live under extremely modest conditions, are much more positive and optimistic about their situation than the relatively well to do Taiwanese, who show a great deal of dissatisfaction. Finally, this new information demonstrates that deep psychocultural insights can be obtained through scientific research and made available to users in the fields of education, communications, international relations, and others.

Generalizability of the Findings

In survey research the generalizability of the results depends on the use of statistically representative samples. Since psycho-cultural characteristics are more widely shared and more evenly distributed throughout the population, their representative sampling poses less stringent requirements. In a culture characterized by strong sex role differentiation, for example, it is not necessary to go through the demanding task of statistically representative sampling of the entire population to arrive at the culturally characteristic male role model or family organization. This does not mean that t here are no individual or class variations but in an intercultural comparison these variations are of secondary importance. To control for them it is helpful to use a strategy of comparing matching samples of similar socio-demographic composition: same age and sex composition, educational level, etc. In this way we are eliminating differences which could be attributable to the most important socio-demographic variables and approximate a situation in which the critical difference between the groups is cultural background. The differences found between such samples can be safely attributed to culture.

This approach of concentration on cultural differences between culture groups of matching socio-demographic composition naturally does not deny the importance of differences within subcultures, social strata, age groups, etc. In the context of the present volume it is important to recognize the considerable intracultural, intrasocietal diversity not only within the United States but also in China where there are large social and economic class differences, sharp rural-urban and regional differences in life conditions. Frequently, populations contain groups of thoroughly different cultural background. Where funding permits, several groups are used from major population strata, e.g., college students, farmers, urban workers, etc. When the financial situation permits the use of only one pair of matching samples, as in the present study, we consider this merely the first critical step in approaching a complex situation. Indeed, in our studies of several other countries, e.g., Korea and Jordan, our first comparative bicultural comparisons have been followed up by scholars from these countries who were interested in extending the comparison to several additional domestic subpopulations.

Our present strategy of focusing first on the intercultural comparison and considering the intracultural differences as somewhat secondary at this point seems to be well justified. In all instances examined up to this point, the psycho-cultural differences within a particular national/cultural sample (e.g., between low and high income groups) were found to be substantially smaller than the differences between two comparable cultural samples (e.g., Hispanic Americans and Anglo Americans (Szalay et al., 1976). Similar results were obtained in a larger cross-cultural study of American and Korean students, workers, and farmers (Szalay & Maday, 1983) and on Anglo, Hispanic, and Latin Americans (Diaz-Guerrerro & Szalay, 1991).

There is a sometimes a tendency to overemphasize the requirements of statistical representativeness by those who lack understanding of the very nature of cultural differences. While the Chinese and American samples may not be statistically representative, they can be considered culturally representative. As the many details on the Chinese groups' perceptual and semantic dispositions indicate, they do show similar trends and patterns when contrasted with Americans. The more empirical data become available, the more it will be possible to move simultaneously in two seemingly opposite directions -- to enhance knowledge on important specifics e.g., particular groups, psycho-cultural dispositions) and to develop a better grasp of how much we share and how much we differ culturally (Szalay, 1982).

Chapter 2

FAMILY

Family is the most universal and elementary human organization common to all cultures. It is also the most popular and widely studied subject of cultural anthropology. The great interest in family arises not only from its universal human importance, but also from the fascinating diversity of inter-family relationships.

These variations follow from cultural views and attitudes that are deeply rooted in early childhood experiences. They involve processes of conditioning and learning, of which people are mostly unaware, such as socialization or enculturation. Since family serves as the main framework for carrying on a particular culture, it offers some unique opportunities for understanding culture and the origin of cultural differences.

Chinese civilization thrived for tens of centuries without so much as the existence of a police force. This is generally attributed to the strong and pervasive role and function of the family in defining and regulating the proper conduct of the individual. Chinese proverbs emphasize that the flourishing of the empire and the prosperity of the province ultimately depend upon harmony in the family and the strict upbringing of youth. Children must be imbued with a deep sense of duty, propriety, and other characteristic traits such as honesty, chastity, loyalty, truthfulness, sincerity, self-restraint, filial piety, etc.

The traditional anthropological interest is in observable cultural differences such as the size of family, its structure, family customs, marriage ceremonies, etc. Our main interest, however, is the foundation of such diversity in psychological dispositions - in perceptions, attitudes, and the subjective worlds of people. This interest is motivated by insights, by the recognition that people's subjective world is the main source of cultural diversity as well as the key to understanding their behavior which appears frequently puzzling. It is the key to understanding our own behavior as well. The more we know about people's subjective worlds, the more we can compare their priorities and perspectives to ours, and the more we will be able to bridge our differences and find common grounds for cooperation.

The domain of family is of special interest since the family is being increasingly recognized as the single most important social institution that shapes and promotes cultural differences. Francis Hsu (1979, 1977) has pointed to an important distinction between Americans and Chinese in their differing emphasis on role and affect in interpersonal relations within and outside the family. The present American-Chinese comparison promises timely insights into how the family functions in promoting those perceptions and attitudes that characterize this post-modern American society, compared to the Chinese societies. By studying the Chinese samples, we can assess how the different backgrounds of controlled socialistic system vs. the free market system may influence people's perspectives and frames of reference.

The comparative analysis of American, Taiwanese, and Mainland Chinese perceptions and attitudes regarding family relations encompass the following eight themes: Family, Parents, Mother, Father, Children, Relatives, Ancestors, and Me (self image).

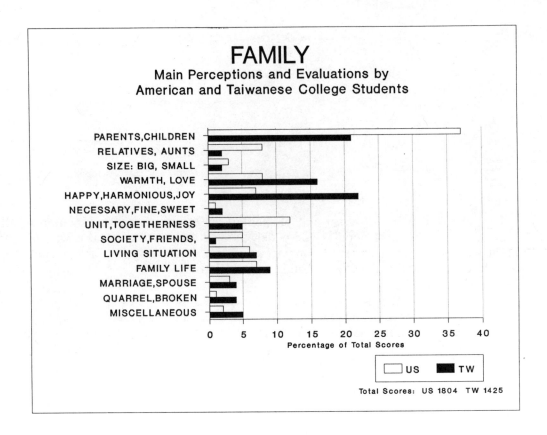

FAMILY
Main Perceptions and Evaluations by
American and Taiwanese College Students

PARENTS,CHILDREN
RELATIVES, AUNTS
SIZE: BIG, SMALL
WARMTH, LOVE
HAPPY,HARMONIOUS,JOY
NECESSARY,FINE,SWEET
UNIT,TOGETHERNESS
SOCIETY,FRIENDS,
LIVING SITUATION
FAMILY LIFE
MARRIAGE,SPOUSE
QUARREL,BROKEN
MISCELLANEOUS

0   5   10   15   20   25   30   35   40
Percentage of Total Scores

☐ US   ■ TW

Total Scores: US 1804   TW 1425

family

American View: Mother, Togetherness. For Americans family depends on the relationship between mother and father, with more attention paid to the mother's central role in the home and family. While mother's role is more important than that of father in all groups except the mainland Chinese, it is nowhere so much emphasized as in the U.S. Females in general, whether mother, sister, or daughter, receive far more emphasis by Americans than their male counterpart. The situation is the opposite in Mainland China. It is surprising to see that it is the Americans who emphasize the extended family -- aunts, uncles, cousins -- and friends. The family unit as an expression of closeness, togetherness, love, and care receives great emphasis. Security, sharing, and helping also appear to be dominant American values. Americans view the family positively as a setting that fulfills their needs and wants. This American life setting includes even such specific details as dogs, reunions, vacations, fun, and outings.

Taiwanese View: Warmth, Responsibility. In defining family the Taiwanese primarily consider parents, children, siblings, with comparatively little emphasis on individual roles such as mother, father, brother, sister. They pay attention to the parent-child relationship within the family. The Taiwanese adults' hope lies on their children: the glory of a child is the glory of his parents. An emotional atmosphere of warmth and love, happiness, safety, comfort, peace and stability is what they hope for. But they express concern about family quarrels, burdens and divorce. More than the other groups, they express anxiety and worry, relating to the pain, and problems associated with family life, including pressures, money, responsibility, and obligations.

American and Taiwanese Contrasts: Needs, Shared Experiences versus Emotional Ties.
Americans much more than Taiwanese, think of relatives as part of the family, which may partially be a semantic difference related to the Chinese ideogram for family. While love and caring are important in American families, Taiwanese stress warmth, concern, and kindness. In general, the Taiwanese are taught to be dependent on their families, while Americans are taught to be independent from their families. The interdependence of the parents and their children is lasting. Taiwanese anticipation of family quarrels, burdens, worries, pressures, and escape is less articulate among Americans. In terms of family life, responsibilities, money, and obligations are much more on the mind of the Taiwanese, while Americans focus on family activities such as reunions, dinner, T.V. shows, vacations, fun, and outings. Perceptions of unity, togetherness, and closeness in the American family are not reflected among the Taiwanese. The latter emphasize family origin and family spirit. The American identification of family ties in home while the Taiwanese relates to haven. Emphasis on family happiness and well being is much stronger among the Taiwanese. Security, sharing, and helping are the dominant American expectations.

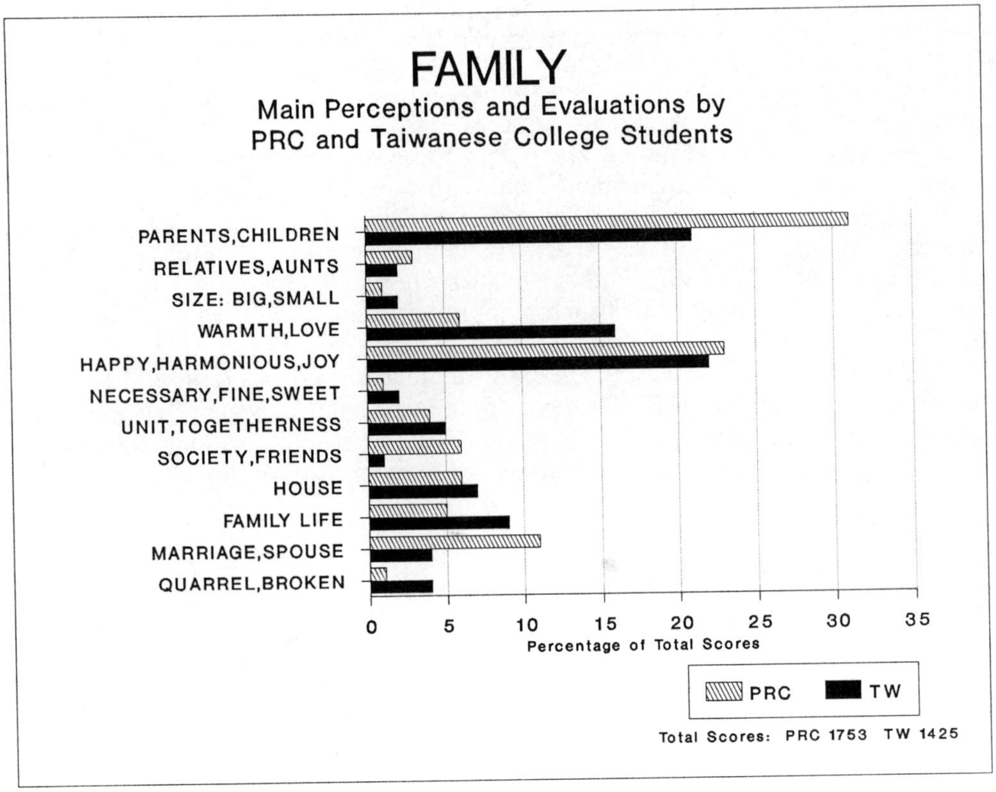
FAMILY
Main Perceptions and Evaluations by
PRC and Taiwanese College Students
PARENTS,CHILDREN
RELATIVES,AUNTS
SIZE: BIG,SMALL
WARMTH,LOVE
HAPPY,HARMONIOUS,JOY
NECESSARY,FINE,SWEET
UNIT,TOGETHERNESS
SOCIETY,FRIENDS
HOUSE
FAMILY LIFE
MARRIAGE,SPOUSE
QUARREL,BROKEN
0 5 10 15 20 25 30 35
Percentage of Total Scores
PRC
TW
Total Scores: PRC 1753 TW 1425

PRC Chinese view: A Yen for Marriage. The Mainland Chinese, like the Taiwanese and the Hong Kong Chinese in the previous study, think mainly of the nuclear family -- father, mother, children, brothers and sisters. They do place more weight on the male members: brother, father and son. A major difference between them and all the other groups is their strong interest in marriage. The Mainland China is still a closed society. Marriage brings them not only happiness but also wealth -- if males can marry rich women with a lot of dowry. Harmony within the family is a central idea, and it is closely related in the Chinese mind to general well-being, economic prosperity, and the flourishing of society -- as some of China's most ancient and still popular proverbs attest. It is probably, more than any other concept, at the heart of "Confucianism." By the Chinese view of family harmony is closely tied in with the "Three Obediences" which stress subordination as an indispensable condition for smooth cooperation in any enterprise. Family is seen as a source of well-being, happiness and joy. They also view it as the basic cell of society.

Taiwanese View: Warmth, Responsibility. In defining family the Taiwanese primarily consider parents, children, siblings, with comparatively little emphasis on individual roles such as mother, father, brother, sister. They pay attention to the parent-child relationship within the family. The Taiwanese adults' hope lies on their children: the glory of a child is the glory of his parents. An emotional atmosphere of warmth and love, happiness, safety, comfort, peace and stability is what they hope for. But they express concern about family quarrels, burdens and divorce. More than the other groups, they express anxiety and worry, relating to the pain, and problems associated with family life, including pressures, money, responsibility, and obligations.

PRC and Taiwanese Contrasts: More Idealized versus Balanced Expectations. The Chinese Mainlanders' interest expressed in marriage and spouse is much stronger than that of the Taiwanese, while Taiwanese concern with the responsibility and burdens is stronger than that of the Mainlanders. The focus on family members siblings, parents, and children, particularly males is much stronger on the mainland. Males are traditionally; they are considered the direct descendants, the ones who burn incense for the dead parents or relatives -- a practice handed down from generation to generation. Also, males can make money to support their families, particularly in an agricultural society like Mainland China. The Taiwanese think of the family much more in the emotional terms of warmth and love, while the mainlanders see it primarily in terms of interpersonal relations in a framework of harmony and joy. They also consider family to be the basic building block or cell of society. Mainlanders do not share Taiwanese concern with quarrels, disputes, worry, and pains.

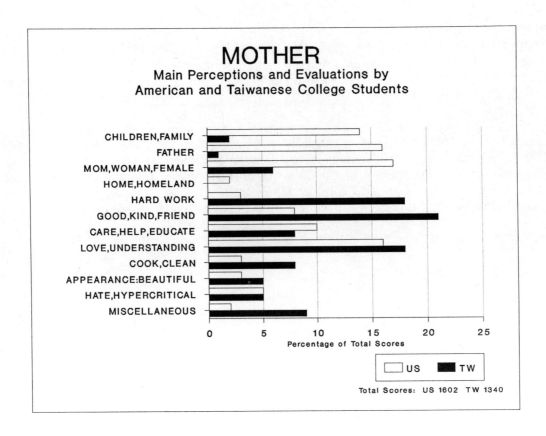

MOTHER
Main Perceptions and Evaluations by
American and Taiwanese College Students

Percentage of Total Scores

US   TW

Total Scores: US 1602 TW 1340

mother

American View: Female Identity, Love, Criticism. The Americans' image of mother centers on her female identity -- woman, wife, female. Mother is seen in direct relation to father, a partnership that is not stressed by any of the Chinese groups. Other family members to which she is linked are children, sons and daughters. Americans believe in individualism Mother and her children are generally on an equal position. Mother brings love, warmth and understanding. She provides help and care in teaching her children. While the positive responses far outweigh the few negative characterizations, Americans are more critical than any other group, and are the only ones to indicate feelings of hatred toward their mothers. Among the negative attributes ascribed to mother are: abusive, bossy, pushy, and nagging. Americans do not describe "mother" as the Chinese do as kind, gentle, great, and dear person; however, they do consider her a friend.

Taiwanese View: Hardworking, Talkative. Taiwanese ascribe to mother such positive qualities as being kind, great, gentle, and amiable. The image of mother elicits strong feelings of love, affection, and warmth. The Taiwan group focuses on the mother's role in educating and disciplining the children. They also emphasize other duties such as cooking and cleaning, and characterize her as toilsome and hardworking. They also criticize mothers for talking too much, and being hypercritical. Most Taiwanese mothers have to toil to help support the families, particularly in the old days. Their hope for their children is high. To the adolescents, however, mothers are at times talkative & nagging. More often than not, a Taiwanese mother spends more time with her children than does a Taiwanese father, because a Taiwanese father is the major supporter (breadwinner) of the family. Generally, the mother is the one who educates the children.

American and Taiwanese Contrasts: Female versus Hard Worker. Taiwanese are far more impressed by their mothers' hard work than are Americans. Americans, in strong contrast to Taiwanese, relate mother to father and to other family members. American emphasis on mother being female is also much greater. Taiwanese exceeding the attention to negative aspects of mother is about the same for both cultures. Unlike Americans, however, the Taiwanese focus on both extremes of idealism and drudgery -- seeing mother as the epitome of kindness and gentleness as well as of much talk and hard work. The Taiwanese regards a woman as of the "weaker" sex, but once a woman becomes a mother, she becomes strong-willed and works hard without complaint.

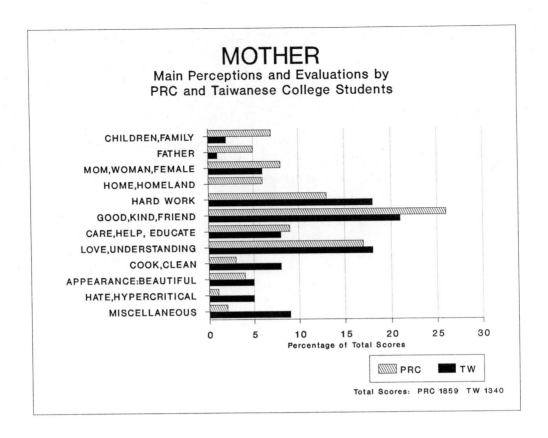

MOTHER

Main Perceptions and Evaluations by
PRC and Taiwanese College Students

Percentage of Total Scores

PRC   TW

Total Scores: PRC 1859 TW 1340

PRC Chinese View: Kindhearted, Beautiful. The PRC group focuses on the personality characteristics of mother; she is seen as a kindhearted, gentle, virtuous, selfless, lovable, and dear person. Maternal love and affection are extremely important. The Chinese mother is also described as industrious and hard-working. There is some recognition of her role in the care and upbringing of her children. The PRC group is the only one which associates mother with their native country (motherland). The only clearly negative attribute (if this is a negative characteristic in the Chinese view) mentioned was severity. More than any other group the Mainlanders consider their mothers beautiful (Chinese proverb: "A child never feels disgusted with his mother's ugliness").

Taiwanese View: Hardworking, Talkative. Taiwanese ascribe to mother such positive qualities as being kind, great, gentle, and amiable. The image of mother elicits strong feelings of love, affection, and warmth. The Taiwan group focuses on the mother's role in educating and disciplining the children. They also emphasize other duties such as cooking and cleaning, and characterize her as toilsome and hardworking. They also criticize mothers for talking too much, and being hypercritical. Most Taiwanese mothers have to toil to help support the families, particularly in the old days. Their hope for their children is high. To the adolescents, however, mothers are at times talkative & nagging. More often than not, a Taiwanese mother spends more time with her children than does a Taiwanese father, because a Taiwanese father is the major supporter (breadwinner) of the family. Generally, the mother is the one who educates the children.

20

PRC and Taiwanese Contrasts: Caring versus Homemaking. The Chinese Mainlanders' consideration of mother in relation to other family members, while where no equal to that of the American's, is much stronger than the Taiwanese. Mother's relation to father in particular is much stronger on the Mainland than on Taiwan. In contrast, the Taiwanese give more attention to the mother's explicit and detailed household tasks such as cooking, kitchen work, and washing clothes. In most other respects the attributes of mother are very similar, except that the Taiwanese mention more negative aspects. Mainlanders are concerned about showing their mothers sufficient love, respect, and consideration -- and giving them every care. Mainlanders consider their mothers overworked and bearing hardships. Taiwanese consider their mothers making sacrifices, being frugal, and suffering. Both consider their mothers great.

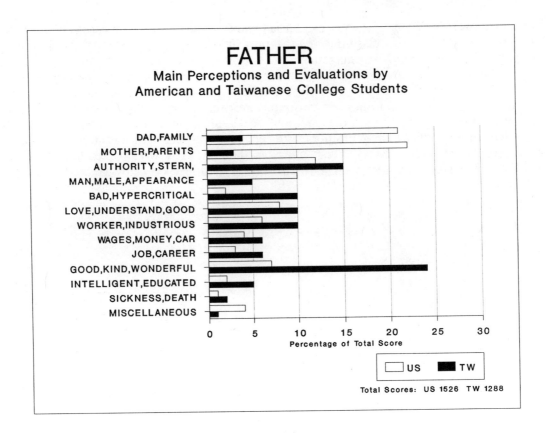

FATHER
Main Perceptions and Evaluations by
American and Taiwanese College Students

Percentage of Total Score

US   TW

Total Scores: US 1526 TW 1288

American View: Male, Provider, Friend. Americans particularly emphasize father in relation to son, family, children, and parents. Father elicits strong feelings of love, but not with much intensity as mother. Likewise the negative attributes are fewer than with mother, and far less intense. The only specific ones mentioned were alcoholism and divorce. Father's personal qualities and characteristics receive relatively less attention; strength, respect, and authority are the more dominant ones mentioned, but not nearly as much as with the Chinese groups. Sexual identity as man and male is a very important element in the image of father. His role as provider is also emphasized, as is his job and career. Americans see father as a friend.

Taiwanese View: Solemn, Authority, Money-maker. The Taiwanese also focus on the personality characteristics of father: he is most often described as solemn but also as kindly and affable. To a lesser extent he is considered silent, cordial, honest, and a friend. His position involves hardship, love and responsibility. The father serves as the pillar of the family, a strong and severe authority. This group expresses the most negative attitude toward father, describing him as hypercritical, unreasonable, cold, bad tempered, unable to bridge the generation gap, diseased and hedonistic. The father and the children belong to different generations, growing up in two different periods and two different societies -- an agricultural society and an industrial society. Naturally, their value judgments are vastly different. But generally the Taiwanese children never contradict their parents (fathers) in public. The generation gap in Taiwan is more obvious; Taiwanese youth are more Westernized. This Chinese group, more than the others, seems to emphasize the father's responsibility to have a job and make money. His intelligence and education are also of importance.

American and Taiwanese Contrasts: Love versus Authority. Generational tension on Taiwan seems to be particularly hard on fathers whose role is increasingly seen as being primarily economic. Both positive and negative feelings toward father are more emphatic on Taiwan than in the U.S. Taiwanese fathers are considered more affable and kinder than American ones, as well as more of an authority and model; but also more bad-tempered, cold and unreasonable. By comparison American fathers are rather neutral. Negative attributes of fathers on Taiwan are at a magnitude of five to one in relation to the U.S. Note the cultural differences between U.S. and Taiwan: at the age of 18 an American child is supposed to be independent of his father (and mother), but a Taiwanese is forever his father's child -- he can always come back to ask his father's help, spiritually and materially.

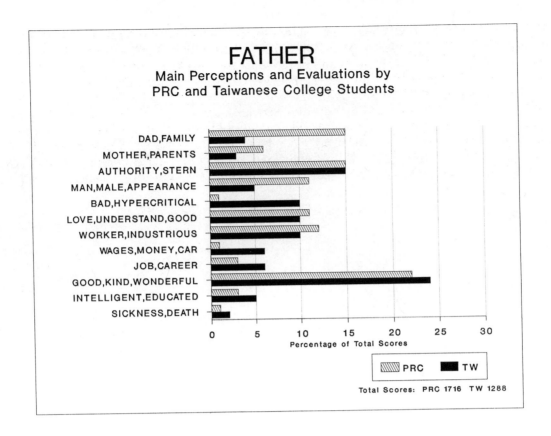

FATHER
Main Perceptions and Evaluations by
PRC and Taiwanese College Students

Categories (top to bottom): DAD,FAMILY; MOTHER,PARENTS; AUTHORITY,STERN; MAN,MALE,APPEARANCE; BAD,HYPERCRITICAL; LOVE,UNDERSTAND,GOOD; WORKER,INDUSTRIOUS; WAGES,MONEY,CAR; JOB,CAREER; GOOD,KIND,WONDERFUL; INTELLIGENT,EDUCATED; SICKNESS,DEATH

Percentage of Total Scores

PRC   TW

Total Scores: PRC 1716   TW 1288

PRC Chinese View: Revered, Kind, Fair-minded. As with mother, the PRC Chinese focus on the personality characteristics of father: kind, good, earnest, lovable, dear; but at the same time forceful, bold and resolute. Of the three Chinese groups, they come closest to Americans (but with less emphasis) in placing father in relation to other family members: children, sons, brothers and sisters, grandfather. They see father as head and pillar of the family, as a teacher, and respectable person of lofty status, dignity, and strength. He may be severe but fair-minded. He may also be industrious, diligent, hard-working and reliable. As was the case with mother, the PRC Chinese express almost no bad feelings toward father. On the contrary, they verbalize their need to show filial obedience, which involves an almost religious awe and reverence which absolutely excludes contradiction, defiance, or direct criticism. Money-making is of negligible importance in Communist society.

Taiwanese View: Solemn, Authority, Money-maker. The Taiwanese also focus on the personality characteristics of father: he is most often described as solemn but also as kindly and affable. To a lesser extent he is considered silent, cordial, honest, and a friend. His position involves hardship, love and responsibility. The father serves as the pillar of the family, a strong and severe authority. This group expresses the most negative attitude toward father, describing him as hypercritical, unreasonable, cold, bad tempered, unable to bridge the generation gap, diseased and hedonistic. The father and the children belong to different generations, growing up in two different periods and two different societies -- an agricultural society and an industrial society. Naturally, their value judgments are vastly different. But generally the Taiwanese children never contradict their parents (fathers) in public. The generation gap in Taiwan is more obvious; Taiwanese youth are more Westernized. This Chinese group, seems to emphasize the father's responsibility to have a job and make money. His intelligence and education are also important.

PRC and Taiwanese Contrasts: Moral Qualities versus Material Provider. The most striking difference between the two groups is that negativity is much stronger on Taiwan than on the Mainland. The father's ability to provide wealth, security, property, a car -- and to make money in general -- are also much more important on Taiwan. In short, a father's status on the Mainland depends on his moral qualities and his living up to his traditional role as pillar, protector, model, disciplinarian, and teacher. In contrast, his esteem and self-respect on Taiwan depend largely on his ability to provide material well-being, status, and economic security for his family. Taiwan is a growing industrial society with a high living standard next only to Japan and Singapore in Asia. The competition in society is keen. Money is an important status symbol in society.

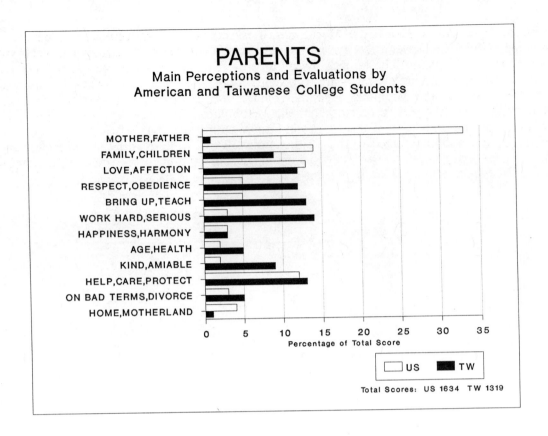

PARENTS

Main Perceptions and Evaluations by
American and Taiwanese College Students

MOTHER,FATHER
FAMILY,CHILDREN
LOVE,AFFECTION
RESPECT,OBEDIENCE
BRING UP,TEACH
WORK HARD,SERIOUS
HAPPINESS,HARMONY
AGE,HEALTH
KIND,AMIABLE
HELP,CARE,PROTECT
ON BAD TERMS,DIVORCE
HOME,MOTHERLAND

0   5   10   15   20   25   30   35
Percentage of Total Score

☐ US   ■ TW

Total Scores: US 1634 TW 1319

American View: Mother, Love, and Home. For Americans mother plays a more central parental role than father, but each is valued for his or her contribution to the family. There is particularly strong emphasis on love as well as friendship; parents are characterized as loving, caring, giving, and helping. They are also seen as protectors and guardians. There are indications in the Chinese responses that the love is expressed more by the parents to the children rather than from the children to the parents. The Chinese groups are much more likely to describe their parents as kind and amiable. Negative associations with parents have to do with fighting and divorce. In contrast to the Chinese, Americans indicate no concern about their parents' health. Americans, much more than the Chinese, consider their parents as friends, and love is more frequently expressed by Americans.

Taiwanese View: Upbringing, Obedience, Indebtedness. In extreme contrast to both the American and the Mainlander groups, the Taiwanese make almost no reference to father, mother, or their partnership. They do refer to family and children in general and to the extended family. The Taiwanese stress the role of parents in bringing up children, educating and directing them. They appreciate the parents' hard work and sacrifice,and acknowledge their obligation to repay and take care of their parents for their watchful and protective upbringing. They are acutely aware of their indebtedness. They know that they are required to show respect and loving obedience to parental authority. Their expression of love and affection is exceeded only by the American group. Yet more than the other groups, Taiwanese say they are on bad terms with their parents; this tension takes the form of arguments, irritation, shouting. Taiwan is in a transitional period, so many problems are surfacing.

American and Taiwanese Contrasts: Love and Mother versus Gratitude and Obedience. Americans see their parents as friends, a source of love, support and discipline, and strongly relate them to other relatives. Compared to the Taiwanese they are less of parental authority, and much more likely to consider parents to be guardians and friends. Unlike the Taiwanese, American students give indication of believing that their parents understand them, and they consider them guardians and guides. The Taiwanese are far more aware of their parents' contribution in terms of toil, work and money - and the sacrifices they have made. But, in general, they express ambivalent feelings on gratitude and resentment of parental pressures.

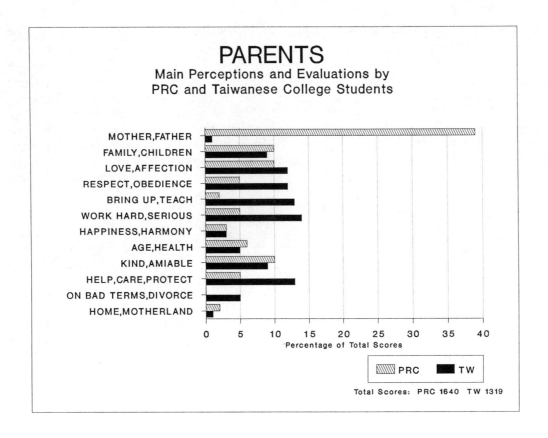

PARENTS
Main Perceptions and Evaluations by
PRC and Taiwanese College Students

PRC ▨ TW ■

Total Scores: PRC 1640 TW 1319

PRC Chinese View: Positive and Middle of the Road. For the PRC Chinese the combined parental role has greater importance than the individual roles of father and mother. However, more attention is paid to father than to mother. The grandparents, particularly on the father's side, are recognized as additional parental models. The qualities the Mainlanders most often ascribe to their parents are kindly, amiable, respectable, healthy, lovable and dear. They are clearly aware of their parents' love and of the education their parents' work has provided. That their parents are in harmony is important to them. One of the most significant contrasts is the total absence of negative feelings about parents among Chinese Mainlanders. They have a very deep commitment to taking care of, and providing support for, their parents.

Taiwanese View: Upbringing, Obedience, Indebtedness. In extreme contrast to both the American and the Mainlander groups, the Taiwanese make almost no reference to father, mother, or their partnership. They do refer to family and children in general and to the extended family. The Taiwanese stress the role of parents in bringing up children, educating and directing them. They appreciate the parents' hard work and sacrifice, and acknowledge their obligation to repay and take care of their parents for their watchful and protective upbringing. They are acutely aware of their indebtedness. They know that they are required to show respect and loving obedience to parental authority. Their expression of love and affection is exceeded only by the American group. Yet more than the other groups, Taiwanese say they are on bad terms with their parents; this tension takes the form of arguments, irritation, shouting. Taiwan is in a transitional period, so many problems are surfacing.

PRC and Taiwanese Contrasts: Harmony versus Tension. Of the groups compared, parents' relationship to each other and to other members of the family was the most important to the Mainlanders and the least important to the Taiwanese. Whereas five percent of the Taiwanese responses indicated tension and friction, none of the Mainlanders did. On the other hand, the notions of respect are much stronger among and obedience is two-and-a-half times as strong among the Taiwanese, compared to the Mainlanders, as is the awareness of the obligation to help and care for one's parents. The Taiwanese also pay more attention to the parents' hard work and efforts to bring up and educate the children. Taiwan is one of the four "dragons" in Asia, because the Taiwanese are hard-working and economically productive. They are especially attentive to the education of the young.

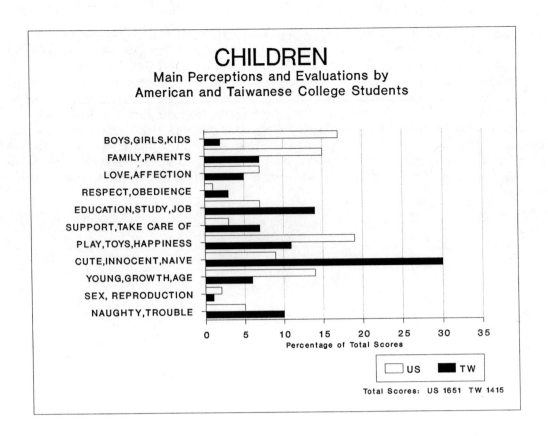

CHILDREN
Main Perceptions and Evaluations by
American and Taiwanese College Students

Percentage of Total Scores

US   TW

Total Scores: US 1651 TW 1415

American View: Babies, Games. The Americans' image of children is dominated by ideas of play, toys, games, and other activities characteristic of young people. Interestingly, Americans have a strong tendency to emphasize young age and size as distinguishing characteristics. The most important characterizations are cute, innocent, helpless. Family and parents receive considerable attention, as do babies. Mother is linked more closely with children than is father.

Taiwanese View: Innocent and Knowledge. Taiwanese think of children as lovely, naive and pure, and needing to be protected, far more than do the other groups. Compared to the other groups, they place less emphasis on children within the context of family or the role of parents,but this may be a reflection on the perspectives of your students than adults, which is somewhat unexpected. This observation conflicts however with others, such as how a baby boy becomes the center of attention of the entire family. Some of this contradiction may be explained by the young age of the students. Mastering a field of knowledge and cultivating their mind are perhaps the most important demands made on children. Being smart is emphasized here more than among the other three groups. The Taiwanese consider children very innocent, but they are also described as naughty, disobedient, and a burden to others.

American and Taiwanese Contrasts: Carefree Youth versus Burden and Seriousness.
Probably the greatest contrast between Taiwanese and American children is the former's early seriousness in relation to studies and the pressure put on children to master their subjects.[1] A Taiwanese child has to pass many examinations to be admitted to various kinds and levels of schools. Studies are their life-long jobs. Taiwanese are most like Americans in their emphasis on toys, playing, and happiness. Americans are, in great contrast to the Taiwanese, only slightly concerned about children's behavior. The major exceptions are fighting and being noisy. For the Taiwanese, children being naughty or disobedient is a major concern. Unlike Americans, Taiwanese do not think of sex in the context of children.

---

[1] Historically this dates back to the influence of the Japanese, who ruled Taiwan in the early decades of this century, and who were determined to demonstrate to other imperial powers such as the U.S. (in the nearby Philippines), Britain, and France that they were as capable colonial masters as those "bearing the white man's burden."

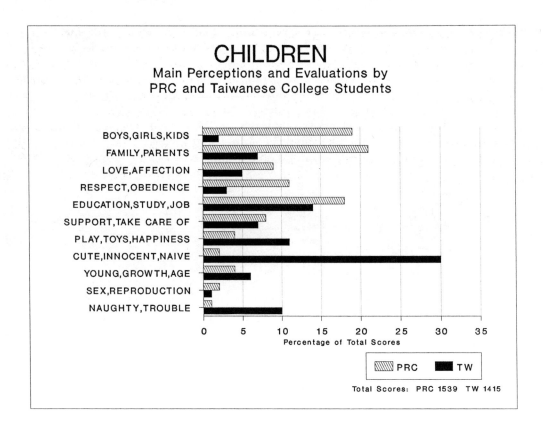

CHILDREN
Main Perceptions and Evaluations by
PRC and Taiwanese College Students

Percentage of Total Scores

PRC TW

Total Scores: PRC 1539 TW 1415

PRC Chinese View: Home and School. For the PRC Chinese children are viewed in two major contexts: at home and at school. At home much attention is placed on the various family roles: on the one hand, to the collective partnership of the parents and, on the other, to the sons and daughters and younger/older brothers and sisters. Children are expected to be obedient, show respect, and provide for and support their parents. At school children's responsibilities including studying and reading, with some career implications (job, employment, profession).[2] No other group indicates as much love and affection for their children and so few problems with discipline or behavior -- a phenomenon which could be related to their "one-child" policy. Other than dolls, there are no toys or playthings mentioned, nor are children considered cute, innocent, or naive. But they are considered "the sweet of parents," beautiful, and nice.

Taiwanese View: Innocent and Knowledge. Taiwanese think of children as lovely, naive and pure, and needing to be protected, far more than do the other groups. Compared to the other groups, they place less emphasis on children within the context of family or the role of parents,but this may be a reflection on the perspectives of young students than adults, which is somewhat unexpected. This observation conflicts however with others, such as how a baby boy becomes the center of attention of the entire family. Some of this contradiction may be explained by the young age of the students. Mastering a field of knowledge and cultivating their mind are perhaps the most important demands made on children. Being smart is emphasized here more than among the other three groups. The Taiwanese consider children very innocent, but also described as naughty, disobedient, and a burden to others.

---

[2]One reason parents have no qualms about giving their offspring over to be educated is that the values of obedience, diligence, and respect for authority demanded in the classroom are also those expected in the home. In class most of the teachers are still very Confucian in their strictness with their students. (Mosher, 1983)

PRC and Taiwanese Contrasts: Respect versus Toys. Children's relationship with family and parents is about much stronger on the Mainland. There is similarly large disparity regarding respect, obedience, and duty. Love and affection are also more emphasized on the Mainland. On the other hand, the negatives of misbehavior is a more serious Taiwanese concern. Preparation for job prospects in the future is stressed more on the Mainland. According to Taiwanese experts this may be a consequence that Mainland China is becoming more and more capitalistic: they are seeking for <u>wealth</u> and their promising children are where all the rosy future lies. In comparison, Taiwanese parents are convinced that no more how weak their children may be, they still can have a good future. Toys, games, and playthings for children are more important to the Taiwanese.

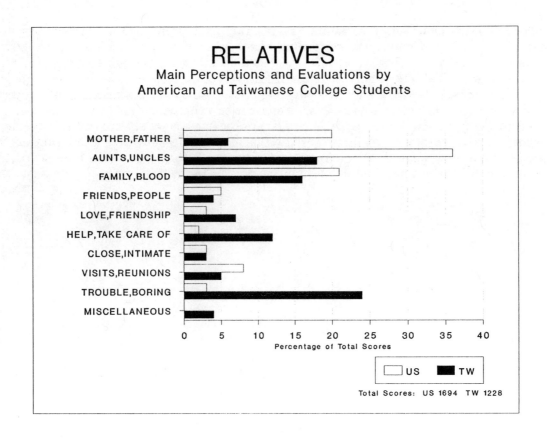

RELATIVES
Main Perceptions and Evaluations by
American and Taiwanese College Students

Percentage of Total Scores

US   TW

Total Scores: US 1694 TW 1228

American View: Aunts, Cousins, Grandfather, Reunions. For Americans relatives are predominantly cousins, aunts, uncles, and grandparents. Father and mother, brothers and sisters are also included. Relatives are an integral part of the American family. Blood relationship is a critical factor, especially in identifying ancestors. Love among relatives is mentioned but not emphasized. Little reference is made of helping or supporting relatives. The dominant mode of connection is through visits, reunions, and family gatherings. Generally, relatives are considered family.

Taiwanese View: Mixed Feelings, Including Alienation, Disgust. The Taiwanese barely mention parents, children, or siblings -- as relatives). Of the groups compared they show the most estranged critical attitudes toward their relatives who include mostly nieces, nephews, cousins, grandparents, aunts, and uncles. The negative terms used to describe these relatives as being disgusting and boring, having no warmth, and being involved in conflicts and quarrels. Taiwanese make practically no mention of the nuclear family but consider mostly their various aunts and uncles and grandparents. Blood relationships are important, to be considered as relative. To be a relative is for them a basis for giving and receiving money and help. Relatives are considered frequently as meddlesome, but realities that they have to be lived with. In Taiwan, a competitive society, "Familiarity breeds contempt" is to the point.

American and Taiwanese Contrasts: Free Choice versus Obligations. To Americans relatives are optional family members whom they consider sometimes friends or people, kin or distant, and boring. But mainly relatives are thought of in terms of friendship, visits, and reunions. Feelings of love are stronger among Americans than Taiwanese. On Taiwan relatives are seen sometimes as dear persons or friends, but more often as a bothersome and alienated. Relatives may involve warmth and affection, but in any case involve inescapable duties and obligations -- such as help in time of trouble; gifts, greetings, invitations to weddings -- and a financial drain if they are in need. The perception of having many relatives is stronger among the Taiwanese. To have influential relatives is helpful to the Taiwanese, generally speaking. On the other hand, if one's relatives are poor and disadvantaged, they may come to ask for help, thus becoming a burden.

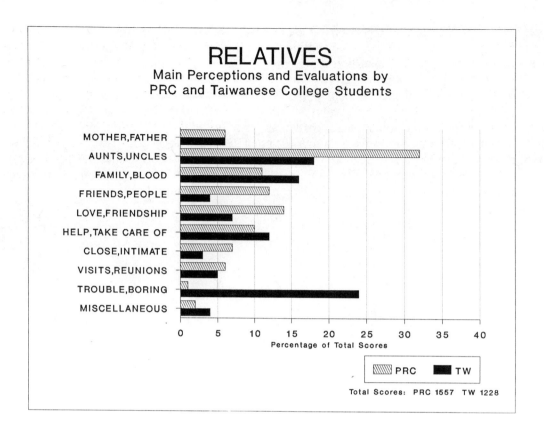

RELATIVES
Main Perceptions and Evaluations by
PRC and Taiwanese College Students

Percentage of Total Scores

PRC   TW

Total Scores: PRC 1557 TW 1228

PRC Chinese View: Good Relations. Aunts and uncles head the list of relatives for the PRC Chinese. Other relations receive little attention and there are few references to family. This suggests a conceptual shift away from what anthropologists consider as nuclear family. The demarcations vary as much as life settings. For instance, when living under the same roof uncles and aunts are treated as family. The Chinese used to extol the case of "four generations under the same roof." The PRC Chinese seem to be more interested in personal rapport than in blood relationship, as evidenced by their references to friends, classmates, comrades, teachers. The dominant sentiment is intimacy rather than love, although, to the Chinese these two words are two sides of the coin. Relatives are described as dear and warm-hearted. The PRC Chinese stress the importance of mutual assistance and help among relatives as well as the need for good, harmonious relations. Unlike the Taiwanese they give almost no negative responses. Generally, the conflicting interests are few, but opportunities of cooperation are more.[3]

Taiwanese View: Mixed Feelings, Including Alienation, Disgust. The Taiwanese barely mention parents, children, or siblings -- as relatives). Of the groups compared they show the most estranged critical attitudes toward their relatives who include mostly nieces, nephews, cousins, grandparents, aunts, and uncles. The negative terms used to describe them are disgusting and boring, having no warmth, and being involved in conflicts and quarrels. Taiwanese barely mention the nuclear family but consider their various aunts, uncles and grandparents as relatives. To be a relative is for them a basis for giving and receiving money and help. Although relatives are considered meddlesome, reality is that they have to be lived with.

---

[3]In the famine of 1960-1962, when millions starved to death, and during the many more recent periods of hardship and turmoil, most Chinese found that mutual dependence upon relatives was often the only means of survival. It is the closest thing that they have to an effective social security system. Shared hardships and dangers have created enduring personal bonds.

PRC and Taiwanese Contrasts: Intimate Rapport versus Preoccupation with Frictions, Problems. Visits to relatives play an important role on the Mainland; visits are barely mentioned by the Taiwanese. The PRC Chinese may have more time to visit; in communist China a "model" worker needs only to work for six hours a day. The help given to relatives on the Mainland has many forms; whereas the Taiwanese tends to focus on lending money. Quarrels between relatives are mentioned much more often by the Taiwanese. The general tenor of relationship with relatives on the Mainland is one of intimate friendship and mutual help. On Taiwan it maybe one of fulfilling unpleasant obligations, but this is not always so. It depends on what kind of relatives one has. "Blood is thicker than water" is still true of the case in Taiwan.

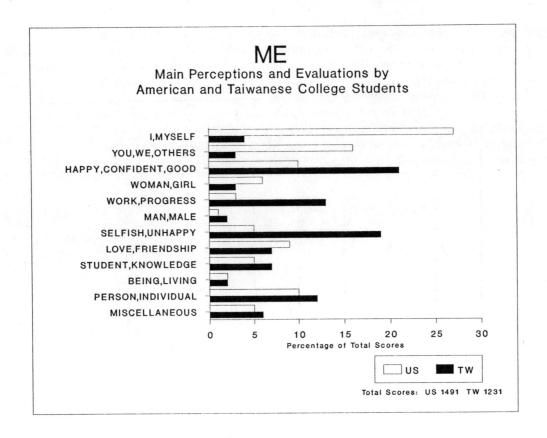

ME
Main Perceptions and Evaluations by American and Taiwanese College Students

Percentage of Total Scores

US   TW

Total Scores: US 1491 TW 1231

American View: Individual, Happy. Americans concentrate attention on the self first -- myself, I -- and secondly in relation to others -- you, we. The point of reference, in other words, is the self as an individual who may relate to others in his world. The desired relationship is love and friendship. Americans basically have a positive image of self and mention very few negative characteristics. More than any of the Chinese groups, Americans consider themselves happy. Interestingly, self is identified with female much more than male. The Americans do not strongly identify themselves in terms of their student or national status. Unlike Chinese, Americans identify little with their work or with progress. On the other hand, individualism and youth emerge far more strongly among Americans, which has to do with American.

Taiwanese View: Industrious, Self-critical. The Taiwanese, much more than the other Chinese groups or the Americans, describe themselves in terms of positive and negative personality characteristics. They apparently weigh themselves on a scale of self confidence and importance: either as very self confident, good and strong or as feeling inferior. They blame themselves mainly for lacking self-confidence, being contradictory, and lonely. However, they also pride themselves on being lovely, handsome, and Confucian. They focus less on being a student than on their general motivation to work industriously toward future achievements. They think little of their sexual or national identity.

American and Taiwanese Contrasts: Satisfied versus Ambivalent. In contrast to Americans, the Taiwanese do not focus on self relation to others but rather a personal trait and character, both positive and negative. Being happy and individualistic are two of the most important aspects of the Americans' self-image, while the Taiwanese pride themselves most on self-confidence, good looks, happiness, and industriousness -- in that order. These positive traits are counterbalanced by critical observations; concerned with lack of self-confidence, selfishness, inferiority. The identification of oneself with struggle and achievement particularly in regard to school-work is strong among the Taiwanese. The Taiwanese have to pass numerous examinations in order to be admitted to colleges and without a college diploma one could hardly secure a "good" job -- that is, a well-paid job. Fun is mentioned by the Americans, but not by the Taiwanese (or other Chinese). Both the Mainlanders and Taiwanese believe in hard work as the goal of life ("We are born to suffer").

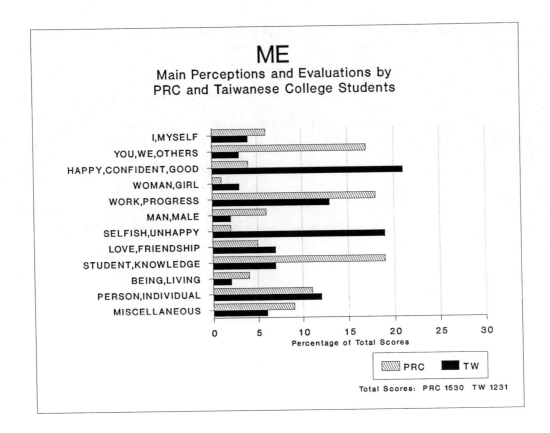

ME

Main Perceptions and Evaluations by
PRC and Taiwanese College Students

PRC Chinese: Patriotic, Hard-Working, Student. The PRC Chinese strongly identify self as student, and emphasize the importance of studying and gaining knowledge. They also pay attention to their personal responsibilities to work, achieve and pursue a career, make a contribution to the future. They tend to think of "me" in relation to "you" and others (parents, friends) rather than of self alone (oneself, individual, person). In traditional Chinese society one's glory is not his alone, but the glory of his parents and relatives as well. Sexual identity is expressed almost exclusively by the male respondents. The PRC Chinese express strong national identification and patriotism: Chinese, motherland. They are not inclined toward introspection, judging how they feel about themselves emotionally. This is probably influenced by Confucius and Mencius.

Taiwanese View: Industrious, Self-critical. The Taiwanese, much more than the other Chinese groups or the Americans, describe themselves in terms of positive and negative personality characteristics. They apparently weigh themselves on a scale of self confidence and importance: either as very self confident, good and strong or as feeling inferior. They blame themselves mainly for lacking self-confidence, being contradictory, and lonely. However, they also pride themselves on being lovely, handsome, and Confucian. They focus less on being a student than on their general motivation to work industriously toward future achievements. They think little of their sexual or national identity.

40

PRC and Taiwanese Contrasts: Work, Future versus Self-Awareness. For Chinese Mainlanders nothing is as important as being identified with working for the progress of China. In great contrast to this, self-awareness (self-confidence; self-importance; self-satisfaction) accompanied by self criticism and doubt are more characterized) to the Taiwanese. Linkage of self and parents is much stronger among the Mainland Chinese, as is their identification with the collective and society. Being a patriotic Chinese is important in the self image of the Mainlanders. The Chinese have over the years been taught that China was bullied by many superpowers in the past. Now they have stood firm in the world.

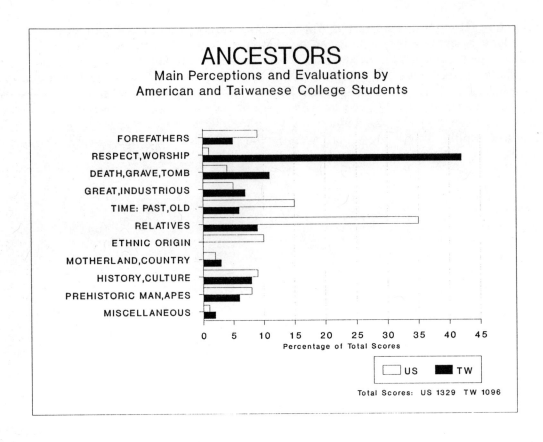

ANCESTORS
Main Perceptions and Evaluations by American and Taiwanese College Students

Percentage of Total Scores

US   TW

Total Scores: US 1329 TW 1096

American View: Deceased Relatives, Mayflower. For Americans ancestors are assigned to the past, to ancient times, and are not an active part of their daily lives. The image of the family tree and its roots is strong. Ancestors refer to old and deceased relatives, to one's forefathers of diverse national, ethnic origin: Europe, Africa. Israel. They are the ones who have shaped history and tradition. The Mayflower, forefathers, pilgrims, George Washington, pioneers, and slaves are the images that come frequently to mind. Far more than the Chinese, Americans relegate ancestors to the distant past, historic past, of little contemporary, practical relevance. American history is relatively short, which may be why Americans tend to look forward rather than backward. Ancestors does not have any religious connotation but is associated more with Darwinian theory among Americans than among other Chinese except the Mainlanders.

Taiwanese View: Respect, Sacrifice, Worship. The Taiwan group expresses the traditional Confucian view of ancestors. They concentrate on the idea of ancestor worship and paying respect and homage to the dead. They speak of the need to remember one's ancestors and to express their respect not only through prayer but also by offering sacrifices to their ancestors and worshiping them by burning incense in a temple. Also, the Taiwanese believe that the spirits of the dead can bless them. They also burn paper money for them. They don't see them from the perspectives of evolution or civilization, although they make some references to history and tradition.

American and Taiwanese Contrasts: Ethnic Forefathers versus Respected Spirits? Historic past and foreign cultural roots are predominate for Americans Taiwanese. The focus on veneration respect, and paying homage respect to their recent predecessors whose names are listed on the ancestor tablets, whose graves are regularly swept, and to whom sacrifices are offered and incense is burned. While American images come largely from the way history is taught in the U.S. school system, the Taiwanese images are very closely tied up with religious upbringing in the home.

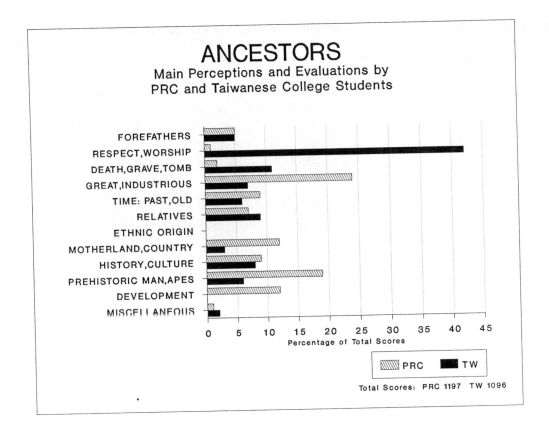

ANCESTORS
Main Perceptions and Evaluations by
PRC and Taiwanese College Students

FOREFATHERS
RESPECT, WORSHIP
DEATH, GRAVE, TOMB
GREAT, INDUSTRIOUS
TIME: PAST, OLD
RELATIVES
ETHNIC ORIGIN
MOTHERLAND, COUNTRY
HISTORY, CULTURE
PREHISTORIC MAN, APES
DEVELOPMENT
MISCELLANEOUS

0 5 10 15 20 25 30 35 40 45
Percentage of Total Scores

PRC   TW

Total Scores: PRC 1197 TW 1096

PRC Chinese: Glorious, Hard-Working, Darwin. The Mainland Chinese proudly point to the greatness of their ancestors to whom they attribute their national character. The most important qualities are industrious, hard-working and brave. The PRC view ancestors as the source of their history, culture and civilization and are proud of their famous inventions and achievements. On a parallel line, their thinking shows a strong influence of Darwinian theory in tracing the human developed back to animal origin. Of all the groups they express the strongest national identification and historic awareness, as indicated by their references to home and motherland. For the Mainland-China college student ancestors have essentially no religious connotation.[4] But even here there is a significant sense of the need to pay respect to the memory of one's ancestors; if for no other reason, because their ancestors were, in addition to the qualities mentioned above, clever, proud, and wise.

Taiwanese View: Respect, Sacrifice, Worship. The Taiwan group expresses the traditional Confucian view of ancestors. They concentrate on the idea of ancestor worship and paying respect and homage to the dead. They speak of the need to remember one's ancestors and to express their respect not only through prayer but also by offering sacrifices to their ancestors and worshiping them by burning incense in a temple. They also burn paper money for them. They don't see them from the perspectives of evolution or civilization, although they make some references to history and tradition (Taiwan's history is relatively shorter than that of Mainland China).

---

[4]This appears to be in conflict with Western missionaries, who claimed that the Chinese could never be influenced to give up ancestor worship.

44

PRC and Taiwanese Contrasts: Great Heritage versus Ancestor Tablets. The notion of paying respect, homage, and worship to ancestors is pervasive for the Taiwanese and almost non-existent for the Mainlanders. On the other hand, admiration for the great achievements of the past is much stronger among the Mainlanders. Identification with motherland or country is also intense on the Mainland. The Taiwanese made more references to death and the grave. Many responses indicate that Mainlanders are more conversant with ancient legends [such as those written down by Han Fei twenty three centuries ago] than the Taiwanese.

FAMILY
MAIN COMPONENTS AND RESPONSES

PARENTS,CHILDREN,SIBLINGS	US	PRC	TW
	664	541	297
parent,s	62	11	92
child,ren	52	78	29
mother,mom	153	84	-
brother,s younger/elder	81	102	-
father	93	67	-
sister,s	86	79	-
member	-	42	23
dear people	-	17	41
brothers & sisters	-	13	37
dad	27	33	14
my, mine	25	-	-
daughter,s	23	-	-
mum	-	-	23
son,s	16	9	-
kids	13	-	-
oneself	-	-	-
siblings	9	-	-
younger brother	-	-	9
us	8	-	-
elder sister	-	-	8
me	-	-	7
pop	7	-	-
babies	5	-	-
in-laws	4	-	-
single-parent	-	-	5
younger sister	-	-	5
father & son/daughter	-	6	4

RELATIVES,AUNTS,UNCLES	US	PRC	TW
	146	51	25
relatives	44	-	-
relations	2	28	-
uncle,s	20	-	-
aunt,s	21	-	-
cousins	15	-	-
kin,ship	11	-	-
grandmother	7	11	-
grandmother,mother's side)	-	-	3
grandfather	6	9	-
grandfather,father's side	-	-	3
relationship	3	-	7
base of growth	-	-	7
grandparents	7	-	-
architecture (structure)	-	-	5
roots	7	-	-
-- trees	-	3	-
nieces	3	-	-

WARMTH, LOVE	US	PRC	TW
	139	107	229
warm,th	8	73	176
love,ing	99	27	24
affection	3	-	-
care,ing	18	7	8
concern	-	-	10
trust	9	-	-
lovable	-	-	8
understand	2	-	-
kind & friendly	-	-	3

HAPPY,HARMONIOUS,JOYFUL	US	PRC	TW
	123	410	317
happy,ness, well-being	20	98	94
harmony,ious	-	151	-
perfectly	-	73	47
joyous,ful (happy)	-	52	4
safe	-	-	29
security	29	-	-
comfortable	-	6	27
peaceful	-	-	23
support	18	-	-
stable	-	4	16
share,ing	15	-	2
relax	-	-	12
freedom	-	8	14
help,ing	11	2	11
peace	4	-	-
quiet	-	-	10
politely	-	3	10
hope,s	8	2	6
esteem each other	-	8	-
strength	8	-	1
health	7	-	-
please	-	-	5
comfort	-	-	3
equality	-	3	-
communication	3	-	-
cooperation	-	-	3

NECESSARY, FINE, SWEET	US	PRC	TW
	20	24	32
necessary	-	6	19
fine	-	18	-
sweet	-	-	10
need	7	-	-
good	6	-	-
want	5	-	-
great	2	-	3

UNIT, TOGETHERNESS	US	PRC	TW
	217	71	77
unit	62	-	-
together,ness	61	-	4
cells, of the society	-	37	6
united,y	24	26	-
nuclear family	22	-	-
origin	-	-	21
close,ness	20	-	2
family spirit	-	-	15
bind	-	-	11
ties	10	-	-
collective	-	8	3
belonging, sense of	-	-	-
part of soc. organization	-	-	8
gathering	7	-	-
bond	6	-	-
unite	-	-	7
tight	5	-	-

SOCIETY,FRIENDS,PEOPLE	US	PRC	TW
	95	107	13
society	-	43	-
population	-	34	4
friend,s,ship	34	6	5
group	34	-	-
people	14	-	-
social organization	-	9	-
community	7	-	-
boyfriend	-	-	4
aged	-	6	-
adult	-	9	-
companions	6	-	-

HOUSE,LIVING SITUATION	US	PRC	TW
	110	99	97
house,hold	47	24	18
home	58	-	-
haven	-	-	40
furniture,ishings	-	39	12
housing	-	23	2
country	-	9	3
nest	-	-	8
yard	-	4	8
room	5	-	4
space	-	-	2

FAMILY LIFE	US	PRC	TW
	123	95	130
daily life	-	38	-
t.v.	-	5	-
dog	21	-	8
life	19	-	-
responsibility	-	-	18
motion	-	-	18
reunion,s	9	17	-
meal,s	2	2	-
dinner	7	-	5
money	3	6	10
t.v. show	12	-	-
obligation	-	-	9
vacation,s	8	-	-
conversation	-	-	8
entertainment	-	8	2
food	-	4	8
fun	8	-	-
eating	-	-	8
family plan	-	-	7
affair	7	-	-
planning	6	-	-
work	3	6	-
meeting	-	-	5
living together	-	-	4
living	-	-	4
holidays	3	-	-
Thanksgiving	5	-	-
chatting and laughing	-	5	5
station wagon	3	-	-
housework	-	4	-
Christmas	2	-	-
videotape machine	-	-	2
eating together	-	-	4
outing	5	-	-
book	-	-	5

MARRIAGE, SPOUSE	US	PRC	TW
	46	185	59
wife	17	62	14
husband	7	44	5
marry,iage	15	19	10
husband and wife	-	16	-
woman	-	12	3
man	7	10	-
male	-	8	3
get married	-	-	7
form a family	-	6	7
monogamy	-	-	7
housewife	-	6	-
sex	-	-	3
production relation	-	2	-

SIZE: BIG, SMALL	US	PRC	TW
	57	9	23
big, extended	17	9	4
small	13	-	-
large	11	-	-
four	9	-	-
little family	-	-	8
limit	-	-	5
crowded	-	-	6
structure	3	-	-
growth	4	-	-

QUARREL,BROKEN,DIVORCE	US	PRC	TW
	26	22	56
quarrel	-	-	16
burden	-	-	16
contradiction	-	9	-
dispute	-	7	4
divorce	4	-	3
feud	8	-	-
worry	-	-	6
split	-	6	-
pain	-	-	5
problems	5	-	-
hate	5	-	-
struggle	4	-	-
escape	-	-	3
pressure	-	-	3

MISCELLANEOUS	US	PRC	TW
	38	32	70
future	-	6	2
sleep	-	-	19
mafia	10	-	-
education	-	8	5
income	-	7	-
status	-	5	2
crush	-	-	10
realistic	-	-	7
study	-	6	-
mob	6	-	-
pregnant	-	-	10
upbringing	6	-	-
fancy	-	-	5
chance (spiritual)	-	-	3
memorize	-	-	3
God	4	-	-
religion	4	-	-
Catholic	5	-	-
homesick	-	-	4
always	3	-	-

SUMMARY

Main Components	Percentage of Total Score		
	US	PRC	TW
PARENTS,CHILDREN,SIBLINGS	37	31	21
RELATIVES, AUNTS, UNCLES	8	3	2
SIZE: BIG, SMALL	3	1	2
WARMTH, LOVE	8	6	16
HAPPY, HARMONIOUS, JOYFUL	7	23	22
NECESSARY, FINE, SWEET	1	1	2
UNIT, TOGETHERNESS	12	4	5
SOCIETY, FRIENDS, PEOPLE	5	6	1
HOUSE, LIVING SITUATION	6	6	7
FAMILY LIFE	7	5	9
MARRIAGE, SPOUSE	3	11	4
QUARREL, BROKEN, DIVORCE	1	1	4
MISCELLANEOUS	2	2	5
Total Scores	1804	1753	1425

MOTHER
MAIN COMPONENTS AND RESPONSES

CHILDREN, FAMILY MEMBERS	US	PRC	TW
	223	127	26
child,ren	60	33	9
brother,s (younger/elder)	-	36	-
daughter	35	-	-
family	34	10	3
sister,s (younger/elder)	25	27	-
son	27	-	-
my, mother	19	-	-
childhood	-	10	2
-- in law	9	-	-
me	9	-	7
foster	-	6	-
for children	-	5	-
generation gap	-	-	5
kids	5	-	-

FATHER	US	PRC	TW
	264	99	16
father	264	99	13
husband	-	-	-
father's wife	-	-	3

MOM, WOMAN, FEMALE	US	PRC	TW
	265	150	75
mum	-	69	-
mom	66	-	-
woman	50	24	15
bear,s child,ren	-	12	35
wife	34	-	-
baby	27	-	-
female	21	-	7
grandmother,mother's side	-	20	-
parent	20	-	-
milk	-	4	3
breast-feed	-	-	8
life	7	5	1
lady	7	-	-
birth	12	-	-
maternal instinct	-	4	-
maternal	8	-	-
give birth	-	6	-
grandmother	-	-	2
pregnant	7	-	1
spouse	-	6	-
person	6	-	-

HARD WORK, INDUSTRIOUS	US	PRC	TW
	56	244	235
industrious	-	66	-
toil,some	-	26	94
hardworking, and thrifty	-	43	-
work,ing	13	24	-
work hard	-	22	-
labor	-	21	-
every way possible	-	-	-
in every possible way	-	-	7
busy	5	-	4
hardworking	-	-	16
excitability	-	-	14
work	-	-	14
daily life	-	14	-
money	5	-	13
support,ive	13	6	5
overworked	-	11	-
hardship, bear	-	11	-
sacrifice	-	-	10
frugal	-	-	9
suffer	-	-	9
petty cash	-	-	2
provider	8	-	-
security	7	-	-
earns money	-	-	6
uptight (highstrung)	-	-	5
workhorse	-	-	5
great expectations	-	-	4
responsibility	-	-	6
pressure	-	-	6
brave	-	-	6
career	5	-	-

COOK, CLEAN	US	PRC	TW
	56	47	109
cook	-	-	42
cook,s,ing	25	-	-
housework	-	10	9
wash,es clothes	-	-	20
feed	4	16	-
clothes	-	3	3
kitchen	3	-	12
free service	-	-	10
bring up	-	10	-
meal	-	4	8
homemaker	8	-	-
food	7	-	-
housewife	5	-	-
diapers	2	-	-
clean	2	-	-
sewing	-	4	-
baby basket	-	-	5

GOOD, KIND, FRIEND	US	PRC	TW
	135	483	280
kind,ly merciful	14	113	-
kind,ly	-	-	102
gentle, and mild	-	82	-
great, person	7	56	-
amiable	-	20	19
great	-	-	57
kindhearted	-	56	4
dear person	-	41	-
friend,ly	40	-	16
lovable	-	37	5
respectable, and lovable	-	27	-
gentle and soft	-	-	23
selfless	-	15	-
happy,ness	14	5	6
virtuous	-	13	4
good	11	-	-
fun	11	-	-
nice/good	11	6	-
sweet	11	-	-
spiritual strength	-	-	14
strength	7	-	-
strong	-	-	4
healthy	-	-	4
superior	2	-	-
patience	-	-	9
generous	-	-	8
funny	7	-	-
glad	-	6	-
normal	-	-	5
courtesy	-	6	-

CARE, HELP, EDUCATE	US	PRC	TW
	157	171	104
cares,ing	72	-	-
care/solicitude, take go	-	25	-
care, take every care fo	-	47	-
help,er,ful	37	-	-
teacher,ing (education)	16	20	10
lofty	-	20	-
take care	-	-	-
give every care to	-	-	19
filial, show - obedience	-	16	-
education	-	-	17
careful	-	15	-
care, give every care to	13	9	-
show filial obedience	-	-	13
strict	-	-	12
safe feeling	-	-	11
take care of	-	-	8
take care of children	-	8	-
take every care for	-	-	7
discipline	7	-	-
glory	-	6	-
health	-	5	-
protector	5	-	-
need	4	-	-
remind	-	-	4
haven (safe harbor)	-	-	3
guidance	3	-	-

LOVE, UNDERSTANDING	US	PRC	TW
	256	308	237
love,s,ing	176	51	-
maternal love	-	117	-
love	-	-	103
affection,ate	14	56	10
cherish	-	12	-
respect, and love	-	8	-
warm,th	16	16	37
consideration, show peop	-	22	-
understand	19	-	-
loving care	-	-	16
love,s children	-	7	6
esteem	-	-	8
cherish,es child,ren	-	-	10
show utmost solicitude	-	-	2
respect	-	-	10
intimate	-	-	3
understandable	-	-	9
kiss	-	8	-
loving mother	-	7	-
tender	5	-	-
love deeply	-	4	-
thankful	-	-	4
nostalgia	-	-	5
trust	5	-	2
show solicitude for	-	-	2
cordial	-	-	-
comfort	6	-	4
compassion	7	-	6
concerned	6	-	-
faith	2	-	-

APPEARANCE: BEAUTIFUL,FAT	US	PRC	TW
	47	76	72
beautiful	10	35	-
fat	9	-	10
beauty	-	-	25
smiling face	-	9	-
white hair	-	-	15
wrinkle	-	-	11
old,aged	-	6	6
breast	11	-	-
simple	-	8	-
Spanish	6	-	-
round	5	-	-
soft	6	-	-
pretty	-	4	-
age	-	8	-
appearance	-	6	-
hand	-	-	5

HATE, HYPERCRITICAL	US	PRC	TW
	81	13	61
hate	18	-	-
hypercritical	-	-	13
fucker	11	-	-
ignorant	-	-	7
strange	9	-	-
worry	-	-	5
busybody	-	-	5
fight,ing	3	-	4
fearful	-	-	3
bossy	7	-	-
stubborn	-	-	7
fear	4	-	-
pushy	7	-	-
nags	5	-	-
horrific	-	-	5
abusive	8	-	-
pain,ful	4	4	-
conflict	5	-	-
severe	-	9	-
tears	-	-	8
self-centered on beauty	-	-	4

HOME, HOMELAND	US	PRC	TW
	37	109	0
home	33	12	-
house	4	-	-
homeland	-	85	-
hometown	-	6	-
out of hometown, person	-	6	-

MISCELLANEOUS	US	PRC	TW
	25	32	125
wordy, verbose	-	-	40
repay	-	11	8
long-breath	-	-	-
Mother's Day	-	-	14
missing	-	11	-
study	-	10	-
Carnation	-	-	12
conservative	-	-	2
has rights	-	-	10
independent	-	-	5
girlfriend	-	-	6
nature	3	-	-
future	-	-	4
earth	6	-	-
divorce	7	-	-
expect	-	-	4
freedom	-	-	6
flower,s	4	-	3
present	-	-	3
silent	-	-	5
night	5	-	-
May	-	-	3

SUMMARY

Main Components	Percentage of Total Score		
	US	PRC	TW
CHILDREN, FAMILY MEMBERS	14	7	2
FATHER	16	5	1
MOM, WOMAN, FEMALE	17	8	6
HOME, HOMELAND	2	6	0
HARD WORK, INDUSTRIOUS	3	13	18
GOOD, KIND, FRIEND	8	26	21
CARE, HELP, EDUCATE	10	9	8
LOVE, UNDERSTANDING	16	17	18
COOK, CLEAN	3	3	8
APPEARANCE: BEAUTIFUL, FAT	3	4	5
HATE, HYPERCRITICAL	5	1	5
MISCELLANEOUS	2	2	9
Total Scores	1602	1859	1340

FATHER
MAIN COMPONENTS AND RESPONSES

DAD,FAMILY	US 318	PRC 259	TW 51
dad,dy,pop,father	93	64	14
son	50	13	3
family	37	47	5
children	32	36	8
daughter	30	-	-
parent,s	26	34	3
my, mine	17	-	-
brothers & sisters	13	6	2
baby	7	-	-
grandfather	6	31	-
relative	5	-	-
me	2	-	-
brother,s younger/elder	-	13	-
foster children	-	8	-
grandmother	-	7	-
generation gap	-	-	16

MOTHER,PARENTS,MARRIAGE	332	107	41
mother,mom	294	101	26
husband	33	-	8
marriage	5	-	7
wife	-	6	-

AUTHORITY, STERN, STRICT	176	249	196
strong, and forceful	24	13	-
severe,stern,strict	21	41	15
guide,ance,leader	21	-	-
head of family,patriarch	17	12	13
esteem, respect,able	15	58	15
authority	14	-	38
model,figure	14	-	17
teacher,ing	11	13	-
hard,tough	10	-	-
tyrant,ruler	10	-	-
boss	8	-	2
discipline,spanking	7	-	-
sire	4	-	-
dignity,fied,presitge	-	28	-
fair-minded	-	24	-
lofty,status	-	22	-
pillar of family	-	9	25
bring up, rear	-	8	16
powerful	-	8	2
bold and resolute	-	7	-
behave	-	6	-
strong	-	-	15
power	-	-	8
teacher	-	-	8
argue	-	-	7
judges wisely,decision	-	-	6
punishment	-	-	5
master	-	-	4

MAN, MALE, APPEARANCE	151	185	59
man	67	44	4
male	26	27	10
tall, big	17	41	4
aged, old	10	16	18
boy	10	-	-
person	7	-	-
human	6	-	-
sex,sexual	5	-	8
masculine	3	-	-
older generation	-	27	5
age	-	15	-
oneself	-	9	-
appearance	-	6	-
white hair	-	-	6
fat	-	-	4

BAD, HYPERCRITICAL	29	10	131
bad	13	-	-
divorce	7	-	3
alcoholic	7	-	-
anger,angry	2	-	5
frightful	-	7	-
chide	-	3	-
hypercritical	-	-	21
unreasonable	-	-	20
bad temper	-	-	12
stubborn	-	-	12
cold	-	-	11
horrific, terrifying	-	-	7
communication distance	-	-	7
hedonistic	-	-	5
fear	-	-	5
strange	-	-	5
suffer	-	-	5
beating	-	-	5
action without thought	-	-	4
blame	-	-	4

LOVE, UNDERSTAND, GOOD	US 119	PRC 193	TW 128
love,ing	80	19	-
paternal	14	-	-
trust	8	9	-
need	7	-	-
caring	6	-	-
miss	4	-	-
father love	-	47	-
show consideration for	-	28	-
affection	-	24	4
I love father	-	15	-
remember with longing	-	15	-
love children	-	9	-
show every care of	-	7	-
hope	-	6	-
harmonious	-	6	-
show filial obedience	-	5	7
deep love	-	3	-
affable	-	-	43
love between family member	-	-	36
cherishes children	-	-	11
concern	-	-	6
dependent on	-	-	4
care	-	-	4
good person	-	-	4
love(between boy & girl)	-	-	3
relationship	-	-	3
like	-	-	3

WORKER, INDUSTRIOUS	98	198	127
work,er	37	44	-
provider	29	-	-
protector,tion	10	16	2
breadwinner	10	-	-
responsibility	8	-	23
goal	4	-	-
industrious, diligent	-	46	-
toil,some	-	31	7
hard-working	-	26	7
rely on	-	20	-
daily life	-	10	-
labor	-	5	-
hardship	-	-	47
sport, exercise	-	-	12
busy	-	-	9
burden	-	-	6
planting	-	-	4
free service	-	-	4
diligent	-	-	3
outdoor recreation	-	-	3

GOOD, KIND, WONDERFUL	109	379	304
friend	22	-	16
good	17	15	-
kind,kindhearted,kindly	7	155	49
helper,ful	14	-	-
great	11	14	8
benevolent	6	-	8
happiness	6	-	-
dependable	5	-	-
quiet	5	-	-
warm	4	6	-
fun	4	-	4
wonderful	4	-	-
there	4	-	-
dear person	-	51	-
lovable	-	35	-
earnest, solemn	-	24	-
cordial	-	21	7
noble,brave	-	14	-
honest and tolerant	-	14	-
simple	-	9	-
steady	-	8	-
sincere	-	7	-
selfless	-	6	-
solemn	-	-	106
silent	-	-	25
freedom	-	-	16
honest	-	-	12
smiling	-	-	9
humor	-	-	8
diplomat (sociable)	-	-	8
entertaining	-	-	7
safe	-	-	5
happy	-	-	5
generous	-	-	5
have a meal	-	-	3
stable	-	-	3

INTELLIGENT, EDUCATED	US 26	PRC 47	TW 64
smart,intelligent	10	-	-
wise	9	-	-
successful	7	-	-
educate,study	-	26	-
knowledge	-	8	-
talent	-	7	-
hobby	-	6	-
high quality	-	-	8
newspaper	-	-	8
wordy, verbose	-	-	8
video machine	-	-	7
helps people	-	-	7
clever	-	-	6
reads books	-	-	5
school	-	-	5
watches movies	-	-	5
confidence	-	-	5

WAGES, MONEY, CAR	55	25	77
home,house	23	6	-
makes money,money	22	6	44
car	10	-	6
repay	-	7	5
wages	-	6	-
supporter	-	-	7
rich	-	-	6
house manager	-	-	6
property	-	-	3

JOB, CAREER	39	49	73
job	19	-	51
doctor	11	-	4
accountant	5	-	-
career	4	-	-
factory director	-	10	-
capable	-	8	2
engineer	-	6	-
farming	-	6	-
society	-	5	-
factory	-	5	-
occupation	-	5	-
guard	-	4	-
stock market	-	-	5
experience	-	-	5
security (insurance)	-	-	4
cook	-	-	2

SICKNESS,DEATH	10	15	30
sickness	7	-	-
death	3	-	6
smoking	-	8	7
died	-	7	-
disease	-	-	13
hospital	-	-	4

MISCELLANEOUS	64	0	7
priest	21	-	-
Father's Day	11	-	3
God	7	-	4
Robert	7	-	-
Oedipus	7	-	-
Simon Deda	6	-	-
time	5	-	-

SUMMARY

Main Components	Percentage of Total Score		
	US	PRC	TW
DAD,FAMILY	21	15	4
MOTHER,PARENTS,MARRIAGE	22	6	3
AUTHORITY, STERN, STRICT	12	15	15
MAN, MALE, APPEARANCE	10	11	5
BAD, HYPERCRITICAL	2	1	10
LOVE, UNDERSTAND, GOOD	8	11	10
WORKER, INDUSTRIOUS	6	12	10
WAGES, MONEY, CAR	4	1	6
JOB, CAREER	3	3	6
GOOD, KIND, WONDERFUL	7	22	24
INTELLIGENT, EDUCATED	2	3	5
SICKNESS,DEATH	1	1	2
MISCELLANEOUS	4	0	1
Total Scores	1526	1716	1288

PARENTS
MAIN COMPONENTS AND RESPONSES

MOTHER,FATHER	US 536	PRC 638	TW 14
mother	180	158	-
father	147	178	-
dad	57	-	-
mom	51	-	-
two	29	-	-
mom & dad,dad & mum	25	23	-
marriage,married	24	7	7
grandparents	15	-	-
folks	8	-	-
father and mother/parent	-	194	-
grandmother (dad's side)	-	26	-
grandfather (dad's side)	-	22	-
parents unite	-	12	-
grandmother (mom's side)	-	9	-
grandfather (mom's side)	-	9	-
parents	-	-	7

FAMILY,CHILDREN,RELATIVES	US 230	PRC 165	TW 115
children	78	35	28
family	63	28	56
my	15	-	-
sister,s	12	19	-
people	11	-	-
brother,s	7	11	-
son,s	7	7	-
baby,ies	7	-	-
birth	7	-	-
kids	6	-	-
mine	6	-	-
offspring	6	-	-
daughters	5	-	-
uncle (mother's brother)	-	11	-
man	-	9	-
uncle (dad's younger br)	-	8	-
friends and relatives	-	8	-
person	-	7	-
uncle (dad's elder br)	-	6	-
aunt (father's sister)	-	5	-
me	-	4	8
younger brother	-	4	-
aunt (mother's sister)	-	3	-
family spirit	-	-	8
childhood	-	-	5
blood relationship	-	-	5
relatives	-	-	5

LOVE, AFFECTION	US 209	PRC 162	TW 153
love,loving	146	19	75
friend,s,friendship	30	18	10
understand	17	-	-
loved ones	7	-	-
sex	5	-	-
cherish	4	-	2
motherlove	-	19	-
love children	-	17	4
dear	-	16	-
affection	-	13	37
have deep love,love dearly	-	24	-
dear persons	-	9	-
love each other	-	9	-
closest	-	7	-
show every care	-	6	-
unite	-	5	-
show consideration to	-	-	14
dear feeling	-	-	8
miss	-	-	3

RESPECT, OBEDIENCE	US 88	PRC 80	TW 153
respect	7	-	25
respect each other	-	8	-
authority	15	-	33
discipline	16	-	-
rules	8	-	-
independent	7	-	7
strict	7	-	-
obey,obedience	6	-	25
restriction	6	-	-
honor	6	-	-
boss	5	-	-
leaders	5	-	-
esteem/respect	-	24	-
show filial obedience	-	15	-
severe	-	14	-
head of the family	-	12	-
win honor for	-	7	-
respect and love	-	-	21
lord	-	-	9
limit	-	-	8
pillar	-	-	7
decision	-	-	7
democracy	-	-	6
conservative	-	-	5

BRING UP, TEACH	US 89	PRC 38	TW 174
guides,guidance	21	-	-
teacher,s	17	-	5
guardians	16	-	-
teach	10	-	6
raise	7	-	-
example	7	-	-
role model	6	-	-
learn	5	-	-
education	-	28	25
knowledge	-	5	-
encourage	-	5	-
bring up	-	-	42
direct	-	-	28
lesson	-	-	16
good example	-	-	14
wordy, verbose	-	-	14
expect	-	-	11
discuss	-	-	7
remind	-	-	6

WORK HARD,SERIOUS	US 51	PRC 89	TW 188
money	21	-	22
work	12	26	25
responsibility	11	-	-
strength	7	-	-
diligent	-	18	-
repay	-	10	15
laborious/hardship	-	10	-
work hard	-	9	-
hardworking	-	8	-
earnest	-	8	-
serious	-	-	38
toil	-	-	38
earn money	-	-	14
pressure	-	-	9
capable	-	-	6
burden	-	-	6
sacrifice	-	-	5
petty cash	-	-	5
business	-	-	5

HAPPINESS, HARMONY	US 44	PRC 54	TW 42
funny,fun	12	-	-
together	11	-	-
happy	9	-	3
togetherness	8	-	-
smiles	2	-	-
holidays	2	-	-
harmony	-	24	19
family happiness	-	8	-
hopes	-	8	-
joyful/happy	-	6	-
happiness	-	5	7
future	-	3	5
freedom	-	-	8

AGE, HEALTH	US 40	PRC 101	TW 69
adults	14	-	-
old	11	-	23
forever	7	-	-
grow up,growing up	6	8	-
living,live	2	-	4
health,healthy	-	26	10
senior/old	-	19	-
living in good health	-	17	-
long life	-	11	-
old people	-	8	-
age	-	6	4
older generation	-	6	-
generation gap	-	-	18
elders	-	-	7
diseased	-	-	3

KIND, AMIABLE	US 39	PRC 167	TW 124
good	15	-	-
nice	14	-	-
great	7	12	27
blessed	3	-	-
kindly	-	50	5
amiable	-	28	12
respectable	-	26	-
lovable	-	18	-
intimate/cordial	-	13	-
warm	-	12	18
nice and pretty	-	8	-
kind-hearted	-	-	21
carefree	-	-	13
peaceful	-	-	8
patient	-	-	8
cordial	-	-	7
generous	-	-	5

HELP, CARE, PROTECT	US 190	PRC 79	TW 174
caring,care	52	-	-
helpful,help	41	7	-
need,needed	18	-	-
supportive	11	-	-
giving	11	-	-
protect,-or,-ive	10	-	33
support	8	-	30
providers	8	-	-
security	8	-	-
provide for/support	7	17	-
nurture	7	-	-
caretakers	6	-	-
worry	3	-	-
show consideration for	-	21	-
help each other	-	13	-
show solicitude	-	9	-
worry about	-	6	-
support me	-	6	-
take care of	-	-	59
watchful	-	-	23
important	-	-	14
manage house	-	-	11
show solicitude to	-	-	4

ON BAD TERMS, DIVORCED	US 44	PRC 0	TW 63
divorced	13	-	1
hate	9	-	-
hurt	7	-	-
fight, ing	7	-	-
bad	6	-	-
argue	2	-	18
on bad terms	-	-	16
irritate	-	-	7
tragedy, drama	-	-	6
shouting	-	-	6
distant	-	-	5
beating	-	-	4

HOME, MOTHERLAND	US 66	PRC 36	TW 9
home	46	13	-
house	20	-	-
motherland	-	12	-
hometown	-	6	-
country	-	5	-
haven (safe harbor)	-	-	6
return home	-	-	3

MISCELLANEOUS	US 8	PRC 31	TW 41
poor	8	-	-
daily life	-	31	-
response	-	-	29
eat meal	-	-	12

SUMMARY

Main Components	Percentage of Total Score		
	US	PRC	TW
MOTHER,FATHER	33	39	1
FAMILY,CHILDREN,RELATIVES	14	10	9
LOVE, AFFECTION	13	10	12
RESPECT, OBEDIENCE	5	5	12
BRING UP, TEACH	5	2	13
WORK HARD,SERIOUS	3	5	14
HAPPINESS, HARMONY	3	3	3
AGE, HEALTH	2	6	5
KIND, AMIABLE	2	10	9
HELP, CARE, PROTECT	12	5	13
ON BAD TERMS, DIVORCED	3	0	5
HOME, MOTHERLAND	4	2	1
MISCELLANEOUS	0	2	3
Total Scores	1634	1640	1319

CHILDREN
MAIN COMPONENTS AND RESPONSES

BOYS, GIRLS, KIDS	US 286	PRC 292	TW 34
kids	62	-	-
children	-	52	12
baby,ies	61	9	-
boy,s	40	23	6
girl,s	34	23	3
many	27	-	-
offspring	19	-	-
siblings	12	-	-
younger/elder,sister	9	27	-
son,s	8	40	-
brother,s,elder brother	8	28	2
daughter,s	6	29	-
male	-	27	-
female	-	19	-
flesh and blood	-	9	-
son and daughter	-	6	-
children's day,childhood	-	-	11

FAMILY, PARENTS	US 243	PRC 318	TW 100
parent,s	71	134	15
family	55	33	18
mother	36	20	5
father,daddy	28	20	-
marriage,marry	14	21	3
nephew,niece	17	-	7
people	10	-	-
me	7	15	-
wife	5	-	12
next,future generation	-	50	20
relations	-	15	-
independent, oneself	-	10	4
husband	-	-	8
home	-	-	4
descendant	-	-	4

LOVE, AFFECTION	US 116	PRC 138	TW 65
love,loving	87	-	19
lovable	2	41	21
want	8	-	-
union,unite	7	11	-
friend,s,friendly	10	3	-
enjoy	2	-	-
love the parents	-	18	-
missing,miss dear ones	-	22	-
love dearly	-	13	-
fruit of love	-	10	-
love friendly affection	-	7	-
contact	-	7	-
dear people	-	6	-
like	-	-	10
affection	-	-	8
tender solicitation	-	-	4
parental love	-	-	3

RESPECT, OBEDIENCE, DUTY	US 21	PRC 165	TW 44
responsibility	12	-	-
trusting	5	-	-
honest	4	4	-
filial obedience	-	58	12
respect parents,respect	-	54	-
duty,ies	-	22	18
obey	-	8	1
obligation	-	7	-
esteem	-	4	-
win honor for	-	4	-
subject them to discipline	-	4	-
faithful	-	-	13

SUPPORT, TAKE CARE OF	US 49	PRC 122	TW 93
caring,care	19	-	-
money	8	-	3
babysitter,babysitting	7	-	-
expensive	7	-	-
give	5	-	-
helpful	3	-	-
support	-	20	-
take good care of/protect	-	26	-
bring up	-	13	5
provide for the parents	-	21	-
help each other	-	11	-
provide for	-	11	-
contribute	-	8	-
provide for the old	-	5	-
management	-	5	-
care for, show solicitude	-	2	-
be protected	-	-	57
child welfare	-	-	11
pampers (diapers)	-	-	8
danger, peril	-	-	5
spent	-	-	4

EDUCATION, STUDY, JOB	US 111	PRC 277	TW 204
school,s,go to school	42	37	7
education / foster	-	25	41
learn,learning	27	-	6
teach,teacher	19	-	9
impression	11	-	-
potential	7	-	-
kindergarten	5	-	13
study,homework,studious	-	48	2
job,career	-	36	-
reading in school	-	20	-
employment,labor	-	25	-
hope,s	-	16	21
cultivate	-	15	17
hope son become imperial	-	11	-
become worthy people/talent	-	10	-
profession	-	9	-
smart	-	7	14
attend university	-	6	-
achievement,accomplishment	-	6	4
moral character	-	4	-
intelligence	-	2	-
master	-	-	42
questioning	-	-	8
thought, idea	-	-	5
talent class	-	-	4
computer	-	-	4
encourage	-	-	4
exam	-	-	3

PLAY, TOYS, HAPPINESS	US 313	PRC 61	TW 158
play,playing	79	-	3
happy,happiness	48	-	25
fun	34	-	-
toy,s	25	-	19
playful	24	-	-
game,s	20	-	5
laughter,laughing	18	-	2
joy	17	-	14
smile,s	10	-	10
run,running	10	-	-
energetic	7	-	-
playmates	6	-	-
camp	5	-	-
funny	5	-	-
Christmas	3	-	-
playground	2	-	-
give presents to	-	17	-
vigor,vivid	-	14	33
daily life	-	12	-
eat	-	9	-
play and joy happy	-	7	-
wear	-	2	-
good cooking	-	-	13
milk	-	-	8
candy	-	-	8
carefree	-	-	7
freedom	-	-	5
t.v.	-	-	4
doll	-	-	2

CUTE, INNOCENT,NAIVE	US 151	PRC 37	TW 425
cute	43	-	-
innocent,innocence	41	-	23
helpless	18	-	-
vulnerable	8	-	-
beautiful,good looking	7	11	-
wonderful	7	-	6
curious	7	-	-
good	6	-	3
sweet	5	-	-
precocious	5	-	-
adorable	4	-	-
sweet of parents	-	16	-
nice	-	10	-
lovely	-	-	180
naive	-	-	134
purity, pure	-	-	28
good-hearted	-	-	20
no trouble	-	-	7
precious	-	-	7
angel	-	-	6
paradise	-	-	6
elegant	-	-	5

SEX, REPRODUCTION	US 33	PRC 29	TW 8
sex	12	-	-
two	10	-	-
life	6	-	-
pregnant	5	-	2
only one child	-	12	-
reproduction	-	11	-
bear children	-	6	-
assn. of family planning	-	-	3
nipple	-	-	3

YOUNG, GROWTH, AGE	US 229	PRC 63	TW 91
young,youth	100	-	-
small,little	59	-	-
future	21	11	19
grow,growth,growing	31	-	12
adults	7	-	-
youngsters	5	-	-
immature	6	-	-
grow up	-	29	3
the aged	-	14	-
the old and the young	-	9	-
very young	-	-	25
chubby	-	-	12
health	-	-	8
weak	-	-	5
strong	-	-	5
gap	-	-	2

NAUGHTY, TROUBLE, BRATS	US 90	PRC 19	TW 141
fight,quarrel	10	7	-
noisy,very noisy	9	-	13
cry,ing	7	6	15
brats	7	-	-
problems	7	-	-
snot	7	-	-
cruel	6	-	-
insecure	5	-	-
messy,dirty	10	-	-
loud	5	-	-
mean	5	-	-
lost	4	-	-
sneaky	4	-	-
pain	4	-	-
weakly learned	-	6	-
naughty	-	-	27
burden	-	-	19
childish	-	-	18
be not obedient	-	-	15
pity	-	-	10
boring	-	-	8
abduction	-	-	7
worry	-	-	5
stupid	-	-	4

MISCELLANEOUS	US 9	PRC 18	TW 52
important	9	-	6
country	-	6	-
frank	-	1	-
beating and blame	-	-	8
forge	-	-	7
eternal	-	-	7
government,society	-	-	9
circumstance	-	-	5
foster,orphanage	-	-	10
motherland	-	5	-
beam and pillar	-	6	-

SUMMARY

Main Components	Percentage of Total Score		
	US	PRC	TW
BOYS, GIRLS, KIDS	17	19	2
FAMILY, PARENTS	15	21	7
LOVE, AFFECTION	7	9	5
RESPECT,OBEDIENCE,DUTY	1	11	3
EDUCATION, STUDY, JOB	7	18	14
SUPPORT, TAKE CARE OF	3	8	7
PLAY, TOYS, HAPPINESS	19	4	11
CUTE, INNOCENT,NAIVE	9	2	30
YOUNG, GROWTH, AGE	14	4	6
SEX, REPRODUCTION	2	2	1
NAUGHTY, TROUBLE, BRAT	5	1	10
MISCELLANEOUS	1	1	4
Total Scores	1651	1539	1415

RELATIVES
MAIN COMPONENTS AND RESPONSES

MOTHER,FATHER,CHILDREN	US	PRC	TW
	338	91	76
mother,s	65	-	2
father	62	15	-
brother,s	57	8	8
sister,s	57	2	-
parents	35	24	6
wedding,s	14	-	-
kid,s	8	-	4
in-laws	7	-	-
children	7	-	-
dad	6	-	-
brother-in-law	6	-	-
folks	6	-	-
mother-in-law	5	-	-
marriage	3	-	18
girl and sister-in-law	-	10	-
sister (younger)	-	9	-
brother (older)	-	8	-
sister (older)	-	7	-
sister-in-law	-	5	-
brothers and sisters	-	3	-
parents and brothers	-	-	22
get married	-	-	16

AUNTS,UNCLES,GRANDPARENTS	610	497	216
cousin,s	163	-	21
aunt,s	157	15	12
uncle,s	134	12	10
grandparent,s	63	-	-
grandma/mother	51	-	-
grandpa/father	24	-	-
nephews	15	-	-
niece	3	-	-
aunt-mother's sister	-	105	23
uncle-father's brother	-	91	5
aunt-father's sister	-	88	27
uncle-mother's brother	-	75	26
uncle-father's older broe	-	38	-
grandmother-mother's side	-	16	22
aunt-father's bro's wife	-	16	-
grandmother-father's side	-	15	8
uncle-mother's sis' husband	-	13	-
aunt- dad's old bro's wife	-	7	-
cousin (female)	-	6	-
grandfather-mother's side	-	-	24
cousin (younger female)	-	-	15
cousin (older,female)	-	-	8
grandfather-father's side	-	-	8
cousin (male)	-	-	7

FAMILY, BLOOD, RELATION	349	171	196
family	179	8	33
relaions, -ship	27	40	-
ancestor,s	27	-	-
distant	21	-	-
kin	17	-	-
few	16	-	7
blood	16	-	-
many	13	-	32
far away	7	-	-
related	6	-	-
roots	5	-	-
family tree	4	-	-
loved ones	4	-	-
blood relationship	-	39	-
dear person	-	31	25
family members	-	15	-
clan	-	9	-
blood relations	-	7	89
relatives and friends	-	6	-
remote relatives	-	4	-
elder generation	-	-	6
countryside	-	-	4
city	-	4	-
country	4	8	-
Spanish	3	-	-

FRIENDS,PEOPLE,CLASSMATES	85	183	53
friend,s	64	118	25
people	21	5	-
classmates	-	25	-
society	-	9	-
comrade	-	8	-
neighbor,s	-	6	15
teacher	-	6	-
social relations	-	6	-
kind friends	-	-	8
company	-	-	5

LOVE,FRIENDSHIP	US	PRC	TW
	53	217	92
love (friendly)	34	14	-
friendly	7	-	-
warm,th	5	3	22
miss	4	-	-
respect	3	-	-
friendship	-	60	-
intercourse	-	24	-
dear	-	23	-
sincere	-	12	-
very intimate terms	-	10	-
warmhearted	-	10	-
lovable	-	10	-
friendly affection	-	8	-
courteous	-	7	-
ordinary sentiments	-	6	-
sympathize	-	6	-
courtesy demands recipr.	-	6	-
esteem	-	6	-
feelings (sentiment)	-	5	-
understanding	-	4	-
friendly feelings	-	3	-
affection	-	-	27
love	-	-	14
human relationship	-	-	14
treat with courtesy	-	-	8
concern	-	-	7

HELP,TAKE CARE OF, SUPPORT	29	163	142
help,ful	11	82	-
support	5	10	-
dependable	5	-	-
caring	3	-	-
faith	3	-	-
need	2	-	-
help each other	-	33	-
take good care/show ever	-	19	-
share joy and sorrow	-	6	-
rely on, reliable	-	4	-
encourage	-	3	-
help	-	-	70
negotiate	-	-	21
borrow money	-	-	11
dependent on	-	-	4
money	-	-	19
money gift	-	-	10
status	-	6	-
rich	-	-	4
property	-	-	3

CLOSE, INTIMATE	47	104	41
close,ness	15	-	-
together	7	-	-
group	7	-	-
ties	6	-	-
unite,d	5	10	-
close ties	4	-	-
unity	3	-	-
intimate	-	47	23
good	-	16	13
close relationship	-	11	-
harmony	-	10	-
good relations	-	7	-
equality	-	3	-
happy	-	-	5

VISITS,REUNIONS,HOLIDAYS	139	88	66
visit,s,ing	38	44	2
reunion,s	19	-	-
holiday,s	16	-	-
gathering,s	10	-	-
Thanksgiving	8	-	-
letters	8	-	-
home	6	9	-
get together	6	8	3
fun	6	-	-
traditions	5	-	-
dinner	5	-	-
write	4	-	-
birthday,s	3	-	2
food	3	-	-
funerals	2	-	-
daily life	-	9	-
contact	-	7	-
gift,s	-	6	12
ceremony	-	5	-
New Year	-	-	12
greeting	-	-	12
communication	-	-	10
wish Happy New Year	-	-	7
play	-	-	4
eat	-	-	2

TROUBLE,BORING,ESTRANGED	US	PRC	TW
	44	17	292
boring	7	-	15
bothersome	6	-	-
forced	6	-	-
crazy	5	-	-
gone	3	-	-
dead	3	-	-
death	3	-	-
no good	-	8	-
quarrel	-	5	14
trouble	-	-	43
become estranged	-	-	41
disgusting	-	-	21
meddlesome	-	-	17
complex relationship	-	-	13
no warmth (cold)	-	-	12
conflict	-	-	12
difficult to visit each	-	-	11
cold	-	-	9
false kindness	-	-	9
snobbish	-	-	9
argue	-	-	9
strange	-	-	8
helpless	-	-	8
fighting	-	-	7
fighting each other	-	-	7
indifferent	-	-	6
bullying	-	-	5
nothing	-	-	5
put on airs	-	-	5
stingy	-	-	4
unnecessary	-	-	2
pretend	-	4	-
different	11	-	-

MISCELLANEOUS	0	26	54
justice	-	10	-
political party	-	9	-
study	-	7	-
exciting	-	-	20
realities	-	-	10
mainland China	-	-	8
convenience	-	-	6
ambitious	-	-	6
chance	-	-	4

SUMMARY

Main Components	Percentage of Total Score		
	US	PRC	TW
MOTHER,FATHER,CHILDREN	20	6	6
AUNTS,UNCLES,GRANDPARENTS	36	32	18
FAMILY, BLOOD, RELATION	21	11	16
FRIENDS,PEOPLE,CLASSMATES	5	12	4
LOVE,FRIENDSHIP	3	14	7
HELP,TAKE CARE OF, SUPPORT	2	10	12
CLOSE, INTIMATE	3	7	3
VISITS,REUNIONS,HOLIDAYS	8	6	5
TROUBLE,BORING,ESTRANGED	3	1	24
MISCELLANEOUS	0	2	4
Total Scores	1694	1557	1228

ME
MAIN COMPONENTS AND RESPONSES

I, MYSELF	US 401	PRC 98	TW 44
myself	197	-	8
I	125	-	-
self,one,oneself	43	78	8
unique	12	-	-
me, mine	7	-	14
name	6	-	-
mirror	6	-	-
soul	5	-	3
personal	-	20	-
spirit	-	-	11

YOU, WE, OTHERS	US 245	PRC 255	TW 32
you	132	135	7
us,we	56	11	-
them, they	15	-	-
others,people	15	24	-
and my shadow	8	-	-
family	7	9	16
generation	6	-	-
together	6	-	-
parents	-	22	7
collective,all	-	23	-
society	-	13	2
unite	-	7	-
father,elder brother	-	11	-

HAPPY, CONFIDENT, GOOD	US 152	PRC 56	TW 262
happy,happiness	44	-	37
good,fine	26	-	18
fun	16	-	-
nice	11	10	-
strength	11	-	-
independent	9	-	14
friendly	7	-	5
important	7	-	-
free,dom	5	-	-
content,satisfied	9	-	-
mature	5	-	-
polite	2	3	-
ideal,idealist	-	24	14
self-confident,-ence	-	8	63
proud	-	4	5
morality	-	4	-
glad	-	2	-
humor	-	1	-
beautiful	-	-	22
optimistic	-	-	14
peaceful	-	-	10
great	-	-	10
freedom	-	-	8
good (heart)	-	-	8
self-satisfaction	-	-	8
pleasant	-	-	6
special,precious	-	-	10
dreamer	-	-	5
righteous	-	-	3
brave	-	-	2

WOMAN, GIRL	US 93	PRC 17	TW 43
girl	40	-	12
woman	34	-	11
wife	9	-	-
mother	7	17	7
daughter	3	-	-
girlfriend	-	-	13

SELFISH, UNHAPPY	US 68	PRC 28	TW 238
alone,lonely	26	-	13
selfish	7	25	10
self-importance	-	-	36
tired	9	-	-
unhappy,sad	11	-	-
lazy	6	-	5
useless	6	-	-
restless	3	-	-
frustration	-	3	-
lack of self-confidence	-	-	42
contradiction	-	-	14
dependent on	-	-	10
to feel inferior	-	-	10
ugly	-	-	10
cold	-	-	10
arrogant,stubborn	-	-	14
sad view of life	-	-	7
suffering	-	-	7
stupid,stupidity	-	-	12
disorder	-	-	6
hedonist	-	-	6
overripe	-	-	5
evil,vain	-	-	10
nervous,afraid of tests	-	-	8
escape from world	-	-	3

WORK, PROGRESS	US 50	PRC 275	TW 161
work	7	25	-
career	-	19	-
potential	7	-	-
busy	7	-	-
education	6	-	-
changing	5	-	-
achievement	4	13	18
responsible	4	-	-
goals	4	-	-
future	3	34	8
ambitions,-ious	3	7	-
hobby	-	25	-
strive	-	18	-
effort,s	-	17	-
hardworking	-	14	-
contribution	-	14	-
capable	-	11	5
forward,start	-	11	-
objective, target	-	10	-
assiduous	-	9	-
pursue	-	7	-
fond of labor	-	6	-
grow up,growth	-	6	3
prospect	-	5	6
devote oneself	-	5	-
do	-	5	-
exercise	-	5	-
advanced	-	5	-
hopes	-	2	-
demand	-	2	-
industrious	-	-	25
pursuit of true,good,beauty	-	-	20
struggle	-	-	18
responsibility	-	-	16
money	-	-	8
make progress	-	-	6
further one's studies	-	-	5
subsist	-	-	5
insist	-	-	5
examination	-	-	4
job	-	-	3
undertaking	-	-	3
active	-	-	2
movement	-	-	1

MAN, MALE	US 20	PRC 85	TW 23
male	9	23	12
man	6	16	4
husband	5	-	-
he, him	-	37	-
boy	-	9	-
he	-	-	7

LOVE, FRIENDSHIP	US 134	PRC 70	TW 87
love,ing	42	7	23
friend,s,friendship	19	23	16
be in love,lover	19	5	-
caring,helpful,ing	24	-	-
like	8	-	-
respect	7	3	-
kind,hearted,compassion	10	9	4
courteous,share	5	10	-
relations	-	8	-
faith	-	5	-
full of desire (desire)	-	-	14
human relationships	-	-	7
like to help people	-	-	7
sensitive	-	-	6
trust	-	-	6
marriage	-	-	4

STUDENT, KNOWLEDGE	US 72	PRC 287	TW 90
intelligent,smart	20	-	13
study	3	93	-
student	15	89	-
understand	13	-	-
complex	6	-	13
writer	6	-	-
interest,ing	3	10	-
teacher	3	10	-
school,-work	3	6	6
knowledge	-	29	-
class,-mates	-	19	-
university,student	-	8	32
scientist,science	-	11	-
willpower	-	7	-
think,thought	-	5	7
conservative	-	-	7
open-minded	-	-	7
thinking constantly	-	-	5

BEING, LIVING	US 35	PRC 58	TW 27
life,alive,lively	13	36	-
health	10	-	3
human,human life	5	-	12
sports,sport	4	-	10
age	3	7	-
play ball,recreation	-	12	-
run	-	3	-
behavior	-	-	2

PERSON, INDIVIDUAL	US 150	PRC 166	TW 153
individual	38	17	-
person	36	23	23
young	12	-	-
ego	16	-	-
character	-	-	5
personality	9	11	-
short	9	-	-
single	8	-	-
good looking,handsome	7	17	16
physical	6	-	-
tall	5	-	12
shy	4	-	4
Chinese,China	-	29	-
patriotic	-	21	-
height	-	15	-
feature,appearance	-	15	-
tiny,thin	-	13	7
lovely	-	-	37
ordinary	-	-	23
fat,weight	-	5	16
outfit important	-	-	10

MISCELLANEOUS	US 71	PRC 135	TW 71
Gary	11	-	-
home,-town	10	5	-
Christian	9	-	2
pronoun	8	11	-
David	7	-	-
John	7	-	-
first	6	-	-
give	5	-	-
it	5	-	-
too	3	-	-
country	-	27	-
nature	-	26	-
motherland, love of	-	13	-
eat	-	13	-
temperature	-	10	-
now	-	10	-
rest	-	8	-
past	-	6	-
hostel	-	6	-
Confucian	-	-	29
sanguine	-	-	11
western	-	-	10
world	-	-	7
Eastern people	-	-	7
animal, monkey	-	-	5

SUMMARY

Main Components	Percentage of Total Score		
	US	PRC	TW
I, MYSELF	27	6	4
YOU, WE, OTHERS	16	17	3
HAPPY, CONFIDENT, GOOD	10	4	21
WOMAN, GIRL	6	1	3
WORK, PROGRESS	3	18	13
MAN, MALE	1	6	2
SELFISH, UNHAPPY	5	2	19
LOVE, FRIENDSHIP	9	5	7
STUDENT, KNOWLEDGE	5	19	7
BEING, LIVING	2	4	2
PERSON, INDIVIDUAL	10	11	12
MISCELLANEOUS	5	9	6
Total Scores	1491	1530	1231

ANCESTORS
MAIN COMPONENTS AND RESPONSES

FOREFATHERS	US	PRC	TW
	124	58	56
Mayflower	28	-	-
forefather	27	23	-
people, old	21	9	-
predecessor	12	-	-
pilgrims	10	-	-
pioneer,s	7	8	-
George Washington	7	-	-
forebearer	7	-	-
slaves	5	-	-
person, ancient	-	18	-
ancient people	-	-	21
Ching Ming holiday	-	-	20
self	-	-	8
human being	-	-	7

RESPECT, WORSHIP	US	PRC	TW
	16	13	460
religious,religion	11	-	15
faith	5	-	-
respect, pay respect to	-	13	59
pay respect to	-	-	86
pay homage to dead	-	-	33
sweep a grave	-	-	32
worship	-	-	26
thinking of someone	-	-	25
offer sacrifice to	-	-	23
blessing	-	-	18
think of ancestors	-	-	15
incense pot,burn incense	-	-	20
commemorate	-	-	14
awe	-	-	13
temple	-	-	10
glorify one's ancestors	-	-	10
glory	-	-	8
soul	-	-	8
God	-	-	7
blindly believe	-	-	5
filial pie	-	-	5
duty	-	-	5
don't forget benefactor	-	-	5
enjoy what ancestors gave	-	-	5
burn paper money for dead	-	-	5
prayer	-	-	4
spirit	-	-	4

DEATH, GRAVE, TOMB	US	PRC	TW
	54	21	123
dead	30	-	-
die,d	-	11	5
dead man	-	10	-
cemetary	7	-	-
bones	7	-	-
gone	6	-	-
grave,s	4	-	-
tablet, w/name of dead	-	-	49
tomb	-	-	34
death	-	-	16
ghost,s & god	-	-	12
die in one's homeland	-	-	4
good shade	-	-	3

GREAT,INDUSTRIOUS,BRAVE	US	PRC	TW
	64	284	78
interesting	11	-	-
great	9	63	12
grand	7	-	-
famous	7	-	-
struggle	7	-	-
wise	6	-	-
love,-able	5	5	-
pride	4	-	3
different	4	-	-
strength	4	-	-
industrious	-	49	-
hard-working	-	35	1
brave	-	24	-
labor	-	22	-
clever	-	21	-
proud	-	18	-
respectable	-	13	-
do pioneering work	-	11	-
wisdom	-	9	2
hero	-	6	-
hardship	-	5	-
kind-hearted	-	3	-
take pains	-	-	16
pioneering	-	-	10
respectful	-	-	8
shedding blood & sweat	-	-	5
kind	-	-	5
reputation	-	-	4
productive	-	-	3
sacrifice,s	-	-	3
tender feeling	-	-	3
mysterious	-	-	3

TIME: PAST, OLD	US	PRC	TW
	202	106	62
past	59	6	3
old	50	-	3
ancient	45	9	4
before	15	-	-
long ago	11	-	-
time, antiquity	7	12	-
antiques	7	-	-
generation, later	5	8	-
future	3	3	-
generation, former	-	31	-
generation, older	-	23	-
backward	-	14	-
long time	-	-	48
lunar New Year	-	-	4

RELATIVES,FAMILY TREE	US	PRC	TW
	462	79	100
relatives	93	-	3
family	80	-	11
root,s	63	-	5
family tree	41	-	3
grandparents	30	-	14
grandfather	25	16	18
descendant,s	23	10	5
father,s	18	-	3
geneology	14	-	-
parents	13	-	2
grandmother	12	13	8
lineage	12	-	-
mother	11	-	-
great great grandparents	10	-	-
great grandparents	9	-	-
blood line	4	-	-
trace	4	-	-
former father	-	12	-
dependents of imperial	-	10	-
me	-	10	-
surname, (with same --)	-	8	1
blood relationship	-	-	11
offspring	-	-	6
children	-	-	5
heritage	-	-	5

ETHNIC ORIGIN	US	PRC	TW
	138	3	0
Europe	23	-	-
German	17	-	-
Irish	14	-	-
English	11	-	-
Italy	11	-	-
England	9	-	-
Africa	7	-	-
Spain	7	-	-
Indians	7	-	-
Israel	7	-	-
foreign	7	-	-
Scotland	5	-	-
Ireland	5	-	-
Africans	5	-	-
Jewish	3	-	-
world	-	3	-

MOTHERLAND, COUNTRY	US	PRC	TW
	26	143	36
American	9	-	-
New York	7	-	-
old country	7	-	-
home	3	-	-
motherland	-	34	-
China (old name)	-	22	-
Yellow river	-	19	-
China	-	14	5
Chinese nation	-	12	-
children of China	-	10	-
Great Wall	-	10	-
ancient civilized countr	-	8	-
homeland, hometown	-	6	3
Yangtze river	-	5	-
country	-	3	-
mainland China	-	-	22
Chinese	-	-	4
countryside	-	-	2

DEVELOPMENT, CIVILIZATION	US	PRC	TW
	0	146	2
developed,-ment	-	40	-
civilization	-	31	-
four ancient inventions	-	23	-
study	-	11	-
progress	-	10	-
cultivate	-	9	-
invention	-	7	-
contribution	-	7	-
science	-	5	-
society	-	3	-
teach	-	-	2

HISTORY,CULTURE	US	PRC	TW
	123	105	87
long history	43	5	-
heritage/inheritance	37	16	-
background	12	-	-
tradition	11	-	13
culture	7	35	5
picture,s	7	-	12
farmer,s	6	-	4
emperor	-	26	8
history	-	14	20
Imperial	-	5	-
language	-	4	-
inherit	-	-	10
farming	-	-	7
rice field	-	-	5
inheritance	-	-	3
portrait of the decs'd	-	-	-

PREHISTORIC MAN, APE	US	PRC	TW
	107	232	66
monkey,s	22	10	6
caveman,-men	15	-	-
ape,s	13	89	-
primitive	12	14	-
anthropological	10	-	-
prehistoric	9	-	-
evolution	5	9	2
origin	5	-	30
caves	5	-	-
animals	4	-	6
Darwin	4	-	-
stone age	3	-	-
primitive man	-	25	-
creation	-	13	-
primitive society	-	13	-
life	-	13	-
forest	-	12	-
anthropoid	-	10	-
mankind	-	7	-
fire	-	7	-
walk	-	4	-
contemporary ape	-	3	-
subsistence	-	3	-
Peking man	-	-	8
Adam & Eve	-	-	6
hunting	-	-	5
incarnation	-	-	3
human history	-	-	-

MISCELLANEOUS	US	PRC	TW
	13	7	26
unknown	13	-	-
wealth	-	5	-
property,ies	-	2	3
no feeling	-	-	8
forget	-	-	6
rich man's mansion	-	-	6
February 28 incident	-	-	3

SUMMARY

Main Components	Percentage of Total Score		
	US	PRC	TW
FOREFATHERS	9	5	5
RESPECT, WORSHIP	1	1	42
DEATH, GRAVE, TOMB	4	2	11
GREAT,INDUSTRIOUS,BRAVE	5	24	7
TIME: PAST, OLD	15	9	6
RELATIVES,FAMILY TREE	35	7	9
ETHNIC ORIGIN	10	0	0
MOTHERLAND, COUNTRY	2	12	3
HISTORY,CULTURE	9	9	8
PREHISTORIC MAN, APE	8	19	6
DEVELOPMENT,CIVILIZATION	0	12	0
MISCELLANEOUS	1	1	2
Total Scores	1329	1197	1096

SUMMARY OF TRENDS IN THE FAMILY DOMAIN

Cultural and Systemic Influences

The alternatives examined here offer a comparison of our own post-modern American culture and social development with Chinese alternatives of socialization. As most anthropologists will agree, these alternatives represent classical contrasts of broad, contemporary relevance. They are similarly interesting because they offer details on those key psychological variables, such as the development of self image, relationship to the social environment, and other important dimensions of the socialization process that are powerful yet too subjective to be reached through the more direct and conventional methods of assessment.

The response trends registered across key roles in the family domain reveal consistent perceptual and attitudinal dispositions informative on the different perspectives and characteristics of the groups compared.

Image of Family. The Americans' image of family involves the togetherness of people who assume individual roles (e.g., mother, father) and who are bound by affective ties of love and friendship. Family is for them a framework for life, a home, a social setting judged by its potential to meet their individual, psychological, and physical needs.

The Chinese think of family more as a group that serves a common purpose and shared objectives. The Chinese place more weight on the educational goals, the task of raising children, to train them for maintaining proper interpersonal relations. They place special emphasis on harmony and mutual obligations. The personal aspirations of the individual members receive less attention, compared to the group as a whole. The PRC group appears in this respect the strongest contrast to the Americans. The Taiwanese, more westernized, are more similar to the Americans, paying more attention to individual feelings, differences, and conflicts.

Family Members. Americans tend to think of individual roles such as mother, father, daughter, and son. The Chinese, particularly the Taiwanese, think of family members in broader, collective categories rather than in individual roles. For example, they tend to think of parents rather than father or mother, and of siblings rather than brother or sister.

There is an essential agreement between the Americans and the Chinese that relatives include aunts, uncles, cousins, etc. However, there is a remarkable difference in that Americans include parents, father, mother, and children as relatives, while the Chinese barely mention them. Furthermore, the Chinese mention friends and classmates with relatives, but rarely "family". Both Chinese groups think of warm, intimate interpersonal relationships with relatives and sharing with them. Americans, on the other hand, think more of occasional visits and reunions. One main difference is that the Chinese feel a stronger sense of obligation. The Taiwanese are highly ambivalent about it, showing critical attitudes and sentiments of rejection and alienation. The Mainland Chinese express predominantly positive attitudes, more readiness to honor obligations and responsibilities regarding relatives.

In contrast, the American attitudes toward relatives are characterized much more by individual rapport based on personal feelings rather than by a sense of universal

obligation. Toward those relatives whom Americans maintain rapport with, they fee'
and friendship. Relatives with whom such rapport is lacking are virtually non-existen
even toward relatives who are loved and considered as friends, just being a relativ
not imply obligation. However, in the case of the Mainland Chinese, it does, and
universal obligation toward relatives is generally accepted. In the case of the Taiwanes
this sense of obligation is felt, yet is frequently resented.

Family Organization. Americans focus on individual roles and their affective ties,
while for the Chinese, family is more a social unit which serves a common purpose. The
American family is seen as built on love, particularly on the affective ties between father
and mother. References to father-mother relations are in every context the strongest by
Americans; these references are negligible by the Taiwanese, who concentrate their
attention on the climate of the family and its goals and activities essential to its existence
and obligations. In the American image of family, the role of the mother is the most
central. The mother receives the most attention in practically all contexts. This tendency
is less heavy in the Chinese groups; in a few instances, the Mainlanders place more weight
on the father. These differences are influenced by the general American tendency to pay
stronger attention to sex-role differences and focus more on females than males in the
context of family. A contrasting tendency is observable among the Chinese, particularly the
Mainlanders, who emphasize more male roles (males are supposedly stronger than females
in China).

Goals and Functions. By analyzing response trends across family roles in order to
reconstruct interpersonal relations within the family, American and Chinese comparisons
reveal perceptions and attitudes that suggest fundamental differences in what they see as
the actual goal or purpose of the family.

The predominance of American references to love and affective ties suggests a
tendency to view the family as a source for satisfying personal needs and emotions as well
as identification, longing for love, security, happiness, joy, etc. There are many indications
indeed that Americans view family from the angle of their own emotional, social, and
physical needs; their attitudes on family reflect the extent to which they feel their needs are
being met. Family is the personal network, home is the place, and holidays, outings, shared
experiences are the occasions which make family a source of happiness and joy.

The Chinese view family not so much from the angle of personal satisfaction as
from the benefit it offers to the group or collective. This is clearly expressed by the strong
Chinese references to obligations, duties, and responsibilities in general. In a similar way,
the Chinese think also in more specific terms of hard work, toil, labor, effort across the
board in the context of practically all adult family roles. The responsibilities and chores
may vary from father to mother or parents in general but the emphasis on obligation and
work is universal. The emphasis on obligation and responsibility involves education and
upbringing of children in the case of adult family members; in the case of children, it
involves the obligation to care for their parents once they become old and sick. To prepare
people to meet these mutual obligations, the Chinese place heavy emphasis on interpersonal
relations characterized by harmony and warm feelings. The emphasis on harmony is
particularly strong among the Mainlanders who convey generally more idealistic normative
expectations, compared to the Taiwanese who express more concern with actual conflicts,
quarrels, contradictions.

The Chinese view family as a source or tool that serves their personal needs, but more as a group or collective which is important for its own sake, a common goal above and beyond its utility to the individual. To the Chinese, particularly to the Mainlanders, family is an institution which has to be served and attended by all members. The maintenance of family obligations and duties receives heavy emphasis. In general as well as in terms of specific chores and responsibilities, hard work is similarly emphasized with regard to father and mother by both Chinese groups.

Personality Traits. The Chinese think less in terms of role relations and focus heavily on personal characteristics. Sexual identity receives relatively little attention. While some of the attributes are relatively gender-specific, a larger part of these characteristics involve general human qualities. Father is characterized, for instance, as respectable, severe, dignified, fair-minded more than mother is, but they have in common such attributes as love, affection, kind, dear, great, and kindhearted. Yet these latter characterizations are intensively used in relationship to mother, along with more feminine attributes such as gentleness and beauty. It is remarkable that, despite a strong sex role differentiation in the Chinese family, the Chinese images of these family roles are focused on general human qualities, actually more so than in the American images. The Mainland Chinese sample also emphasizes in all these contexts the qualities of being industrious and hardworking, and the importance of upbringing and education.

Both Chinese groups pay more attention to the hard work and industriousness in the context of both the mother and father. The Taiwanese Chinese think in more traditional terms of dignity, esteem, and respect, while the Mainland Chinese place more emphasis on kindness, and on affective ties with the parents. Mother brings out identification with the motherland from this population, which show numerous signs of nationalistic pride and identification across the board. The Mainlanders show no bad feelings, but the Taiwanese are critical particularly toward the mother, indicating conflict, alienation, and erosion of values of respect.

Parent-Child Relationship. While Americans think more in terms of the individual parent, father and mother, the Chinese tend to think of parents collectively. Also the American students think of parents more in terms of love, care, and help received, and the Chinese stress more the proper attitudes toward parents along such traditional values as esteem, respect, and filial obedience. These same attitudes are emphasized by the Mainland Chinese also in the context of children, thinking more of their upbringing along these values. The Americans' view of children centers more on young age, age-specific entertainment through play and toys, their cuteness and innocence.

In regard to parents, both Chinese groups think of the proper attitudes with focus on such traditional values as esteem, respect, filial obedience. While Americans think more of the special age characteristics of young children, the two Chinese groups show more awareness of the age of the parents and express concern with their health, well-being, and their harmonious and happy social climate. These traditional trends are stronger among the Taiwanese, except that the Mainlanders show more concern with the grandparents and certain relatives. With regard to children, the above traditional values show similar dominance in the case of both Chinese groups, except that the Mainlander students appear to show stronger interest in children and convey a stronger motivation to have children, while the Taiwanese appear less favorable, more concerned with the associated burden and inconvenience. The Mainlanders think also more of such traditional values as obedience, respect, filial duty, and the obligation of children to take care of their parents.

Self and Others. It is relevant to examine how the individual person fits into the family, how the image of self or "me" relates to the subjective view of the family. The image of "me" by Americans shows very strong emphasis on the "I", the individual self. The most important nexus for Americans is between the individual "me" and the individual "you". The strong individualistic emphasis conveyed by the American self image supports the position of Francis Hsu, who traces some of the most characteristic differences in the American and Chinese interpersonal relations to a contrast between American individualism and the Chinese family or group orientation. According to Hsu, this American emphasis on the autonomous individual is a product of the American family and upbringing. It is also the source of the American emphasis on individual roles, a tendency observed across the board in the context of the family roles examined.

In their self image, the Chinese place little emphasis on "I" and "self", but place much more on "you" and "others". This suggests a stronger collectivistic group orientation particularly by the Mainland Chinese. The stronger Taiwanese emphasis on self-importance, self-confidence and happiness suggests, however, a more individualistic focus by this group. Mainland China is a relatively closed society Taiwan is more open. The Mainlanders also show a strong nationalistic collectivistic orientation through such self-identifications as patriotic, Chinese, idealist, as well as references to China, country, and motherland. In the case of the Taiwanese, such indicators of nationalistic identification are missing.

Ancestors, Relatives. The differences observed with regard to ancestors are particularly dramatic. The Taiwanese view ancestors in the framework of essentially Confucian religious views and perspectives: veneration, respect, graves, rituals. The Mainland sample from the PRC attaches apparently no such religious connotations to ancestors, but view them more as historic predecessors characterized as brave, civilized and industrious people. References to Chinese history, culture, nation, and motherland again convey strong national identification.

While in the context of ancestors the Confucian value considerations have rather completely disappeared from the perspectives of the PRC students, in the context of parents and children, respect of the elderly and the virtues of filial obedience are distinctly active and operative. This applies to relatives as well. The conditions on the Mainland may severely restrict opportunities to maintain contact with relatives living in distant places; nonetheless, the attitudes toward relatives are more positive and the sense of obligation is more active. In the case of the Taiwanese, the attitudes toward relatives are predominantly alienated and hostile, suggesting a broad rejection of such obligations.

The comparison of American and Chinese response trends is informative on those different perceptions and attitudes which lie at the foundation of those differential processes of socialization which members of these two cultures pass through in evolving the traits that characterize members of these two great world cultures. These contrasting traits are frequently identified as representing individualistic vs. collectivistic alternatives of human development.

Individualistic Americans vs. Collectivistic Chinese Perspectives. The U.S. emphasis on love is predominant across all themes used in the representation of this domain. It conveys a preoccupation with the subjective need of the individual to love and to be loved which is particularly strong in a post-modern social environment in which people frequently feel alone and alienated. The American emphasis on individual roles, compared to the stronger Chinese tendency to consider more collective roles -- parents, children -- is another sign of a more individualistic orientation. Family is looked at from the American perspective in terms of what it offers in satisfying the psychological and physical needs of the individual family members. This contrasts with the Chinese focus on obligations and respect.

The American emphasis on I, ego, and the self observed in the context of "me" represents similarly a propensity to view the world, including family, more narrowly from the angle of the personal needs and aspirations of the autonomous individual. The Chinese, in contrast, pay little attention to the individual but focus on the goals and objectives dictated by the group as a collective.

With regard to family and family roles, Americans pay the most attention to individual attributes such as sex, age, appearance, weak, strong, tall, etc. The Chinese emphasize social and interpersonal traits -- fairminded, affectionate, kind, gentle, understanding, kindhearted, respectable. While the Americans think that love requires mutuality and may change rather freely depending on conditions and circumstances (e.g., divorce), the Chinese consider more commitments, obligations, respect, duty, sacrifice which depend less on mutuality and suggest more long--range involvement.

The Chinese -- particularly the Mainlanders -- relate family and family roles such as mother more to society, to nation, carrying connotations of motherland and national identification, compared to Americans who view mother as a private person. Similarly, to Americans ancestors are mainly deceased relatives of foreign background; to the Chinese, particularly the Mainlanders, ancestors represent their great civilization, representatives of the nation's past remembered with sentiments of patriotism and pride.

The Taiwanese and the Mainland Chinese show across the board major differences. These differences do not supersede but merely modulate the fundamental contrast of individualism vs. collectivism as it applies to the American and Chinese cultures.

Influences of the Economic-Political Systems on the Chinese

In contrast to the American-Chinese comparison, which reflects on psychological dispositions and the resulting perspectives that are characteristically cultural, the comparison of the PRC and Taiwanese groups reflects the impact of two economic and political systems on people characterized originally by common cultural roots.

Image of Family and Family Members. Both groups, the Mainlanders as well as the Taiwanese, think of family as a group, focusing on the emotional climate and paying more attention to parents and children than to individual roles. This focus on the internal climate and obligations is particularly strong among the PRC group. For them the climate of harmony and warm interpersonal relations is particularly important. These tie people to the family as a whole in a stronger and more lasting way than the personal ties between individual family roles (e.g., father and mother), which is the foundation of the American family, according to Francis Hsu (1981), a rare scholar with similarly deep insights into both

58

American and Chinese family relations. They pay little attention to the feelings of love and affection of individual family members. Their focus is on a positive climate reflecting interpersonal relations which appear ideal.

The Taiwanese think more of love, friendship, personal feelings, including negative feelings, criticism, and personal resentment as well. They are not only critical and resentful of relatives but also express some negative sentiments toward parents, father and mother as well. They speak of obligational respect but find this Confucian virtue frequently annoying and more of a burden. Compared to the Mainlanders, who appear to idealize Confucian virtues of harmony and subordination, the Taiwanese make many references to internal conflicts, intrafamily arguments and fights, suggesting that the reality of their family life is far from the Confucian ideas. These dimensions further suggest that the Mainlanders show more conformity with the traditional ideals compared to the Taiwanese, whose contemporary life is facing contradictions in an ever-changing transitional period. Again, this shows Taiwan as a society affected by both America & Mainland China.

Personality Traits and Attributes. The dominant characteristics of family members perceived by the two groups show some characteristic differences as well. Father is perceived by both as hard working and industrious. The Mainland group thinks of the father only in terms of positive qualities, high moral standards, characterizing him as kind hearted, a pillar, teacher, and educator. This may partially be due to the circumstance that the Mainland as a closed society, does not allow people to have too much freedom of speech. The Taiwanese group sees him as positive, solemn and kind but expresses also negative attitudes in describing him as critical and unreasonable, cold and hedonistic.

With regard to mother, there is again more positive identification expressed by the Mainlanders. At the same time, the Taiwanese show again a stronger contrast between positive and negative traits. The positive traits include heavy work, cooking and cleaning, caring and providing, along with making sacrifices. Her personality is seen as kind and gentle, loving and affectionate. On the negative side, the Taiwanese view mother as nervous and stubborn.

Parents are viewed again in exclusively positive terms as kind, amiable, and child loving, by the Mainlanders. They make no references to any conflict, alienation, antagonism. The Taiwanese group shows predominately positive attitudes and evaluations, placing special emphasis on the hard work of parents, on their involvement in bringing up and educating children, on taking care of and protecting them. There are also several references to negative experiences of arguing, shouting, even beating. The attributes and characterizations offered by these two groups suggest stronger conformity with tradition and Confucianism among the Mainlanders. At the same time, the Taiwanese reactions reflect more conflict, internal contradiction, alienation, or what is frequently characterized as a generation gap. This shows that western value judgments have a far-reaching impact on the Taiwanese.

Self Image. Students from the Mainland show stronger emphasis on their male identity. They convey also strong awareness of being a student. Whether this emphasis is more a function of being proud of this status or a sign of intensive involvement in learning and education is not clear at this point. Nonetheless, independent references to studying, hard work, and being industrious suggest a strong emphasis on what they do. Whether that is an expression of activism, a strong motivation to produce will require further examination. This student group shows little doubt or uncertainty about its identity or self-confidence. Their references to society suggest strong group identification, and their references to Chinese past and to Chinese culture show a patriotic national identification.

The Taiwanese group shows much more uncertainty with equally strong positive and negative self-characterizations. They list several positive attributes such as being industrious, loving, happy, self-confident, important, beautiful, and optimistic. At the same time they characterize themselves as lacking self-confidence, feeling inferior, stupid, ugly, lonely, etc. Although the positive attributes are predominant, the proportion of negative qualities suggest a strong split of uncertainty, confusion, and ambivalence.

These differences between the two groups suggest again an interesting differential impact of the two social environments. The students in Mainland China project a self-image which may appear to be simplistic in expressing almost exclusively positive features, action orientation, and strong social and national identification. On the other hand, the Taiwanese raised under the conditions of free market systems express more confusion and uncertainty, a competition between positive and negative qualities and self-identification.

Ancestors. The students from Mainland China show two main images of ancestors. The references to apes and cavemen reflect the influences of Darwinism and modern evolutionary theory. The discovery of the Peking Man in northern part of china is worth noting, as well. A stronger and more dominant image involves, however, a strong historical awareness of and pride toward their Chinese predecessors, who are described as hardworking, productive people, recognized for their role in developing the world's greatest civilization. This second image reflects strong affective identification and emphasis on the great historical past. It has no religious element, no reference to Confucian or religious practices. The identification of ancestors with apes appears even as a strong contrast to the traditional ancestor cult.

The Taiwanese image of ancestors is dominated by the Confucian precept. It reflects both religious practices and rituals, celebrations at graves and on holidays. It also conveys an identification with the ideals of respect, veneration, obligation, filial piety, and duty. The major components of the Taiwanese image tie in with the Confucian precept of the ancestor. At the same time, ancestors has negligible nationalistic, patriotic connotations, which are strong in the case of the Mainland group. We observe here an interesting reversal. While in most previous contexts the Mainland Chinese have shown a stronger traditional value orientation, a heavier influence of the Confucian past, in the context of ancestors the case is opposite, apparently in the field of religious thinking. The centrally controlled socialistic system was successful in substituting the Confucian precepts by a more up to date national identification rooted in an action-oriented interpretation of the historic past (the Confucian precepts were severely criticized during the Cultural Revolution -- c. 1966-1971).

60

Chapter 3

NATIONAL IMAGES

Mental images are selective, often affect-laden representations of reality. Whether the mental representations are of simple objects or of complex problems, they are all shaped by the frame of reference of the observer, by his or her own perspective. In international contacts people of different national backgrounds are frequently influenced by the collective images people and nations have of each other. In countries where the national image of Americans tends to be negative, individual Americans are more likely to be received and treated with skepticism and hostility as well. These collective images generate strong subconscious dispositions that influence how words, actions, and intentions are interpreted and understood.

The following national images offer new insights that are informative in several respects. The Americans' images of the Chinese, of the PRC, of Taiwan, and Hong Kong show our dominant trends of perceptions and evaluations compared to their own views and attitudes. Comparison of the images held by the Americans, the Taiwanese, and the PRC reveals their perceptions and attitudes toward each other. In analyzing the dominant perceptual and attitudinal trends, we can see how cultural influences, American and Chinese, become the source of different sensitivities and expectations. Up to date knowledge of our own biases and dispositions can be just as valuable as objective information. It is particularly interesting to see how the different political and economic systems -- the socialistic alternative of the PRC and the free enterprise system of Taiwan - create different perceptual and attitudinal dispositions which influence the relationship of these countries to each other as well as toward the United States.

Subjectivity and selectivity are natural and intrinsic attributes of human perception. Data on contemporary trends of selective perceptions and attitudes are particularly informative on psychological dispositions that are mostly hidden and subconscious and exert powerful influences on human behavior. The nondirective, open-ended nature of the research method used here provides a rare opportunity to look into the highly subjective priorities and perspectives of people whose lives have been shaped by different cultural, economic, and political experiences. The value of these insights comes from the realization that the solutions they are likely to seek are probably influenced more by their subjective perception of reality than by what we may consider to be objective and real.

In this chapter we take a look at the following national images as held by Americans, Taiwanese, and PRC Chinese: United States, PRC, Taiwan, Hong Kong, Country, Americans, Chinese, & Overseas Chinese.

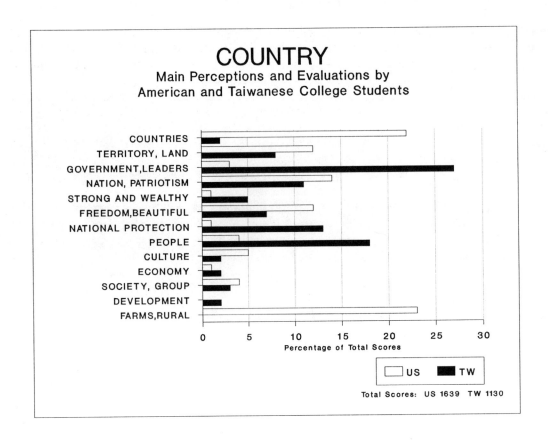

COUNTRY
Main Perceptions and Evaluations by
American and Taiwanese College Students

Percentage of Total Scores

US   TW

Total Scores: US 1639   TW 1130

American View: USA, Freedom, Land. For Americans, country evokes, first of all, names of many countries with the USA predominating. Several European countries come to mind, especially those which contributed heavily to U.S. immigration in the 19th and 18th centuries: Ireland, England, and Germany. Land comes second. In English, the word country has two very distinct meanings: a political, territorial, unit, on one hand, and a rural -- as opposed to urban or suburban -- region, on the other. The Chinese assign only the first meaning, not the second. American references to trees, home, farms, and various farm animals reflect this second meaning not shared by the Chinese. Freedom is an important attribute, followed by love and beauty. The nation and patriotism are part of the American image of country as well.

Taiwanese View: Territory, People, Government. Taiwanese focus on government, and especially on the president and on politics. "People as a whole" is a very important concept for the Taiwanese, possibly reflecting a strong Taiwanese predisposition to consider China indivisible. This may be a carryover from the older generation. The importance they give to "territory" may have the same significance. Nationalism and patriotism are also of great significance, as is the concept "people-centered." Taiwanese indicate great concern with national protection and defense. "Protect the people" is an important concept. This may be because Taiwanese people did not want to be communist. The separation of Taiwan from Mainland China for over 40 years has rendered Taiwan a different entity from Mainland China in many ways, culturally and politically.

American and Taiwanese Contrasts: Land versus People. The American inclination to list many nations, beginning with one's own, is virtually absent among the Taiwanese. On the other hand, the very strong Taiwanese tendency to see countries in terms of government and politics is minimal among Americans. National defense is a much greater concern for Taiwanese than for Americans. Both groups see a country as territory or land, but this focus is much stronger among the Americans when the second meaning of country [the idea of a rural area which is not part of the Chinese word] is included. The Taiwanese emphasize more the connection between the country and its people. In country translates literally as "nation home", meaning the whole country is like a home. In this sense, the Taiwanese emphasis on people (family members or fellow-countrymen) is understandable.

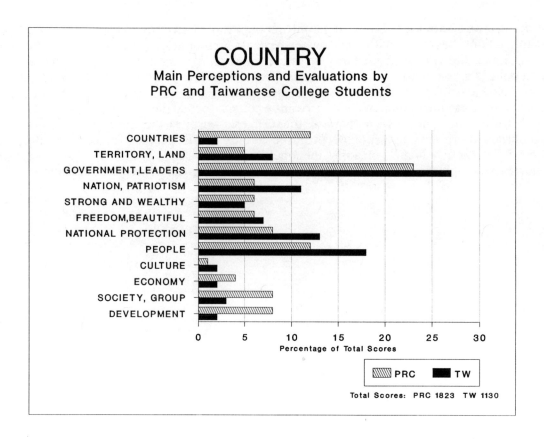

COUNTRY
Main Perceptions and Evaluations by
PRC and Taiwanese College Students

Percentage of Total Scores

PRC   TW

Total Scores: PRC 1823 TW 1130

PRC Chinese View: China, Leadership.   Nearly as emphatically as the Taiwanese, Mainlanders see countries in terms of politics and government -- and specifically in terms of leadership and power.   Mainland Chinese style of leadership affects people's life tremendously. So they have to be concerned about who are leading them. Their inclination to list countries, beginning with their own, is strong, but not quite as strong as that of Americans. Interestingly, they do not mention Taiwan. National protection and defense are important to the Mainlanders; they think especially of the army and wars. The country's development is also important, especially in terms of technology and science. They give significance to a country being strong and wealthy. In contrast to the others, Mainlanders do not see great significance in land or territory. People, however, are fairly important in relation to the country. Together with people and population, Mainlanders focus on society, the collective, group, and unity.

Taiwanese View: Territory, People, Government. Taiwanese focus on government, and especially on the president and on politics. "People as a whole" is a very important concept for the Taiwanese, possibly reflecting a strong Taiwanese predisposition to consider China indivisible. This may be a carryover from the older generation. The importance they give to "territory" may have the same significance. Nationalism and patriotism are also of great significance, as is the concept "people-centered." Taiwanese indicate great concern with national protection and defense. "Protect the people" is an important concept. This may be because Taiwanese people did not want to be communist. The separation of Taiwan from Mainland China for over 40 years has rendered Taiwan a different entity from Mainland China in many ways, culturally and politically.

PRC and Taiwanese Contrasts: National Development versus Protection and Nationalism.
Both groups see countries strongly in terms of political leadership, with greater emphasis among the Mainlanders on leadership, and among the Taiwanese on politics. Mainlanders strongly identify with their own country, while the Taiwanese think more generally of territory. People as a whole are emphasized much more by the Taiwanese. Nationalism and patriotism protection of the people also receive more attention from the Taiwanese. [Mainland China and Taiwan are still enemies.] At least 35% of the money is spent on national defense in Taiwan. Strength and prosperity of the country capture more attention from the Mainlanders. The Mainlanders' focus on collectivism, development, and technology is virtually absent among the Taiwanese.

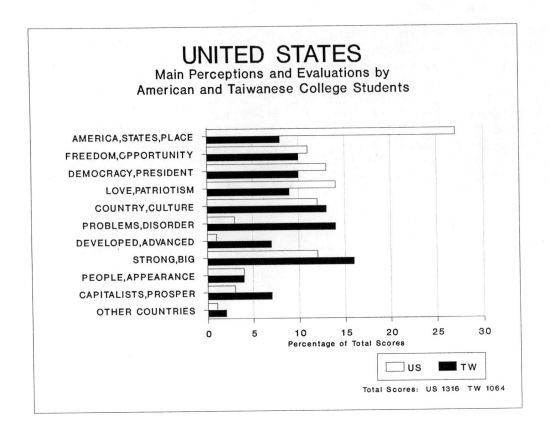

UNITED STATES
Main Perceptions and Evaluations by
American and Taiwanese College Students

AMERICA,STATES,PLACE
FREEDOM,OPPORTUNITY
DEMOCRACY,PRESIDENT
LOVE,PATRIOTISM
COUNTRY,CULTURE
PROBLEMS,DISORDER
DEVELOPED,ADVANCED
STRONG,BIG
PEOPLE,APPEARANCE
CAPITALISTS,PROSPER
OTHER COUNTRIES

0   5   10   15   20   25   30
Percentage of Total Scores

☐ US   ■ TW

Total Scores: US 1316   TW 1064

American View: Freedom, Democracy. Americans think of the United States in terms of America, states, and cities. Freedom, history, liberty, and justice are important aspects. Government and democracy are among other attributes most frequently thought of. Americans express strong national identification with the US as home, with the flag, and with feelings of pride in their country (proud, great). They also indicate awareness of the superpower status of their country.

Taiwanese View: Large, Strong, Democracy. Taiwanese think of the United States first and foremost as a superpower, and its government being an open democracy. It is strongly perceived as covering a large area of land in America. They view the United States as a strong, rich, big country, which is a wonderful land for study -- in part because of its freedom and opportunity. They are impressed with its open democracy, its president, and its high technology. On the negative side, they view the United States as having serious domestic problems with crime and a decline in morals, as well as being an international busybody.

American and Taiwanese Contrasts: Home States and Cities versus Superpower with Problems. Americans show naturally greater familiarity and focus on different perspectives within the United States. The Taiwanese look at various aspects of US culture and are impressed with US power. Americans show more interest in the functioning of the US government. US prosperity and technology impress the Taiwanese much more. Reactions of national identification such as home, flag, pride, and patriotism are significant to Americans. On the other hand, the attention given to US problems, such as exploitation, unemployment, and decline of morals, reflect critical views by the Taiwanese. The Taiwanese perceive the United States as selfish and ethnically self-centered.

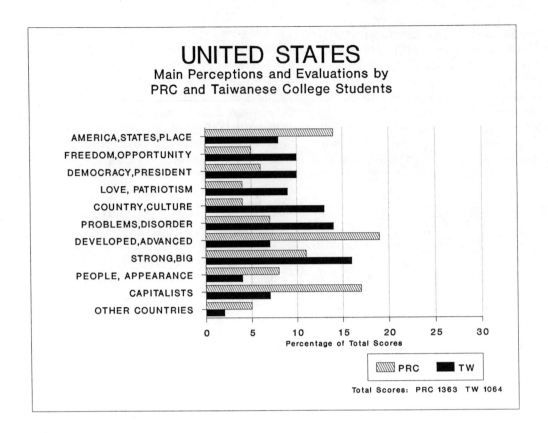

UNITED STATES
Main Perceptions and Evaluations by
PRC and Taiwanese College Students

PRC Chinese View: Capitalist, Developed, Superpower. Mainland Chinese are most impressed by US capitalism, technical and economic development, and super-power status. In significant numbers, they also consider the United States to be a beautiful and friendly nation which has freedom and is open. On the negative side, they perceive acutely US social disorder, crime, and "lack of spiritual ballast." The Mainlanders think of the people and their physical and racial characteristics. From their point of view, the most significant aspect of the appearance of Americans is what they perceive to be big noses. During the Period when Mao Tse Tung ruled, however, people were brainwashed and referred to U.S. as a "paper tiger" -- big but powerless.

Taiwanese View: Large, Strong, Democracy. Taiwanese think of the United States first and foremost as a superpower, and its government being an open democracy. It is strongly perceived as covering a large area of land in America. They view the United States as a strong, rich, big country, which is a wonderful land for study -- in part because of its freedom and opportunity. They are impressed with its open democracy, its president, and its high technology. On the negative side, they view the United States as having serious domestic problems with crime and a decline in morals, as well as being an international busybody.

PRC and Taiwanese Contrasts: Prosperous Capitalism versus Freedom and Democracy. Both groups of Chinese perceive the United States to be highly developed and advanced, but this is much more pervasive in the Mainlanders image than in the Taiwanese image. American cities also make much more impression upon the Mainlanders. US strength is more significant to the Taiwanese, although the military aspect of this makes a greater impression upon the Mainlanders. Mainland China has long considered the U.S. the no. 1 enemy, military speaking. Experts disagree as to what extent this may have really changed. The US as a land of freedom and democracy is important to the Taiwanese, as is American culture in general. However, American prosperity is much more impressive to the Mainlanders. In regard to US problems, the Mainlanders are critical of US social disorder, crime, and unemployment, while the Taiwanese focus more on flaws in national character (self-centered, selfish).

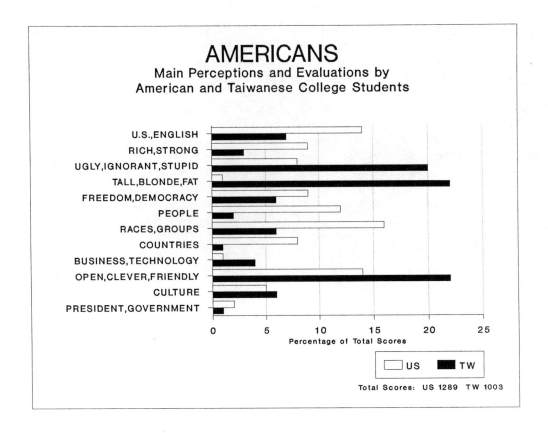

AMERICANS
Main Perceptions and Evaluations by
American and Taiwanese College Students

Percentage of Total Scores

US   TW

Total Scores: US 1289 TW 1003

American View: Identity, Diversity, Pride. Americans express a strong sense of national identity. Attention given to people and the United States are the most dominant. The sense of racial and ethnic diversity is strong, with Indians receiving the most attention along with white and black. Characteristics attributed to Americans by Americans are rich, free, proud, good, strong, best, great and loyal. References to symbols, such as flag, and red, white, and blue reflect identification, which appear in contrast to such critical observations as ignorant, spoiled, and wasteful.

Taiwanese View: Open, Friendly, Haughty. Taiwanese focus on personality and character traits and are inclined to see Americans largely in very positive terms, such as open, candid, friendly, kind, enthusiastic and generous. Taiwanese, often remembering American aid from 1950-1965, are still pro-American, by and large. Criticisms, which encompass close to one-fifth of the responses, focus on Americans being perceived as haughty, over-proud, naive, self-centered busy bodies who practice racial discrimination. Independence, boldness, and liveliness attributes may have been noticed as Americans because they are contrary to the type of personality characteristically formed by Confucian values. Their dominant physical image is one of big and tall, blond and blue-eyed persons with big noses, who speak English. Black people are mentioned but with far less frequency. Americans are also seen as represented by cowboys, TV-serials, and rock-and-roll music -- showing the influence of the American mass media.

American and Taiwanese Contrasts: Diverse and Free versus Strong, Free, and Proud. In both positive and negative perceptions of Americans, the Taiwanese are broader and more contrastive than Americans. Positive attributes and character traits are nearly twice as strong among Taiwanese responses, and negative perceptions are nearly three times as strong among the Taiwanese. Nevertheless, Taiwanese positive responses outnumber their negative ones. Physical features of Americans are much more significant to the Taiwanese than to Americans. The Taiwanese make no link between Americans and the United States. They are more positively disposed toward the latter than toward the former.

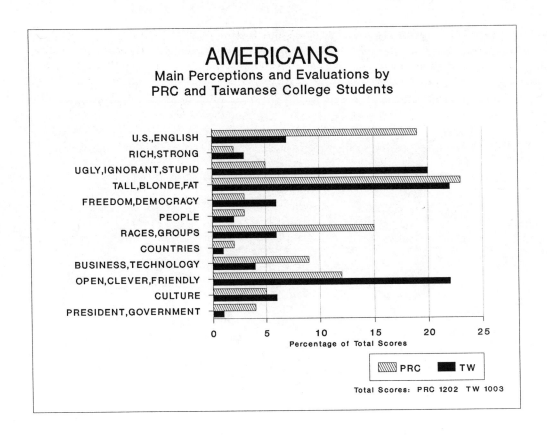

AMERICANS
Main Perceptions and Evaluations by
PRC and Taiwanese College Students

PRC 1202 TW 1003

PRC Chinese View: Tall, Golden-Haired, Clever. American physical features attract strong attention from the Mainlanders, possibly because they are less frequently found in the PRC. Americans are seen as tall, with golden hair, blue eyes, big noses, and skin color (white,black). Mainlanders show an acute awareness of racial differences, mentioning White people, Black and White mixture, Chinese, and Black people -- in that order. In regard to personality and character Mainlanders perceive Americans as clever, open and forthright, hardworking, friendly, and romantic. There are fewer negative perceptions of Americans by Mainlanders. It was not so in the past, particularly with the older generation growing up under Mao's rule. Unemployment, bad, and arrogant are the main ones mentioned.

Taiwanese View: Open, Friendly, Haughty. Taiwanese focus on personality and character traits and are inclined to see Americans largely in very positive terms, such as open, candid, friendly, kind, enthusiastic and generous. Taiwanese, often remembering American aid from 1950-1965, are still pro-American, by and large. Criticisms, which encompass close to one-fifth of the responses, focus on Americans being perceived as haughty, over-proud, naive, self-centered busy bodies who practice racial discrimination. Independence, boldness, and liveliness attributes may have been noticed as Americans because they are contrary to the type of personality characteristically formed by Confucian values. Their dominant physical image is one of big and tall, blond and blue-eyed persons with big noses, who speak English. Black people are mentioned but with far less frequency. Americans are also seen as represented by cowboys, TV-serials, and rock-and-roll music -- showing the influence of the American mass media.

PRC and Taiwanese Contrasts: Tall, Clever, and Multiracial versus Virtues and Vices. The Mainland Chinese are more restrained in expressing both positive and negative perceptions. The Taiwanese are most emphatic, in both directions. American cleverness impresses the Mainlanders, while American candid openness sticks most in the Taiwanese mind. Physical features and racial distinctions are more important to the Mainlanders. American unemployment is the strongest concern among the Mainlanders, while character trait deficiencies, such as haughtiness, self-centeredness, naivete, and meddling, preoccupy the Taiwanese. American freedom and democracy are more important to the Taiwanese than to the Mainlanders, but they are less significant to either group than they are to Americans. Of the three groups, the Mainlanders are most impressed by American science and technology. They pay also more attention to the English language. As experts observe, Mainland China is still a very poor country, economically. But Mainland Chinese are still preoccupied with military development, believing it's the short cut to make China the first-rate country in the world. People on the Mainland have since their childhood been taught to sacrifice "self" for the good of the country.

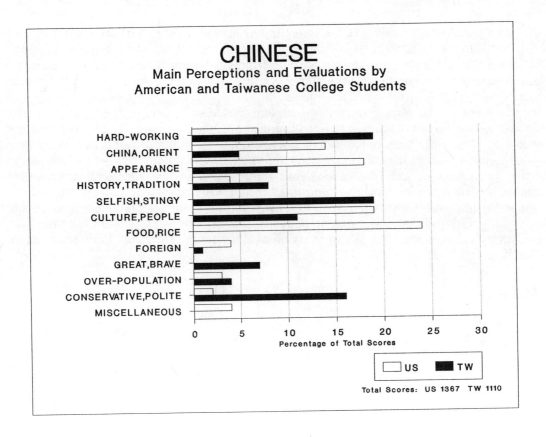

CHINESE
Main Perceptions and Evaluations by
American and Taiwanese College Students

Percentage of Total Scores

US   TW

Total Scores: US 1367 TW 1110

American View: Smart People, Oriental, Food. For Americans Chinese food is the dominant thought, followed by language, people, and culture. The American image of Chinese people is dominated by a perception of intelligence and industriousness. Chinese are seen, first of all, as Oriental, with eyes being the dominant feature. There is also a perception of short stature, black hair, and yellow skin. Americans show very little familiarity with Chinese people, beyond their physical appearance and an impression of their being nice, polite, and quiet.

Taiwanese View: Hard-Working, Wise, Selfish. Taiwanese focus on the Chinese character. They consider Chinese to be primarily hard-working -- and wise. They are perceived as having yellow skin, black hair, and black eyes. The Taiwanese stress on Chinese having human feelings may relate to a concern that Chinese reticence, modesty, and self-restraint are mistaken as indicators of lack of feelings. Nevertheless, Taiwanese are strongly critical of Chinese for being selfish. In general, the Taiwanese are far more critical of Chinese than either of the other groups. They also view Chinese as being conservative -- and great. The dragon appears to be the most important symbol. The Chinese consider themselves descendants of the dragon. To Westerners dragons are big snakes -- a symbol of ill omen or evil, but the Chinese think otherwise. Chinese are seen as being friendly, plain, hospitable, modest, and patient. Confucianism and long history are mentioned.

American and Taiwanese Contrasts: Smart versus Hard-Working. Americans describe the Chinese as smart and intelligent. While the Taiwanese describe the Chinese as wise people. However, to the Taiwanese the most striking Chinese trait is that they are hard working people. Oriental appearance and eyes are the outstanding physical characteristics of Chinese to Americans -- while yellow skin is to the Taiwanese. Chinese language and culture are very significant to Americans, but far less so to the Taiwanese who can communicate with the PRC Chinese in Mandarin Chinese. The Taiwanese mention of human feelings of the Chinese has no counterpart among American perceptions. One of the strong contrasts between the two groups is the great emphasis which Americans place on Chinese food while that subject barely occurs to one Taiwanese because Taiwanese food and Chinese food are basically the same. Americans also show stronger interest in specific countries, especially in linking Chinese to China. The Taiwanese image of Chinese is many-faceted to an extreme; both positive and negative perceptions are numerous.

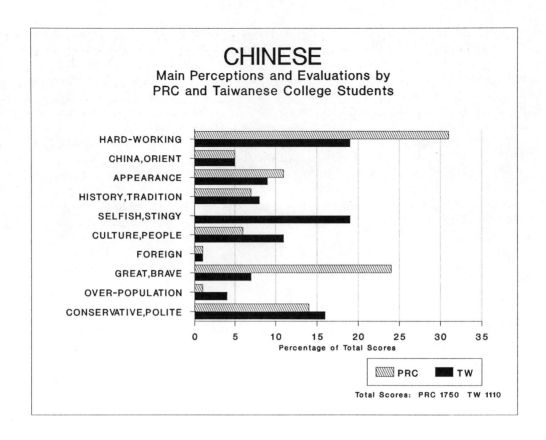

CHINESE
Main Perceptions and Evaluations by
PRC and Taiwanese College Students

Percentage of Total Scores

PRC   TW

Total Scores: PRC 1750   TW 1110

PRC Chinese View: Industrious, Clever, and Brave. Nearly a third of Mainlanders' reaction relates to their perception of Chinese as being industrious and clever. Next in importance is their collective self-perception of being great, brave, proud, and full of integrity. This is followed by the self-image of being kind-hearted, simple, polite, friendly, fair-minded, and warm. In terms of physical features, their perception of themselves as being of the yellow race -- or having yellow skin -- exceeds other physical attributes, such as black hair and black eyes (the first legendary emperor in china is the Yellow Emperor -- the origin of their yellow skin). As a symbol of Chinese culture the Great Wall is important. Mainlanders attribute almost no negative traits to Chinese -- the Chinese are proud people.

Taiwanese View: Hard-Working, Wise, Selfish. Taiwanese focus on the Chinese character. They consider Chinese to be primarily hard-working -- and wise. They are perceived as having yellow skin, black hair, and black eyes. The Taiwanese stress on Chinese having human feelings may relate to a concern that Chinese reticence, modesty, and self-restraint are mistaken as indicators of lack of feelings. Nevertheless, Taiwanese are strongly critical of Chinese for being selfish. In general, the Taiwanese are far more critical of Chinese than either of the other groups. They also view Chinese as being conservative -- and great. The dragon appears to be the most important symbol. The Chinese consider themselves descendants of the dragon. To Westerners dragons are big snakes -- a symbol of ill omen or evil, but the Chinese think otherwise. Chinese are seen as being friendly, plain, hospitable, modest, and patient. Confucianism and long history are mentioned.

PRC and Taiwanese Contrasts: Industrious and Kind-Hearted versus Conservative and Stingy. Industriousness is a far more important Chinese attribute to the Mainlanders than to the Taiwanese. The latter mention that Chinese are good at making money, which aspect is not part of the Mainlander perception. Regarding Chinese culture, the Great Wall is not mentioned by the Taiwanese, nor is the dragon mentioned by the Mainlanders. Being kind-hearted is a far more important Chinese attribute for the Mainlanders, while being conservative is a Chinese trait far more strongly for the Taiwanese. The very strong Taiwanese sense of collective self-criticism, in terms of Chinese being selfish, stingy, not unified or cooperative, has no counterpart in Mainlanders' image. On the contrary, the Mainlanders indicate an extremely positive view of the Chinese as a great and brave people. There is a very small component of self-identification as Chinese among both groups.

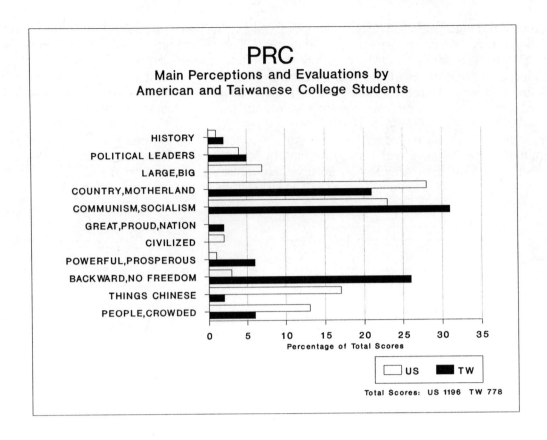

PRC
Main Perceptions and Evaluations by
American and Taiwanese College Students

HISTORY
POLITICAL LEADERS
LARGE,BIG
COUNTRY,MOTHERLAND
COMMUNISM,SOCIALISM
GREAT,PROUD,NATION
CIVILIZED
POWERFUL,PROSPEROUS
BACKWARD,NO FREEDOM
THINGS CHINESE
PEOPLE,CROWDED

0   5   10   15   20   25   30   35
Percentage of Total Scores

US   TW

Total Scores: US 1196 TW 778

American View: Large Country, Communist. The largest component of the American image identifies the PRC as a country among other countries, mainly in the Orient. However, Communist is the single most important label given to the Country. Another dominant component of the Americans' image of the PRC has to do with things Chinese, such as rice and the Great Wall. Americans also perceive the People's Republic as being crowded or over-populated with people. The only other significant component in the American image of the PRC is that it is a large country. Most of the remaining aspects of the PRC which impress Mainlanders about their own country, such as their sense of their country's greatness and glory, its power, and history, make only a marginal impression on Americans.

Taiwanese View: Red China, Communist, Backward. For the Taiwanese, their dominant image of the PRC has to do with communism, which accounts for nearly one third of all responses. Red China is the closest equivalent, and Taiwanese make only minor references to their own country in relation to the PRC. In view of the fact that both sides have been separated from each other for over 40 years, this observation is quite natural. The Taiwanese have a strongly negative view of the PRC as backward and poor and as a country with no freedom. Communist political leaders, Mao Tse-tung and Teng Hsiao-ping, are frequently mentioned. They do show some identification with the PRC in their references to "out people" and visiting one's relatives.

78

American and Taiwanese Contrasts: Large and Crowded versus Backward and Poor. The second most important component for Americans -- communism -- is the most important one for the Taiwanese. From that point on, however, the images of Americans and Taiwanese diverge widely. The PRC's perceived backwardness is little noted by the Americans. On the other hand, the strong American identification of the PRC with things Chinese is nearly totally absent among the Taiwanese. The Americans' perceptions of crowded and over-populated condition of the PRC is not shared by the Taiwanese -- who, nevertheless, refer to the people on the Mainland as "our people." One likely reason for the different perceptions is that Taiwan is not only far more heavily populated than the United States, it is even more densely settled than the Chinese Mainland -- as is Hong Kong. Taiwan has about 1,600 people per square mile, Hong Kong 12,500, China 270, and the US 60.

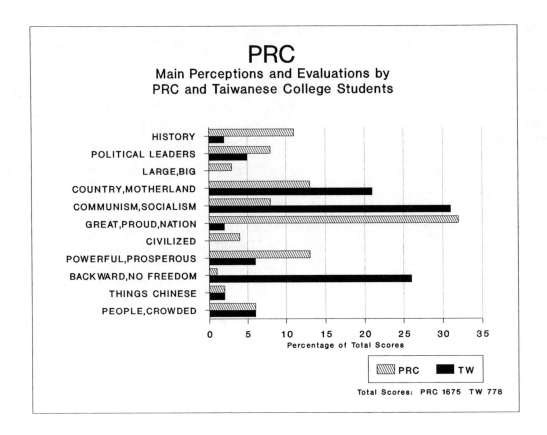

PRC

Main Perceptions and Evaluations by
PRC and Taiwanese College Students

Percentage of Total Scores

Total Scores: PRC 1675 TW 778

PRC Chinese View: Great, Prosperous, Motherland. The Mainland Chinese view the PRC as their motherland and as "great", which is by far their most frequent description. They express immense national pride and patriotism. Their perception of it as powerful and prosperous is also a dominant feature of their image of the PRC. Another very significant aspect is their emphasis on history, development, and the founding of the nation. They describe their system of government more as socialist than communist. Other than a very minor acknowledgement of poverty and backwardness there is no indication of negative characteristics. Theirs is a tightly controlled society without much freedom of speech.

Taiwanese View: Red China, Communist, Backward. For the Taiwanese, their dominant image of the PRC has to do with communism, which accounts for nearly one third of all responses. Red China is the closest equivalent, and Taiwanese make only minor references to their own country in relation to the PRC. In view of the fact that both sides have been separated from each other for over 40 years, this observation is quite natural. The Taiwanese have a strongly negative view of the PRC as backward and poor and as a country with no freedom. Communist political leaders, Mao Tse-tung and Teng Hsiao-ping, are frequently mentioned. They do show some identification with the PRC in their references to "out people" and visiting one's relatives.

PRC and Taiwanese Contrasts: Great and Prosperous versus Backward and Poor. The fact that the PRC is communist is much more heavily stressed by the Taiwanese than by the Mainlanders. To the Taiwanese communism has such bad connotations as tyranny, backwardness, poverty, etc. The greatest divergence of the two views is probably the contrast between the Mainlander perception of greatness and glory, power and prosperity, and the Taiwanese view of the PRC as backward, poor, and lacking freedom. Neither group pays much attention to the dominant American perception of overcrowding. The strong Mainlander emphasis on history is of marginal interest to the Taiwanese.

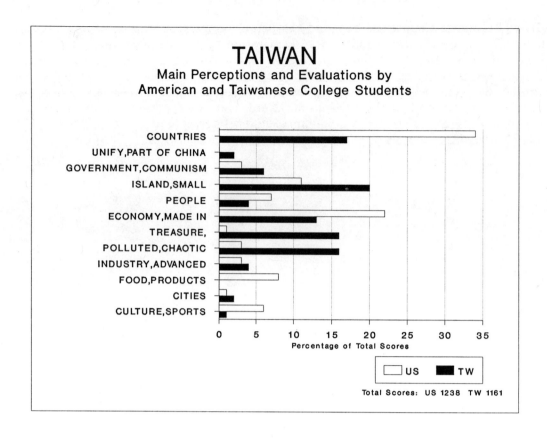

TAIWAN
Main Perceptions and Evaluations by
American and Taiwanese College Students

Percentage of Total Scores

US ☐   TW ■

Total Scores: US 1238 TW 1161

American View: China, Island, Made in Taiwan. China is the most frequent representation of Taiwan for Americans. They also view it as a small island. There are various references related to manufacturing, particularly the familiar phrase "made in Taiwan." Cheap products and cheap labor are dominant American perceptions of Taiwan. Food and industrial products have some relevance only to Americans. Taiwan is seen as a foreign culture far away in the Orient.

Taiwanese View: Small Island, Rich, Beautiful. Physical descriptions dominate the Taiwanese image of Taiwan. It is viewed predominantly as a rich and beautiful small island, but also as free and independent, peaceful and happy. The former name of Taiwan is Formosa, meaning "beautiful island." Nearly as important as these aspects, however, are the perceptions of pollution, chaos, disorderly traffic, and crowding. Economic progress and economy are other important concerns. Taiwan is a small island with scanty natural resources; thus, exports are its lifeblood.

American and Taiwanese Contrasts: Chinese Island versus Beauty and Pollution.
Americans and Taiwanese agree that Taiwan is a small island, with the latter placing more emphasis on the size. That Taiwan and its people are Chinese receives much more stress in the American image. Economic aspects are important to both groups manufacturing for Americans and economic progress for the Taiwanese; exports and imports are only an American concern. Taiwan's beauty is much more present in the Taiwanese mind. So too are its pollution, disorder, and crowding.

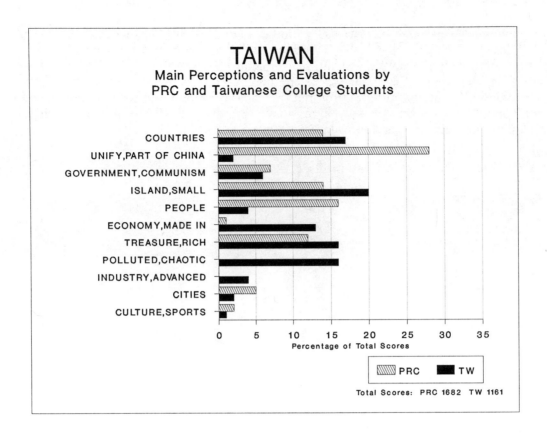

TAIWAN
Main Perceptions and Evaluations by
PRC and Taiwanese College Students

Percentage of Total Scores

PRC   TW

Total Scores: PRC 1682   TW 1161

PRC Chinese View: Unify, Return Part of China. Nearly a third of Mainlander responses relate to the return to China of part of its national territory. Next in importance are the people, whom they call compatriots, followed by a description of physical geography such as island, mountain, Sun Moon Lake. Treasure Island, beautiful, wealthy, and peace are other frequent Mainlander representations. The Mainland Chinese think of Taiwan's relationship to the US much more than do the Taiwanese or Americans.

Taiwanese View: Small Island, Rich, Beautiful. Physical descriptions dominate the Taiwanese image of Taiwan. It is viewed predominantly as a rich and beautiful small island, but also as free and independent, peaceful and happy. The former name of Taiwan is Formosa, meaning "beautiful island." Nearly as important as these aspects, however, are the perceptions of pollution, chaos, disorderly traffic, and crowding. Economic progress and economy are other important concerns. Taiwan is a small island with scanty natural resources; thus, exports are its lifeblood.

PRC and Taiwanese Contrasts: National Territory versus Progress and Disorderly Traffic.
The dominant image of Taiwan for Mainlanders is that of a beautiful and wealthy Treasure Island which "belongs to our country," is part of China, and must be unified with the Mainland. This issue has only a tiny fraction of the Mainlander importance to the Taiwanese. The latter are much more intensively aware of both positive and negative aspects of rapid economic progress. Neither group pays much attention to governmental politics.

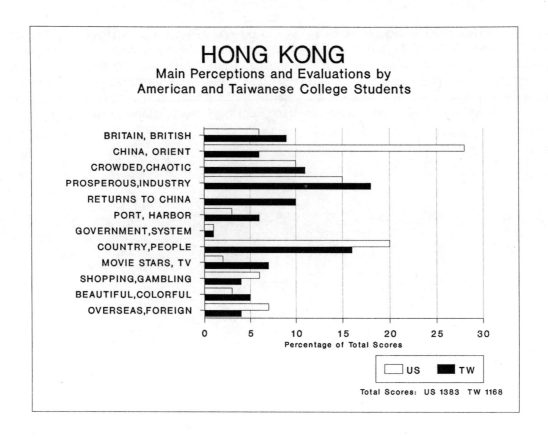

HONG KONG
Main Perceptions and Evaluations by
American and Taiwanese College Students

BRITAIN, BRITISH
CHINA, ORIENT
CROWDED, CHAOTIC
PROSPEROUS, INDUSTRY
RETURNS TO CHINA
PORT, HARBOR
GOVERNMENT, SYSTEM
COUNTRY, PEOPLE
MOVIE STARS, TV
SHOPPING, GAMBLING
BEAUTIFUL, COLORFUL
OVERSEAS, FOREIGN

Percentage of Total Scores

US   TW

Total Scores: US 1383 TW 1168

American View: China, City, Crowded. More than one quarter of American responses link Hong Kong to China and the Orient and Crowded city life. The people and culture attract Americans' attention, particularly the food. Hong Kong's manufacturing industry is characterized by cheap labor and products -- "made in Hong Kong."

Taiwanese View: Prosperous, Trade. Hong Kong is one of Taiwan's major trade partners. For the Taiwanese, prosperity and trade are the most significant aspects of Hong Kong. This is followed by their interest in the people and culture. Here what makes the greatest impression upon the Taiwanese is the Cantonese dialect, the small area, and the Cantonese inhabitants. The crowded and chaotic streets of Hong Kong are part of their vivid city imagery. Movie stars and TV programers are also linked to Hong Kong. Hong Kong is strongly identified as the beautiful Pearl of the Orient. The Taiwanese are strongly aware of the 1997 reversion date when the British colony is to be returned to China.

American and Taiwanese Contrasts: Chinese City versus Prosperous British Colony. That Hong Kong is Chinese and part of the Orient is the most significant aspect of the American image. This aspect is only marginally meaningful to the Taiwanese. The latter are much more impressed with the colony's prosperity and trade. The cultural aspect that the Taiwanese emphasize is Hong Kong ties with Canton. Americans have very different cultural images, relating mainly to the food and city life.

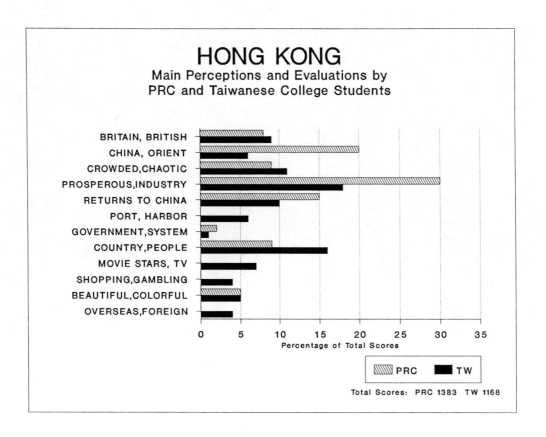

HONG KONG
Main Perceptions and Evaluations by
PRC and Taiwanese College Students

Percentage of Total Scores

PRC   TW

Total Scores: PRC 1383 TW 1168

PRC Chinese View: Prosperous, Territory of China. The Mainlanders are interested in the economic prosperity of Hong Kong, its development, capitalism, and industry. An important issue for the PRC Chinese is consideration of Hong Kong as a "territory of China" and their determination to "regain sovereignty." The negotiation and treaty between Britain and China are emphasized. Another significant image of Hong Kong for Mainlanders is the perception of chaos and crime: disorder, disgrace, crime, the dark side, riots, and bustle.

Taiwanese View: Prosperous, Trade. Hong Kong is one of Taiwan's major trade partners. For the Taiwanese, prosperity and trade are the most significant aspects of Hong Kong. This is followed by their interest in the people and culture. Here what makes the greatest impression upon the Taiwanese is the Cantonese dialect, the small area, and the Cantonese inhabitants. The crowded and chaotic streets of Hong Kong are part of their vivid city imagery. Movie stars and TV programers are also linked to Hong Kong. Hong Kong is strongly identified as the beautiful Pearl of the Orient. The Taiwanese are strongly aware of the 1997 reversion date when the British colony is to be returned to China.

PRC and Taiwanese Contrasts: Prosperous Part of China versus Trade in Pearl of Orient.
While Hong Kong's prosperity is a very important characteristic to both groups of Chinese, this aspect is far more important to the Mainlanders than to the Taiwanese. Trade and commerce are the elements that most impress the Taiwanese, while the developed economy and capitalism are the most significant to the Mainlanders. The Mainlanders focus on the issue of Hong Kong "belonging to China," and its "return to the motherland." Taiwanese interest in these issues is marginal. Taiwan does not have much to say about the future of Hong Kong, because Hong Kong is so close to Mainland China. In regard to culture, Taiwanese focus on the Cantonese speech or the Cantonese inhabitants of Hong Kong -- an issue not at all significant to the Mainlanders. This may reflect the fact that the dominant language of Hong Kong is unintelligible to the Taiwanese -- who speak and understand Mandarin and several Southeast China dialects. The Taiwanese interest in Hong Kong movie stars and TV programs is not shared by the Mainlanders. The Taiwanese view Hong Kong more as a British colony than as a Chinese territory because Hong Kong is market-oriented like Taiwan, whereas the opposite is true for the Mainlanders.

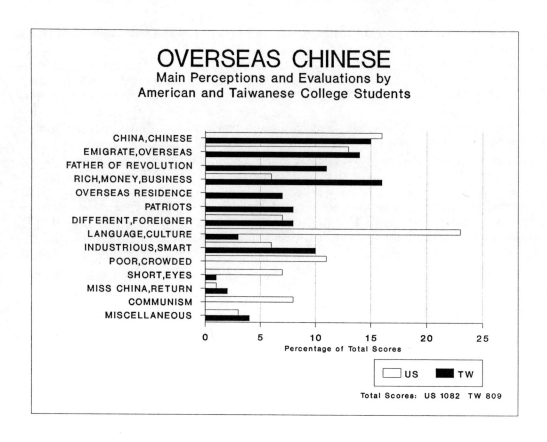

OVERSEAS CHINESE
Main Perceptions and Evaluations by
American and Taiwanese College Students

Percentage of Total Scores

US   TW

Total Scores: US 1082 TW 809

American View: Rice, Boats, Communism. Americans tend to link overseas Chinese to their culture and heritage, especially to food. In American minds Overseas Chinese are also linked to Communism. They are also viewed as immigrants from far away who left by boat or ship. Another interesting aspect is what is perceived by Americans as Chinese over-population, crowded, poor, many, population, and billion. Americans describe Overseas Chinese as short, small, and Oriental.

Taiwanese View: Wealthy People, Abroad. The Taiwanese perceive Overseas Chinese as wealthy people living abroad. They are characterized as rich, toiling, industrious, and struggling. Taiwanese think of "foreigners" who are "not accurate in pronunciation." The Taiwanese link overseas Chinese to Hong Kong, South Asia, and American-born Chinese. The Taiwanese refer strongly to the "Father of the Revolution" -- Sun Yat-sen, who himself used to be an overseas Chinese and enlisted the aid of overseas Chinese during his revolutions.

American and Taiwanese Contrasts: Food versus Father of the Revolution. The American focus on foreign culture food and boats is not shared by the Taiwanese. Whereas Americans characterize overseas Chinese as smart and intelligent, the Taiwanese view them as toilsome, industrious, and struggling -- but above all these traits: wealthy and rich. The important Taiwanese perception of Sun Yat-sen having been an overseas Chinese is not part of the American image.

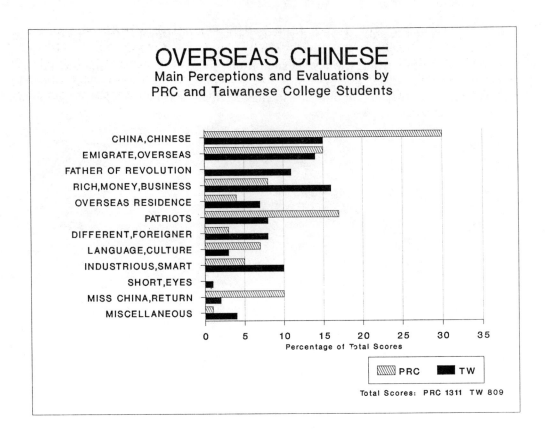

OVERSEAS CHINESE
Main Perceptions and Evaluations by
PRC and Taiwanese College Students

PRC Chinese View: Chinese, Foreign Country, Rich. The Mainlanders focus on being Chinese, the motherland, China, China streets, and hometown. There is some attention given overseas emigration and distance. Countrymen living in a foreign country, abroad, and residing abroad are the dominant images. Overseas Chinese are seen as patriots missing home and yearning to return. "Falling leaves settle on roots" is a popular saying reflecting a very deep and widespread desire of Chinese to come home to die. One of the strongest perceptions is that overseas Chinese are rich.

Taiwanese View: Wealthy People, Abroad. The Taiwanese perceive Overseas Chinese as wealthy people living abroad. They are characterized as rich, toiling, industrious, and struggling. Taiwanese think of "foreigners" who are "not accurate in pronunciation." The Taiwanese link overseas Chinese to Hong Kong, South Asia, and American-born Chinese. The Taiwanese refer strongly to the "Father of the Revolution" -- Sun Yat-sen, who himself used to be an overseas Chinese and enlisted the aid of overseas Chinese during his revolutions.

PRC and Taiwanese Contrasts: Patriot from Motherland versus Wealthy People. The Mainlanders focus on being Chinese and having a common heritage -- and on patriotism. The Taiwanese show more awareness of struggle and toil and its resulting wealth. Only the Taiwanese refer to the "Father of the Revolution" in this context. Unlike the Americans, neither Chinese group sees Communism as having a role in the life of overseas Chinese.

COUNTRY
MAIN COMPONENTS AND RESPONSES

COUNTRIES	US 359	PRC 226	TW 28
USA, United States	141	42	6
America	68	-	-
Ireland	18	-	-
England,Britain	16	7	-
Germany	14	-	-
France	11	-	-
Canada	10	-	-
Russia	9	-	-
Europe	8	-	-
foreign,countries	7	8	-
S America	7	-	-
Africa	7	-	-
Spain	7	-	-
Asia	6	-	-
China	5	141	4
Japan	5	20	-
Sweden	5	-	-
Italy	5	-	-
Portugal	4	-	-
Switzerland	4	-	-
Poland	2	-	-
Soviet Union	-	8	-
R.O.C. Taiwan	-	-	13
int'l relationship	-	-	5

TERRITORY, LAND	196	92	96
territory	6	-	81
territories of a country	-	11	-
land	52	-	-
city	33	-	-
state,s	28	11	-
place	17	-	-
road,s	14	-	-
space	11	-	-
Earth	10	6	-
continent	10	-	-
water	9	-	-
world	6	30	-
map	-	19	-
resources	-	8	2
size	-	6	-
energy resources	-	1	-
settled	-	-	13

GOVERNMENT,LEADERS	45	417	302
government	15	26	49
president	11	6	51
politics,politician	7	13	38
democracy	7	9	18
law,s, legal system	5	22	14
leader,leadership	-	58	-
power	-	35	-
regime	-	31	2
chairman	-	28	-
system, of a country	-	40	2
system of government	-	9	-
organ of power	-	17	-
rule	-	15	6
policy	-	12	10
sovereign right,sovereignty	-	19	-
represent the people	-	11	-
political party,ies	-	10	2
Socialism	-	10	-
organization	-	9	2
nerve	-	9	-
management	-	7	-
diplomacy	-	6	2
center	-	6	-
reform	-	5	-
capital	-	4	-
authority	-	-	34
ideology,abstract	-	-	24
empowered	-	-	16
Congress	-	-	12
Communism,-ists (Chinese)	-	-	15
repression	-	-	5

NATION, PATRIOTISM	229	109	125
patriotism,patriot,-ic	37	-	29
home	34	-	-
nation,national,-ism	41	62	31
national flag,flag	25	-	23
mine,my	21	-	-
loyalty	20	-	16
God	18	-	-
pride,proud	19	-	-
allegiance	10	-	-
honor	4	5	-
motherland	-	27	-
fond of the country	-	8	-
national banner	-	7	-
glory	-	-	12
national anthem	-	-	7
national flower	-	-	7

STRONG AND WEALTHY	11	107	57
big country, big	6	-	20
prosperous,rich,wealth	5	14	3
strong and wealthy	-	60	-
status	-	15	2
strong,strength	-	14	28
inviolable	-	4	-
magnetic power	-	-	4

FREEDOM,BEAUTIFUL,LIVING	189	106	82
freedom, free	44	8	8
living,life,live	39	-	-
love	28	-	13
beauty,beautiful	33	6	-
peace	15	29	12
quiet	12	-	-
good	7	-	-
liberty	6	-	-
respect	5	-	-
great	-	22	-
independence	-	16	5
stability (and peace)	-	13	-
friendly	-	6	-
happiness	-	6	-
solidity	-	-	30
dignified	-	-	6
cooperation	-	-	4
contract	-	-	4

NATIONAL PROTECTION,DEFENSE	16	151	149
protect the people	-	-	35
people are protected	-	-	10
war,s	11	29	-
fighting, fight	5	-	21
army	-	75	16
aggression,aggressive	-	14	5
violence	-	10	-
military affairs	-	9	-
weak	-	5	7
national defense	-	5	4
cannot be bullied	-	4	-
safety	-	-	14
defensive unit	-	-	9
struggle	-	-	8
revolution	-	-	6
guilt	-	-	6
military,soldiers	-	-	8

PEOPLE	58	214	198
people, as a whole	34	88	91
composed of people	-	-	29
group of people	-	-	4
folk	6	-	-
American	6	-	-
family	4	9	10
citizen	4	-	-
European	4	-	-
individual	-	24	4
population	-	24	2
person	-	22	-
people of a country	-	10	-
worker	-	8	-
farmer	-	8	-
master	-	7	-
me	-	7	-
mankind	-	7	-
people centered	-	-	42
Chinese	-	-	16

CULTURE	78	21	19
customs	12	-	-
cultural,tradition	11	-	6
origin	10	-	-
simple	10	-	-
culture	7	13	-
different	7	-	-
identity	5	-	-
religion	5	-	-
history	4	6	-
songs	4	-	-
heritage	3	-	-
sports	-	2	-
root	-	-	8
image	-	-	5

ECONOMY	11	74	24
work	6	-	-
needs	5	-	-
economy	-	31	16
benefit	-	16	-
backward	-	11	-
people's life (livelihood)	-	8	-
job	-	5	-
living standard	-	3	-
welfare	-	-	8

SOCIETY, GROUP	66	139	31
us	43	-	-
unite,united	7	11	-
belong,belonging	7	-	-
club	5	-	-
together	4	-	-
society	-	40	18
group	-	28	13
unity,and integrity	-	20	-
collective	-	20	-
classes	-	11	-
whole	-	9	-

DEVELOPMENT,TECHNOLOGY	8	154	19
school,education	8	9	-
development,developed	-	46	-
science,and technology	-	19	4
machine	-	15	-
future	-	12	-
industry	-	10	-
advanced	-	10	-
develop vigorously	-	7	-
knowledge	-	6	2
construction	-	6	2
seek progress,progress	-	5	11
contribution	-	4	-
strive	-	3	-
civilization	-	2	-

FARMS,RURAL	373	13	0
trees,woods	64	-	-
farm,s	41	-	-
green,grass	51	-	-
rural	23	-	-
cows,horses	27	-	-
travel	14	-	-
fresh air, air	21	-	-
house,s	13	-	-
side	11	-	-
animals, barn	18	-	-
vacation,camping	17	-	-
store	8	-	-
pigs,chickens	11	-	-
fresh	6	-	-
wild,nature	11	-	-
mountains	6	-	-
easy, slow	8	-	-
food, ham,eggs	14	-	-
kitchen	3	-	-
skiing	3	-	-
tractor	3	-	-
agriculture	-	13	-

SUMMARY

Main Components	Percentage of Total Score		
	US	PRC	TW
COUNTRIES	22	12	2
TERRITORY, LAND	12	5	8
GOVERNMENT,LEADERS	3	23	27
NATION, PATRIOTISM	14	6	11
STRONG AND WEALTHY	1	6	5
FREEDOM,BEAUTIFUL,LIVING	12	6	7
NATIONAL PROTECTION	1	8	13
PEOPLE	4	12	18
CULTURE	5	1	2
ECONOMY	1	4	2
SOCIETY, GROUP	4	8	3
DEVELOPMENT,TECHNOLOGY	0	8	2
FARMS,RURAL	23	1	0
Total Scores	1639	1823	1130

UNITED STATES
MAIN COMPONENTS AND RESPONSES

AMERICA, STATES, PLACES	US	PRC	TW
	353	189	88
USA, of America	209	67	-
nation, my country	40	-	-
50 states,fifty, 50	27	-	3
states, city	22	-	-
California	14	-	2
united, one	11	-	-
Wash. D.C., Washington	9	52	-
map	9	-	-
Alaska	7	-	-
Maryland	5	-	-
New York	-	33	9
Los Angeles, Hollywood	-	22	4
Atlantic Ocean	-	9	-
America (N&S America)	-	6	-
large areas of land	-	-	57
Grand Canyon	-	-	5
great lakes area	-	-	4
San Fransisco Bridge	-	-	4

FREEDOM, OPPORTUNITY	US	PRC	TW
	144	67	105
freedom,free,liberty	100	16	37
justice	11	-	-
opportunity	9	-	-
independent, people	5	8	5
travel	5	-	5
rights, equality	10	-	-
life	4	-	-
system,social system	-	14	-
open	-	11	-
Olympic Games	-	8	-
education	-	7	2
university student	-	3	-
wonderful land for study	-	-	31
green card	-	-	7
pioneer	-	-	7
Harvard University	-	-	6
academic	-	-	3
education and research	-	-	2

DEMOCRACY, PRESIDENT	US	PRC	TW
	167	83	109
democracy	63	-	31
government, govt	59	-	-
president	13	24	-
Carter, Jimmy Carter	13	-	-
politics, political	12	6	-
Congress	7	-	4
Ronald, Pres Reagan	-	17	30
Lincoln	-	13	-
diplomacy	-	8	-
White House	-	7	2
poll	-	5	-
election contest	-	3	-
open democracy	-	-	33
selection of president	-	-	9

LOVE, PATRIOTISM	US	PRC	TW
	190	60	94
home	52	-	-
great, best,good	43	-	7
flag	28	-	4
proud, pride	15	-	-
beautiful	9	28	-
love	9	-	-
patriotism	7	-	-
red/white/blue	7	-	-
Uncle Sam	6	-	2
stable	6	-	-
happiness	5	-	-
help	3	-	-
friendly	-	12	-
flag, stars & stripes	-	8	-
romantic	-	8	-
general mood	-	4	-
warm affection	-	-	14
rich in resources	-	-	14
peaceful and rich land	-	-	6
Statue of Liberty	-	-	10
love peace	-	-	7
generous	-	-	5
eagle	-	-	5
confidence	-	-	5
beautiful forests & lakes	-	-	4
truthful	-	-	4
paradise	-	-	4
beautiful natural scenes	-	-	3

OTHER COUNTRIES	US	PRC	TW
	16	74	23
Soviet Union	8	-	13
Iran	8	-	-
Taiwan	-	20	-
world	-	11	-
Europe	-	11	-
Japan	-	10	-
Britain	-	9	-
overseas	-	8	-
China street	-	5	-
Red China	-	-	10

COUNTRY, CULTURE	US	PRC	TW
	153	51	140
country	102	6	-
history	12	7	-
revolution, 1776	12	-	-
melting pot	7	-	-
variety	7	-	-
baseball	6	-	-
colonies	5	-	-
Civil War	2	-	-
English,speaking	-	11	20
civilization	-	10	8
liv. condition	-	10	-
culture	-	5	5
custom	-	2	-
culture mix	-	-	24
immigration	-	-	14
movie, TV program	-	-	12
complicated	-	-	8
Indian people	-	-	8
western cowboy	-	-	8
complex heritage	-	-	7
Qefl exam	-	-	6
McDonalds	-	-	6
international level	-	-	5
rock and roll music	-	-	5
blue jeans	-	-	2
Michael Jackson	-	-	2

PROBLEMS, DISORDER, CRIME	US	PRC	TW
	34	91	148
wasteful	8	-	-
stupid	5	-	-
problems	5	-	-
trouble	5	-	-
inflation,recession	7	-	-
greed	4	-	-
disorder,social disorder	-	22	-
crime, much crime	-	17	2
unemployment	-	13	5
lack spiritual ballast	-	9	-
corrupt	-	8	4
fight,rape	-	7	-
drug taking	-	7	-
tense	-	6	-
prostitute	-	2	-
selfish and proud people	-	-	19
busy body	-	-	18
ethnically self-centered	-	-	15
attacker, oppressor	-	-	9
confuse	-	-	7
short of culture	-	-	7
sick of	-	-	7
exploitation	-	-	6
trade deficit	-	-	6
FBI	-	-	6
big brother	-	-	5
degenerate	-	-	5
evil and ugly	-	-	5
decline of morals	-	-	5
negative	-	-	4
self-protective	-	-	4
many social problems	-	-	4
New York subway train	-	-	3
sex	-	-	2

DEVELOPED, ADVANCED	US	PRC	TW
	18	262	75
developed, country	-	115	-
developed economy,industr	y	14	-
much, competition	-	7	2
high tech, technology	12	-	20
potential	6	-	-
high building	-	21	-
developed science	-	19	-
industry	-	16	7
advanced, technology	-	21	-
flourishing	-	9	-
electronic	-	9	-
modernization	-	8	-
powerful nuclear energy	-	6	6
science	-	6	-
developed production	-	5	-
future	-	3	-
highway	-	3	-
energetic,people work har	d	-	12
progress	-	-	8
airplane,space shuttle	-	-	8
clean environment	-	-	6
scientific development	-	-	6

STRONG, BIG, SUPERPOWER	US	PRC	TW
	153	151	167
power, super power	46	42	-
big, large	34	12	-
army, navy	22	-	-
war	10	5	2
strong country	9	20	55
world power	7	-	-
draft	6	-	-
powerful country	5	-	17
coast guard,marines	10	-	-
military strength,force	4	12	8
hegemony,hegemonism	-	11	8
strong,rich	-	11	-
imperialist	-	8	-
big country, big state	-	7	32
oppress other countries	-	7	-
invasion	-	7	-
nuclear weapon,atomic bom	b	7	4
relationship	-	2	-
Vietnam War,Korean War	-	-	12
negotiation of US and Ch	-	-	8
empire builders	-	-	6
great authority	-	-	4
veto of trade bill	-	-	4
deployment	-	-	3
weapon	-	-	4

PEOPLE, APPEARANCE	US	PRC	TW
	50	105	41
people	34	12	-
citizen	6	-	-
taller people, tall	4	-	16
American,s	3	33	-
hostages	3	-	-
big nose	-	24	-
black/white	-	10	-
blue eyes	-	7	-
Amer. Chinese	-	7	-
white skin,white person	-	6	4
Robert	-	3	-
worker	-	3	-
foreigner	-	-	12
negro (black)	-	-	9

CAPITALISTS, PROSPEROUS	US	PRC	TW
	38	230	74
gold & treasure everywhere	-	-	5
rich, wealth	27	-	30
capitalist,capitalism	8	64	8
money	3	10	-
money, powerful	-	4	-
rich people, wealthy	-	30	-
capitalist system,society	-	25	-
prosperous	-	17	2
automobile, car	-	17	2
economical system,economy	-	24	4
ambitions	-	11	-
economic crisis	-	8	-
status	-	8	-
salary,big	-	6	-
housing	-	6	-
economic	-	-	11
money centered	-	-	8
trade	-	-	4

SUMMARY

Main Components	Percentage of Total Score		
	US	PRC	TW
AMERICA, STATES, PLACES	27	14	8
FREEDOM, OPPORTUNITY	11	5	10
DEMOCRACY, PRESIDENT	13	6	10
LOVE, PATRIOTISM	14	4	9
COUNTRY, CULTURE	12	4	13
PROBLEMS, DISORDER, CRIME	3	7	14
DEVELOPED, ADVANCED	1	19	7
STRONG, BIG, SUPERPOWER	12	11	16
PEOPLE, APPEARANCE	4	8	4
CAPITALISTS, PROSPEROUS	3	17	7
OTHER COUNTRIES	1	5	2
Total Scores	1316	1363	1064

AMERICANS
MAIN COMPONENTS AND RESPONSES

U.S., ENGLISH	US	PRC	TW
	186	223	75
U.S.,USA	116	-	-
United States	25	54	-
citizen,s	20	-	-
America	9	11	-
American,s	-	8	7
English	6	45	3
speak English	-	41	47
states	6	-	-
here	4	-	-
Washington,D.C.	-	32	4
New York	-	17	4
British	-	15	-
Anglo Saxons	-	-	10

RICH,STRONG	US	PRC	TW
	116	22	31
rich	34	-	-
too rich	-	-	8
capitalism,capitalist	7	8	3
strong	18	-	-
powerful	16	-	-
united	16	-	-
wealth,wealthy	16	10	2
money	9	4	-
bold and unconstrained	-	-	10
self-confidence	-	-	8

UGLY,IGNORANT,STUPID	US	PRC	TW
	107	58	203
ugly	14	-	-
ignorant,stupid	18	-	5
materialistic	11	-	-
crazy	9	-	4
spoiled	9	-	-
wasteful,waste	8	-	2
greedy	7	-	-
loud	7	-	-
prejudice	7	-	-
bad	5	15	-
arrogant	5	9	-
violent	5	-	-
lost	2	-	-
unemployment	-	18	-
pass off fisheyes as pea	-	11	-
prostitute	-	5	-
haughty	-	-	35
naive	-	-	33
racial discrimination	-	-	16
self-centered,selfish	-	-	24
busy body	-	-	12
over proud	-	-	10
self-important	-	-	8
childish behavior	-	-	8
social indifference	-	-	7
cool and strange	-	-	7
eat a lot	-	-	6
non-communication	-	-	5
shocking act	-	-	5
exaggeration	-	-	4
self centered ideas	-	-	4
oppress people	-	-	4
people who worship money	-	-	4

TALL,BLONDE,FAT	US	PRC	TW
	19	273	216
fat	19	-	12
golden hair	-	50	-
big and tall person	-	92	96
blonde hair and blue eyes	-	-	49
blue eyes	-	40	-
big nose	-	36	21
white skin	-	29	10
yellow eyes	-	10	-
curly hair	-	8	-
eyes	-	5	-
goodlooking	-	3	-
robust	-	-	13
lovely	-	-	8
beard	-	-	4
beautiful physical body	-	-	3

FREEDOM, DEMOCRACY	US	PRC	TW
	121	33	61
free,freedom	41	22	12
democratic,democracy	24	6	2
patriotic,patriots	18	-	-
independent	9	-	-
together,togetherness	14	-	-
unity	6	-	-
revolution	5	-	-
travel	4	-	-
thought	-	5	-
independence	-	-	18
liberty	-	-	10
freedom worshiper	-	-	10
democracy and freedom	-	-	5
equality	-	-	2
peace	-	-	2

PEOPLE	US	PRC	TW
	152	33	22
people	80	-	-
me	46	-	-
hostages	7	-	-
friends	6	-	-
poor	5	-	-
many	4	-	-
farmers	4	-	-
person	-	14	-
don't know	-	9	-
you	-	7	-
family	-	3	-
foreigner	-	-	22

COUNTRIES	US	PRC	TW
	98	20	7
country	37	9	-
south	21	-	-
north	14	-	-
nation	9	-	-
central	7	-	-
North America	5	-	-
South America	5	-	-
world	-	6	-
Vietnam	-	5	-
emigration	-	-	4
U.S.S.R.	-	-	3

BUSINESS, TECHNOLOGY	US	PRC	TW
	15	109	40
business	11	-	-
advance,advanced	4	5	6
developed	-	18	2
science	-	13	-
modernization	-	11	-
living standard	-	9	-
competition	-	9	-
scientific technology	-	8	11
job	-	8	-
economy	-	7	2
tall buildings	-	6	-
industrious	-	6	-
technology	-	5	-
invention	-	2	-
contribution	-	2	-
utilitarianism	-	-	11
good ideas	-	-	4
developing	-	-	4

OPEN, CLEVER, FRIENDLY	US	PRC	TW
	178	144	218
proud	35	-	-
good	28	10	4
best	15	-	-
great	11	-	-
loyal	11	-	-
helpful	9	-	-
happy	7	-	4
lucky	7	-	-
loving	7	-	-
healthy	6	-	-
friendly and kindly	-	-	36
our friends	-	-	7
friendly	5	11	3
loved	5	-	-
unique	5	-	-
individual	4	-	-
generous	4	-	16
intelligent	4	-	-
famous	4	-	-
worthy	4	-	-
concerned	4	-	-
resourceful	3	-	-
clever	-	36	-
open	-	15	38
hardworking	-	15	-
forthright	-	12	-
romantic	-	11	-
some friendly some not	-	10	-
humor, ous	-	7	12
enthusiasm	-	6	26
lovable	-	6	-
brave	-	5	4
candid	-	-	18
pragmatism	-	-	9
honest	-	-	8
active,activist	-	-	15
wise	-	-	7
pure heart	-	-	5
sense of responsibilities	-	-	4
optimistic	-	-	2

RACES, GROUPS	US	PRC	TW
	202	181	60
Indian,s	61	-	4
diverse	25	-	-
white,people	17	39	16
black,people	16	23	13
melting pot	9	-	-
Canadians	9	-	-
Latin	9	-	-
nationality	8	-	-
natives	8	-	-
Afro	7	-	-
Russian,s	5	4	-
Jews	5	-	-
mixture,mixed	9	-	-
red	5	-	-
Irish	4	-	-
society	3	11	-
class	2	-	-
black, white mixture	-	35	-
Chinese	-	27	4
yellow skin	-	11	-
Japanese	-	9	-
race	-	8	-
French	-	8	-
white and black people	-	6	-
multi-racial	-	-	8
common people	-	-	8
multi-cultured	-	-	7

CULTURE, ENTERTAINMENT	US	PRC	TW
	63	56	60
red,white & blue	13	-	-
flag	12	-	-
cars	10	-	-
culture	6	-	7
food	6	-	-
apple pie	5	-	-
baseball,football	8	-	-
different	3	-	-
young	-	15	-
basketball	-	11	2
daily life	-	9	-
be fond of dressing	-	7	-
wear western clothes	-	6	-
custom	-	5	-
status	-	3	-
lively, brisk	-	-	13
western cowboy	-	-	10
Rambo	-	-	7
curious	-	-	6
cultural	-	-	6
TV serials	-	-	5
rock and roll music	-	-	4

PRESIDENT, GOVERNMENT	US	PRC	TW
	32	50	10
war	16	-	-
government	9	-	-
leaders	5	-	-
army	2	-	-
Ronald	-	18	-
Lincoln	-	15	2
White House	-	11	-
system	-	6	-
President Reagan	-	-	8

SUMMARY

Main Components	Percentage of Total Score		
	US	PRC	TW
U.S., ENGLISH	14	19	7
RICH,STRONG	9	2	3
UGLY,IGNORANT,STUPID	8	5	20
TALL,BLONDE,FAT	1	23	22
FREEDOM, DEMOCRACY	9	3	6
PEOPLE	12	3	2
RACES, GROUPS	16	15	6
COUNTRIES	8	2	1
BUSINESS, TECHNOLOGY	1	9	4
OPEN, CLEVER, FRIENDLY	14	12	22
CULTURE, ENTERTAINMENT	5	5	6
PRESIDENT, GOVERNMENT	2	4	1
Total Scores	1289	1202	1003

CHINESE
MAIN COMPONENTS AND RESPONSES

HARD-WORKING, CLEVER	US	PRC	TW
	94	551	215
smart, intelligent	43	-	-
computer, s science	16	-	-
industrious	11	174	-
math, engineering	12	-	-
efficient	6	-	-
educated	4	-	-
acrobats	2	-	-
clever	-	120	-
wisdom, wise, people	-	64	70
ambitious, ambition	-	60	-
hard-working	-	28	92
strive	-	12	-
competent	-	12	-
worker, labor	-	10	-
creation, creative	-	16	-
invention	-	9	-
construction	-	6	-
enterprising	-	6	-
be self-possessed	-	6	-
knowledge	-	6	-
ability	-	5	-
modernization	-	3	-
assiduous	-	3	-
make progress	-	3	-
science	-	3	-
seek to win	-	3	-
contribution	-	2	-
strong willed	-	-	13
good at making money	-	-	11
suffering	-	-	8
strong	-	-	7
burden	-	-	7
penny wise pound foolish	-	-	7

CHINA, ORIENT	US	PRC	TW
	196	91	59
China	61	19	-
Japanese	26	5	-
Hong Kong	18	5	2
Taiwan	11	10	10
nation	9	-	-
Peking	9	-	-
country	7	9	2
Asia	7	-	-
land	7	-	-
Korea	7	-	-
Vietnam	7	-	-
red	6	-	-
Peoples Republic	6	-	-
Chinatown	5	-	-
mainland	5	-	-
Orient	5	-	-
motherland	-	16	-
Yellow River	-	9	6
Yangtze River	-	9	-
Russia	-	6	-
world	-	3	-
mainland China	-	-	29
mainland China in trouble	-	-	6
scenery of fatherland	-	-	4

APPEARANCE, ORIENTAL	US	PRC	TW
	251	195	100
Oriental, Asian	83	-	-
eyes, slanted eyes	55	-	-
short	30	-	-
black hair, hair	23	39	16
skinny	11	-	-
yellow	11	-	-
chink	10	-	-
race	10	-	-
slant	7	-	-
small	6	-	-
smell	5	-	-
yellow skin	-	60	33
yellow race	-	41	-
black eyes	-	33	16
pretty, beautiful, lovely	-	22	7
Mongol race	-	-	12
near-sighted	-	-	12
too short	-	-	4

FOOD, RICE	US	PRC	TW
	323	0	0
food	207	-	-
rice	53	-	-
egg roll, s	16	-	-
chopsticks	13	-	-
restaurant	11	-	-
Chow Mein	6	-	-
soup	6	-	-
fish	11	-	-

HISTORY, TRADITION	US	PRC	TW
	54	114	86
communist, s, communism	37	-	2
communist party	-	6	-
ancient, old	11	-	-
Mao, Zedong	4	8	-
history	2	12	18
later gen. of emperor	-	42	-
imperial	-	15	-
descendant of imperial	-	14	-
socialism	-	8	-
four inventions in histor	y	5	-
ancient, stick to old way	s	4	-
Confucionism	-	-	22
long history	-	-	22
5000 years' history	-	-	6
tradition	-	-	4
deep rooted	-	-	4
offspring of Huan Ti	-	-	2
unified	-	-	6

SELFISH, STINGY	US	PRC	TW
	0	0	211
selfish, stingy	-	-	71
not unified	-	-	23
no moral sense	-	-	17
miserable	-	-	12
idle	-	-	10
infighting	-	-	10
false	-	-	10
not cooperative	-	-	10
afraid of troubles	-	-	9
no self-confidence	-	-	8
corrupt	-	-	8
not abiding by the law	-	-	5
not live up to a standard	-	-	5
dull	-	-	5
inflexible	-	-	4
not self loving	-	-	4

CULTURE, PEOPLE	US	PRC	TW
	266	109	124
language	79	2	-
people	70	12	-
culture	47	7	19
Mandarin	10	-	-
art	9	-	-
Kung Fu, karate	14	-	-
bicycles	7	-	-
dragon	6	-	24
movies	6	-	-
customs	6	-	-
silk	5	-	-
tea	4	-	-
clothes	3	-	-
civilized	-	38	-
Great Wall	-	17	5
unite	-	15	-
Chinese (language)	-	5	-
woman volleyball team	-	5	-
male and female	-	3	-
economy	-	2	11
equality	-	2	-
farmer	-	1	-
human feelings	-	-	26
sheet of loose sand	-	-	10
worship anything western	-	-	8
long garment	-	-	8
many dialects	-	-	6
eating	-	-	7

FOREIGN	US	PRC	TW
	58	9	9
foreign, foreigner	29	3	-
far, far away	13	-	-
different, culture	16	-	-
foreign countries	-	6	-
Overseas Chinese	-	-	9

GREAT, BRAVE, ENDURE	US	PRC	TW
	6	412	77
big	6	-	-
great, great nation	-	136	26
brave	-	107	-
be proud, of, proud	-	46	12
full of integrity	-	36	-
lofty	-	16	-
me	-	15	16
love the country	-	14	-
be patriot	-	12	-
glory	-	11	5
force	-	11	-
firm	-	8	-
confidence	-	-	7
public morality	-	-	5
sense of mission	-	-	4
passionate	-	-	2

OVER-POPULATION, POOR	US	PRC	TW
	40	25	48
many	11	-	-
poor	7	-	3
crowded	6	-	-
over-populated, -tion	5	13	-
population	5	-	-
1 billion people, billion	4	-	8
birth control	2	-	-
backward	-	9	-
family	-	3	9
very dirty	-	-	9
populous and spacious	-	-	9
chaotic	-	-	5
Chinese populated area	-	-	4

CONSERVATIVE, POLITE, KIND	US	PRC	TW
	23	244	181
nice	13	-	-
quiet	7	-	-
friendly, friends, -ship	3	19	26
kind-hearted	-	33	-
simple	-	26	-
conservative	-	16	29
polite	-	19	7
fair-minded	-	14	-
warmly	-	13	-
elegant, behavior	-	11	-
have self-confidence	-	10	-
help each other	-	15	2
good and honest, honesty	-	19	10
peace, peaceful	-	9	10
happiness	-	9	-
amiable and kindly	-	8	-
simple and unadorned	-	6	-
have ideal	-	6	-
harmony	-	5	-
good	-	3	-
friendly affection	-	3	-
plain	-	-	19
hospitable	-	-	18
modesty	-	-	17
patient	-	-	13
face saving	-	-	11
tender	-	-	10
seek for approximation	-	-	5
easy going	-	-	4

MISCELLANEOUS	US	PRC	TW
	56	0	0
American, s, America	16	-	-
checkers	8	-	-
College Park	7	-	-
blue	6	-	-
markets	5	-	-
boat	4	-	-
cheap	4	-	-
hard	6	-	-

SUMMARY

Main Components	Percentage of Total Score		
	US	PRC	TW
HARD-WORKING, CLEVER	7	31	19
CHINA, ORIENT	14	5	5
APPEARANCE, ORIENTAL	18	11	9
HISTORY, TRADITION	4	7	8
SELFISH, STINGY	0	0	19
CULTURE, PEOPLE	19	6	11
FOOD, RICE	24	0	0
FOREIGN	4	1	1
GREAT, BRAVE, ENDURE	0	24	7
OVER-POPULATION, POOR	3	1	4
CONSERVATIVE, POLITE, KIND	2	14	16
MISCELLANEOUS	4	0	0
Total Scores	1367	1750	1110

97

PRC
MAIN COMPONENTS AND RESPONSES

HISTORY	US 10	PRC 184	TW 13
ancient country, old	7	9	-
history	3	20	-
October 1 (national day)	-	48	-
civilized ancient country	-	25	-
four modernizations	-	20	-
found of the country	-	15	-
have a long history	-	13	-
found	-	11	-
found in 1949	-	11	-
cultural revolution	-	6	9
35th national day	-	6	-
history & culture	-	-	4

POLITICAL LEADERS	42	139	40
Mao Tse-Tung	24	-	23
Mao Zedong	-	42	-
Chairman Mao	-	24	-
Nixon	14	-	-
leader	4	8	-
Tian An Men	-	30	-
Deng Xiao Ping	-	13	-
Zhou Enlai	-	13	-
Liu Shao Qi	-	5	-
Chairman	-	4	-
Teng Hsiao-Ping	-	-	17

LARGE, BIG	86	42	0
large,big	80	-	-
many	6	-	-
extensive	-	11	-
vast territory	-	11	-
land	-	8	-
8 hundred million farms	-	6	-
abundant resources	-	6	-

COUNTRY, MOTHERLAND	338	216	160
Chinese	66	-	18
China	22	45	-
Red China	8	-	90
Hong Kong	15	-	-
Taiwan	13	-	20
country	42	17	-
oriental, orient	37	-	-
Asia	27	-	-
foreign	24	-	-
Korea	13	-	-
far	11	-	-
Peking	9	-	2
mainland	9	-	-
Far East	7	-	-
island	7	-	-
east	7	-	-
distant	7	-	-
Japan	6	-	-
Russia, USSR	4	-	4
Canton	4	-	-
motherland	-	65	-
mother	-	34	-
Beijing	-	29	-
Chinese nation, the	-	10	-
Britain	-	10	-
foreign countries	-	3	-
China (ancient name)	-	2	-
world	-	1	-
hometown	-	-	10
nation	-	-	8
fatherland	-	-	8

COMMUNISM,SOCIALISM	274	127	241
Communist	143	-	-
Red	47	-	8
Communism	34	4	7
government	28	3	-
commie	7	-	-
politics	6	-	-
relations	5	-	-
ally	4	-	-
socialist country	-	28	-
Socialism	-	26	-
Communist Party	-	24	83
Chinese Communist party	-	18	-
system	-	13	-
economy	-	6	-
imperial	-	5	-
communists (bandits)	-	-	83
power struggle	-	-	14
totalitarianism	-	-	14
Communist government	-	-	6
Communist system	-	-	6
espionage	-	-	6
Communist country	-	-	5
iron curtain	-	-	5
Viet Cong	-	-	4

GREAT, PROUD, NATION	US 5	PRC 537	TW 19
friend	5	-	-
great	-	212	-
glory	-	43	-
long life	-	29	-
be proud of	-	26	-
national flag	-	25	-
ardently love	-	24	-
happiness,of the people	-	19	-
bless	-	17	-
beautiful	-	15	2
dignified	-	15	-
great nation	-	14	-
equality	-	14	-
lovable	-	13	-
good,fine	-	11	-
national anthem	-	11	-
hope	-	11	-
great motherland	-	10	-
national emblem	-	9	-
greatest country	-	6	-
peace	-	5	-
honor	-	3	-
living	-	3	-
ideal	-	2	-
love motherland	-	-	14
liberty	-	-	3

CIVILIZED, DEVELOPMENT	23	63	0
Olympics	7	-	-
changing	7	-	-
production	5	-	-
industry	4	-	-
civilized	-	18	-
modernization	-	11	-
future	-	10	-
construction	-	7	-
advanced	-	6	-
develop vigorously	-	5	-
efforts	-	2	-
creation	-	2	-
development	-	2	-

POWERFUL AND PROSPEROUS	14	218	47
smart	7	6	-
strong,country	4	5	-
powerful	3	-	8
powerful and prosperous	-	49	-
prosperous	-	34	4
rich	-	22	-
unity,unite	-	17	-
diligent	-	12	-
unity of country	-	11	-
strong and wealthy	-	11	-
brave	-	10	-
long standing	-	10	-
bright	-	9	-
sovereign right	-	7	-
wealthy	-	6	-
safe & stable	-	5	-
wisdom	-	4	-
fertile & plentiful land	-	-	18
absolute	-	-	7
recovery of the lost land	-	-	6
militarily strong	-	-	4

BACKWARD,NO FREEDOM,POOR	38	18	200
poor,poverty	13	12	30
little	6	-	-
conflict	5	-	-
screaming	5	-	-
cold	5	-	-
dirty	4	-	-
backward	-	6	64
no freedom	-	-	27
occupied land	-	-	18
pitiable people	-	-	10
men live like dogs	-	-	7
confuse nations in world	-	-	7
repress the people	-	-	6
enemy	-	-	5
purge	-	-	5
corrupt government	-	-	5
catastrophe	-	-	5
tragedy	-	-	4
need to be destroyed	-	-	4
suffering	-	-	3

THINGS CHINESE	US 205	PRC 36	TW 12
rice	39	-	-
Great Wall	31	17	5
different	13	-	-
food	12	-	-
culture	10	3	-
bicycle,s	10	-	-
dragon	8	-	-
small	8	-	-
wall	7	-	-
chinese food	7	-	-
bikes	7	-	-
friendly	7	-	-
pandas	6	-	-
green	6	-	-
chopsticks	5	-	-
language	5	-	-
yellow	4	-	-
mountains	4	-	-
bamboo	4	-	-
karate	3	-	-
short	3	-	-
black hair	3	-	-
music	3	-	-
Yellow River	-	8	-
Yangtze river	-	8	-
blue shirts	-	-	5
Yantze & Yellow Rivers	-	-	2
five-starred red flag	-	-	-

PEOPLE, CROWDED	161	95	46
crowded	32	-	-
people	30	43	-
over populated	20	-	-
overpopulation	18	-	-
population	16	15	-
large population	9	-	-
birth	7	-	-
millions	6	-	-
crowd	6	-	-
billions	5	-	-
birth control	5	-	-
one billion	4	-	-
populated	3	-	-
one billion people	-	16	-
full of people	-	15	-
proletariat, the	-	6	-
our people	-	-	22
visit one's relatives	-	-	18
populous	-	-	6

SUMMARY

Main Components	Percentage of Total Score		
	US	PRC	TW
HISTORY	1	11	2
POLITICAL LEADERS	4	8	5
LARGE, BIG	7	3	0
COUNTRY, MOTHERLAND	28	13	21
COMMUNISM,SOCIALISM	23	8	31
GREAT, PROUD, NATION	0	32	2
CIVILIZED, DEVELOPMENT	2	4	0
POWERFUL AND PROSPEROUS	1	13	6
BACKWARD,NO FREEDOM,POOR	3	1	26
THINGS CHINESE	17	2	2
PEOPLE, CROWDED	13	6	6
Total Scores	1196	1675	778

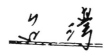

TAIWAN
MAIN COMPONENTS AND RESPONSES

COUNTRIES	US 422	PRC 229	TW 199
China	105	51	36
Oriental,Orient	62	-	-
nation	42	6	14
foreign	40	-	-
Asia,Asian	51	-	-
Japan,Japanese	43	-	-
far	23	-	-
East	12	-	-
far away	11	-	-
R.O.C.	7	-	7
overseas	7	-	-
Far East	6	-	-
Korea	6	-	-
distant	5	-	-
United States,U.S.A.	2	29	4
mainland	-	37	32
motherland	-	37	-
territory	-	29	-
Hong Kong	-	26	-
South Korea	-	11	-
world	-	3	3
Formosa	-	-	72
home	-	-	18
go abroad	-	-	6
international	-	-	4
Taiwan	-	-	3

UNIFY, PART OF CHINA	US 0	PRC 478	TW 22
unify	-	166	-
part of China	-	102	10
return	-	43	-
territory of China	-	40	-
national territory	-	36	-
belongs to our country	-	26	-
territory of our country	-	21	-
return to motherland	-	17	-
get together	-	13	-
return to country a.s.a.p.	-	5	-
regain	-	5	-
unify peacefully	-	4	-
Taiwan independent movemt	-	-	8
reunify China	-	-	4

GOVERNMENT, COMMUNISM	US 31	PRC 120	TW 67
capitalism,capitalist	7	-	4
nationalist	7	-	-
democracy,democratic	6	-	11
not communist	6	-	-
ally	5	-	-
Guomingtang	-	82	13
capitalist system	-	10	-
coop. betw com par&guom	-	8	-
government	-	8	-
communist party	-	6	-
politics	-	3	14
system	-	3	-
dem. progressive party	-	-	12
ruled	-	-	5
anti-communist to the end	-	-	4
anti-communist bastion	-	-	4

ISLAND,SMALL	US 140	PRC 235	TW 233
island	75	90	60
small,little	49	-	46
water	7	-	-
jungle	4	-	-
hot	3	-	4
rock	2	-	-
Ali mountain	-	86	4
sun and moon pond	-	49	-
ocean	-	9	9
small land,many people	-	-	41
settlement	-	-	18
shaped like banana leaf	-	-	10
banana like plants	-	-	8
banana	-	1	-
four clearcut seasons	-	-	7
mountainous	-	-	7
Cho-Swei river	-	-	5
isolated	-	-	5
central mountain series	-	-	5
crossing island highway	-	-	4

PEOPLE	US 91	PRC 275	TW 42
Chinese	43	-	-
people	37	30	-
immigrant	6	-	-
population	5	-	-
Tiang Tieshi	-	64	4
compatriots,in Taiwan	-	48	-
Tiang Tinguo	-	35	-
dear person	-	16	-
Huang Zhicheng	-	14	-
Taiwanese,people	-	19	-
Kaoshan nationality	-	9	-
Zheng Cheung Gong	-	8	-
farmer	-	7	2
lead by Jiang Jingguo	-	7	-
Zhang Xinoliang	-	6	-
children of imperial	-	6	-
worker	-	3	-
friends and relatives	-	3	-
birthplace	-	-	12
history	-	-	5
aboriginals in Taiwan	-	-	5
Ching Ching Kuo	-	-	4
mountainous people	-	-	4
soldier recruit	-	-	4
Koxinga	-	-	2

ECONOMY, MADE IN	US 271	PRC 9	TW 149
made, made in	82	-	-
cheap	52	-	-
manufacture, -ing	26	-	-
manufacturer,s	12	-	-
export,s, imports	24	-	-
factory,s	16	-	-
cheap labor	12	-	-
production	8	-	-
products	7	-	-
goods	7	-	-
competition	6	-	-
trade	5	-	14
business	5	-	6
money	5	-	-
labor	2	-	4
label	2	-	-
economy	-	8	32
economic progress	-	-	47
economically strong	-	-	4
bustling	-	-	14
foreign exchange reserve	-	-	13
developing country	-	-	10
third world	-	-	5
job	-	1	-

TREASURE,RICH,BEAUTIFUL	US 9	PRC 203	TW 185
rich	5	-	48
independent	4	-	12
treasure island	-	64	-
beautiful	-	29	35
peace	-	24	4
wealthy	-	24	-
rich and popular	-	20	-
friendly	-	9	-
good place	-	9	-
Taiwan treasure island	-	9	-
inviolable	-	5	-
villa	-	4	-
wealthy and strong	-	3	-
resolve	-	3	-
free	-	-	18
peaceful and happy	-	-	13
beautiful scenery	-	-	11
miracle	-	-	11
safety	-	-	6
newly rich	-	-	6
equality	-	-	6
free China	-	-	5
happiness	-	-	5
hope	-	-	5

INDUSTRY, ADVANCED	US 43	PRC 8	TW 47
industry	28	-	-
car,s	9	-	-
plane	4	-	-
build	2	-	-
developed	-	8	-
rapid development	-	-	13
Japanization	-	-	9
transportation	-	-	9
industrialization	-	-	8
diligent	-	-	4
reeducation	-	-	4

POLLUTED, CHAOTIC	US 38	PRC 3	TW 186
crowded	9	-	14
disease	8	-	-
poor	7	-	-
mean	5	-	-
tough	5	-	-
war	4	1	2
interference	-	2	-
polluted	-	-	27
polluted air	-	-	12
disorderly traffic	-	-	27
chaotic	-	-	20
too crowded	-	-	12
too much	-	-	12
dirty	-	-	9
lousy	-	-	8
no public morality	-	-	7
dirty water	-	-	6
too many road side vendors	-	-	6
crisis	-	-	5
inconvenient transportation	-	-	4
too many cars	-	-	4
self-deception & deception	-	-	4
illegal gambling	-	-	4
struggle	-	-	3

FOOD, PRODUCTS	US 105	PRC 0	TW 0
clothes	24	-	-
food	15	-	-
plastic	14	-	-
produce	9	-	-
fish	9	-	-
stereo	9	-	-
toys	8	-	-
items	6	-	-
tv	4	-	-
straw	4	-	-
rice	3	-	-

CITIES	US 11	PRC 87	TW 21
Taipei	11	36	9
Taiwan straits	-	47	8
Tainan (city in NE Taiwan)	-	4	-
Taichung	-	-	4
Sun Yat-Sen	-	-	-

CULTURE, SPORTS	US 77	PRC 35	TW 10
culture	17	-	-
soccer	14	-	-
baseball	11	-	-
boat,s	10	-	-
different	7	-	-
language	7	-	-
bicycles	6	-	-
speak	5	-	-
uniform of country	-	28	-
blue	-	4	-
custom	-	3	-
Taiwanese language	-	-	10

SUMMARY

Main Components	Percentage of Total Score		
	US	PRC	TW
COUNTRIES	34	14	17
UNIFY, PART OF CHINA	0	28	2
GOVERNMENT, COMMUNISM	3	7	6
ISLAND,SMALL	11	14	20
PEOPLE	7	16	4
ECONOMY, MADE IN	22	1	13
TREASURE,RICH, BEAUTIFUL	1	12	16
POLLUTED, CHAOTIC	3	0	16
INDUSTRY, ADVANCED	3	0	4
FOOD, PRODUCTS	8	0	0
CITIES	1	5	2
CULTURE, SPORTS	6	2	1
Total Scores	1238	1682	1161

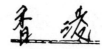

HONG KONG
MAIN COMPONENTS AND RESPONSES

BRITAIN, BRITISH	US	PRC	TW
	77	124	107
British	38	-	-
Britain, Great Britain	16	60	-
England English	16	6	28
British colony, colony	7	6	79
joint stmt of Brit & China	-	14	-
treaty betw China & Brit	-	13	-
special zone	-	12	-
talks betw China & Britain	-	6	-
treaty	-	5	-
negotiation	-	2	-

CROWDED,CHAOTIC,CRIME	US	PRC	TW
	137	147	130
crowded	42	8	25
junk,s	20	-	-
busy	11	-	5
phooey	11	-	-
dirty	9	-	7
cars	8	-	-
mysterious	6	-	-
bustle	6	-	-
opium, drugs	10	-	-
poor	6	-	-
lights	5	-	-
bustling	3	11	10
disorder, riot	-	45	-
disgrace	-	15	-
crime	-	14	-
opium war	-	11	2
much dark side	-	8	-
unemployment	-	6	-
dark	-	6	-
morals	-	6	-
automobile	-	6	-
bar	-	6	-
prostitute	-	3	-
gangster	-	2	-
populous	-	-	27
chaotic	-	-	20
guilty	-	-	8
refugees	-	-	7
violence	-	-	6
night scene,s	-	-	6
gang ring	-	-	5
full of cars and people	-	-	2

PROSPEROUS, INDUSTRY	US	PRC	TW
	205	479	214
prosperous, city	-	272	71
made in, made	41	-	-
money, capital	24	21	-
factory,s	21	-	-
cheap labor	13	-	-
industry	11	10	4
trade	11	-	31
products	10	-	-
toys	9	-	-
plastic	9	-	-
manufacture	8	-	-
business	8	-	-
labor	7	-	-
import, export	10	-	-
rich	6	-	9
electronics	6	-	-
market	5	-	-
commercial,city, aura	3	-	20
tourism	3	-	-
developed	-	28	2
capitalism	-	27	3
capitalist, society, syst	em	20	-
wealthy	-	13	-
economy,developed economy	-	15	-
complex	-	9	12
rich & populous	-	8	-
development	-	8	-
worker	-	7	-
science	-	7	-
modernization	-	6	2
property	-	6	-
high salary	-	6	-
high building, mansion	-	5	-
efforts	-	5	-
work	-	3	-
advanced science	-	3	-
transfer post	-	-	21
economic development	-	-	11
money worship	-	-	7
tax-free	-	-	6
imperialism	-	-	5
precious stones	-	-	4
business field	-	-	4
commerce	-	-	2

CHINA, ORIENT	US	PRC	TW
	390	319	72
China, Chinese	233	70	10
Japan, Japanese	54	-	-
Oriental,s, Orient	54	-	-
Asia, Asian	20	-	-
eastern, east	15	-	-
Peking	9	-	-
Taiwan	5	23	1
territory of China	-	89	-
part of China	-	44	-
belonging to China	-	26	21
motherland	-	22	-
territory of motherland	-	15	-
compatriots	-	14	-
uniform of motherland	-	7	-
Macao	-	6	4
mainland	-	3	-
communist China	-	-	29
near mainland China	-	-	4
Chinese university	-	-	3

RETURNS TO CHINA	US	PRC	TW
	0	233	116
expired in 1997	-	80	107
regain	-	48	-
return	-	26	-
regain sovereignty	-	22	-
territory	-	17	-
sovereign rights	-	16	-
return to motherland	-	12	-
H K returns to China	-	7	-
nat'l sovereign rights	-	5	-
new territory	-	-	9

GOVERNMENT, SYSTEM	US	PRC	TW
	9	35	16
government	5	-	-
communist	4	-	-
system	-	13	-
democracy	-	10	-
one country, two systems	-	6	2
freedom	-	3	7
status	-	3	-
open	-	-	7

COUNTRY,PEOPLE,CULTURE	US	PRC	TW
	279	146	186
city	66	31	-
food, Chinese food	32	-	2
island	22	-	-
rice	22	-	-
people	20	19	2
Hong Kong people	-	6	-
country	19	-	-
culture	17	-	-
different	11	-	-
big, large	18	-	-
Buddha	8	-	-
language	8	-	-
dragon	7	-	-
ancient	7	-	-
metropolis	6	-	-
chopsticks	4	-	-
old	4	-	-
bikes	3	-	-
schools	3	-	-
society	2	5	-
utilitarianism	-	-	14
Hong Kong	-	12	-
living	-	12	-
Kowloon	-	11	14
red lanterns & green wine	-	9	-
relationship,betw people	-	9	-
skyscraper,tall buildings	-	7	8
nation	-	7	-
person	-	7	-
Qing dynasty	-	6	2
university	-	5	-
Kwantong dialect	-	-	38
Kwantong inhabitants	-	-	26
small area, island	-	-	48
hometown	-	-	10
eating	-	-	10
underground	-	-	7
realities	-	-	5

MOVIE STARS, TV	US	PRC	TW
	28	6	81
King Kong	20	-	-
Godzilla	3	-	-
movies	5	-	16
singing star	-	6	-
movie stars	-	-	34
Hong Kong TV programs	-	-	22
Hong Kong films	-	-	9

SHOPPING, GAMBLING	US	PRC	TW
	78	3	45
cheap	45	-	-
clothing, clothes	20	-	-
goods	8	-	-
souvenirs	5	-	-
material life	-	3	-
inexpensive commodities	-	-	20
purchase	-	-	16
materialism	-	-	6
gamble	-	-	3

BEAUTIFUL, COLORFUL	US	PRC	TW
	42	77	61
exotic	12	-	-
beautiful	8	27	3
friend, friendly	8	6	-
popular	7	-	-
fun	5	-	-
interesting	2	-	-
colorful,world	-	35	3
pearl of orient	-	9	55

PORT, HARBOR	US	PRC	TW
	41	3	69
port	21	-	25
fish	8	-	-
boats	7	-	-
harbor	5	-	-
sea	-	3	-
ships	-	-	20
entry to Kwantong	-	-	10
free port	-	-	7
oceanworld	-	-	4
open sea	-	-	3

OVERSEAS, FOREIGN	US	PRC	TW
	97	7	41
foreign	33	-	-
overseas	13	-	-
far, distant,far away	25	-	-
travel	11	-	-
vacation	10	-	-
south	5	-	-
foreigner	-	7	-
overseas chinese students	-	-	21
visit relatives	-	-	20

MISCELLANEOUS	US	PRC	TW
	0	27	30
unity	-	18	-
support	-	7	-
ally	-	2	-
airplane	-	-	14
athlete's foot	-	-	11
bridge of two sides	-	-	5

PERCEPTIONS AND EVALUATIONS

Main Components	Percentage of Total Score		
	US	PRC	TW
BRITAIN, BRITISH	6	8	9
CHINA, ORIENT	28	20	6
CROWDED,CHAOTIC,CRIME	10	9	11
PROSPEROUS,INDUSTRY	15	30	18
RETURNS TO CHINA	0	15	10
PORT, HARBOR	3	0	6
GOVERNMENT,SYSTEM	1	2	1
COUNTRY,PEOPLE,CULTURE	20	9	16
MOVIE STARS, TV	2	0	7
SHOPPING,GAMBLING	6	0	4
BEAUTIFUL,COLORFUL	3	5	5
OVERSEAS,FOREIGN	7	0	4
MISCELLANEOUS	0	2	3
Total Scores	1383	1606	1168

OVERSEAS CHINESE
MAIN COMPONENTS AND RESPONSES

CHINA, CHINESE	US	PRC	TW
	172	388	124
China	31	46	10
Chinese	-	165	58
Taiwan	16	4	-
Peking	7	-	-
Hong Kong	6	26	13
Macao	-	8	-
people	25	7	-
Asian,Asia	25	-	-
Great Wall,wall	25	-	-
country	15	-	-
Orient	12	-	-
hometown, home	10	16	2
motherland	-	49	5
Chin live in foreign place	-	21	-
China street	-	20	21
native	-	8	-
Chinese heart	-	7	-
Fujian province	-	6	-
Guanzhou	-	5	-
Kwantang	-	-	8
China town	-	-	5
fatherland	-	-	2

EMIGRATE, OVERSEAS, FAR	US	PRC	TW
	146	199	117
far, far away	47	-	-
boat,s	30	-	-
immigration,immigrants	15	-	14
ship	11	-	-
ocean	11	-	-
travel	9	-	-
Pacific	7	-	-
water	7	-	-
distant	5	-	-
Far East	4	-	-
foreign country	-	90	-
countrymen reside abroad	-	21	-
abroad	-	21	68
live in foreign country	-	16	-
live abroad	-	13	-
overseas Chinese	-	12	-
out-of-town	-	8	21
worthy son live abroad	-	7	-
overseas	-	6	-
be forced to leave native	-	5	-
forget one's origin	-	-	6
remote	-	-	4
committee of overseas chinese	-	-	4

FATHER OF REVOLUTION	US	PRC	TW
	0	0	85
father of revolution	-	-	72
founding father	-	-	7
revolution	-	-	6

RICH, MONEY, BUSINESS	US	PRC	TW
	62	105	132
trade	10	-	-
industry	9	-	-
money	7	-	6
technology	7	-	-
import	7	-	-
power	6	8	-
advanced	6	-	-
rich	5	56	28
respect	5	-	-
status	-	9	-
investment	-	6	12
powerful	-	6	-
construction	-	6	-
job	-	5	-
development	-	5	-
undertakings	-	4	-
wealthy people	-	-	62
restaurant	-	-	10
power of attraction	-	-	6
make money	-	-	4
economize	-	-	4

OVERSEAS RESIDENCE	US	PRC	TW
	0	46	53
reside in	-	16	-
western countries	-	8	-
nationality	-	6	4
Singapore	-	6	2
overseas Chin in America	-	5	-
New York	-	5	-
South Asia	-	-	12
American born Chinese	-	-	11
every nation in world	-	-	10
Southeast Asia	-	-	6
Taiwan young students study	-	-	4
Indonesia	-	-	2
Vietnam	-	-	2

PATRIOTS	US	PRC	TW
	0	222	68
be patriot	-	75	-
some are patriots	-	49	-
compatriots	-	21	-
patriot,s	-	17	47
love homeland	-	10	-
love country	-	10	-
compatriots of country	-	9	-
support	-	9	-
unite,(integrate)	-	11	-
for the country	-	6	-
get together	-	5	-
fellowmen	-	-	11
unified	-	-	10

DIFFERENT, FOREIGNER	US	PRC	TW
	72	41	67
foreign	39	-	-
foreigner,s	8	14	14
different	25	-	5
foreign merchants	-	11	-
having foreign nationality	-	7	-
be underestimated	-	9	-
inaccurate pronunciation	-	-	23
English	-	-	8
unable to speak Mandarin	-	-	7
be discriminated	-	-	4
discrimination	-	-	2
green card	-	-	4

LANGUAGE,CULTURE	US	PRC	TW
	249	96	22
rice	52	-	-
food	48	-	-
fish	23	-	-
language	22	8	2
culture	22	-	-
family	13	-	-
friend,s	12	-	4
chopsticks	10	-	-
history	7	4	-
ancient	7	-	-
karate	7	-	-
kung fu	7	-	-
hats	7	-	-
junks	6	-	-
mysterious	4	-	-
Buddha	2	-	-
life	-	20	-
descendants	-	16	-
later gen of emperor	-	15	-
ancestors	-	13	4
dear person	-	11	-
descendants of imperial	-	6	-
flesh and blood	-	3	-
Chinese (language)	-	-	5
offspring of Huang Ti	-	-	4
sell piglet	-	-	3

INDUSTRIOUS,SMART	US	PRC	TW
	60	68	84
smart	20	-	-
industrious	10	-	20
intelligent	10	-	-
productive	8	-	-
intelligence	4	-	-
discipline	4	-	-
happy	4	7	-
contribution	-	16	2
good person	-	12	-
clever	-	12	-
work hard to honor country	-	11	-
help each other	-	6	-
work very hard	-	4	-
toil	-	-	23
struggle	-	-	17
extra pts in coll ent exam	-	-	8
persevering	-	-	6
have achievements	-	-	5
helper	-	-	3

POOR,CROWDED	US	PRC	TW
	114	6	0
crowded	22	-	-
poor	20	-	-
many	13	-	-
population	10	6	-
billion	10	-	-
big,large	15	-	-
over population,-tion	14	-	-
little	7	-	-
birth control	3	-	-

SHORT,EYES	US	PRC	TW
	81	0	7
short	18	-	7
eyes	14	-	-
small	13	-	-
oriental	11	-	-
smell	7	-	-
black hair	6	-	-
black	5	-	-
skinny	4	-	-
hair	3	-	-
stupid looking	-	-	7

MISS CHINA, RETURN	US	PRC	TW
	11	126	20
visit	11	-	-
missing hometown	-	28	-
return to country	-	18	-
falling leaves settle on root	-	16	-
welcome	-	15	-
yearn for	-	11	-
return to homeland	-	11	-
missing homeland	-	8	-
intend to return to country	-	8	-
think of	-	7	-
tour	-	4	-
enthuslastic in public welcome	-	-	6
sightseeing	-	-	6
back to mainland for visit	-	-	4
prone to fatherland	-	-	2
go back to die in hometown	-	-	2

COMMUNISM	US	PRC	TW
	84	0	0
communist,s	53	-	-
communism	14	-	-
red	17	-	-

MISCELLANEOUS	US	PRC	TW
	31	14	30
Nixon	14	-	-
please	10	-	-
navy	7	-	-
dressing	-	6	-
donation	-	5	-
force	-	3	-
savior	-	-	10
countryside	-	-	5
contradictory	-	-	5
fool around	-	-	4
selfish	-	-	4
bumming	-	-	2

SUMMARY

Main Components	Percentage of Total Score		
	US	PRC	TW
CHINA, CHINESE	16	30	15
EMIGRATE, OVERSEAS, FAR	13	15	14
FATHER OF REVOLUTION	0	0	11
RICH, MONEY, BUSINESS	6	8	16
OVERSEAS RESIDENCE	0	4	7
PATRIOTS	0	17	8
DIFFERENT, FOREIGNER	7	3	8
LANGUAGE,CULTURE	23	7	3
INDUSTRIOUS,SMART	6	5	10
POOR,CROWDED	11	0	0
SHORT,EYES	7	0	1
MISS CHINA, RETURN	1	10	2
COMMUNISM	8	0	0
MISCELLANEOUS	3	1	4
Total Scores	1082	1311	809

101

SUMMARY OF TRENDS IN THE DOMAIN OF NATIONAL IMAGES

The American Image -- From American and Chinese Perspectives

The following trends of perceptions and attitudes emerged from American responses to United States, to Americans, and to country. They are reviewed in contrast to the Chinese images of Americans and the United States.

Americans think foremost of their country, of their homeland, the fifty states, regions and geography. In comparison, the PRC interest is very much focused on the large cities -- Washington, D.C., New York and Los Angeles while the Taiwanese students are more captivated by the large territory of the United States.

The single most outstanding feature of the United States in the eyes of the Americans is its freedom, its liberty. This is also a prominent feature in the eyes of the Taiwanese students as well. It is relatively little recognized by the mainland Chinese. The Taiwanese emphasize freedom of opportunities, especially for study. They see the United States as a wonderful land for study. Another particularly salient feature is democracy, which is closely tied in with government and political organization. The Taiwanese recognize this dimension quite intensively as well. The Mainlanders speak little of democracy but do mention American leaders and presidents and refer to politics as well. Americans characterize the United States as their home and homeland and describe the U.S. and Americans in very positive terms such as great, best, good, beautiful and make many references to national symbols such as flag and the national colors. These are obviously signs of national identification expressing patriotism and pride.

Americans show considerable awareness of the strength, power, and the superpower status of the U.S. They are also aware of its large size and vast territory. They show a moderate level of historical identification speaking mostly of the Revolution of 1776 and the colonies. Compared with the image of the country, the image of the American people is only a little different. Thinking of Americans brings in more emphasis on people, including themselves, and a great variety of ethnic, racial identifications. Indians are the most frequently mentioned, but they also think of blacks, whites, and pluralism. Freedom and independence are still among the most salient characteristics recognized. The racially diverse composition of Americans also receives much attention from the PRC group except that their focus is different. They think of whites and blacks and American Chinese. Another large cluster of reactions shows that they are particularly sensitive and aware of the physical appearance and distinguishing characteristics of Americans. They pay a great deal of attention to the size of Americans -- big and tall; they speak of blonde, golden hair, blue eyes and big noses. This awareness of racial differences represents the most predominant single feature of the American image for the PRC group and for the Taiwanese as well. These Chinese groups, and also the Hong Kong Chinese in our earlier study, seem to have a strong sensitivity to racial differences and differences in appearance. America is a "melting pot", but Mainland Chinese cherish the "purity" of blood.

Both the PRC and the Taiwanese groups focus on the personality characteristics of Americans. The PRC group sees Americans particularly as clever, hard working, forthright, romantic, optimistic and generally good and open. The Taiwanese admire the openness of Americans and their social qualities, such as friendliness, enthusiasm, generosity, candidness, humor, liveliness and activism.

Compared to these positive characterizations, there are few negative characterizations of Americans from the PRC group, but similarly intensive negative characterizations from the Taiwanese group. Experts observe that the Mainland Chinese youth admire Americans whole-heatedly the way the Taiwanese did two or three decades ago. Now that the Taiwanese have known Americans more. They can view Americans in a more objective, critical way. Foremostly, they describe Americans as haughty, naive, selfish and self-centered, guilty of racial discrimination, overly proud, self important, etc. The Americans view themselves mainly in positive terms as proud, good, best, friendly, great, loyal, and loving, with only a few minor critical references to ignorance, stupidity, and being materialistic.

Compared to the Americans, both Chinese groups give much more attention to the interpersonal, social characteristics of Americans and the United States. The Taiwanese think more of selfishness, social disorder, crime, and unemployment in connection with the United States and with Americans as well. The Mainland Chinese are particularly impressed by the highly developed nature of the United States. They think of development in general as well as scientific development, economic production, technology, and industry. The Mainland Chinese tend to identify the United States and Americans closely with capitalism, the capitalist system, capitalist economy. Nonetheless, there are relatively few negative references which would suggest that this identification has a critical undertone. Rather, they speak of wealth, rich people, rich resources, economic welfare, and many cars and tall buildings. Their references to capitalism show no indication of a critical evaluation of capitalism along the logic of classical Marxism.

In general, the Americans and the Chinese show considerable agreement as well as some substantive differences in their image of Americans and the United States. Compared to Americans who express a great deal of personal identification and positive feelings, the Chinese are predominantly positive in their attitudes as well but in somewhat different ways. The Taiwanese show the most positive attitudes, most appreciation, but they are the most critical, pointing out the variety of problems and weaknesses which they perceive as characteristic of the American environment and people. The Mainlanders are essentially positive but not to the extent of the Taiwanese. On the other hand, they show very little critical observations and attitudes.

Probably most important is the fact that these three groups are predisposed to look at quite different characteristics of Americans and the United States. The Americans think predominantly of the country, the land, the freedom of opportunities, and the democratic system, and they express a great deal of identification and affection. All three groups recognize the United States as being a superpower, as being strong and powerful. The Chinese in general think more about the social and human dimension of the United States and Americans. The Taiwanese are particularly impressed by the freedom, openness and friendly social characteristics of Americans and the country in general. The PRC are particularly cognizant of the smartness and intellectual qualities of Americans and their success in a variety of fields. They focus attention on the advanced American technology, the high level of American progress and industrial development, and on American affluence and economic success which they consider exemplary. The PRC group pays less attention to democracy and politics in American terms, including the American government. They have since childhood been indoctrinated to believe that the Chinese-style socialism (not communism) is the best political system on earth. Nonetheless, they do think intensively of capitalism because of Teng Hsiao-ping's advocacy of free market in certain coastal areas.

Whether used in more political or economic terms does not become clear from the data presented here. The Taiwanese criticism and skepticism regarding American problems show no sign of hostility, but rather awareness of the same type of problems that they have to cope with in their own environment.

Chinese Images -- From American Perspectives

The Americans' image of Chinese reveals a set of perspectives which reflect American experiences and priorities. One major perspective involves the language and culture of China, which appeals greatly to the American imagination. Also, China, the country, its size, its overcrowding and over-population, and its Oriental surroundings receive a great deal of attention and interest. This interest and curiosity is probably stimulated by the different appearance of the people; their Oriental features, black hair, slanted eyes, yellow skin color receive attention. The Americans think highly of the intelligence of Chinese and recognize their success with computers, their skills in math, and their generally industrious approach to life. Finally, the source of most attention from Americans is the Chinese contribution of great popularity -- namely, Chinese food. This trend reflects a fundamental feature of subjective images -- how our priorities and pragmatic interests are potent forces which reorder the world along our subjective, self-centered interests and perspectives.

It is interesting to see how this general image of Chinese varies depending on which particular population of Chinese we have in mind. We are considering here Mainlanders, Taiwanese, and Hong Kong Chinese.

The Americans' image of the PRC reflects a fundamental recognition that the PRC has essentially a Chinese, Oriental population, is a large country situated in Asia, and is related to Taiwan and Hong Kong. Also in connection with PRC, the perception of many people, crowded conditions, overpopulation and related miseries receives considerable attention. Americans view the PRC to a certain degree as backward and poor, in contrast to the PRC's image of themselves as affluent and prosperous. From the cultural viewpoint, elements which capture the Americans' imaginations are the Great Wall, bamboo and again Chinese food. An entirely new and very prominent feature which emerges in the context of the PRC involves its Communist political structure and background. Communism, the Communist government, the symbols of red and the insignia are dominant in the American mind and capture about one quarter of all the attention received by the PRC. There are also references to the Communist leadership.

The Americans' view of Taiwan is similar to their image of the PRC. The main focus is on the Chinese population, the Oriental background, the national identity. Also, people get a great deal of attention and there are no references to over-population. The role of the culture is emphasized but with more emphasis on some differences from the mainland Chinese, speaking of the Taiwanese dialect, customs, they speak of soccer, baseball, the food, and other products. But there is a great deal of emphasis of industrial products, stereos, toys and the inexpensive nature of these products. That is a part of this interest comes up more explicitly with references to manufacturing, industry and economy - references which emphasize the characteristic contribution of the Taiwanese economy, its high level of productivity, its manufacturing success, cheap labor, and the multiplicity of goods produced and marketed successfully. Americans have an awareness of the small island nature of this country, the shape of the island, the relative smallness of the island and its local scenery. Compared to the Mainland, the small size of the country receives recognition as well as its achievement in the field of industrial production.

In the Americans' image of Hong Kong the most central issue is its close connection with China. It is characterized as China, as Chinese but it is also recognized for the time being as a British colony, a part of England. Hong Kong's relationship to Japan and the Orient also receives considerable attention. Among its most intrinsic features, Americans think of Hong Kong as a highly crowded, bustling, active city. Its role in industrial production and commerce captures a great deal of American attention, especially the cheap labor and products, and capital available. It is characterized also as a city, an island, as well as a country. The opportunities for shopping and buying inexpensive products are mentioned. It is also characterized as exciting, friendly, colorful and beautiful.

The Americans' image of the overseas Chinese is similar to their image of Hong Kong Chinese. Immigration and living abroad, travelling by boat and ship are some of the distinct features. Overseas Chinese are described in somewhat contrasting ways both as rich and affluent with reference to trade, as well as being poor, crowded, and facing problems of overpopulation. With regard to cultural heritage, the standard items of language, culture, and food items, such as fish and rice, are mentioned. Americans describe overseas Chinese as being industrious, smart, intelligent, productive, advanced. Their intellectual performance and motivation also receive recognition. There are some references which identify them with Communism, characterized as red and communist in orientation. Finally, the ideas of returning to China and visiting China receive some attention.

In general, the Americans' images of the different Chinese populations contain a common core which reflects recognition of the Chinese culture, such as the language and certain observable features. Also, the ethnic identity of the Chinese and their origin receive considerable attention. There are consistent references to the overcrowded living conditions and overpopulation, large masses of people associated with China. There are also distinguishing characteristics, such as communism in connection with the Mainland Chinese. With regard to both Hong Kong and Taiwan, industrial performance and success are mentioned; they are characterized as rich and prosperous states and populations. The talent, intelligence, and work motivation of the Chinese are generally appreciated, more in connection with the free market places like Hong Kong and Taiwan and less in connection with the Chinese Mainland.

The Chinese Images -- From Chinese Perspectives

The Mainland Chinese stress a number of outstanding qualities of the Chinese, involving industrious hard work, smartness, cleverness, wisdom, intelligence, ambition, problem solving capabilities, and creative thinking. This focus suggests strong pride and self-awareness. Interestingly, the PRC group also shows a high degree of awareness of racial, physical characteristics, such as yellow skin, yellow race, black hair, black eyes and slanted eyes. They describe the Chinese as pretty, lovely and beautiful. They think of China as the motherland and their home. They show a strong awareness of Chinese history, descendants of the imperial past, and people as later generations of the emperors. References to Communism are few and do not show any particular sign of identification. References to the Chinese past, Chinese culture, Chinese civilization and the symbols of the Great Wall do reflect a high degree of identification. In terms of human qualities the PRC

Chinese describe Chinese in general as great, brave, full of integrity, proud people with love of their country, loyalty and glory. They characterize the attitudes of the Chinese as conservative, kind-hearted, friendly, nice, fair-minded, honest, self-confident, amiable, peaceful and happy. The PRC Chinese heavily emphasize human social characteristics, motivation and character. In their characterization of Chinese more than two thirds of their attention given over to human qualities.

In the Mainlanders' image of the PRC the single most dominant feature used in their own characterization involves glory, national identification, pride, ardent love, very strong identification with the Chinese nation. Again, the focus is on human attributes and strong connection with the past and population. There are also heavy references to the motherland, country and China. They identify PRC as a civilized nation with a long historical past. There are references to holidays, October 1st, National Day, the 31st National Day, and others which tie in more with the modern history of China under Communism. There are some references to Communism and the Communist Party, but they identify more with socialism and consider themselves a socialist country. With regard to the economic situation of the country, the PRC response is positive and optimistic. They describe the PRC as powerful and prosperous, strong and wealthy, rich, affluent, stable, unified, sovereign. There are only a very few reactions which deal with poverty or backwardness.

The PRC's image of Taiwan deals primarily with unification and characterization of Taiwan as a part of China. Taiwan is also described as a national territory which belongs to Mainland China. There are many references calling for its unification with the Mainland. The PRC Chinese relate Taiwan to the nation, to motherland, to China in general. The same trend is seen in reference to Hong Kong. There is strong association of Taiwan with the Cuomingtang government, along with a few minor references to the capitalist system. Taiwan is characterized as an island, rich in mountains, the Sun Moon Lake, the ocean, describing its scenery. In describing Taiwan, there are many references to the population, the different rulers and dynasties associated with the history of Taiwan. The Taiwanese are described as compatriots, dear persons, children of the imperial past. The island is characterized as a Treasure Island of China, rich and popular, wealthy and strong and peaceful. There are many references to cities, particularly to Taipei and also to the Taiwan straits.

The PRC's image of Hong Kong also deals with the return of Hong Kong to the Mainland. The PRC Chinese emphasize the expiration of the British mandate in 1997, and refer to sovereignty and Hong Kong's return to China. It is considered related to China, a territory of China and being essentially Chinese and belonging to the motherland. The PRC Chinese characterize Hong Kong as a very rich, very prosperous country, highly developed. It has a capitalist system, a great deal of money and wealth, a prosperous economy characterized by a capitalistic society. They characterize Hong Kong as plagued by disorder, crime, too much traffic, the dark sides of life, prostitution and riots as well as moral problems and unemployment. It is defined as a British territory and colony. The PRC views Hong Kong as a beautiful and colorful city, a city with friends, freedom and democracy. These characterizations by the PRC show a strong national pride and determination to unite these territories.

Chapter 4

RELIGION

Most educated Chinese would likely admit to being at least influenced by Confucianism, but many would deny that this has anything to do with religion. A popular saying has it that "Every Chinese is a Confucian in good times, and a Taoist in times of disaster." In prosperous and secure times one sees the practical, skeptical, and socially correct side of Chinese behavior. In times of stress and danger the Chinese are inclined to show their mystical and spiritual side.

Westerners have many associations with the concept of "religion" which are alien to most Chinese. For example, we could expect a person to be a Muslim, Catholic, or Methodist, but not all three at the same time. Also, when we say that a person is very religious, this is often meant to convey certain positive notions regarding personal ethics, conscientiousness, and strength of character.

Although there is no general agreement on this issue, for many Chinese Confucianism is an ethical and philosophical system and a code of manners and behavior, as well as a system of mutual obligations, especially in regard to family relationships. For many Chinese Confucianism has no relationship to faith or worship.[1] However this does not necessarily imply agnosticism or atheism.

The following comparisons of American, Taiwanese, and PRC students' understanding of religion, Christianity, Buddhism, faith, morals, conscience, guilt, and shame provide some insights and at least partial answers to several questions. Some of the fundamental questions the comparison may bear on relate to how different historical roots may produce the different logic and cosmologies. The Chinese are not heirs of Mesopotamian, Egyptian, Judeo-Christian, Greco-Roman, or Germanic concepts which have shaped our Western subjective world. It appears that they have a different understanding of the concept of religion than do Westerners or many other Asians (eg. Arabs, Iranians, Hindus).

Comparing the subjective meaning of religion for Americans, PRC Chinese and Taiwanese raises many intriguing questions. What aspects of life are considered to be within the domain of religion by the three groups studied? How has communism had a measurable effect on PRC students? Has the rapid rise in wealth on Taiwan affected faith and morals? What are the effects of Buddhism and Christianity on the Taiwanese? Which aspects of these religions impress the Mainland Chinese? How have modern Western influences modified Chinese views of religion? What impact does individualism and materialism have on the religious beliefs and practices of the three societies?

---

[1]"The Analects of the sage [Confucius] have... been annotated, taught, and reinterpreted throughout the last twenty centuries. But,...for the scholars who thus engaged themselves, Confucius was not a god and Confucianism was not a religion." - Hsu, p. 264.

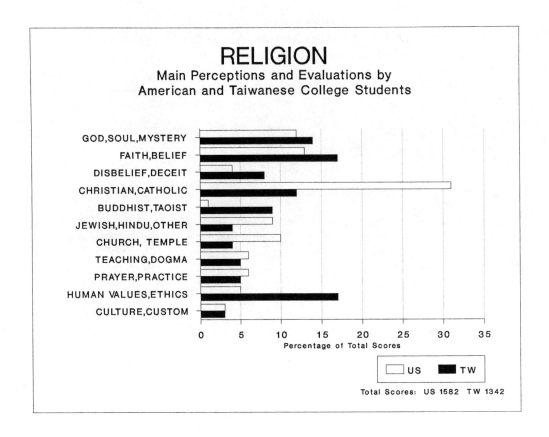

RELIGION
Main Perceptions and Evaluations by American and Taiwanese College Students

GOD,SOUL,MYSTERY
FAITH,BELIEF
DISBELIEF,DECEIT
CHRISTIAN,CATHOLIC
BUDDHIST,TAOIST
JEWISH,HINDU,OTHER
CHURCH, TEMPLE
TEACHING,DOGMA
PRAYER,PRACTICE
HUMAN VALUES,ETHICS
CULTURE,CUSTOM

0   5   10   15   20   25   30   35
Percentage of Total Scores

US   ■ TW

Total Scores: US 1582   TW 1342

American View: God, Church, Christian. American views regarding religion reflect broad pluralism and the principle of free choice. Larger and more influential denominations receive greater attention. There is a strong focus on tangibles such as the Bible, Church, denominations such as the Catholic, Protestant, Baptist, activities such as Worship and Prayer. Teaching, preaching, and doctrine are of somewhat lesser importance. Unlike Chinese, Americans tend to identify with a specific denomination [e.g. "I am a Methodist"]. God, church and the Bible receive significantly more emphasis from Americans than from either of the Chinese groups. American place relatively little emphasis on human values and ethics in the context of religion.

Taiwanese View: Faith, Buddhism, Ethics. The Taiwanese emphasize the mystery of God and the soul. Human values and ethics are a far more important part of religion to them than to the other respondents. Thinking of religion primarily in terms of faith in Buddhism and Christianity, they focus on religion's role as a force for social amelioration and for instilling proper ethical values. They attribute to religion the responsibility for encouraging people to be kind and sincere toward others. A religious person is expected to exhibit benevolent behavior and attitudes such as kindness, peace-making, sincerity, strength, and love. Religion is seen as a source of spiritual sustenance and consolation. In practicing religion, they emphasize worship.   Religion is an everyday must to the Taiwanese. They worship not only the tablet representation of their ancestors but also such natural objects as earth, trees, etc. To them religion is also more a ritual.

American and Taiwanese Contrasts: Denominations and Sunday School versus Faith and Ethics. Faith is the focus of the Taiwanese, while individual Christian denominations are the focus of Americans. God receives greater emphasis in the U.S., while human values and ethics are stressed on Taiwan. Buddhism, Taoism, and Islam receive greater attention in Taiwan while Judaism receives more attention in the U.S. The Taiwanese view religion mostly in terms of faith, ethics and worship: to the taiwanese the purpose of religion worship is to be a righteous person. While these things also receive prominence among the Americans, they are exceeded by emphasis on denominations, God, and tangibles such as church, the Bible, and activities.

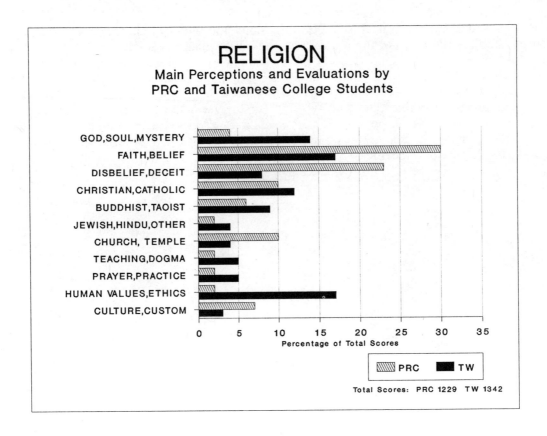

RELIGION
Main Perceptions and Evaluations by
PRC and Taiwanese College Students

Total Scores: PRC 1229 TW 1342

PRC Chinese View: Faith, Superstition. Far more than anything else, and far more than the other respondents, Mainland Chinese consider religion a matter of faith and belief. There is a great expression of disbelief and disapproval of religion as unscientific as well as a concern with the possible negative influences of religion through deceit of the ignorant. They see religion as false, unbelievable, no good, and harmful. After the Cultural Revolution Maoism aimed to replace the traditional Chinese religious beliefs. With more emphasis than that of the other two groups they view religion in terms of culture and tradition, and associate it with foreign ideas. Catholicism is uppermost in their minds. The Mainland China students view religion as a matter of faith and belief and a result of culture and tradition reflects the dozen or more years of classroom indoctrination when they declare religion to be false, and unbelievable, suggesting that modern "scientific" thinking will eventually dispel the darkness of religious deceit.

Taiwanese View: Faith, Buddhism, Ethics. The Taiwanese emphasize the mystery of God and the soul. Human values and ethics are a far more important part of religion to them than to the other respondents. Thinking of religion primarily in terms of faith in Buddhism and Christianity, they focus on religion's role as a force for social amelioration and for instilling proper ethical values. They attribute to religion the responsibility for encouraging people to be kind and sincere toward others. A religious person is expected to exhibit benevolent behavior and attitudes such as kindness, peace-making, sincerity, strength, and love. Religion is seen as a source of spiritual sustenance and consolation. In practicing religion, they emphasize worship. Religion is an everyday must to the Taiwanese. They worship not only the tablet representation of their ancestors but also such natural objects as earth, trees, etc. To them religion is also more a ritual.

110

PRC and Taiwanese Contrasts: Disbelief versus Spiritual Sustenance. The emphasis on faith as a dominant factor in religion is much stronger among Mainland Chinese than among the Taiwanese, as are references to Catholicism. The Mainlanders' negative attitudes toward religion presents a stark contrast to the Taiwanese approach of religion as a vehicle for transmitting human values and ethics. The Mainlanders see religion as an undesirable influence in modern China carried over from earlier times by weight of tradition and conservatism -- and possibly as a wedge of foreign influence and an instrument of deceit. The Taiwanese, by contrast, see religion -- whether Buddhist, Protestant, or Catholic -- as a major force of social amelioration and an internal motivating force in instilling benevolent behavior. Again, these contrasts reflect the respective influence of Communism on the Mainlanders and western influences on the Taiwanese.

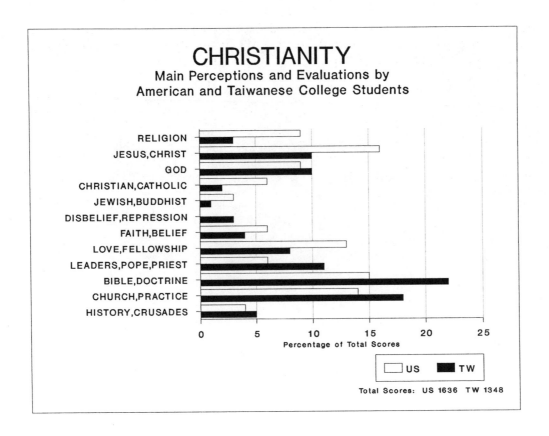

CHRISTIANITY
Main Perceptions and Evaluations by
American and Taiwanese College Students

American View: Jesus, Church, Love. Focus on Jesus Christ exceeds all other aspects of Christianity for Americans. Other significant components are the church, God and love. A very important component of Christianity has to do with the Bible and doctrine. Christ's redemptive sacrifice on the cross for the salvation of mankind and the forgiveness of sins receives attention. Heaven is mentioned, but hell is not. Christianity is expected to help people be good, improve their morals, and live in peace, especially in the family. Prayer is important, as is the role of the church. The fellowship aspect of Christianity is extremely important to Americans, who speak of love, peace, good, and people. Practices most significant to Americans include the celebration of Christmas, prayers, the experience of being born again, Sunday observance, and communion. The leadership aspect also receives some emphasis: pope, priest, preacher/pastor/minister.

Taiwanese View: Jesus, God, the Bible. Jesus, God, the Bible, and Christian doctrine are the focal points in the Taiwanese view of Christianity. The cross, Jerusalem, and Rome are the most important symbols. Living among polytheists, Taiwanese give some importance to the fact that Christianity is a monotheistic religion. The religious practice of Sunday church-going, prayers, hymns, and baptism are mentioned more by them than the other groups because the Taiwanese see them practiced in the "foreign" churches in Taiwan. Taiwanese emphasize religious leadership: missionaries, priests, fathers, nuns, and the pope. The Taiwanese link Christianity to foreigners, the West, and medieval Europe. They show greater awareness of Christian missionary work than do Americans. In regards to negative attitudes toward Christianity, Taiwanese are in an intermediate position between the very negative responses of the Mainland Chinese and the nearly non-existent negative responses of the Americans.

American and Taiwanese Contrasts: Christ and Love versus the Bible and Cross. There is basically strong overlap in the outward structure of Christianity as seen by Americans and Taiwanese. Church related practices are very important aspects of Christianity to the Taiwanese, while the church itself is more important for Americans, as is Jesus Christ. The Bible and cross are more important symbols of Christianity to the Taiwanese than to Americans. Sunday church-going means more to the Taiwanese, as do prayers, hymns and baptism. Beyond these tangible, observable elements, Americans find in Christianity a strong component of love and fellowship.

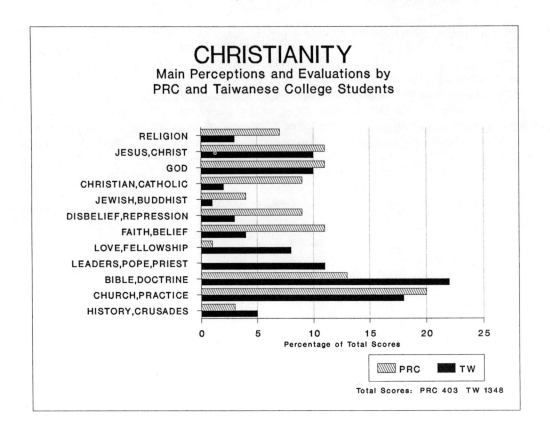

CHRISTIANITY
Main Perceptions and Evaluations by
PRC and Taiwanese College Students

PRC Chinese View: Church, Don't Believe it. Responses from the Mainland Chinese indicate little familiarity with Christianity and apparently very little interest. Their response rate on this topic was less than a third of that of the other groups and of their own in all other themes. Their knowledge seems to be limited to very few basic facts: Christianity is centered on the story of Jesus, as related in the Bible. They indicate that church, the Bible, Jesus, the Christian God, and cross are important, in that order. Less significant, but more important than for the other groups, are the negatives: don't believe it, meaningless, ridiculous. Because the Chinese have had many unpleasant experiences with the "barbarian" foreigners, they tend to link Christianity to imperialism.

Taiwanese View: Jesus, God, the Bible. Jesus, God, the Bible, and Christian doctrine are the focal points in the Taiwanese view of Christianity. The cross, Jerusalem, and Rome are the most important symbols. Living among polytheists, Taiwanese give some importance to the fact that Christianity is a monotheistic religion. The religious practice of Sunday church-going, prayers, hymns, and baptism are mentioned more by them than the other groups because the Taiwanese see them practiced in the "foreign" churches in Taiwan. Taiwanese emphasize religious leadership: missionaries, priests, fathers, nuns, and the pope. The Taiwanese link Christianity to foreigners, the West, and medieval Europe. They show greater awareness of Christian missionary work than do Americans. In regards to negative attitudes toward Christianity, Taiwanese are in an intermediate position between the very negative responses of the Mainland Chinese and the nearly non-existent negative responses of the Americans.

PRC and Taiwanese Contrasts: Meaningless versus Jesus. The Mainland Chinese consider Christianity principally as an institution based on the Bible and Jesus. They are inclined to see it as a meaningless religion imposed upon blind believers and symbolized by the cross. The Taiwanese stress the importance of Jesus, the Bible, and Sunday attendance. Both the Bible and the cross are significantly more important to them than to the Mainlanders. Among the Taiwanese important images, which are not among the PRC Chinese, are details about Christian doctrine and practice: missionary work, prayers, hymns, baptism, Holy Mother, great love, sins, God loves everyone, and pope. In general, the PRC response indicates a lack of interest in the subject.[2]

---

[2] "With the beginning of the Cultural Revolution, all places of worship in the country were closed or put to other uses and religious personnel were made to do labor reform and sometimes even tortured and killed. *** Like Islam and Catholicism, Protestantism is a recreationary feudal ideology...with foreign and contacts... We are atheists; we believe only in Mao Tse-tung." -Julia Ching. Probing China's Soul (1990), pp.128-129.

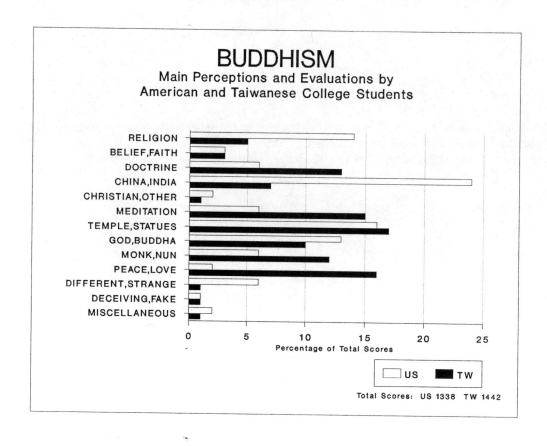

BUDDHISM
Main Perceptions and Evaluations by
American and Taiwanese College Students

Percentage of Total Scores

US   TW

Total Scores: US 1338   TW 1442

Taiwanese View: Temple, Monks, Sakyamuni. The Taiwanese show accurate and detailed familiarity with Buddhism. Temples, Buddhist monks, and the figure of Buddha are the most prominent images of Buddhism for the Taiwanese. They place the historic origins of Buddhism in India and acknowledge Sakyamuni (honorific of the founder of the historic origins of Buddhism). They know that Taiwanese Buddhists worship or pray to Kuan Yin (goddess of mercy, with attributes similar to those of the Catholic Madonna). They also indicate familiarity with more universal practices of Buddhism, such as burning joss sticks, vegetarianism and praying to Buddha. They are familiar with Buddhist scripture and the teachings regarding reincarnation and heaven. The Taiwanese have a very positive image of Buddhism -- in great contrast to the Mainlanders -- considering them to be good, peaceful people of dignity and love who can be counted on for help. Buddhism is considered mysterious.

American View: Fat, Bald, Idol. Americans strongly label Buddhism as a religion but show little familiarity with something so distant and foreign to them. They describe Buddhism as different and strange. They focus on the outer trappings. A very heavy proportion of American responses deal with geographic location, especially China, India, and Asia. Americans also think of the person of Buddha and describe the physical features of Buddha statues: fat, bald, stomach/belly. They give relatively little attention to meditation and prayer. In regard to doctrine, cows and reincarnation are mentioned. American interest in Buddhism is minimal and knowledge of it very superficial. There is confusion between Hindu and Buddhist beliefs and practices. The physical appearance of Buddha's statues is what impresses them most. However, they are aware of the Buddhist emphasis on peace.

American and Taiwanese Contrasts: Foreign Eastern Religion versus Temple Worship and Peaceful Lifestyle. Physical descriptions of Buddha statues dominate American images while Taiwanese mention familiar temples and specific artifacts related to temple worship, such as wooden drums, beads, residues of human remains, and bells. India figures prominently in both groups' images. The religious leaders -- monks as well as nuns -- are emphasized more by the Taiwanese. Buddhist practices, such as head shaving, ritual, fasting, and Buddhist Mass are mentioned by the Taiwanese but not by the Americans. Positive images, among the Taiwanese, related to peace and love, far outnumbering those of Americans.

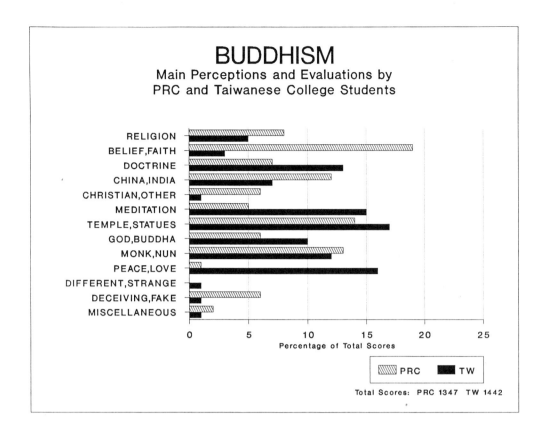

BUDDHISM
Main Perceptions and Evaluations by PRC and Taiwanese College Students

Total Scores: PRC 1347 TW 1442

PRC Chinese View: Buddhist Monk, Blindly Believing. Mainlanders are not very familiar with either doctrine or practices of Buddhism. They see Buddhism as just another religion, like Christianity and Hinduism, which calls for blindly believing in something that is not scientifically proven and perhaps deceiving. It was not so before the Cultural Revolution. Buddhist monks present the most prominent image of Buddhism. References are made to India, Buddhist nuns and Sakyamuni. Other imageries evoked for them include temples, statues, and geographic locations important to Buddhism. Six percent of their responses [compared to one percent from the other groups] reflect negative attitudes toward Buddhism: deceptive, senseless, unscientific. Unlike the other groups, Mainland Chinese found nothing strange or mysterious about Buddhism. The respondents from Mainland China indicate a great deal of hostility and misinformation, such as attributing violence and bloodthirstiness to Buddhism.

Taiwanese View: Temple and Sakyamuni. The Taiwanese show accurate and detailed familiarity with Buddhism. Temples, Buddhist monks, and the figure of Buddha are the most prominent images of Buddhism for the Taiwanese. They place Buddhism in India and acknowledge Sakyamuni (honorific of the founder of the historic origins of Buddhism). They know that Taiwanese Buddhists worship or pray to Kuan Yin [goddess of mercy, with attributes similar to those of the Catholic Madonna]. They also indicate familiarity with more universal practices of Buddhism, such as burning joss sticks, vegetarianism and praying to Buddha. They are familiar with Buddhist scripture and the teachings regarding reincarnation and Heaven. The Taiwanese have a very positive image of Buddhists -- in great contrast to the Mainlanders -- considering them to be good persons of dignity and love who can be counted on for help. Buddhism is considered mysterious.

PRC and Taiwanese Contrasts: Deceiving and Unconscious versus Peace and Love. For both groups temples and statues, as well as monks and nuns, are important. Surprisingly, it is on the Mainland that monks and nuns take precedence over temples and statues, and the reverse takes place on Taiwan. Location, history, and origin of Buddhism are more important on the Mainland. The God, Buddha component is much stronger for the Taiwanese in comparison with the Mainlanders. Religious practices, such as meditation, are very much emphasized on Taiwan but not on the Mainland. Doctrine is also more important in Taiwan, but the Taiwanese make little mention of the aspect of belief or faith; rather, they focus on the practice of Buddhism as a way of life. What most distinguishes the Taiwan group from the Mainlanders are the positive attributes associated with Buddha and Buddhism: peace, purity, sincerity, dignity, love, and benevolence.

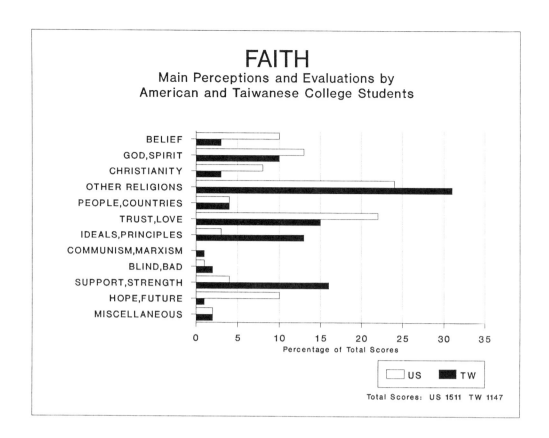

FAITH

Main Perceptions and Evaluations by
American and Taiwanese College Students

American View: God, Trust, Belief. In thinking of faith, Americans place great emphasis on belief in God and religion, particularly Christianity. Trust, love, loyalty, and confidence are much more important aspects of faith to Americans than to Chinese. An American's faith engenders hope and an optimistic confidence in the future. Faith healing is mentioned exclusively by Americans. Faith is considered as a help to understanding life and tied to Biblical teaching.

Taiwanese View: Spiritual Sustenance, God, Principles. For Taiwanese, faith is a source of support, spiritual sustenance, and power. It brings a sense of confidence, peace, comfort, and safety. For them faith is strongly connected to freedom, thought, knowledge, and truth. This shows the western influence in general and American influence in particular. However, mystery and mysterious forces are also elements in their faith. Faith is strongly associated with religion, more so with the Christian God than with Buddhism.

American and Taiwanese Contrasts: Trust versus Mystery. God receives much more emphasis among Americans than among Taiwanese, and the component of trust and love is also much more important in the meaning of faith to Americans. The pattern is similar regarding hope and the future. Faith is less concrete and specific for Taiwanese than for Americans. Mystery is a significant part of faith for the Taiwanese, who believe in reincarnation and karma, but not for Americans.

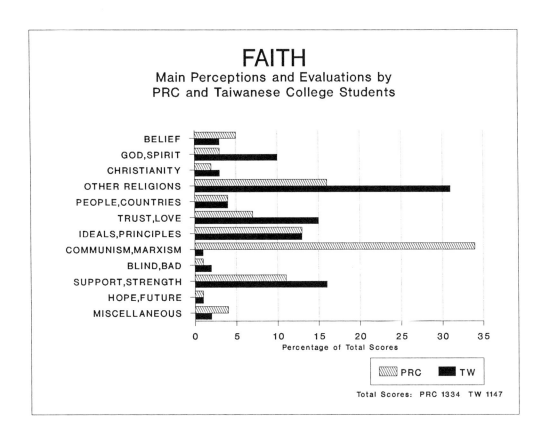

FAITH

Main Perceptions and Evaluations by
PRC and Taiwanese College Students

Percentage of Total Scores

PRC   TW

Total Scores: PRC 1334 TW 1147

PRC Chinese View: Communism, Ideals. The most overwhelming response to faith, among the Mainlanders, is Communism. More than one third of all responses fall into the component dealing with Communism and Marxism. Another important component has to do with ideals and principles, where they emphasize freedom, ideals, world outlook, truth and science. For Mainland Chinese, Communism, rather than religion, is the proper object of faith. They are convinced that faith in Marxism, as a world outlook, will bring about freedom and an ideal world based on scientific truth. There is a strong motivational component of faith indicating the pursuit of ideals to be achieved through the study of Marx, Lenin, and Mao tse-tung's thought.

Taiwanese View: Spiritual Sustenance, God, Principles. For Taiwanese, faith is a source of support, spiritual sustenance, and power. It brings a sense of confidence, peace, comfort, and safety. For them faith is strongly connected to freedom, thought, knowledge, and truth. This shows the western influence in general and American influence in particular. However, mystery and mysterious forces are also elements in their faith. Faith is strongly associated with religion, more so with the Christian God than with Buddhism.

PRC and Taiwanese Contrasts: Marxism versus God. Although faith is placed in the realm of religion by all groups, the differences on this concept are extreme. The PRC Chinese place their faith squarely in Communism and Marxism, which neither the Taiwanese nor the Americans mention at all. That faith is a source of motivation and power. Other religions capture more attention from the Taiwanese, compared to the Mainlanders, as does the component of trust and love. Both groups emphasize ideals and principles; however, the God and spirit component has much more importance to the Taiwanese.

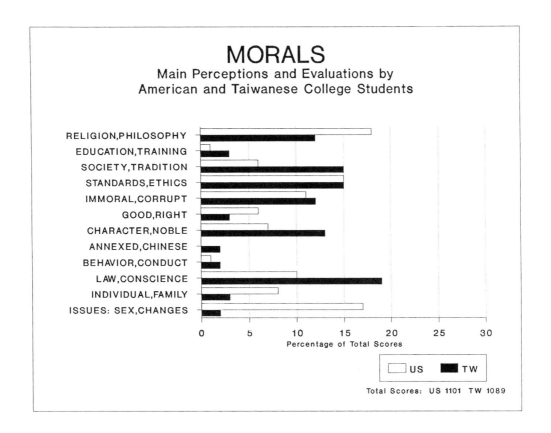

MORALS
Main Perceptions and Evaluations by American and Taiwanese College Students

RELIGION,PHILOSOPHY
EDUCATION,TRAINING
SOCIETY,TRADITION
STANDARDS,ETHICS
IMMORAL,CORRUPT
GOOD,RIGHT
CHARACTER,NOBLE
ANNEXED,CHINESE
BEHAVIOR,CONDUCT
LAW,CONSCIENCE
INDIVIDUAL,FAMILY
ISSUES: SEX,CHANGES

Percentage of Total Scores

☐ US   ■ TW

Total Scores: US 1101 TW 1089

American View: Religion, Sex, Conscience. For Americans morals are closely tied to religion and to some extent to society. They are related to values and ethics. Sex is the major moral issue along with concern with perceived changes in morality. Conscience and sin play significant roles. Morals are a measure of goodness and love, and inform laws and rules. Honesty and decency are indicators. Moral failure results in feelings of guilt. There is recognition of the existence of external, objective, moral standards, and to some extent social pressures and public opinion have an effect in the determination of individual morality. However, every person's own conscience is considered the ultimate judge of the correctness of his or her moral behavior.

Taiwanese View: Falling Standards. For Taiwanese, morality means living up to a standard or criterion of behavior. It is closely related to public spirit and ethics and is seen as a constraint on behavior through laws and regulations. There is strong awareness in Taiwan of falling morality, as well as of hypocrisy. Among Taiwanese there is broad agreement that morality is not relative or subjective but precisely defined in Confucianism, which is almost universally accepted as the criterion. Proper moral behavior is guided by the Three Obediences (subject to ruler, wife to husband, and children to parents) and the four virtues (filial piety, loyalty, benevolence, and integrity). It is the old day criterion, though. All of these are considered to be enforced by sense of shame. Law and the court system are seen as back-up mechanisms to enforce morality. Laws are seen as based on morality.

American and Taiwanese Contrasts: Individualism versus Societal Standards. Religion is stressed much more by Americans as a determinant of moral standards, thus evoking the notion of sin in failing to follow those standards. Americans view morality as a matter of individual conscience and decision-making, while this concept is wholly absent among the Taiwanese. The issue of sexuality is not mentioned at all by the Taiwanese. The Taiwanese stress the importance of character development and training much more than Americans do.

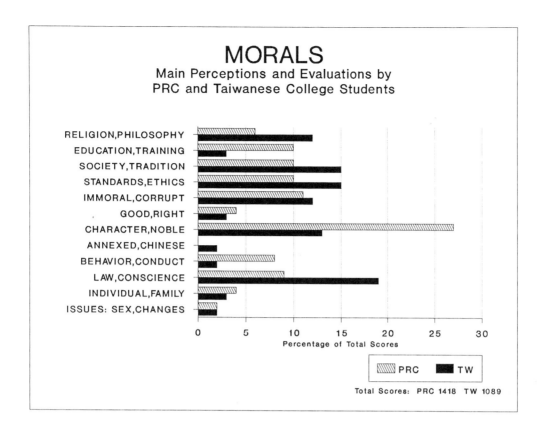

MORALS
Main Perceptions and Evaluations by
PRC and Taiwanese College Students

Percentage of Total Scores

PRC   TW

Total Scores: PRC 1418 TW 1089

PRC Chinese View: Noble Character, Corruption, Training. For Mainland Chinese, a person is admired as noble on the basis of moral character and qualities, and being in harmony with social morality. Corruption and immorality receive much prominence and are closely associated in their minds. Law is closely linked with morality. Moral training as part of education is seen as a major factor in creating individuals of noble and moral character. In general, for at least thirty centuries, morality in China has been thought of largely in terms of fulfilling one's obligations to different categories of persons: younger or older siblings, parents, spouses, and rulers. This has involved playing clearly defined roles in a prescribed manner. The strong concern with moral corruption, which is not mentioned at all by the Americans or the Taiwanese, may reflect an awareness among Mainland Chinese of the prevalence of the "back-door" dealing as a means of circumventing laws and red tape (Mosher, 1983).

Taiwanese View: Falling Standards. For Taiwanese, morality means living up to a standard or criterion of behavior. It is closely related to public spirit and ethics and is seen as a constraint on behavior through laws and regulations. There is a strong awareness in Taiwan of falling morality, as well as of hypocrisy. Among Taiwanese there is broad agreement that morality is not relative or subjective but precisely defined in Confucianism, which is almost universally accepted as the criterion. Proper moral behavior is guided by the Three Obediences (subject to ruler, wife to husband, and children to parents) and the four virtues (filial piety, loyalty, benevolence, and integrity). It is the old day criterion, though. All of these are considered to be enforced by sense of shame. Law and the court system are seen as back-up mechanisms to enforce morality. Laws are seen as based on morality.

PRC and Taiwanese Contrasts: Noble Moral Character versus Societal Standards and Constraint. Traits related to a person's character play a much greater role in morals for the PRC Chinese than for the Taiwanese. Standards and ethics figure more prominently in the Taiwanese understanding of morals. Law and the court system are important in regulating morals for both Chinese groups, although the connection between law and morality is stronger on the Mainland. Education and moral training are stressed much more on the Chinese Mainland. Divorce is seen as a moral issue on the Mainland, but not on Taiwan. More than anything else, morals for the PRC Chinese refer to the character or moral quality of a person; the ideal is one who is noble and polite. These qualities are not considered innate but rather the result of proper education and training. The Taiwanese place greatest emphasis on society and tradition. They tend to view morals partly as inner personal qualities but more as standards that are imposed from the outside - society, traditions, laws -- for regulation and constraint of human behavior.

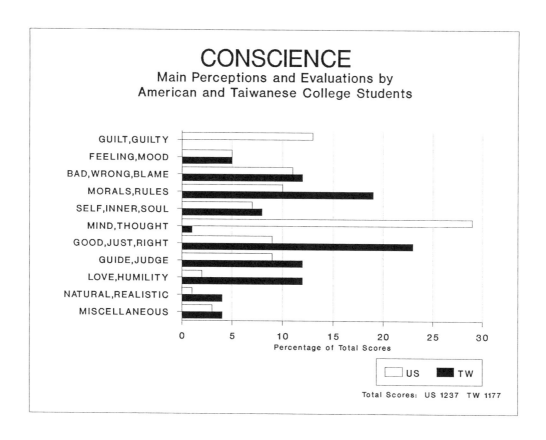

CONSCIENCE
Main Perceptions and Evaluations by
American and Taiwanese College Students

American View: Mind, Guilt. In general, Americans think of conscience in relation to self whereas Chinese think of it in relation to society. Conscience for Americans is a matter of mind and thought, an inner guidance in making moral decisions. When a person makes the wrong decision he suffers from a bad conscience and feelings of guilt. The dominance of the mental aspect in the American mind probably comes from a close connection between the words conscience and conscious. The Freudian influence is clear here: id, ego, superego, etc. Guilt is an especially prominent American response and totally absent among those of the other groups.

Taiwanese View: Morality, Goodness, Humility. Emphasis is on character; one is brought up to be a good and just person, a humble and responsible member of society. Conscience for them relates directly to self and inner feelings. Although they do not see the conscience as guide, they do speak of judgment between right and wrong behavior. And there is a very close connection between conscience and morality. They see education playing a major role in forming conscience. They also view humility, responsibility, and compassion as traits which will insure a quiet and peaceful heart. They consider conscience as a reliable guide in distinguishing right and wrong, and believe it to be closely tied up with one's self or essence.

American and Taiwanese Contrasts: Freud and the Mind versus Moral Upbringing. American responses to conscience are very heavily laden with Freudian concepts and notions of guilt. The mental aspect is almost totally missing for the Taiwanese as well as PRC Chinese views of conscience. The Taiwanese, on the other hand, see the formation of conscience and the building of moral character as an important function of education and see conscience as a source of humility and peace of heart.

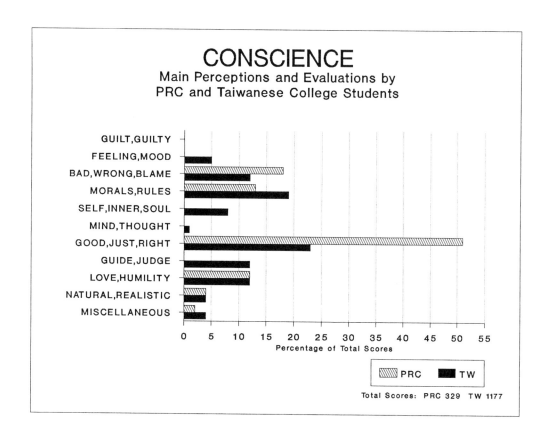

CONSCIENCE
Main Perceptions and Evaluations by
PRC and Taiwanese College Students

Percentage of Total Scores

PRC   TW

Total Scores: PRC 329 TW 1177

PRC Chinese View: Goodness, Morality. Conscience elicits very few responses from the PRC Chinese group, and those fall mainly into the categories of good and bad. Goodness, good, just, good heart, good person comprise more than half of all Mainland China responses. Bad and blame are also emphasized. Sincerity, honesty and humility figure prominently in their image of a person of good conscience. For the Mainlanders a person with conscience is a moral person, and there is no relativity involved. There is no reference to personal thought or inner feelings, no mention of guilt, feeling, or mood. Guilt in the Chinese context refers predominantly to judgments made within the legal system. Conscience is a moral issue of living justly in relation to society.

Taiwanese View: Morality, Goodness, Humility. Emphasis is on character; one is brought up to be a good and just person, a humble and responsible member of society. Conscience for them relates directly to self and inner feelings. Although they do not see the conscience as guide, they do speak of judgment between right and wrong behaviors. And there is a very close connection between conscience and morality. They see education playing a major role in forming conscience. They also view humility, responsibility, and compassion as traits which will insure a quiet and peaceful heart. They consider conscience as a reliable guide in distinguishing right and wrong, and believe it to be closely tied up with one's self or essence.

PRC and Taiwanese Contrasts: Moral Goodness versus Self judgement. The Taiwanese convey much more strongly than the PRC Chinese the idea of living within the moral structure of society. In some components, such as love and humility as well as natural and realistic, PRC Chinese and Taiwanese respond very similarly. In others, however, such as feelings and mood or self, inner, and soul, the Taiwanese respond like Americans. In still others, such as bad and wrong, blame and good, just and right, the Taiwanese occupy a clearly intermediate position. Just as the PRC Chinese, the Taiwanese do not at all relate conscience to guilt, but they do relate it to blame and shame. The most prominent response of the Taiwanese was moral, which was about equally important to the Mainlanders. Goodness was the most emphatic response of the Mainlanders, and it was nearly as important to the Taiwanese.

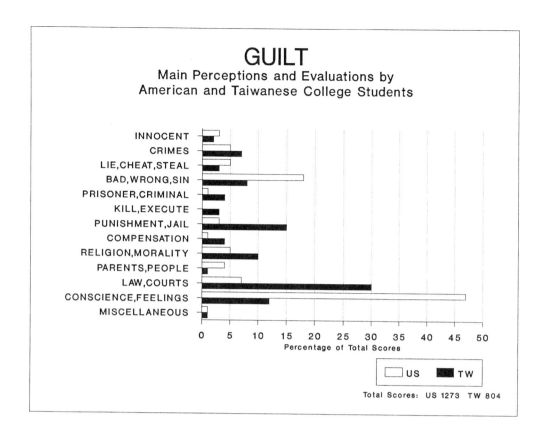

GUILT

Main Perceptions and Evaluations by
American and Taiwanese College Students

INNOCENT
CRIMES
LIE,CHEAT,STEAL
BAD,WRONG,SIN
PRISONER,CRIMINAL
KILL,EXECUTE
PUNISHMENT,JAIL
COMPENSATION
RELIGION,MORALITY
PARENTS,PEOPLE
LAW,COURTS
CONSCIENCE,FEELINGS
MISCELLANEOUS

0 5 10 15 20 25 30 35 40 45 50
Percentage of Total Scores

US ☐   TW ■

Total Scores: US 1273 TW 804

American View: Bad Conscience. Americans internalize ideas of improper behavior or thinking and therefore judge themselves as guilty. Nearly half the American responses have to do with conscience and feelings of shame, hurt, and anxiety. Americans are very concerned about the possibility of doing wrong, committing sin, and being bad. Bad behavior which invokes guilt includes lying, stealing, cheating, and sex. Guilt is focused on the family, parents, particularly mother. For Americans guilt is mainly an individual subjective reaction to conscience. It is accompanied by fear and anxiety and feelings of hurt, pain, sadness, and sorrow. Guilt also results in bad feeling and embarrassment. To a limited extent, guilt feelings are attributed to the moral teachings of various religions and in the Christian context arise from sin.

Taiwanese View: Law, Judge, Court. Although guilt is a relatively less important concept for the Taiwanese , they define guilt primarily in legal terms, something to be decided by the courts, which may result in imprisonment. What is clearly noticeable about the Taiwanese is that they also view guilt as a religious issue within Christianity. Perhaps it is this religious internalization of guilt that links them with Americans in their awareness of conscience and feelings of guilt and regret. Most of Taiwanese attention is turned toward the law and courts. They indicate a preoccupation with law and the judge. Acting against the law may bring them into court, or even to jail as a prisoner.

American and Taiwanese Contrasts: Personal Feelings versus Legal Judgement. For Americans guilt refers to inner feelings of conscience arising from a person's sense of doing wrong. This is the major distinction in the meaning of guilt between the Americans and the Taiwanese: one is mainly inner-directed and personal; the other is largely outer-directed and social. For Americans guilt is overwhelmingly a subjective feeling, while for the Taiwanese it is, more than anything else, a formal determination of a legal system. The difference is one of emphasis, as both meanings exist within each cultural setting. References to conscience, for example, are much stronger by Americans, while law is much more predominant in the Taiwanese view of guilt. Punishment and jail are greater concerns for the Taiwanese than the Americans. Negative references -- bad, wrong, sin -- are made more by Americans. On the other hand, the Taiwanese stress the role of religion: Christianity, God, Jesus, original sin. In contrast, Americans think in general of the church and morals.

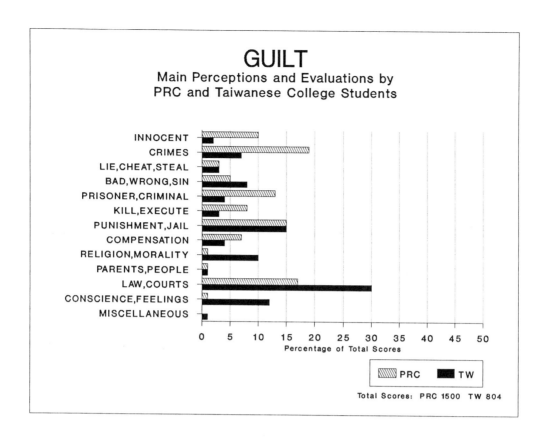

GUILT
Main Perceptions and Evaluations by
PRC and Taiwanese College Students

INNOCENT
CRIMES
LIE,CHEAT,STEAL
BAD,WRONG,SIN
PRISONER,CRIMINAL
KILL,EXECUTE
PUNISHMENT,JAIL
COMPENSATION
RELIGION,MORALITY
PARENTS,PEOPLE
LAW,COURTS
CONSCIENCE,FEELINGS
MISCELLANEOUS

0   5   10   15   20   25   30   35   40   45   50
Percentage of Total Scores

PRC   TW

Total Scores: PRC 1500   TW 804

PRC Chinese View: Commit a Crime, Serve a Jail Sentence. The PRC Chinese view guilt predominantly as a legal term in connection with determining responsibility for a crime committed against society. A great deal of attention is directed toward obtaining a confession and sentencing the offender. One who is condemned as an enemy of the state may expect to be imprisoned or executed if found guilty. Apparently the concept of guilt is not generally used in reference to inner, personal feelings. The most emphatic concerns in the PRC deal with determining guilt or exonerating the innocent who did not commit a crime or violate the law, as a guilty verdict can lead to execution. There is a high level of interest in prisoners, courts, and law as a means of punishing criminals.

Taiwanese View: Law, Judge, Court. Although guilt is a relatively less important concept for the Taiwanese , they define guilt primarily legal terms, something to be decided by the courts, which may result in imprisonment. What is clearly noticeable about the Taiwanese is that they also view guilt as a religious issue within Christianity. Perhaps it is this religious internalization of guilt that links them with Americans in their awareness of conscience and feelings of guilt and regret. Most of Taiwanese attention is turned toward the law and courts. They indicate a preoccupation with law and the judge. Acting against the law may bring them into court, or even to jail as a prisoner.

PRC and Taiwanese Contrasts: Kill versus Religion. Compared to the Taiwanese, the PRC Chinese place much less emphasis on law and courts but have about the same emphasis on punishment and jail. Perhaps because of the more severe consequences of a legal judgement of guilt in the PRC, the Mainlanders also stress the alternative of innocence. The Mainlanders express a great deal of concern about crime, but rape and arson are the only specific crimes mentioned. In contrast to the PRC Chinese, the Taiwanese see guilt not only as a legal issue but also very much as a religious and moral issue and as a personal matter of conscience.[3]

---

[3] This may be due to the recent rehabilitation in the PRC of many political prisoners previously condemned as rightists. Responses in the category of kill and execute receive nearly three times as much emphasis among PRC Chinese - a possible reflection of the government's proclivity toward executions, even for economic, non-violent, crimes.

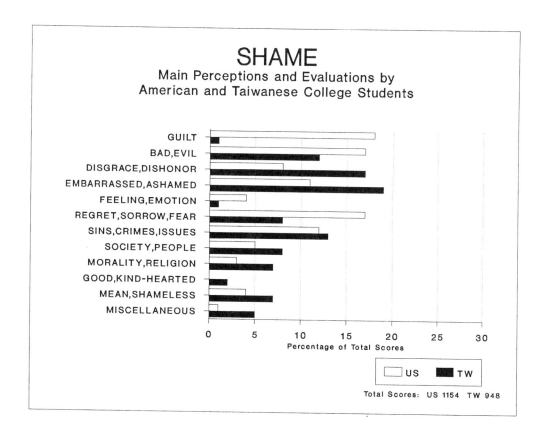

SHAME
Main Perceptions and Evaluations by
American and Taiwanese College Students

American View: Guilt, Embarrassment, Wrong. For Americans shame brings about strong emotional feelings of embarrassment, as well as regret, sorrow, and fear within the individual. That the heavy emphasis on sin may be related to a sexual context is indicated by references to sex, nudity, abortion, adultery. Shame has strong moral connotations of being guilty of doing something wrong or bad. While Americans connect shame very closely with guilt, neither of the Chinese groups make this connection at all.

Taiwanese View: Disgrace, Blush. The Taiwanese blush with shame at the disgrace that one brings upon oneself for things such as being denounced for stealing, cheating, making mistakes, or committing sins, especially those related to sex. Being naked is also mentioned in this context. This group seems to be the most aware of negative personality and character traits - being mean, immoral, shameless, ignorant; or having disrespect for other human beings - that may lead to shame.

American and Taiwanese Contrasts: Feeling Guilty and Embarrassed versus Disgrace and Dishonor. Among offenses, sex came in second place -- only sin had greater emphasis -- among American responses. It appeared in fifth place among Taiwanese responses. Among Americans, being poor or in poverty can be a source of shame, but not among Taiwanese. To the Taiwanese poverty is not necessarily a shame; it is lack of good ambition. Being accused of being shameless, or of having lost the ability to blush, is one of the most devastating insults among the Taiwanese. This concept does not appear among the American responses. The strong shame associated with being accused of theft on Taiwan is not reflected among American responses.

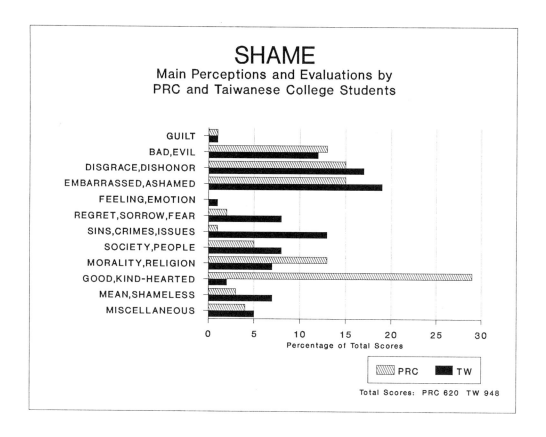

SHAME
Main Perceptions and Evaluations by
PRC and Taiwanese College Students

Percentage of Total Scores

PRC   TW

Total Scores: PRC 620 TW 948

PRC Chinese: Good Shame. Shame has relatively little meaning for the PRC. Chinese culture has often been described as a shame culture, rather than a guilt culture. Children are taught to behave by being shamed, and it is assumed that the individual will go to great lengths to avoid being publicly humiliated (Pye, 1972). For the PRC Chinese shame is a matter of moral character rather than a social issue. The most frequent responses indicate that for the Mainland Chinese shame has strong positive connotations. The most frequent responses were kind-hearted, good, sincere, honest, and having good intentions. These together added up to 29% of the responses -- more than any other category. The explanation is that, from the perspective of traditional Chinese literature and drama, the hero or heroine are very sensitive, uncomplicated persons with a highly developed and delicate conscience which causes them to blush and feel shame at the slightest transgression of morality or propriety. In contrast, the villain -- who may be a Westerner -- blushes at nothing.

Taiwanese View: Disgrace, Blush. The Taiwanese blush with shame at the disgrace that one brings upon oneself for things such as being denounced for stealing, cheating, making mistakes, or committing sins, especially those related to sex. Being naked is also mentioned in this context. This group seems to be aware of negative personality and character traits -- being mean, immoral, shameless, ignorant; or having disrespect for other human beings -- that may lead to shame.

139

PRC and Taiwanese Contrasts: Good Versus Bad Thing. The notion that shame is good and that it contributes to positive moral character like kind heartedness, honesty, and sincerity is almost exclusively held by the PRC Chinese. Feeling embarrassed or ashamed, particularly to blush with shame, receives more emphasis on Taiwan than on the Mainland, while the notion that shame is the result of a bad thing receives more emphasis on the Mainland. That a mistake brings shame is a strong concern among Taiwanese, but is not even mentioned by the Mainlanders. The explanation may be that the Japanese schooling to which Taiwanese were subjected for three decades instilled among the islanders the same horror of making mistakes which is characteristic of the Japanese. Disgrace is a frequent response among both groups with somewhat more emphasis among Taiwanese. The latter also very strongly associate shame with sins and crimes, while the Mainlanders associate it with neither.

RELIGION
MAIN COMPONENTS AND RESPONSES

GOD, SOUL, MYSTERY	US	PRC	TW
	192	48	194
God	192	18	-
God (Christian)	-	22	19
spirit	-	8	-
god,deity	-	-	66
soul	-	-	47
mysterious	-	-	46
supernatural	-	-	7
only one god	-	-	5
belief in many gods	-	-	4

FAITH, BELIEF	US	PRC	TW
	200	374	226
faith	93	219	148
belief,s	87	18	3
hope	11	-	-
trust	5	-	5
creed	4	-	-
blindly believe	-	70	37
believer of a religion	-	42	2
follower of a religion	-	16	11
idealism	-	9	-
devotion	-	-	8
rely on	-	-	7
confidence	-	-	5

DISBELIEF, DECEIT, WAR	US	PRC	TW
	61	284	114
atheism,t	24	-	-
bad	13	-	-
crutch	10	-	-
opiate	6	-	-
hypocritical	5	-	-
war,s	3	-	20
deceive	-	65	6
superstitious story	-	64	-
ignorant	-	36	-
Ch. don't believe in rel.	-	24	-
false	-	15	-
don't believe religion	-	14	-
unbelievable	-	13	-
object to	-	13	-
no good	-	12	-
cannot believe	-	9	-
harmful	-	9	-
unscientific	-	6	-
kill people	-	4	-
strange	-	-	14
opium	-	-	10
doubt	-	-	9
vain	-	-	8
escape from the world	-	-	7
fanaticism	-	-	6
senseless	-	-	6
oppression	-	-	5
terrifying	-	-	5
manmade	-	-	5
imagination	-	-	5
terror	-	-	4
lost	-	-	4

CHRISTIAN, CATHOLIC	US	PRC	TW
	484	122	157
Catholic,ism	144	34	21
Protestant	46	-	-
Bible	43	10	19
Baptist	43	-	-
Jesus,- Christ	39	14	2
Christian	39	7	-
priest	23	10	23
Christ	20	8	8
sin	15	-	-
Sunday	14	-	-
Christianity	13	14	59
Methodist	12	-	-
cross	9	25	5
heaven	9	-	8
Sunday school	4	-	-
salvation	3	-	-
Pope	3	-	-
Lutheran	3	-	-
nun,s	2	-	4
hell	-	-	8

BUDDHIST, TAOIST	US	PRC	TW
	23	70	119
Buddhist	15	-	-
Buddhism	8	25	78
Buddhist monk	-	21	10
Taoist priest	-	10	-
Buddhist scripture	-	9	-
Sakyamuni	-	5	-
statue of Buddha	-	-	17
Taoism	-	-	14

JEWISH,HINDU,OTHER	US	PRC	TW
	149	27	51
Jewish	69	-	-
Jew	30	-	-
Islam	11	12	34
Hindu	11	-	-
Muslim	9	-	-
orthodox	8	-	-
Mormon	7	-	-
Hinduism	4	-	-
founder of a religion	-	15	2
local religion	-	-	7
Judaism	-	-	4
pagan	-	-	4

CHURCH, TEMPLE	US	PRC	TW
	151	121	58
church	141	27	-
institution	10	-	-
church (place of worship)	-	94	14
temple	-	-	21
church (organization)	-	-	19
holy place	-	-	4

TEACHING, DOGMA	US	PRC	TW
	90	29	73
structured	14	-	-
philosophy	9	-	5
preacher	9	-	-
science	7	8	6
dogma	7	-	-
restricting	7	-	-
minister	7	-	-
death	6	-	4
Rabbi	5	-	-
preach	4	-	-
taught	4	-	-
strict	4	-	-
eternity	4	-	-
rule,s	3	-	6
disseminate	-	9	-
thought	-	8	5
ghost	-	4	7
doctrine	-	-	11
approach	-	-	10
religious doctrine	-	-	10
pastor	-	-	5
truth	-	-	4

PRAYER, PRACTICE	US	PRC	TW
	94	25	71
worship	19	-	38
money	13	-	-
prayer	12	-	-
pray	11	-	-
Mass	8	-	-
ritual	7	-	-
sing	5	-	-
praise	5	-	-
congregation	5	-	-
choir	5	-	-
service	2	-	-
confession	2	-	-
admire	-	16	-
alms bowl	-	5	-
kneel	-	4	-
ceremony	-	-	15
idol	-	-	11
fragrant	-	-	4
donation	-	-	3

HUMAN VALUES, ETHICS	US	PRC	TW
	83	24	231
morality	12	-	5
good	12	-	-
peace	10	-	22
love	10	-	8
freedom	7	24	4
religious	7	-	-
values	7	-	-
security	6	-	-
help,- people	5	-	5
holy	4	-	5
ethics	3	-	-
spiritual sustenance	-	-	45
teach people to be kind	-	-	33
sincere	-	-	20
strength	-	-	17
quiet	-	-	14
need	-	-	11
good & evil	-	-	10
sustenance	-	-	9
consolation	-	-	6
sense of safety	-	-	5
warm	-	-	5
agree	-	-	4
be kind and honest	-	-	3

CULTURE,CUSTOM,TRADITION	US	PRC	TW
	55	80	44
people	12	-	-
individual	11	-	-
family	10	-	-
personal	9	-	-
old time	6	-	-
community	4	-	-
life	3	-	6
foreign countries	-	18	-
culture	-	10	-
feudal	-	9	-
myth	-	9	-
custom	-	7	-
China	-	6	-
person	-	6	-
movement	-	6	-
history	-	5	-
daily life	-	4	-
civilization	-	-	18
human life	-	-	6
tradition	-	-	4
nature	-	-	4
mythology	-	-	3
grandmother	-	-	3

MISCELLANEOUS	US	PRC	TW
	0	25	4
Marxism	-	10	-
Communism	-	9	-
court	-	6	-
plumb	-	-	4

SUMMARY

Main Components	Percentage of Total Score		
	US	PRC	TW
GOD,SOUL,MYSTERY	12	4	14
FAITH,BELIEF	13	30	17
DISBELIEF,DECEIT,WAR	4	23	8
CHRISTIAN,CATHOLIC	31	10	12
BUDDHIST,TAOIST	1	6	9
JEWISH,HINDU,OTHER	9	2	4
CHURCH, TEMPLE	10	10	4
TEACHING,DOGMA	6	2	5
PRAYER,PRACTICE	6	2	5
HUMAN VALUES,ETHICS	5	2	17
CULTURE,CUSTOM,TRADITION	3	7	3
MISCELLANEOUS	0	2	0
Total Scores	1582	1229	1342

CHRISTIANITY
MAIN COMPONENTS AND RESPONSES

	US	PRC	TW
RELIGION	142	30	36
religion	142	30	36
JESUS, CHRIST	256	44	138
Jesus	153	44	138
Christ	103	-	-
GOD	153	46	135
God (Christian)	148	34	90
lord	5	-	14
god (deity)	-	12	-
monotheism	-	-	13
God loves everyone	-	-	10
Jehovah	-	-	8
CHRISTIAN, CATHOLIC	93	35	32
Catholic,Catholicism	52	10	23
Baptist	13	-	-
Christian	11	25	9
fundamentalists	9	-	-
Protestant	8	-	-
JEWISH, BUDDHIST	42	16	15
Judaism	19	-	-
Jewish	13	-	4
Jews	10	-	-
Buddhism	-	16	-
Muslims	-	-	6
Buddha	-	-	5
DISBELIEF, REPRESSION	4	35	45
confusing	4	-	-
don't believe it	-	16	-
meaningless	-	8	-
ridiculous	-	7	-
difficult to understand	-	4	-
dislike	-	-	9
unable to identify	-	-	8
hypocrite	-	-	7
blind	-	-	6
repression	-	-	6
boring	-	-	5
doubtful	-	-	4
FAITH, BELIEF	93	46	60
faith	50	21	40
belief,s	35	-	-
religious	8	-	12
blindly believe	-	17	-
just blind believer	-	8	-
believe	-	-	4
devotion	-	-	4
LOVE, FELLOWSHIP	208	3	106
love	58	-	-
people	13	-	-
important	13	-	-
good	11	3	7
peace	11	-	-
needed	10	-	-
family	9	-	-
morals	9	-	-
compassion	7	-	-
brotherhood	7	-	-
friends	7	-	-
hope	7	-	-
goodness	7	-	-
helpful	6	-	-
happiness	6	-	-
caring	5	-	-
mercy	4	-	-
kindness	4	-	-
community	4	-	-
strength	4	-	-
help	3	-	-
father	3	-	-
great love	-	-	17
sincere	-	-	15
lead people to do good	-	-	12
peaceful	-	-	10
fellowship	-	-	9
union	-	-	8
help people	-	-	7
joy, happy	-	-	6
love each other	-	-	4
care for society	-	-	4
aspire	-	-	4
do good	-	-	3

	US	PRC	TW
LEADERS, POPE, PRIEST	97	0	152
Pope	46	-	11
priest	22	-	24
preacher	9	-	-
nun,s	7	-	14
pastor	5	-	-
preaching	4	-	6
minister	4	-	-
missionary	-	-	31
to spread the gospel	-	-	30
fathers	-	-	21
elder	-	-	6
prophet	-	-	5
monks	-	-	4
BIBLE, DOCTRINE	239	53	295
Bible	66	17	77
cross	45	36	62
salvation	17	-	-
heaven	16	-	8
forgiveness	10	-	-
Mary	9	-	-
sin,s	8	-	11
Rome	7	-	14
holy	7	-	-
saints	7	-	-
Moses	6	-	-
savior	5	-	4
rules	5	-	-
guilt	5	-	-
Eve	4	-	1
life	4	-	-
Holy Grail	4	-	-
death	4	-	-
calvary	3	-	-
Joseph	3	-	-
Satan	2	-	8
devil	2	-	-
Jerusalem	-	-	17
judgment	-	-	12
salvation thru bel.in chr.	-	-	12
Holy Mother	-	-	12
hell	-	-	10
eternal life	-	-	8
doctrine	-	-	7
Paul	-	-	7
Trinity	-	-	6
blood	-	-	5
New Testament	-	-	4
Ten Commandments	-	-	4
Old Testament	-	-	4
Adam	-	-	2
CHURCH, PRACTICE	236	82	243
church	150	67	86
Christmas	22	6	14
prayer,s	15	-	21
born again	11	-	-
Baptism	6	9	13
Sunday	6	-	-
Communion	6	-	-
baptize	5	-	-
Mass	5	-	-
pray	4	-	-
holidays	4	-	-
Easter	2	-	-
go to church (Sunday)	-	-	34
sing holy hymns	-	-	16
very active	-	-	12
amen	-	-	10
church member	-	-	8
religious school	-	-	7
chorus	-	-	6
Confession	-	-	5
bell (jingle of)	-	-	4
ritual	-	-	4
wedding	-	-	3

	US	PRC	TW
HISTORY, CRUSADES	59	13	65
old	16	-	-
war	14	-	-
crusade,s	12	-	8
western	11	-	-
history	3	-	-
Europe	3	-	-
nation	-	7	-
India	-	6	-
foreigners	-	-	13
the west	-	-	12
medieval Europe	-	-	10
foreign	-	-	7
Israel	-	-	6
religious revolution	-	-	5
Middle Age	-	-	4
MISCELLANEOUS	14	0	26
me	8	-	-
money	6	-	5
compelling	-	-	10
capitalism	-	-	7
science	-	-	4

SUMMARY

	Percentage of Total Score		
Main Components	US	PRC	TW
RELIGION	9	7	3
JESUS, CHRIST	16	11	10
GOD	9	11	10
CHRISTIAN, CATHOLIC	6	9	2
JEWISH, BUDDHIST	3	4	1
DISBELIEF, REPRESSION	0	9	3
FAITH, BELIEF	6	11	4
LOVE, FELLOWSHIP	13	1	8
LEADERS, POPE, PRIEST	6	0	11
BIBLE, DOCTRINE	15	13	22
CHURCH, PRACTICE	14	20	18
HISTORY, CRUSADES	4	3	5
MISCELLANEOUS	1	0	2
Total Scores	1636	403	1348

BUDDHISM
MAIN COMPONENTS AND RESPONSES

RELIGION	US	PRC	TW
	188	102	69
religion	181	56	-
religious	4	-	60
sect	3	-	-
kind of religion	-	36	-
myth	-	6	-
theology	-	4	-
philosophy	-	-	9

BELIEF, FAITH	US	PRC	TW
	34	256	40
belief,s	24	68	15
faith	10	-	-
blindly believe	-	87	7
believer of Buddhism	-	73	8
believe Buddhism	-	12	-
believe,r	-	9	5
heart	-	7	-
ghost	-	-	5

DOCTRINE	US	PRC	TW
	78	101	182
cow,s	28	-	-
reincarnation	11	-	23
grasshopper	9	-	-
oneness	7	-	-
study	7	-	-
nirvana	7	-	-
tree	4	-	-
mountain	3	-	-
karma	2	-	-
science	-	21	-
Buddhist scripture	-	16	28
margin of travelling west	-	16	2
void	-	16	-
tarhagata	-	14	8
maiteya	-	6	2
classroom	-	6	-
learning	-	3	-
influence	-	3	-
ta-sen(heaven)	-	-	20
hsiar-sen (earth)	-	-	18
go out of the world	-	-	12
human being (life)	-	-	12
profound	-	-	10
uplifting one's spirit	-	-	8
without desire	-	-	8
Taoism	-	-	7
consolation of spirit	-	-	6
be born again	-	-	5
lily	-	-	5
understand Tao	-	-	4
cause and effect	-	-	4

CHINA, INDIA	US	PRC	TW
	317	161	97
India	77	58	66
China	57	36	18
Chinese	37	-	-
Asian	20	-	-
foreign	16	-	-
Asia	16	-	-
old	15	-	-
Indian	14	-	-
oriental	10	-	-
culture	9	5	-
Far East	9	-	-
Ghandi	7	-	-
Japan	7	-	-
Thailand	6	-	7
Iran	6	-	-
East	6	-	-
history	3	6	-
Indian style	2	-	-
came from India	-	17	-
Japan, China & India	-	12	-
older	-	8	-
jade emperor	-	8	-
development	-	7	-
feudal	-	4	-
tradition	-	-	6

CHRISTIAN, OTHER	US	PRC	TW
	33	87	10
Hinduism	8	-	-
Christian religion	7	15	2
Mohammed	7	-	-
Mecca	6	-	-
Shinto	5	-	-
Catholicism	-	39	-
Islam	-	12	-
heaven	-	6	2
Bible	-	6	-
Jesus	-	6	-
hell	-	3	6

PRACTICES: MEDITATION	US	PRC	TW
	83	66	212
meditation	37	-	-
pray	8	7	3
sitting	7	-	-
burn	7	-	-
yoga	5	-	-
rub	5	-	-
prayer	4	-	-
follow	4	-	-
worship	3	4	58
sacrifice	3	-	-
pray to Buddha	-	15	16
language of Buddhism	-	9	-
do missionary work	-	7	-
burn joss stick	-	6	45
recite scripture	-	6	-
hit the bell	-	5	2
kneel	-	5	-
manner	-	2	-
vegetarian	-	-	31
complete shaving of head	-	-	12
ritual	-	-	11
Buddhist's amen	-	-	10
fasting	-	-	7
Buddhist mass	-	-	5
spell to drive away spirit	-	-	5
beg for temple	-	-	4
nature	-	-	3

TEMPLE, STATUES	US	PRC	TW
	213	188	238
fat	45	-	-
statue	36	3	-
bald	33	-	-
temple,s	27	49	98
idol,s	21	-	-
pagoda	9	-	-
fat man	9	-	-
incense	9	-	-
stomach	8	-	-
belly	7	-	-
bald head	5	-	-
church	4	-	-
figure of Buddha, idol	-	43	73
church (place of worship)	-	43	-
Shaolin temple	-	27	27
church (organization)	-	11	-
golden statue of Buddha	-	6	2
canon	-	4	3
clay statue	-	2	-
wooden drum	-	-	12
beads	-	-	7
residues of human remains	-	-	5
fo-kuan-shan (holy temple)	-	-	4
bell	-	-	4
cave of 1,000 Buddhas	-	-	3

GOD, BUDDHA	US	PRC	TW
	180	86	141
Buddha	134	6	-
Zen	11	-	-
gods	9	-	-
God	8	22	-
sacred	8	-	-
Allah	7	-	-
holy	3	-	10
Sakyamuni(founder,Buddhism)	-	34	61
Kuan-Yin (Buddha)	-	18	31
lord	-	6	-
Zenism (Sung Dynasty)	-	-	31
holy god	-	-	8

MONK, NUN	US	PRC	TW
	74	181	175
monk,s	48	9	-
orange	11	-	-
priest	10	-	-
robe	5	-	-
Buddhist monk	-	95	86
Buddhist nun	-	42	38
Buddhist monk Tang	-	29	16
pig-monk	-	6	-
high monk	-	-	10
Buddhist's costume	-	-	9
master Ta-Moh(anc. buddhism)	-	-	7
leave home to become nun	-	-	5
master Hsin-Yun(famous monk)	-	-	4

PEACE, LOVE	US	PRC	TW
	27	8	234
peace	21	-	-
quiet	3	-	-
harmony	3	-	-
confidence	-	5	-
content	-	3	-
good	-	-	38
peaceful	-	-	33
purified	-	-	31
benevolence	-	-	27
sincere	-	-	20
dignified	-	-	15
help people	-	-	14
love	-	-	10
passive	-	-	9
temperate	-	-	8
devotion	-	-	8
wisdom	-	-	6
patient	-	-	6
spiritual	-	-	5
kind	-	-	4

DIFFERENT, STRANGE	US	PRC	TW
	76	6	18
different	34	-	-
strange	19	-	-
mysterious	13	-	18
unknown	5	-	-
confusing	5	-	-
be puzzled	-	6	-

DECEIVING, FAKE	US	PRC	TW
	13	80	16
protest	7	-	-
fake	6	-	-
deceive	-	21	-
deceive people	-	17	-
senseless	-	9	-
I do not believe	-	9	-
unscientific	-	8	-
kill people	-	6	-
prohibit	-	6	-
backward	-	4	-
vain	-	-	10
blind chance	-	-	6

MISCELLANEOUS	US	PRC	TW
	22	25	10
towels	7	-	-
good luck	7	-	-
black	5	-	-
important	3	-	-
more	-	15	-
Sunday	-	8	-
socialism	-	2	-
sky	-	-	5
fruit	-	-	5

SUMMARY

Main Components	Percentage of Total Score		
	US	PRC	TW
RELIGION	14	8	5
BELIEF, FAITH	3	19	3
DOCTRINE	6	7	13
CHINA, INDIA	24	12	7
CHRISTIAN, OTHER	2	6	1
PRACTICES: MEDITATION	6	5	15
TEMPLE, STATUES	16	14	17
GOD, BUDDHA	13	6	10
MONK, NUN	6	13	12
PEACE, LOVE	2	1	16
DIFFERENT, STRANGE	6	0	1
DECEIVING, FAKE	1	6	1
MISCELLANEOUS	2	2	1
Total Scores	1338	1347	1442

信仰

FAITH
MAIN COMPONENTS AND RESPONSES

BELIEF	US	PRC	TW
	158	69	30
belief,s	108	-	-
believe,-in	32	46	18
belief, conviction	9	23	12
believing	9	-	-

GOD, SPIRIT	US	PRC	TW
	203	36	114
god,deity	189	8	-
spirit	7	-	-
in God	7	-	-
mystery	-	17	10
God (Christian)	-	11	61
soul	-	-	16
mysterious forces	-	-	10
holy	-	-	6
ghosts	-	-	5
supernatural	-	-	3
the unknown	-	-	3

CHRISTIANITY	US	PRC	TW
	115	30	32
Bible	32	-	-
Catholic	26	-	-
Catholicism	-	16	4
Jesus	25	3	6
Christ	25	-	2
Protestant	7	-	-
Christian religion	-	7	16
cross	-	4	-
Christian	-	-	4

OTHER RELIGIONS,PRACTICES	US	PRC	TW
	359	211	357
religion,s	246	166	180
church	62	7	20
Jewish	16	-	-
prayer	11	-	-
sin	6	-	-
religious	10	-	-
priest	5	-	-
Hindu	3	-	-
worship	-	21	33
Buddhism	-	17	36
temple	-	-	21
idol	-	-	8
atheism	-	-	8
pray	-	-	7
teach people to be kind	-	-	6
theology	-	-	5
ritual	-	-	5
witch	-	-	5
witchcraft	-	-	5
Islam	-	-	4
to go to church (Sunday)	-	-	4
monk	-	-	3
pastor	-	-	3
picture of Buddha	-	-	2
sectarians	-	-	2

PEOPLE, COUNTRIES	US	PRC	TW
	57	52	45
people	13	2	3
life	10	-	2
self	8	-	-
others	8	-	-
girl	7	-	-
family	5	-	5
mother	3	-	-
marriage	3	-	-
society	-	13	3
mankind	-	11	-
motherland	-	11	-
me	-	6	8
foreign countries	-	6	-
world	-	3	-
ancestors	-	-	8
culture	-	-	8
country	-	-	3
human life	-	-	3
father	-	-	2

TRUST,LOVE,CONFIDENCE	US	PRC	TW
	325	87	176
trust	140	11	8
love	55	-	9
charity	25	-	-
healing	18	-	-
healer	14	-	-
loyalty	11	20	2
confidence	10	7	49
faithful	9	-	-
devotion	7	-	-
feeling	7	-	-
honor	6	-	-
courage	5	-	-
security	5	-	-
relax	5	-	-
joy	4	-	5
happy	2	-	-
secure	2	-	-
sincere	-	12	29
respect and admire	-	12	8
noble	-	12	-
esteem	-	9	-
trust firmly	-	4	4
peaceful & quiet	-	-	21
comfort	-	-	18
safety	-	-	10
love passionately	-	-	7
pious	-	-	3
satisfaction(sense of security	-	-	3

IDEALS,PRINCIPLES	US	PRC	TW
	38	169	147
understand	24	-	-
knowledge	7	-	14
learned	7	-	-
freedom	-	39	25
ideal	-	34	3
world outlook	-	16	-
truth	-	14	14
science	-	13	2
study	-	13	-
thought	-	11	25
outlook of human life	-	10	7
research	-	7	2
education	-	6	3
schoolwork	-	3	-
undertakings	-	3	-
principle	-	-	21
ideas	-	-	10
duty	-	-	5
heaven	-	-	3
philosophy	-	-	5
morality	-	-	4
3 principles of the people	-	-	4

COMMUNISM, MARXISM	US	PRC	TW
	0	456	8
Communism	-	252	-
Marxism-Leninism	-	61	-
socialism	-	28	-
Communist party	-	20	-
I believe in Communism	-	19	-
Marx and Lenin	-	18	-
capitalism	-	17	-
Marxism	-	12	-
Communist party of China	-	9	-
Marx	-	7	-
labor force	-	7	-
Mao Zedong thought	-	6	-
law	-	-	5
money	-	-	3

BLIND, BAD	US	PRC	TW
	16	14	24
blind	12	-	-
crutch	4	-	-
don't have	-	7	12
object to	-	7	-
monotonous	-	-	5
blindly	-	-	4
contradictory	-	-	3

SUPPORT, STRENGTH	US	PRC	TW
	58	151	181
strong	11	-	-
strength	10	-	-
fate	9	-	-
death	9	-	-
help	7	-	-
need	7	-	-
keep	5	-	-
pursue	-	35	-
strive	-	27	-
firm	-	19	3
great	-	17	3
spiritual pillar	-	16	-
crisis	-	10	-
power (physical strength)	-	9	39
success	-	9	-
fight for	-	5	-
bright	-	4	3
spiritual sustenance	-	-	61
prompt delivery	-	-	25
dependent	-	-	8
efforts	-	-	7
spiritual support	-	-	7
identified with	-	-	6
necessity	-	-	5
sustenance	-	-	5
power (authority)	-	-	3
having reliance	-	-	2
important	-	-	2
pillar	-	-	2

HOPE,FUTURE	US	PRC	TW
	158	12	15
hope	132	12	15
future	20	-	-
optimism	6	-	-

MISCELLANEOUS	US	PRC	TW
	24	47	18
name	8	-	-
in what	7	-	-
good	5	-	-
will	4	-	-
target	-	20	3
realize	-	7	2
worker	-	7	-
fine	-	7	-
correct	-	6	-
make up for something	-	-	6
act	-	-	4
change of life	-	-	3

SUMMARY

Main Components	Percentage of Total Score		
	US	PRC	TW
BELIEF	10	5	3
GOD, SPIRIT	13	3	10
CHRISTIANITY	8	2	3
OTHER RELIGIONS,PRACTICES	24	16	31
PEOPLE, COUNTRIES	4	4	4
TRUST,LOVE,CONFIDENCE	22	7	15
IDEALS,PRINCIPLES	3	13	13
COMMUNISM, MARXISM	0	34	1
BLIND, BAD	1	1	2
SUPPORT, STRENGTH	4	11	16
HOPE,FUTURE	10	1	1
MISCELLANEOUS	2	4	2
Total Scores	1511	1334	1147

MORALS
MAIN COMPONENTS AND RESPONSES

RELIGION, PHILOSOPHY	US	PRC	TW
	193	82	128
religion	61	-	11
church	39	-	-
belief,s	32	-	-
religious	14	-	-
philosophy	14	-	-
God	13	-	-
Bible	9	-	-
concept	7	11	4
ideas	4	-	-
thought	-	30	-
ideological level	-	9	-
spirit	-	9	-
world outlook	-	8	-
outlook on life	-	6	-
doctrine(ideology)	-	3	-
soul	-	3	-
attitude	-	3	-
Confucius	-	-	27
Confucianism	-	-	18
3 obediences & 4 virtues	-	-	12
theory	-	-	8
Mencius	-	-	8
saint	-	-	7
abstract	-	-	6
theories of Laotze & Chua	n	-	6
nature	-	-	6
old doctrine	-	-	5
Plato	-	-	5
peace	-	-	5

EDUCATION, TRAINING	US	PRC	TW
	6	136	35
upbringing	6	-	-
accomplishment	-	49	-
moral training	-	41	-
well-trained	-	19	-
education	-	11	20
stress morality	-	10	-
cultivate	-	6	-
teacher	-	-	4
influence	-	-	4
force	-	-	4
book learning	-	-	3

SOCIETY, TRADITION	US	PRC	TW
	69	139	158
society	42	40	44
social morality	7	23	-
social	7	-	-
old	7	-	-
opinions	6	-	-
civilization	-	53	-
country	-	10	4
customs	-	7	7
nation	-	6	-
tradition	-	-	27
culture	-	-	23
social order	-	-	12
can be found everywhere	-	-	7
ideal republic	-	-	5
heritage	-	-	5
experience	-	-	5
past	-	-	5
stick to old ways	-	-	5
habit	-	-	5
times	-	-	4

STANDARDS, ETHICS	US	PRC	TW
	162	142	163
values	43	-	-
ethics	34	25	25
morals	30	-	-
moral	14	-	-
relative	11	-	-
standard, criterion	8	49	101
standards	8	-	-
ethical	8	-	-
ideals	6	-	-
level	-	24	-
range	-	15	-
quality	-	13	-
moral principles	-	8	-
style	-	8	-
contracts of life	-	-	10
public opinion	-	-	9
man-made	-	-	8
real or false	-	-	5
stipulation	-	-	3
criterion	-	-	2
principal	-	-	-
quality and style	-	-	-

IMMORAL, CORRUPT	US	PRC	TW
	124	161	131
sin	30	-	7
immoral	15	40	-
immorality	12	-	-
guilt	11	-	-
bad	10	10	-
low	8	13	-
wrong	7	-	-
no	7	-	-
loose	6	-	-
evil	5	-	-
decay	5	-	-
lies	5	-	-
none	3	-	-
corrupt	-	60	-
commit a crime	-	13	-
violate the law	-	7	-
immoral person is bad	-	6	-
kill people	-	5	-
ugly	-	4	-
bad person	-	3	-
fall	-	-	61
hypocritical	-	-	18
shortage	-	-	17
false	-	-	6
empty slogan	-	-	6
lower morality	-	-	5
social problem	-	-	5
moral decline	-	-	3
drop behind	-	-	3

GOOD, RIGHT	US	PRC	TW
	67	61	31
good	33	15	-
right	17	-	-
high	10	9	-
truth	7	-	-
lofty	-	14	-
great	-	12	-
virtue	-	6	12
fine	-	5	-
invisible	-	-	10
good or bad	-	-	5
perfect	-	-	4

CHARACTER, NOBLE, POLITE	US	PRC	TW
	81	387	137
goodness	16	-	-
love	14	-	-
honesty	10	-	-
conscious	10	-	-
righteous	7	-	7
decency	7	-	-
trust	7	-	-
upright	6	-	-
care	4	-	-
noble	-	101	-
moral character	-	89	-
character	-	72	-
sentiments	-	30	-
confidence	-	16	8
moral quality of a person	-	15	-
respect the old&love young	-	11	-
friendly affection	-	11	-
impartial	-	9	-
relationship among people	-	8	-
general mood	-	6	3
selfless	-	6	-
consciousness	-	6	-
good person	-	4	-
warm	-	3	-
moral spirit (public)	-	-	35
edifying	-	-	16
esteem	-	-	13
courage	-	-	12
sense of value	-	-	11
heart	-	-	8
filial piety	-	-	7
conservative	-	-	7
considered by others	-	-	6
happy	-	-	4

ANNEXED, CHINESE	US	PRC	TW
	0	4	18
great China	-	4	8
Chinese	-	-	8
be annexed	-	-	2

BEHAVIOR, CONDUCT	US	PRC	TW
	7	107	27
behavior	7	34	-
polite	-	44	-
friendly	-	10	-
show consideration for	-	8	-
conduct oneself	-	6	-
daily life	-	3	-
help	-	2	14
self-control	-	-	8
do good	-	-	3
self-restrict	-	-	2

LAW, CONSCIENCE	US	PRC	TW
	112	121	205
conscience	30	24	25
law,s	25	54	20
judgement,s	19	-	5
rules	19	-	-
decision	7	-	-
justice	6	5	7
judge	6	-	-
court	-	27	-
legal system	-	6	-
function	-	5	-
constrain	-	-	59
pay attention to	-	-	22
follow	-	-	20
regulation	-	-	20
maintain	-	-	11
obey	-	-	6
do things acc.to one's conscience	-	-	5
tool	-	-	3
pressure	-	-	2

INDIVIDUAL, FAMILY	US	PRC	TW
	93	50	36
individual	37	-	-
parents	16	-	-
people	11	-	18
personal	11	-	-
marriage	8	12	-
men	6	-	-
human	4	-	-
person	-	23	-
family	-	13	11
mankind	-	2	-
personality	-	-	4
old person	-	-	3

ISSUES: SEX, CHANGES	US	PRC	TW
	187	28	20
sex,sexual,sexuality	94	-	-
drugs	20	-	-
death	20	-	-
new	16	-	-
life	12	-	-
changes	10	-	-
issue,s	9	-	-
changing	6	-	-
Communism	-	16	-
divorce	-	12	-
restoration	-	-	15
breakthrough	-	-	5

SUMMARY

Main Components	Percentage of Total Score		
	US	PRC	TW
RELIGION, PHILOSOPHY	18	6	12
EDUCATION, TRAINING	1	10	3
SOCIETY, TRADITION	6	10	15
STANDARDS, ETHICS	15	10	15
IMMORAL, CORRUPT	11	11	12
GOOD, RIGHT	6	4	3
CHARACTER, NOBLE, POLITE	7	27	13
ANNEXED, CHINESE	0	0	2
BEHAVIOR, CONDUCT	1	8	2
LAW, CONSCIENCE	10	9	19
INDIVIDUAL, FAMILY	8	4	3
ISSUES: SEX, CHANGES	17	2	2
Total Scores	1101	1418	1089

CONSCIENCE
MAIN COMPONENTS AND RESPONSES

GUILT, GUILTY	US	PRC	TW
	159	0	0
guilt	125	-	-
guilty	34	-	-

FEELING, MOOD	US	PRC	TW
	64	0	53
feel,ings	54	-	-
emotion	7	-	-
attitudes	3	-	-
natural feeling	-	-	26
mood	-	-	13
changeable	-	-	11
sensitive	-	-	3

BAD,WRONG,BLAME	US	PRC	TW
	134	58	145
bad	37	37	-
worry	14	-	-
bother,ing	13	-	-
none	13	-	-
sin	12	-	-
wrong	11	-	-
evil	9	-	13
objector	7	-	-
devil	7	-	-
fear	6	-	-
nagging	5	-	-
blame	-	15	31
hardship	-	6	-
lost	-	-	10
non-existent	-	-	10
crime	-	-	9
low (none)	-	-	8
empty talk	-	-	8
unrealistic	-	-	7
ashamed	-	-	7
few	-	-	7
person without conscience	-	-	7
no conscience(dog ate it)	-	-	7
shame	-	-	6
punishment	-	-	5
suffering	-	-	5
darkness	-	-	5

MORALS, RULES	US	PRC	TW
	127	44	228
morals	44	-	-
moral	25	44	122
morality	20	-	-
ethics	11	-	-
belief	11	-	-
religion	7	-	6
church	5	-	-
believe	4	-	-
education	-	-	25
law	-	-	17
society rules	-	-	16
standard	-	-	13
value point or view	-	-	7
evil&good exist together	-	-	6
limit	-	-	5
society custom	-	-	5
society product	-	-	5
custom in culture	-	-	1

SELF, INNER, SOUL	US	PRC	TW
	90	0	99
self	16	-	49
personal	12	-	-
inner	12	-	-
soul	11	-	-
spirit,ual	10	-	7
hidden	9	-	8
me	7	-	-
inner self	7	-	-
mine	6	-	-
formless	-	-	11
in the heart	-	-	10
formed inside	-	-	8
self-conscious	-	-	6

MIND, THOUGHT	US	PRC	TW
	357	0	11
mind	80	-	-
think,ing	40	-	-
thought,s	31	-	-
superego	29	-	-
ego	27	-	-
aware,ness	27	-	-
understand	15	-	-
unconscious	14	-	-
id	14	-	-
head	13	-	-
brain	11	-	-
knowledge	10	-	7
sub	10	-	-
Freud	9	-	-
awake	9	-	-
conscious	8	-	-
subconscience	5	-	-
knowing	5	-	-
deep thought	-	-	4

GOOD,JUST,RIGHT	US	PRC	TW
	111	168	271
good	52	61	-
clean	14	-	-
right	13	-	-
clear	13	-	-
important	11	-	18
free	4	-	-
best	4	-	-
goodness	-	75	106
just	-	12	46
good heart	-	12	10
good person	-	8	6
help	-	-	14
very sensible	-	-	12
heart	-	-	12
pure	-	-	12
bright	-	-	10
frankly	-	-	9
always do good thing	-	-	7
positive	-	-	5
strong faith	-	-	4

GUIDE, JUDGE	US	PRC	TW
	108	0	139
guide	30	-	-
regulator	16	-	-
voice, little voice	15	-	-
Jiminy Cricket	9	-	-
guard	7	-	-
behavior	7	-	-
listen	7	-	-
follow	6	-	-
control	6	-	-
guidance	5	-	-
judge between right&wrong	-	-	27
don't want to follow evil	-	-	25
have action (express feeling)	-	-	16
to tell when one is wrong	-	-	10
reconsider when wrong	-	-	9
discover (conscience)	-	-	8
wish to show	-	-	8
body language	-	-	7
suggestive	-	-	7
mirror	-	-	6
give one ideas	-	-	5
wish to discuss	-	-	5
difficult to follow	-	-	3
obey	-	-	3

LOVE, HUMILITY	US	PRC	TW
	29	40	139
love	9	-	12
honest,y	7	13	-
responsible	5	-	19
loving	5	-	-
peace,ful	3	-	7
sincere	-	17	2
human humility	-	10	42
compassion,ate	-	-	12
faith	-	-	10
quiet heart	-	-	8
never cheat	-	-	7
philanthropic	-	-	7
beauty	-	-	5
hope	-	-	4
idealism	-	-	4

NATURAL, REALISTIC	US	PRC	TW
	16	12	48
science	8	-	-
truth	8	-	-
nature	-	12	-
natural	-	-	36
realistic, true	-	-	12

MISCELLANEOUS	US	PRC	TW
	42	7	44
God	9	-	7
life	7	-	-
raising	7	-	-
people	6	-	-
endeavor	5	-	-
parents	5	-	-
waves	3	-	-
have	-	7	-
conquer people	-	-	14
dog	-	-	8
saint	-	-	6
child	-	-	5
ghost	-	-	4

SUMMARY

Main Components	Percentage of Total Score		
	US	PRC	TW
GUILT, GUILTY	13	0	0
FEELING, MOOD	5	0	5
BAD,WRONG,BLAME	11	18	12
MORALS, RULES	10	13	19
SELF, INNER, SOUL	7	0	8
MIND, THOUGHT	29	0	1
GOOD,JUST,RIGHT	9	51	23
GUIDE, JUDGE	9	0	12
LOVE, HUMILITY	2	12	12
NATURAL, REALISTIC	1	4	4
MISCELLANEOUS	3	2	4
Total Scores	1237	329	1177

GUILT
MAIN COMPONENTS AND RESPONSES

INNOCENT	US	PRC	TW
	36	154	18
innocence	25	-	-
innocent	11	154	13
wrong custody of a person	-	-	5

CRIMES	US	PRC	TW
	63	284	55
crime	34	24	-
theft	14	-	-
murder	10	-	-
steal	5	18	-
commit a crime	-	97	14
violate the law	-	79	-
rape	-	19	4
act against law	-	17	27
rob	-	16	-
commit arson	-	13	3
drug smoking	-	1	-
capital crime	-	-	4
gory	-	-	3

LIE, CHEAT, STEAL	US	PRC	TW
	64	42	24
lie	30	-	-
cheat,ing	12	-	-
wrong doing	11	-	-
trouble	7	-	-
make mistake,s	4	12	10
fight	-	9	-
betray one's country	-	9	-
commit error	-	6	-
blunder	-	6	-
errors	-	-	8
derided conduct	-	-	6

BAD, WRONG, SIN	US	PRC	TW
	225	82	66
wrong	70	-	-
sin	63	-	-
bad	38	11	14
unfair	11	-	-
hate	8	-	-
harm,ful	7	19	9
destructive	7	-	-
dishonest	7	-	-
useless	5	-	-
manipulate	5	-	-
sick	4	-	-
detestable	-	27	-
hate bitterly	-	10	-
do evil things	-	9	8
don't do bad thing	-	6	-
evil	-	-	15
immoral	-	-	10
deceiving	-	-	6
dark	-	-	4

PRISONER, CRIMINAL	US	PRC	TW
	7	188	36
criminal,s	7	41	4
prisoner	-	59	21
offender	-	35	6
enemy	-	21	-
bad person	-	19	-
petty thief	-	13	-
rascal	-	-	5

KILL, EXECUTE	US	PRC	TW
	2	114	26
death	2	8	5
kill people	-	44	11
should be killed	-	32	-
execute by shooting	-	22	-
shot to death	-	6	3
capital punishment	-	2	1
kill oneself	-	-	6

PUNISHMENT, JAIL	US	PRC	TW
	43	230	124
jail	15	66	23
punishment	11	-	9
prison	9	6	16
punish	8	42	11
to sentence a criminal	-	75	13
be in jail	-	26	14
serve a sentence	-	8	1
punish severely	-	7	-
penalize	-	-	12
be punished	-	-	10
punishment (physical)	-	-	7
be sent to jail	-	-	5
deserve the punishment	-	-	3

COMPENSATION, CORRECTION	US	PRC	TW
	12	98	30
behavior	6	-	-
school	6	-	-
educate	-	16	2
remould	-	14	-
perf.mer.ser.to atone crime	-	13	-
begin one's life anew	-	9	-
put right	-	8	-
have performed useful service	-	8	-
reform through labor	-	8	-
redemption	-	6	10
correct errors	-	6	6
responsible to the societ y	-	6	-
repentance	-	3	5
study	-	1	-
compensation	-	-	7

RELIGION, MORALITY	US	PRC	TW
	62	13	79
morals	12	13	9
church	12	-	-
religion	7	-	5
Catholics	7	-	-
hell	7	-	-
Jewish	7	-	-
morality	5	-	-
social mores	5	-	-
Christianity	-	-	25
God	-	-	18
original sin	-	-	12
Jesus	-	-	10

PARENTS, PEOPLE	US	PRC	TW
	50	18	7
parents	16	-	-
mother	13	-	-
people	6	-	-
friend	5	6	-
society	5	6	-
family	5	-	-
good person	-	6	-
person	-	-	7

LAW, COURTS	US	PRC	TW
	93	253	240
court	20	49	24
confess,ion	17	-	-
law	11	47	59
guilty	11	-	14
jury	10	-	5
judge(person)	9	15	29
trial	8	-	-
blame	5	-	15
fine	2	-	-
bring to trial	-	28	12
police, -man	-	22	17
plead guilty	-	15	2
make a confession	-	14	-
confess one's crime	-	10	2
criminal law	-	10	-
lawyer	-	9	10
public security officer	-	8	-
frame case against	-	6	3
special agent	-	6	-
legal system	-	5	-
public security	-	4	-
court decision	-	3	10
arrest	-	2	-
appeal	-	-	10
judge(make decision)	-	-	8
justice	-	-	7
accuse	-	-	5
make judgment	-	-	4
limited sentence	-	-	4

CONSCIENCE, FEELINGS	US	PRC	TW
	597	21	94
feeling,s	105	-	-
conscience	88	-	14
shame	61	-	-
complex	40	-	-
fear,ful	25	12	9
hurt	23	-	-
anxiety	20	-	-
emotion	17	-	-
pain,ful	16	6	-
sorry	13	-	-
sadness	13	-	-
worry	13	-	-
sorrow	13	-	-
trip	12	-	-
ashamed	12	-	-
bad feeling	11	-	-
embarrassment	11	-	-
jealous	9	-	-
anger	9	-	-
remorse	8	-	-
regret,ful	7	3	10
burden	7	-	-
ridden	7	-	-
depression	7	-	-
mind	7	-	-
alone	6	-	-
understand	6	-	-
forgive,ing	5	-	8
trust	5	-	-
unhappiness	5	-	-
hide	5	-	-
cringe	4	-	-
inside	4	-	-
afraid	3	-	-
sense of guilt	-	-	17
feel guilty	-	-	14
level	-	-	10
guilty conscience	-	-	7
pang	-	-	5

MISCELLANEOUS	US	PRC	TW
	19	3	5
sex	12	-	-
Nixon	7	-	-
enlist in Army	-	3	-
different definition	-	-	5

SUMMARY

Main Components	Percentage of Total Score		
	US	PRC	TW
INNOCENT	3	10	2
CRIMES	5	19	7
LIE, CHEAT, STEAL	5	3	3
BAD, WRONG, SIN	18	5	8
PRISONER, CRIMINAL	1	13	4
KILL, EXECUTE	0	8	3
PUNISHMENT, JAIL	3	15	15
COMPENSATION, CORRECTION	1	7	4
RELIGION, MORALITY	5	1	10
PARENTS, PEOPLE	4	1	1
LAW, COURTS	7	17	30
CONSCIENCE, FEELINGS	47	1	12
MISCELLANEOUS	1	0	1
Total Scores	1273	1500	804

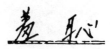

SHAME
MAIN COMPONENTS AND RESPONSES

GUILT	US	PRC	TW
	211	9	10
guilt	184	-	-
conscience	20	9	10
guilt trip	7	-	-

BAD, EVIL	US	PRC	TW
	199	80	118
bad	67	37	-
wrong	55	-	-
awful	25	-	-
evil	13	-	-
mistake	9	-	42
wrong doing	8	-	-
failure	6	-	5
naughty	6	-	-
sick	5	-	7
stupid	5	-	-
bad thing	-	29	17
wrong thing	-	14	8
cannot do it	-	-	5
no good	-	-	14
don't know how to do	-	-	10
to be in the wrong	-	-	5
darkness	-	-	5

DISGRACE, DISHONOR	US	PRC	TW
	92	90	159
disgrace	20	46	77
dishonor	16	-	6
disgust	16	-	-
pride	13	-	-
shameful	10	10	25
ridicule	7	-	-
scold	7	-	-
hate	3	-	-
denounce	-	24	25
disgraceful	-	10	15
scold a person	-	-	6
to be made fun of	-	-	5

EMBARRASSED, ASHAMED	US	PRC	TW
	126	94	184
embarrassment	57	-	-
embarrassed	23	-	-
embarrass	18	-	-
ashamed	16	-	-
blush	12	-	-
blush with shame	-	41	68
feel embarrassed	-	35	38
be ashamed	-	11	42
have	-	7	-
feel ashamed	-	-	15
unable to hide oneself	-	-	7
cover up one's embarrass.	-	-	6
embarrassed(be in dilemma)	-	-	5
to lower down one's head	-	-	3

FEELING, EMOTION	US	PRC	TW
	49	0	14
feeling	30	-	14
emotion	14	-	-
emotional	5	-	-

REGRET, SORROW, FEAR	US	PRC	TW
	193	11	76
hide	30	-	-
sorry	28	-	13
hurt	22	-	-
fear	20	11	5
regret	20	-	-
pity	18	-	-
sorrow	11	-	-
afraid	11	-	-
remorse	8	-	-
crying	7	-	8
anger	6	-	-
unhappy	5	-	-
sad	5	-	-
why	2	-	-
evade	-	-	17
self-reflection (regretful)	-	-	16
purify	-	-	6
agony	-	-	4
angry	-	-	4
feel going to end of world	-	-	3

SINS,CRIMES,ISSUES	US	PRC	TW
	140	6	122
sin,s	31	-	21
sex	17	-	11
crime	16	-	6
naked	12	-	14
poverty	9	-	-
nudity	7	-	-
death	7	-	-
deed	7	-	-
punishment	6	-	5
caught	6	-	-
poor	5	-	-
problems	5	-	-
cheating	4	-	11
abortion	4	-	-
adultery	4	-	-
hardship	-	6	-
steal	-	-	22
no peace	-	-	7
criminal	-	-	7
sense of committing crime	-	-	6
killing a person	-	-	4
suicide	-	-	4
prison	-	-	4

SOCIETY, PEOPLE	US	PRC	TW
	56	34	74
on you	22	-	-
fame	7	-	-
name	6	-	-
pressure	6	-	-
change	5	-	-
friends	4	-	-
parents	3	-	-
mother	3	-	-
nature of people	-	10	14
female	-	9	8
good person	-	8	-
person, human being	-	7	10
education	-	-	7
public opinion	-	-	7
society	-	-	7
Mencius	-	-	6
exam	-	-	5
woman	-	-	5
civilization	-	-	5

MORALITY, RELIGION	US	PRC	TW
	35	79	63
morality	-	-	34
moral ideal	-	-	9
morals,moral	16	9	-
church	11	-	-
religion	8	-	-
moral character	-	44	-
justice	-	12	-
reason	-	10	-
correct	-	4	20

GOOD, KIND-HEARTED	US	PRC	TW
	0	178	20
kind-hearted	-	75	-
good	-	61	-
sincere	-	17	-
honest	-	13	-
good intention	-	12	-
heart	-	-	7
self-respect	-	-	7
self-love	-	-	6

MEAN, SHAMELESS	US	PRC	TW
	47	17	64
disrespect	11	-	-
lie	7	-	-
dog	7	-	-
no	7	-	-
naive	6	-	-
outcast	5	-	-
greed	4	-	-
ignorance	-	9	10
be impolite	-	8	2
shameless (immoral)	-	-	11
shameless	-	-	9
not responsible	-	-	7
lying	-	-	5
mean	-	-	5
deceiving a person	-	-	4
animal	-	-	4
take revenge	-	-	4
insult	-	-	3

MISCELLANEOUS	US	PRC	TW
	6	22	44
song	6	-	-
nature	-	12	34
handle affairs	-	10	-
action	-	-	5
distinguished from others	-	-	5

SUMMARY

Main Components	Percentage of Total Score		
	US	PRC	TW
GUILT	18	1	1
BAD, EVIL	17	13	12
DISGRACE, DISHONOR	8	15	17
EMBARRASSED, ASHAMED	11	15	19
FEELING, EMOTION	4	0	1
REGRET, SORROW, FEAR	17	2	8
SINS,CRIMES,ISSUES	12	1	13
SOCIETY, PEOPLE	5	5	8
MORALITY, RELIGION	3	13	7
GOOD, KIND-HEARTED	0	29	2
MEAN, SHAMELESS	4	3	7
MISCELLANEOUS	1	4	5
Total Scores	1154	620	948

As scholars of comparative religions generally agree, a major difference between western American and eastern Chinese concepts of religion is emphasis on the relationship of man to God versus the relationship of man to man. Western religions are preoccupied with the concept of divinity that theologies and metaphysics elaborate on the concept of God and involve elaborate systems in this respect. In comparison, Buddhism, Confucianism and Eastern religions in general focus more on human qualities which reflect proper interpersonal relationships, acceptance and observance as moral principles. According to Buddhism, every person can become a buddha through self-discipline and self-denial.

Relationship to God

To provide sufficient opportunities for such differences to emerge, we have used four themes on the relationship to God and related theological systems: Religion, Faith, Christianity and Buddhism. The following trends observed across these themes reflect some characteristic dimensions of differences.

Monotheism, Polytheism, and Atheism. A strong monotheistic perspective is expressed by the American references to God, Christ in the context of all four themes included in this section. The references to Buddha and God are somewhat less emphatic. The Taiwanese reactions reflect essentially an atheistic attitude, a fundamental rejection of religion. In the context of Buddhism, they do make some references to Buddha as a central figure. It is interesting to observe that for the Mainlander group, their entire religious attitude is strong and very categorical. The negative sentiments about specific religions like Buddhism and Christianity are less pronounced than the very strong rejection expressed in the context of religion in general. While religion is rejected and treated with contempt, Faith is viewed very positively, except that the context is not religion but faith in the communist party, in Mao Tse Tung, Marxism and Leninism, and the communist doctrine. They speak of high ideals, intensive pursuit, and characterize faith more positively than either of the other two groups.

God, Buddha, Communism. American think mainly of God and Jesus. The Taiwanese also think of a Christian God, mainly of Catholicism, and to a certain degree of Buddha as the representative of the Buddhist religion. The Mainlanders think the least of God, and their predominant expression is a rejection. They place their faith firmly in the Communist ideology in mind.

Affective Ties, Love and Trust. The affective identification is particularly strong on the part of Americans. Americans express strong emotional connection referring predominantly to love, affection and to a lesser extent to trust. The Taiwanese make some references to love as well, but interestingly much less in the context of Buddhism than in the context of the Christian God. That is obviously a dimension of Western influence implying more emotional content as a part of religious identification. The negative feelings and attitudes expressed in the context of religion in general and the particular religions considered here have two dimensions. One is the characterization of religion as fake and deceitful, foreign and alien. They think also intensively of superstition and blindness. The

American emphasis on affective ties reflects a philosophy which stresses a very personal individual based relationship with God where the emotional dimension acquires special importance. This is characteristic of a very individualized relationship to God emphasized by Americans.

As Francis Hsu (1981) observes:

> ...the interest motive and the individualized approach to religion in combination have led to privatization of God in America. God becomes the "hero" of every individual believer's joy or sorrows, successes or disappointments, loves or hates... He wants to be exclusive. But his exclusiveness has no bite unless other likeminded people combine forces with him... The pious in America tend to identify God with themselves and to consider God an intristic part of themselves... The worth and meaning of God are determined by the individual believer.

Personality Attributes: Good and Kind. Emphasis on positive qualities of the religious person goodness, kindness, and sincerity -- is a particularly strong feature of the Taiwanese understanding of religion. It comes out again and again irrespective of the particular religion or whether we think of Religion and Faith in general. The implication of religion, for them, is the good attitudes it requires or promotes among people. They think particularly in the context of faith, of the qualities of strength and the capabilities to make a successful effort. Actually, in this respect, there is some similarity between the Taiwanese and the Mainland Chinese, who both emphasize the positive motivational dimension of faith as resulting in endeavor, active pursuit and positive results.

Practices: Prayer, Worship, Meditation. Most of the American and Taiwanese think of activities related to religion about to the same extent except that their focus is somewhat different. The American emphasis is on prayer and to a lesser extent on teaching. The Taiwanese focus is more on worship which is somewhat similar to prayer. The emphasis on worship from the part of the Taiwanese reflects a strong involvement and active participation. They see apparently worship, prayer and the positive human qualities attached to the religious person as closely interrelated.

Church, Temple, Monks, Representatives. The Americans and the Taiwanese give somewhat similar attention to this concrete dimension of religion, namely to their representatives. While Americans think relatively more of the Pope, the Taiwanese have more missionaries in mind. With regard to religion, the Americans think more of the church; whether the "church" means the building or the body of believers is not clear in this particular context. In the context of Buddhism, the Taiwanese think of temples, also somewhat more than Americans. Monks, nuns and temple receive relatively stronger interest from the Mainland Chinese, who pay little attention to the spiritual context of Buddhism or religion in general but do note the observable elements.

Denominations, Pluralism. It is particularly characteristic of the American meanings of religion, Christianity and Faith that Americans have a broad diversity of denominations in mind. Usually, Catholics receive the most attention, followed by different Protestant denominations, Jews and all the other religions. This widespread of attention reflects the American reality which involves the friendly relationship of a broad variety of denominations which coexist side by side. The Taiwanese, on the other hand, think mostly of two main religions. One is Christianity (mostly Catholicism) and the other is Buddhism. They seem to be equally divided in their attention paid to these two major religions. What is particularly characteristic of the Taiwanese is a strong emphasis on religious values. They think of spiritual sustenance, teaching people to be kind, to give strength, loyalty, sense of security, peace and a variety of other positive characteristics which reflect in their mind the very substance of religious commitment.

Across these dimensions we find fundamental trends which show that in general Americans pay more attention to their personal relationship to God, emphasizing faith and belief, basically monotheistic postures, and very strong personal ties with God. They paid attention to prayer and worship and relatively less attention to positive human qualities. Also one may argue that the feeling of love can be interpreted as goodness. In comparison, the Taiwanese show a somewhat different orientation. They emphasize the human qualities and characteristics of the believing person, the attitudes and values of the believer. And also they place more emphasis on worship with the implication that worship and the development of human qualities may be dominant features of religion.

The meaning of religion for the Taiwanese is apparently influenced by Western thinking in several ways. First of all, they show also now an increasing amount of attention paid to the emotional affective content to the deity. Furthermore, obviously their religious affiliations, at least at the present period, seem to be about equally divided between Christianity and Buddhism. It is interesting that Confucianism does not emerge at all in connection with religion or faith, which essentially underscores the observation of Western scholars who claim Confucianism should not be considered a religion but a compilation of moral principals and moral values.

The meaning of religion and faith emerges from this data with regard to the Mainlanders in a rather conclusive and peculiar way. Religion is essentially rejected by them, and at the same time, faith has a strong positive meaning to them, almost exclusively associated with the Communist doctrine and dogma. All the reactions emerging in connection with these four major stimulus words support such a conclusion. It should be added that Buddhism did not completely lose its meaning but lost its basic doctrinal content and the attention which it receives from the Mainlanders is limited to such external observances as nuns, monks, temples, statues, etc.

Relationship to People

Now that we have examined relationship to God as perceived by Americans and Chinese, in this second section we summarize findings which bear on the question of relationship to people. This relationship is reflected by responses to morality, conscience, guilt and shame.

Morality, Ethics. Morality for Americans reflects strong concerns with religious beliefs and faith. This same relationship is not present, at least not to the same extent, in the case of the Chinese, who consider morality an issue of regulation of behavior by moral principles. Although the Taiwanese do make considerable references to Confucius and some, even to the philosopher Plato, the relationship to people in their mind, is something primarily regulated by moral philosophies which have contemporary timeliness as well as roots in divine regulation.

Values, Standards. Americans are inclined to think primarily of values. They think of ethical and moral values, and more specifically of goodness, honesty, decency, care, sense of value. The PRC Chinese think in terms of standards without going into details. For them it appears that morality is not so much the appreciation of specific attitudes as a matter of character, the combination of personality features which add up to an overall posture characteristic of a human being. The heaviest and most interesting response is the attribute of being noble. Nobility is meant here as a particular feature of moral character. They speak of character of the person, quality of the person, relationship of the person to other people. The Taiwanese think of qualities like moral spirit, public spirit of people, esteem, being a good person. The real Taiwanese focus is however, on law and standards. The Taiwanese look at morality as behavior regulated by law and they consider constraints, regulations, legal matters as being particularly influential and important. While to the Mainland Chinese, the moral character appears to be of primary importance, to the Taiwanese the ethical standards and legal constraints appear to be more important.

The Choice Between Good and Bad. From the American perspective, whether thinking of morality or conscience, guilt or shame, there is a consistently strong emphasis on the contrast of good and bad, right and wrong. The morality dimension involves essentially a decision between two alternatives not so much in adherence to certain laws or regulations as through a personal choice between good and bad. The choice appears to be a consideration independent from formal regulations or laws. The basis of this choice is naturally the conscience of the individual person. This conscience is frequently described as an inner voice which makes the choice between good and bad, right and wrong. This choice making receives much less attention from the two Chinese groups. Of the two, the Taiwanese give more references but they speak more not so much in contrasting good and bad as consider either one or the other. Conscience has an exclusively positive meaning for the PRC group. For them conscience is entirely good, just involves goodness and sincerity. The Mainland group does not show the clear contrasting of good and bad alternatives, which is so characteristic of the American idea of conscience and morality.

Mind, Super Ego. From the American angle, the source of conscience is the human mind or the human soul which makes the choices. The decision is entirely up to the person. From the Mainlander perspectives the choice is decided by the person's character, is given by the character of the person, and if the person has conscience, then the choices will be positive. The Taiwanese emphasize education and the influence of the social environment. The educational emphasis comes out quite strongly from the PRC group, particularly in the context of morality. From the angle of conscience, the PRC group considers mainly the given character.

Moral vs. Criminal vs. Legal Alternatives. From the American perspective, morality, conscience, guilt, and shame involve free choices made by the person listening to his own or her own conscience. From the Chinese angle, the focus is on what is legal and what is not. Particularly in the context of guilt, the PRC group makes a very narrow and categorical distinction between crime and innocence. They are not considering the distinction of the person's motivation or choice, they consider only the act and whether the behavior happens to be criminal or legal. Along these same lines, they think intensively of the punishment, from jailing to execution. They think of correction, redemption and other legal measures. Similarly, the Taiwanese group gives increasingly more attention to the legal dimension, to punishment and jail, to law and courts. Also their references to Christianity and religion suggest that their narrow legalistic traditional thinking may have been influenced by more recent considerations which decide about guilt based on the person's conscience rather than the narrow application of the law.

Sentiments Associated with Moral Decisions. In this context, all three groups consider the options of guilt and shame and the Americans increasingly consider regret and remorse as well as anxiety and uneasy feelings. However, the real source of the these diverse feelings comes essentially from the conscience. The conscience generates positive or negative feelings after a particular moral decision has been made. This logic is entirely consistent with the American moral philosophy of autonomous individualism where the individual makes moral decisions and the consequence of his decision is rewarded or punished by feelings of guilt and shame, a sense of good conscience. Somewhat surprisingly, shame doesn't elicit much negative reaction from the PRC group; rather, the opposite seems to be true. The PRC Chinese recognize the manifestation of blush and embarrassment as negative experiences of shame. On the other hand, relating shame to moral character and goodness and kind-heartedness suggests from the PRC view, shame may be a consequence which honest well-meaning people may suffer under social conditions and circumstances which they cannot control, but for which they are personally responsible. The Taiwanese look at shame entirely negatively. They condemn it and associates it with disgrace and dishonor, sin, and lying. They also relate shame to character weakness and behavior like stealing and cheating.

In General. The trends observed in regard to morality, conscience, guilt and shame indicate that there are indeed some substantive differences between the American and the Chinese interpretations of morality. The single most important difference is that Americans view morality largely as a personal choice between right and wrong. It is a matter of individual conscience. It can be sinful or it can be virtuous. In this sense, it has clear religious overtones. From the Chinese perspectives, the focus is on moral or immoral, legal or illegal behavior alternatives. The motivation to conscience, the internal voice is not examined or questioned. What matters is conformity with the established norms and moral standards. The PRC Chinese see these moral standards very much as a part of the moral character of the person and relate it to the person's education, moral training and upbringing. The Taiwanese accept these Chinese perspectives but at the same time consider morality and conscience somewhat more from a religious, Western angle, recognizing the role of individual conscience. The Taiwanese look at choices of sin vs. proper behavior not exclusively from the angle of their legality or illegality. The findings generally support the notion that the Chinese groups place much more emphasis on behavior or norms of conduct, and their conformity or nonconformity with laws and regulations and standards.

Chapter 5

ECONOMY

The following analysis of the American and Chinese views of economy reflects upon the influences of three characteristically different systems and environments. The first part of this chapter is based on four economic concepts of high level abstraction: economy, development, industry and agriculture. In the second half of this chapter we examine four themes that are much more concrete and bear on fundamental human needs like food and clothing.

America is a highly developed, industrialized country frequently characterized as a post-modern, post-industrial consumer society. The Chinese samples represent two societies and cultures that economic experts place in different categories. The PRC is frequently characterized as a highly centralized Communist economic system built on the Maoist and post-Maoist versions of Communism, a Third World country with a low level of economic development. In partial contrast, Taiwan is often described as the fastest developing country with a booming economy based predominantly on the principles of the free market system.

The comparison of these countries is made increasingly interesting by the fact that two Chinese samples represent people of similar cultural background who have embarked on different paths of economic development which represent two particularly interesting competing alternatives.

During the Sixties, leading development economists such as Rupert Emerson (1966), Edward Shils (1966), Lucian Pye (1963), David Apter (1967), Frederick W. Frey (1967), and Paul Sigmund identified a host of trends, such as psychological forces, nationality, collectivism, ideological blue prints, and centralized planning, that attract leaders of the Third World interested in economic development. A major criticism directed at this school was the objection that their emphasis on common psychological trends was speculative and unverifiable. The present analysis offers new opportunities for reviewing the relevance of these development theories on solid empirical grounds.

It is also relevant to explore how members of these three different social and economic systems perceive their own situation, their problems and achievements. How much are their economic views and attitudes influenced by their different economic experiences, ideologies, culture, etc.? How much are their views influenced by the values and ideals of the free market system, respectively by those of socialist planning, centralization and control?

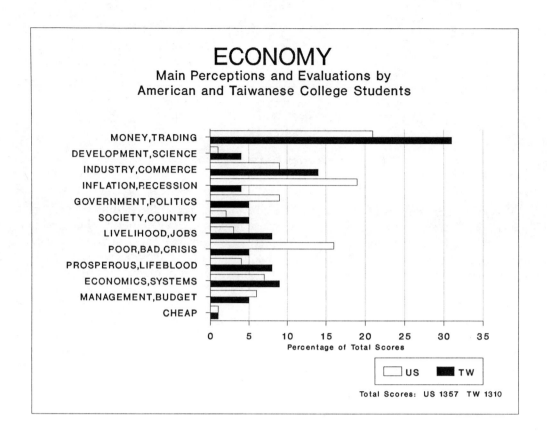

ECONOMY
Main Perceptions and Evaluations by
American and Taiwanese College Students

Percentage of Total Scores

US   TW

Total Scores: US 1357 TW 1310

American View: Money, Inflation. For Americans the economy is seen first of all in terms of money, and then in terms of inflation and recession. Business is an important part of the image, as is the notion that the economy is in poor or bad shape. Politics and the American president are also involved. Economics has some significance, but less than for the Chinese groups. The capitalist system is mentioned.

Taiwanese View: Money, Trading, Stock. More than a third of the Taiwanese picture consists of money, trading, stock, and related factors. Far more than the other groups, Taiwanese see the economy as rich and a source of wealth. Industry and commerce are strong elements of the economy. The economic system and the theory behind it are far more significant to them than to the other groups. Taiwan's continued prosperity rests heavily on its economy.

American and Taiwanese Contrasts: State of the Economy versus Active Trading. Negative views regarding the economy are much stronger among Americans than among Taiwanese, especially in term of the poor state of the economy, plagued with inflation and recession. The role of government and politics is stronger in the American mind compared to the Taiwanese.

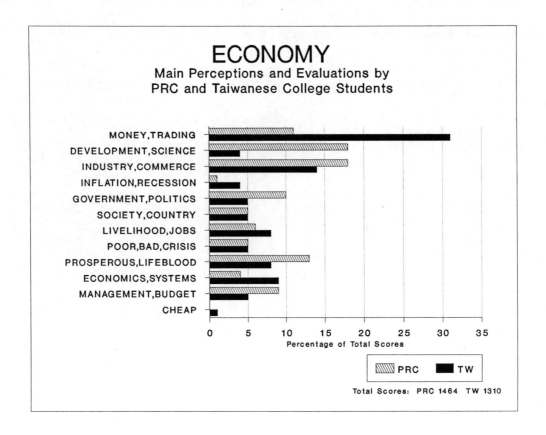

ECONOMY
Main Perceptions and Evaluations by
PRC and Taiwanese College Students

Percentage of Total Scores

PRC   TW

Total Scores: PRC 1464 TW 1310

PRC Chinese View: Political Economics, Development, Management. Industry and agriculture are seen as very vital aspects of the economy. Money, too, receives significant attention, but far less than from the other two groups. Development is uppermost in Mainlander minds -- and science and technology play a role here. More than the other two groups, Mainlanders see the economy of their country as prosperous -- and as the lifeblood of the country. In the past there were cases of dropping dead on the street. Now each Chinese person has rice and basic foodstuff to eat, and people are satisfied, more so that ever before. Management of the economy is very significant to them.

Taiwanese View: Money, Trading, Stock. More than a third of the Taiwanese picture consists of money, trading, stock, and related factors. Far more than the other groups, Taiwanese see the economy as rich and a source of wealth. Industry and commerce are strong elements of the economy. The economic system and the theory behind it are far more significant to them than to the other groups. Taiwan's continued prosperity rests heavily on its economy.

PRC and Taiwanese Contrasts: Political Economics versus Trading and Commerce. In the Taiwanese mind, money, trading stock, commerce, and economic theory are major aspects of the economy. The Mainlanders, by contrast, see the economy principally in terms of political economics, politics, and development. Any Communist country is politics-oriented. And the Chinese Communists are no exception. Industry and agriculture are seen as the foundation by them, while these aspects, particularly agriculture, are less important to the Taiwanese. The Taiwanese concerns have to do with economic crisis, exploitation, and depression. While Mainlanders perceive the existence of an economic crisis, and see their economy as backward, inflation and recession are not part of their picture. Overall, the economy is seen least negatively, of the three groups, by the Mainlanders. As Taiwanese experts observe, the greatest contribution of the Chinese Communists seems to be that the regime has managed to feed every mouth on the Mainland although the living standard there is still very low.

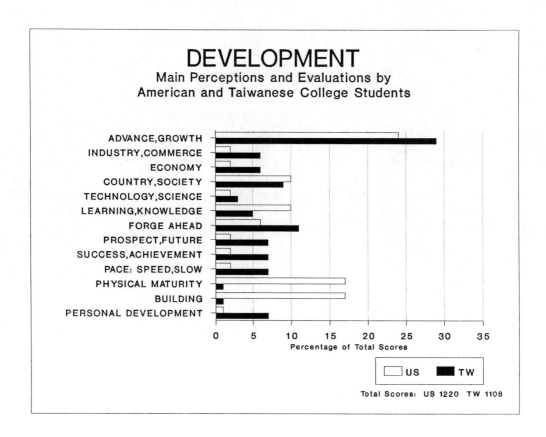

American View: Physiological Growth, Building. In the American mind, growth and physical maturity are the most significant meanings of development. The construction of buildings -- especially housing and apartments -- are next in importance. Learning, and the filling of the mind with knowledge, are also significant. Americans also consider the level of development of various countries, especially those of the Third World.

Taiwanese View: Advance, Struggle, Success. A predominant part of the Taiwanese image of development has to do with advancement, progress, and related concepts. Their understanding of developmental undertaking involves struggle, creativity, and breakthrough. Industry and commerce are significant elements, as is knowledge. Even greater attention is paid to success and achievement. Many people in Taiwan are indeed money-crazy. Thus to them, development means economic development period. There are few references to human development.

American and Taiwanese Contrasts: Physical Maturity versus Advancement and Progress. All three groups, but especially the Taiwanese, pay the most attention to advancement, growth, and progress. After that, physical maturity and human development is more important than any other component of development in the American mind. Within that context, only person, mother, and health are considered by the Taiwanese. Children, physical development, especially in terms of breasts or bust, and maturity, receive significant American attention. The third largest American component, building and construction, receives virtually no notice from the Taiwanese. Success and achievement are more as significant aspects of development to the Taiwanese than Americans.

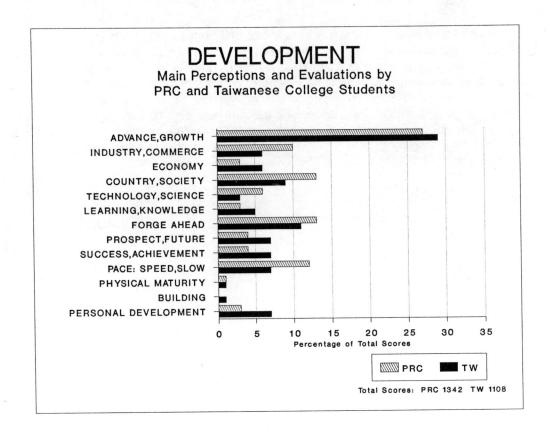

DEVELOPMENT
Main Perceptions and Evaluations by
PRC and Taiwanese College Students

Percentage of Total Scores

PRC   TW

Total Scores: PRC 1342 TW 1108

PRC Chinese View: Advance, Agriculture, Society. The notion of advance is uppermost in Mainlander minds when development is mentioned. That single response is more prominent for them than for either of the other groups. Concepts related to it make up about one fourth of the Mainlander image of development. More than for the other groups, Mainlander focus is on society's development. They see this in terms of forging ahead and pushing forward. National defense is part of the picture, but industry and agriculture are more important. In their view, speed in development is important in overcoming backwardness.

Taiwanese View: Advance, Struggle, Success. A predominant part of the Taiwanese image of development has to do with advancement, progress, and related concepts. Their understanding of developmental undertaking involves struggle, creativity, and breakthrough. Industry and commerce are significant elements, as is knowledge. Even greater attention is paid to success and achievement. Many people in Taiwan are indeed money-crazy. Thus to them, development means economic development period. There are few references to human development.

162

PRC and Taiwanese Contrasts: Society Forging Ahead versus Struggling to Succeed. The societal or collective aspect of development is far more important to the Mainlanders than it is for the Taiwanese. The Mainlanders think in terms of forging ahead, while the Taiwanese view the process as a struggle. Industry is significant for both groups, agriculture is a concern only for the Mainlanders, and commerce is mentioned only by the Taiwanese. Again, this has to do with the types of communities that Mainland and Taiwan represent respectively. Knowledge, in the context of development, is more significant to the Taiwanese. Success, an important aspect of development for the Taiwanese, is not even mentioned by the Mainlanders. The notion that speed in development is important to overcome backwardness is far stronger among the Mainlanders than among the Taiwanese. Science receives somewhat more emphasis than technology among the Mainlanders, while the reverse is true for the Taiwanese. Seeing development in terms of the economy and the future is a more prevalent view among the Taiwanese than among the Mainlanders.

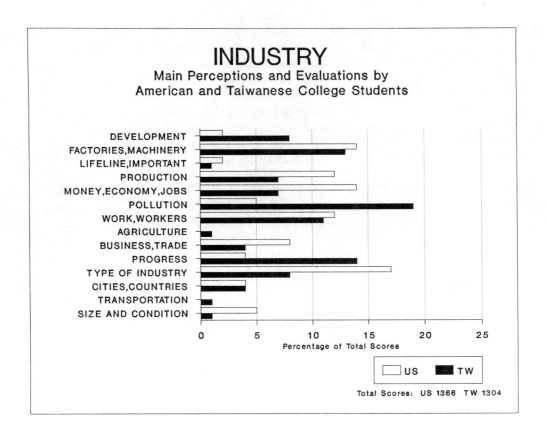

INDUSTRY
Main Perceptions and Evaluations by
American and Taiwanese College Students

Total Scores: US 1366 TW 1304

American View: Fantasies, Money, Business. Fantasies, money, and the mass production are what Americans think of when industry is mentioned. The manufacture or production of cars, as well as labor unions, are important facets of the mental picture of industry. Business is also a significant aspect. There is some concern about pollution, especially through smoke.

Taiwanese View: Pollution and Progress. Nothing about industry impresses the Taiwanese as much as does pollution -- especially of the air. More than one-fifth of all Taiwanese responses relate to pollution -- a far greater emphasis than that of the other two groups put together. Progress, particularly in science and technology, also predominates in Taiwanese thinking about industry. To neither of the other two groups is progress nearly as important. The steel industry is the segment which receives the greatest attention. The manufacture of products is part of the picture, but a bigger part consists of workers. Machines, the economy, and development (including the industrial revolution) are the remaining important facets of industry for the Taiwanese.

American and Taiwanese Contrasts: Labor Unions versus Machines and Workers. Cars and labor unions are an important part of the American image of industry but not for the Taiwanese. The latter are much more concerned about pollution - especially by smoke. Money is much more significant to Americans than to Taiwanese in their view of industry. The disparity regarding business is also large. Both groups think of location, but the Taiwanese think in terms of nations, while Americans picture cities, especially Detroit and Pittsburgh. Progress and technology are far more significant to the Taiwanese than to Americans. Workers, their welfare, and their relation to capital and their boss receive Taiwanese attention; but, unlike Americans, Taiwanese do not think of labor unions. The power of labor unions in Taiwan is still negligible. In local elections, "laborer" candidates were not supported even by their fellow laborers, not to mention other constituents. Machines are mentioned far more by Taiwanese than by Americans.

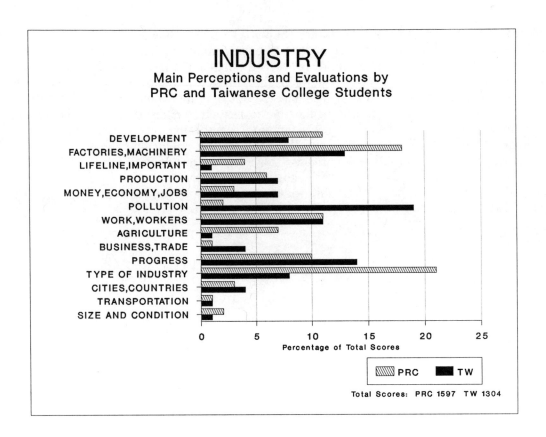

INDUSTRY
Main Perceptions and Evaluations by PRC and Taiwanese College Students

DEVELOPMENT
FACTORIES,MACHINERY
LIFELINE,IMPORTANT
PRODUCTION
MONEY,ECONOMY,JOBS
POLLUTION
WORK,WORKERS
AGRICULTURE
BUSINESS,TRADE
PROGRESS
TYPE OF INDUSTRY
CITIES,COUNTRIES
TRANSPORTATION
SIZE AND CONDITION

0   5   10   15   20   25
Percentage of Total Scores

PRC   TW

Total Scores: PRC 1597 TW 1304

PRC Chinese View: Iron and Steel. Heavy industry, especially iron and steel, dominate the Mainlander image of industry. Light industry also receives considerable attention. The automobile and petroleum industries receive significant mention. In regard to work and workers, workers are, for Mainlanders, a more important part of the picture, by far, compared to the other two groups. In comparison with the intellectuals, workers and farmers are the main contributors to the advancement of socialism -- according to the Communist ideology. The same holds true for agriculture, machinery, and development. Also, more than the other groups, Mainlanders consider industry an important lifeline of the country.

Taiwanese View: Pollution and Progress. Nothing about industry impresses the Taiwanese as much as does pollution -- especially of the air. More than one-fifth of all Taiwanese responses relate to pollution -- a far greater emphasis than that of the other two groups put together. Progress, particularly in science and technology, also predominates in Taiwanese thinking about industry. To neither of the other two groups is progress nearly as important. The steel industry is the segment which receives the greatest attention. The manufacture of products is part of the picture, but a bigger part consists of workers. Machines, the economy, and development (including the industrial revolution) are the remaining important facets of industry for the Taiwanese.

PRC and Taiwanese Contrasts: Iron and Machinery versus Pollution and Progress. For The Mainlanders show almost no concern about pollution whereas it is a major preoccupation among the Taiwanese. Production is about equally significant to both. Factories and machinery are more important to the Mainlanders, as is development. The workers are more strongly connected to industry by the Mainlanders than the Taiwanese. Money is not mentioned by the Mainlanders. In a Communist country workers have fixed pay in most cases. No matter how hard they work, their payment is the same. Agriculture is of great importance to the Mainlanders and of little interest to the Taiwanese.

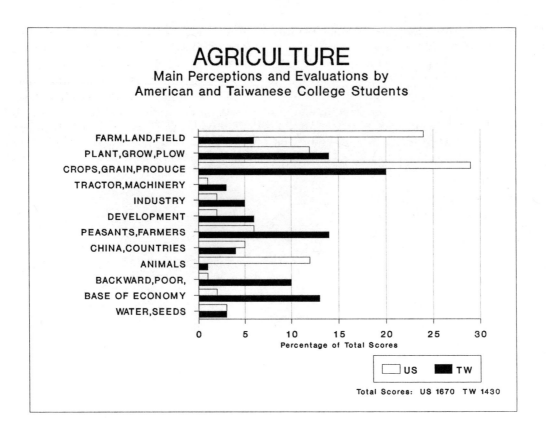

AGRICULTURE
Main Perceptions and Evaluations by
American and Taiwanese College Students

Percentage of Total Scores

US   TW

Total Scores: US 1670 TW 1430

American View: Farms, Food. More than one-fourth of the American image of agriculture consists of food and other crops. Another quarter has to do with farms, land, fields, and similar mental pictures. Activities, such as farming, plowing, growing, and harvesting is the next largest component, followed closely by animals, horses, and pigs. The only other facets of significance for Americans deal with geographic location such as rural, Midwest, Iowa, and Africa; and farmers.

Taiwanese View: Farmers, Peasants, Rice. While not as frequently thought of among the Taiwanese as among the other two groups, food and crops make up the single most significant component of agriculture also for them. Rice, wheat, vegetables, and fruit are the main crops mentioned. The farmers and peasants, and their activities, are the only other sizable facet in the Taiwanese picture of agriculture. Toil, plowing, and harvesting are the principal activities. There is a strong Taiwanese thought that agriculture was the "basis for the founding of the nation." Virtually unique to the Taiwanese perception are the thoughts that agriculture is backward, but also exploited and victimized.

American and Taiwanese Contrasts: Farms and Cows versus Toiling Peasants. Food and crops are a much larger part of the picture for Americans than for Taiwanese. An even greater disparity exists in the importance farms and land have in the American perception. Perhaps the greatest disparity is the virtual absence of animals among Taiwanese responses; while for Americans, cows, animals, horses, pigs, and barns are all significant. The Taiwanese see agriculture as a strong part of their history and economic development; Americans do not. Americans also do not share the view that agriculture is backward or exploited. As noted previously, Taiwan is now undergoing many changes. What was formerly an agricultural society is now almost totally industrialized. Thus people have mixed feelings about agriculture. Farmers nowadays are generally poorer than other people.

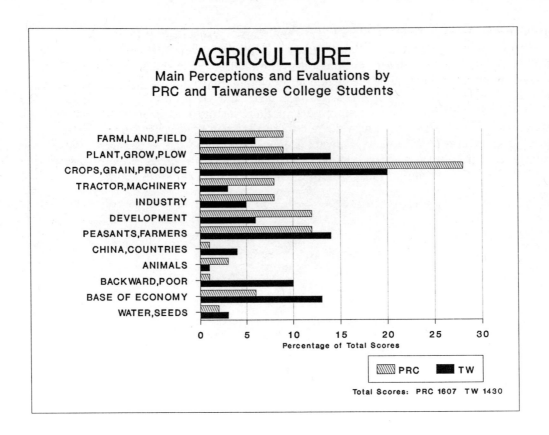

PRC Chinese View: Grain and Industry. Grain crops, especially rice and wheat, account for more than a quarter of the Mainlander image of agriculture. Farmers are next in importance. Development, technology, and industry are other very important aspects, as are farming activities. Tractors and machinery are significant symbols of progress and development in the field of agriculture.

Taiwanese View: Farmers, Peasants, Rice. While not as frequently thought of among the Taiwanese as among the other two groups, food and crops make up the single most significant component of agriculture also for them. Rice, wheat, vegetables, and fruit are the main crops mentioned. The farmers and peasants, and their activities, are the only other sizable facet in the Taiwanese picture of agriculture. Toil, plowing, and harvesting are the principal activities. There is a strong Taiwanese and the thoughts that agriculture was the "basis for the founding of the nation." Virtually unique to the Taiwanese perception are the thoughts that agriculture is backward, but also exploited and victimized.

PRC and Taiwanese Contrasts: Wheat and Tractors versus Toil and Plowing. Grain, crops, wheat, corn and oil crops are much more frequently thought of by Mainlanders than by Taiwanese. Of the various crops mentioned, rice and fruit occur more frequently to the Taiwanese. Livestock is mentioned more frequently by the Mainlanders. In regard to farm lands, earth, fields, and the countryside are mentioned more by the Taiwanese, while concepts related to development and technology are much more typical of the Mainlanders. Tractors and machines are more a part of the Mainlander view, while references to the toil and labor involved in farming are much more prominent in the Taiwanese imagery of agriculture. In this case, it appears that each group is much more aware of what is objectively lacking. Taiwanese agriculture is more productive and advanced technologically than is that on Mainland China. Taiwanese farmers have for decades had access to credit, chemicals, and farm machinery that are only now beginning to appear in Mainland agriculture. It seems that aspects of agriculture which the Taiwanese have long taken for granted are now very important in the subjective world of the Mainlanders. Taiwanese, in reference to agriculture, mention poor, victims, and exploitation. Mainlanders do not.

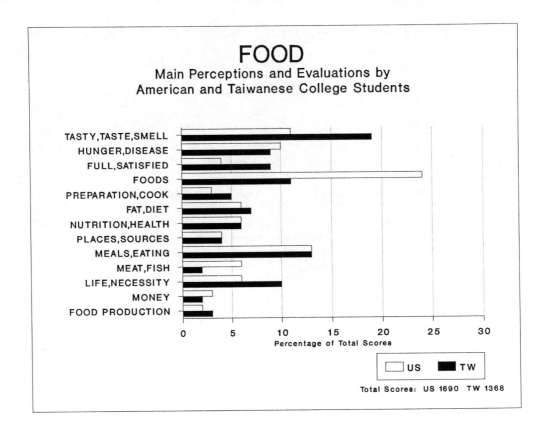

FOOD
Main Perceptions and Evaluations by
American and Taiwanese College Students

Total Scores: US 1690 TW 1368

American View: Hunger, Fruit, Junk. Of the three groups, Americans think of the greatest variety of foods, cuisine, and dishes. Chinese, Italian, and Mexican cuisine are mentioned, the first of these with by far the greatest frequency. Terms related to eating and mealtimes are the next most frequently occurring set of responses, followed by descriptions related to taste, appearance and smell. Paradoxically, Americans are the ones with greatest awareness of hunger -- and Mainlanders with the least! Yet massive famine with millions dying occurred several times this century in Mainland China -- most recently in 1962. Americans, along with Taiwanese, show significant awareness of nutrition and health. Restaurants are mentioned in significant frequency only by Americans. Meat, steak, and hamburger are part of the American picture.

Taiwanese View: Delicious, Necessity. The taste and smell of food is significantly more important to the Taiwanese than to the other two groups and no other aspect of food is so significant to them. Yet they mention relatively few foods, placing their greatest attention on fruit, bread, and rice. Far more than the others, Taiwanese consider food a necessity to keep living -- yet neither of the other groups places more stress on the need to diet and watch fat. Places where food is obtained are as important to them as to Americans -- and they too mention supermarkets.

172

American and Taiwanese Contrasts: Hunger versus Necessity. Of the three groups, Americans think of the greatest variety of foods, and the Taiwanese the smallest. Eating appears to be equally important to both, but taste and smell are far more significant to the Taiwanese. The latter are more emphatic about food being a necessity of life. They also think of being full and satisfied far more frequently than Americans. Awareness of fat in the diet is relatively more conspicuous among Taiwanese. Restaurants are more likely to occur to Americans than to the Taiwanese.

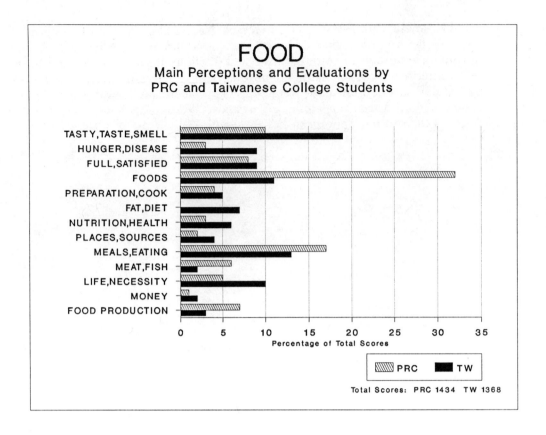

FOOD
Main Perceptions and Evaluations by
PRC and Taiwanese College Students

PRC Chinese View: Eat Rice. For Mainlanders, nearly a third of their responses refer to a variety of different foods and dishes headed by bread, rice, fruit, grain, vegetables, and cake. To no group is eating more important. In contrast to the other two groups, Mainlanders show no interest in diet, fat, or calories. Nutrition and health are of marginal interest in the context of food. That famine does not, and starvation and hunger hardly, appear among Mainlander responses might possibly be due to the fact that the student sample is too young to have a memory of the 1960-62 famine - and to the fact that government control over the mass media has prevented its mention. Places where food is obtained are barely mentioned. Money has the least interest for this group, in the context of food.

Taiwanese View: Delicious, Necessity. The taste and smell of food is significantly more important to the Taiwanese than to the other two groups and no other aspect of food is so significant to them. Yet they mention relatively few foods, placing their greatest attention on fruit, bread, and rice. Far more than the others, Taiwanese consider food a necessity to keep living -- yet neither of the other groups places more stress on the need to diet and watch fat. Places where food is obtained are as important to them as to Americans - and they too mention supermarkets. All this shows that Taiwan is very much influenced by Americans.

PRC and Taiwanese Contrasts: Variety versus Taste. The Mainlanders give a lot more attention to the variety of foods available. Eating is about equally significant to both groups, but taste and smell are mentioned more frequently by the Taiwanese. Although bread, rice, fruit, cake, and eggs are mentioned more frequently by the Mainlanders, it is likely that most of these foods are eaten more frequently by the Taiwanese, who enjoy a much higher standard of living. The Taiwanese are more likely to consider food a necessity of life. That famine, starvation, and hunger are stronger in the awareness of the Taiwanese than Mainlanders may be more of a reflection of what each group of students has read than the historical experience of these two parts of China. The Taiwanese concern with fat in the diet does not appear among Mainlander responses.

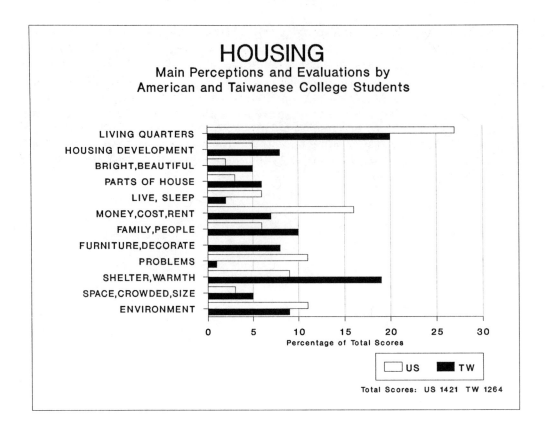

HOUSING
Main Perceptions and Evaluations by
American and Taiwanese College Students

Percentage of Total Scores

US   TW

Total Scores: US 1421 TW 1264

American View: Dorms, Campus, Expensive. More than a quarter of the American mental picture of housing consists of living quarters: dorms, apartments, home, house, etc. Much more than the Chinese groups, Americans are likely to consider housing expensive and be concerned about having money for rent. Also, more than the other groups, Americans show awareness of problems of housing for the homeless and poor. The concept of shelter is more significant to them than to the others. Housing development by the government is also a unique American perception in this context. Living and sleeping are mentioned by all three groups, but significantly more frequently by Americans. The housing environment pictured by the students is predominantly campus-related.

Taiwanese View: Comfortable Family Dwelling. Living quarters, for the Taiwanese, comprise more than a fifth of the housing image. Dwelling, villa, and home are most frequently pictured; apartment, mansion, and building occur far less frequently. They expect a warm, comfortable shelter. Much more than the other two groups, the Taiwanese think of housing in the context of family. Housing that is spacious and contains a yard and garden prominently occupies Taiwanese thinking. The scarcity of land and space makes many people dream of living in a spacious area with their families. The reality is that Taiwan is a small island with a great shortage of space for a dense population of 1600 persons per square mile [by comparison, the US has 60] which has doubled in the past three decades. They also express concern about the cost of housing. Furniture and decoration are also frequently occurring thoughts. In regard to housing development, the construction or building process attracts more attention from the Taiwanese than the two other groups.

176

American and Taiwanese Contrasts: Expensive Dorm versus Villa with Garden. For both groups, living quarters is the most important component, but it is more important to Americans, who think primarily of dorms, and apartments. Taiwanese visualize a spacious dwelling, or even a villa, as housing. That housing is expensive is the second most dominant thought for Americans, while for Taiwanese it is the thought of a warm, comfortable shelter - in a family setting. Problems of the homeless and poor significantly preoccupy American thinking, but not Taiwanese. Likewise, the government role in housing development is noted by Americans but not Taiwanese. Generally speaking, the Taiwanese people are skeptical about the quality of government-supported housing plans. Housing is thought of in relation to living much more frequently by Americans.

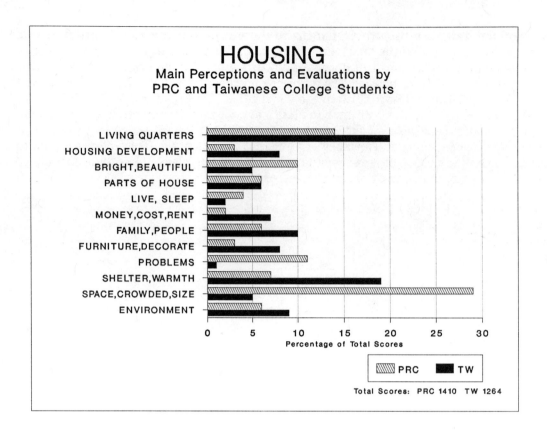

PRC Chinese View: Crowded Building. For the Mainlanders, nothing is more crucial than whether housing is spacious or crowded --- whether it is large or small. Next in importance is the issue of whether the living quarters are in a storied building, a mansion, a one-story house, a thatched cottage, or a hostel. Housing being bright and beautiful is another important aspect. More than the others, Mainlanders think of parts of the dwelling, and, in contrast to the thinking of the others, the bedroom is the most important, followed by the kitchen.

Taiwanese View: Comfortable Family Dwelling. Living quarters, for the Taiwanese, comprise more than a fifth of the housing image. Dwelling, villa, and home are most frequently pictured; apartment, mansion, and building occur far less frequently. They expect a warm, comfortable shelter. Much more than the other two groups, the Taiwanese think of housing in the context of family. Housing that is spacious and contains a yard and garden prominently occupies Taiwanese thinking. The scarcity of land and space makes many people dream of living in a spacious area with their families. The reality is that Taiwan is a small island with a great shortage of space for a dense population of 1600 persons per square mile [by comparison, the US has 60] which has doubled in the past three decades. They also express concern about the cost of housing. Furniture and decoration are also frequently occurring thoughts. In regard to housing development, the construction or building process attracts more attention from the Taiwanese than the two other groups.

PRC and Taiwanese Contrasts: Size and Brightness versus Warmth and Security. In the context of housing, similarities are more conspicuous than contrasts. The type of living quarters, whether villa, mansion, or storied building is important in both images. The environment has similar significance. Both give significance to housing being beautiful and clean -- though here Mainlanders emphasize this more. Furniture and decoration occur more frequently to the Taiwanese, as does family. In contrast to Mainlander thinking about parts of the house, the bedroom is not even mentioned by the Taiwanese, and the kitchen is mentioned less frequently. Ironically, most Taiwanese urban families have their own kitchen, while, as a rule, their counterparts on the Mainland have to share one with their neighbors. Regarding problems, the Mainlanders mention that housing is "in short supply," while the Taiwanese are concerned with the amount of money spent on expensive rent. While the environment the Taiwanese visualize includes a yard and garden, shade trees, and swimming pool, the Mainlanders apparently do not aspire to such a level of life-style. In Taiwan, people often consider themselves to be living in Heaven, and the mainlanders in Hell.

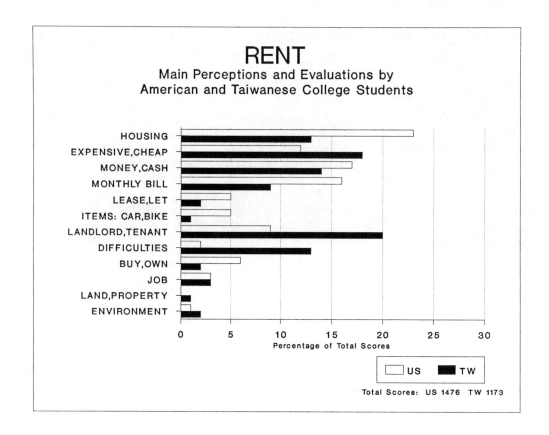

RENT
Main Perceptions and Evaluations by
American and Taiwanese College Students

American View: Money, Apartment. Nothing enters the American mind more often, in response to rent, than housing. Money is the next largest component. Regarding the type of housing, the American students think first of apartments and then of houses. Monthly payment is a strong concern, reflected in the notion that rent is expensive. Americans weigh owning or buying as an alternative to renting. They also frequently consider renting cars. An American's rent is, in his mind, connected with his job.

Taiwanese View: Landlord, Expensive. Of the three groups, the Taiwanese are clearly the most negatively disposed toward rent. Neither of the other groups feel as strongly as the Taiwanese that rent is expensive. The Taiwanese list many difficulties associated with renting. The landlord is a much more predominant figure for the Taiwanese than for either of the other groups. Bad landlords head the list of troubles. Within the context of difficulties rent is frequently seen as a burden. Bad landlords head the list of troubles. The Taiwanese are inclined to consider the rent they pay as irrational exploitation and poor treatment. This happens more so in Taipei than in any other part of Taiwan.

180

American and Taiwanese Contrasts: Money Monthly versus Expensive Burden. Money is more often thought of by Americans, while landlords, including bad ones, occupy Taiwanese thinking. Americans are more likely to think of rent for an apartment than for a house, while Taiwanese think most often of a house. Compared to most Americans, Taiwanese think that rent is expensive -- and they are very much more likely to be preoccupied with difficulties. The monthly bill plays a much bigger part in the American awareness, compared to the Taiwanese. While Americans think frequently of renting cars, this does not occur to the Taiwanese.

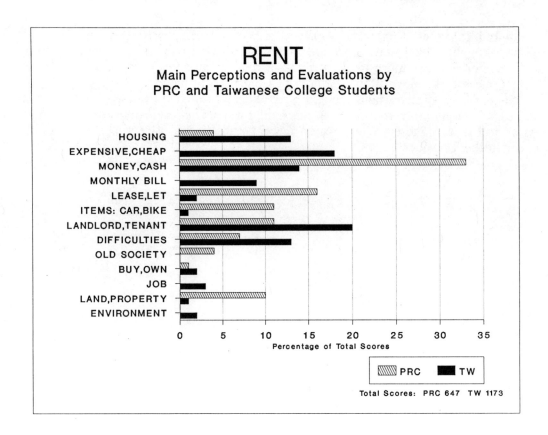

PRC Chinese View: Borrow, Money. Rent did not elicit many responses from the PRC Chinese, indicating it has little importance in meaning. Most of its meaning has to do with money, including the borrowing of it. Landlords play a major role and the notion of renting land are also mentioned most by this group. Mainlanders also think of renting things such as cameras, goods, and bicycles.

Taiwanese View: Landlord, Expensive. Of the three groups, the Taiwanese are clearly the most negatively disposed toward rent. Neither of the other groups feel as strongly as the Taiwanese that rent is expensive. The Taiwanese list many difficulties associated with renting. The landlord is a much more predominant figure for the Taiwanese than for either of the other groups. Bad landlords head the list of troubles. Within the context of difficulties rent is frequently seen as a burden. Bad landlords head the list of troubles. The Taiwanese are inclined to consider the rent they pay as irrational exploitation and poor treatment. This happens more so in Taipei than in any other part of Taiwan.

PRC and Taiwanese Contrasts: Money and Land versus Landlords and Expensive Burden.
Money is a far bigger part of the Mainlanders' perception of rent, while landlords figure more prominently in the Taiwanese perception. The Taiwanese extreme concern is with to cost, indicating that rent is very expensive, is totally absent among the Mainlanders. Burden, bad landlord, and trouble are significant difficulties of renting for Taiwanese but are not mentioned by the Mainlanders. The same holds true for monthly payments. Land rent is an important concept for Mainlanders but is virtually non-existent for the Taiwanese. The latter also link rent to job and salary, neither of which occurs to the Mainlanders.

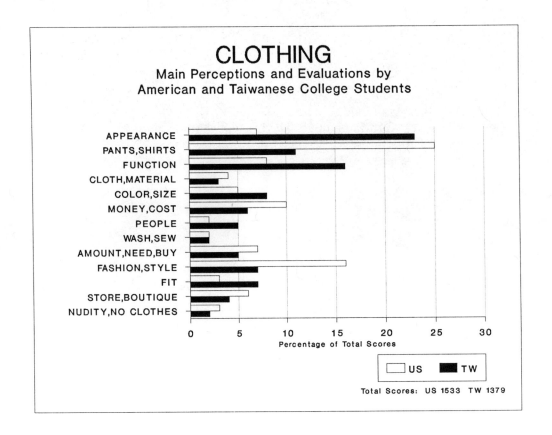

American View: Fashion, Expense. Much of the American image of clothing consists of different items, especially shirts, pants, shoes, jeans, dresses, sweaters, socks, and underwear. Fashion is a very important consideration. This is followed by cost. Stores and shops make up the only other significant component of clothing for Americans.

Taiwanese View: Nice Looking, Warmth. A large part of the Taiwanese image of clothing has to do with beauty and appearance. Next in importance is its function -- especially warmth and heat preservation. At first glance this would seem odd on an island with subtropical climate which is located on the Tropic of Cancer. Yet the northern part of the island, which is the most heavily populated, receives relatively little sunshine, and has an average temperature of under 60 degrees Fahrenheit for two or three months of the year. Since most houses are not heated, clothing fulfills an important function in heat preservation. The third most significant is the component listing kinds of clothing and accessories. Color and shape are also important factors. Fashion comes only in fourth place for the Taiwanese. This is followed by comfortable fit. They think of boutiques and department stores as places to do their shopping.

American and Taiwanese Contrasts: Fashion and Cost versus Beauty and Warmth. The two most important aspects of clothing to Americans, types of clothes and fashion, come in third and fourth place respectively for the Taiwanese. On the other hand, beauty and function, which are the two most important aspects for the Taiwanese, matter very little to Americans. Cost, which is a very important aspect of clothing to Americans, is less a concern to the Taiwanese. The Taiwanese strongly believe that clothing makes the man. They prefer eating cheap food to wearing cheap clothes.

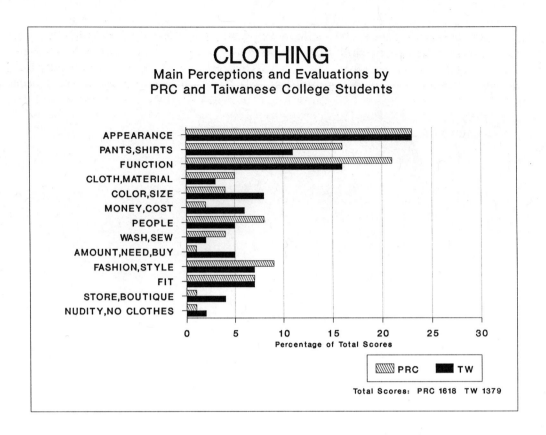

CLOTHING
Main Perceptions and Evaluations by
PRC and Taiwanese College Students

Percentage of Total Scores

PRC   TW

Total Scores: PRC 1618 TW 1379

PRC Chinese View: Beauty and Function. Mainlanders give equal importance to beauty and function as the most important aspects of clothing. "Beautiful" is by far the most frequent description to clothing. "Heat preservation" is second. The third most important component, as in the case of Taiwanese, consists of various kinds of clothing, beginning with jacket, pants, and overcoat. Fashion comes in fourth place, beginning with Western clothes, Chinese clothes, and whatever is in vogue. Color is also important to the Mainlanders as well as fit and material. The maintenance of clothing, cleaning, and washing, is more in the minds of the other two groups.

Taiwanese View: Nice Looking, Warmth. A large part of the Taiwanese image of clothing has to do with beauty and appearance. Next in importance is its function -- especially warmth and heat preservation. At first glance this would seem odd on an island with subtropical climate which is located on the Tropic of Cancer. Yet the northern part of the island, which is the most heavily populated, receives relatively little sunshine, and has an average temperature of under 60 degrees Fahrenheit for two or three months of the year. Since most houses are not heated, clothing fulfills an important function in heat preservation. The third most significant is the component listing kinds of clothing and accessories. Color and shape are also important factors. Fashion comes only in fourth place for the Taiwanese. This is followed by comfortable fit. They think of boutiques and department stores as places to do their shopping.

PRC and Taiwanese Contrasts: Tasteful versus Comfortable. There is very little difference in the subjective meaning of clothing for the two Chinese groups. Beauty is about equally important to the Mainlanders and Taiwanese. Function, dominated by the notion of heat preservation, is emphasized more by the PRC Chinese. Color and fit are of about equal importance to both groups as well. The Mainlanders show more awareness of Western and Chinese styles than do the Taiwanese.

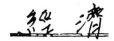

ECONOMY
MAIN COMPONENTS AND RESPONSES

MONEY, TRADING, BANKING	US	PRC	TW
	289	162	411
money	165	67	140
trade,trading	7	14	73
Wall Street	16	-	-
save,savings	15	7	-
stock market	11	-	7
price,s	10	-	-
spend,buy	10	-	-
exchange	8	-	-
gold	8	-	-
interest rate	7	-	-
power	7	-	-
credit	6	-	-
monetary	6	-	-
dollars	4	-	-
bonds	4	-	-
status	3	7	2
wealth,wealthy	2	19	27
store	-	25	-
finance	-	10	9
fund	-	5	-
banking,bank	-	4	9
pay	-	4	-
stock	-	-	46
foreign exchange	-	-	24
investment	-	-	14
expense	-	-	14
tycoon	-	-	12
accumulate	-	-	9
index	-	-	7
U.S. dollars	-	-	6
poor, rich	-	-	5
profit	-	-	4
Taiwan dollar	-	-	3

DEVELOPMENT, SCIENCE	US	PRC	TW
	11	259	56
high	11	-	-
developed	-	100	31
development	-	97	7
level	-	16	-
science	-	13	-
develop economy	-	13	-
science and technology	-	12	14
make progress	-	5	-
develop vigorously	-	3	-
technological people	-	-	4

INDUSTRY,AGRIC,COMMERCE	US	PRC	TW
	127	266	182
business	35	8	-
oil	14	8	-
supply	14	-	-
car,s	12	-	-
export,s	11	-	12
import,s	10	-	8
production force	7	5	-
sales	7	-	-
energy	7	-	-
industry	5	56	20
wheat	5	-	-
agriculture	-	52	1
merchandise	-	17	12
production	-	16	6
commerce	-	15	31
circulation	-	15	-
market	-	11	5
light industry	-	11	-
grain	-	10	-
factory	-	8	-
non-staple food	-	7	-
heavy industry	-	7	-
property	-	6	4
farmer	-	4	-
rice	-	4	-
enterprise	-	3	-
product	-	3	-
resources	-	-	22
industry and commerce	-	-	14
farm products	-	-	7
surplus	-	-	7
land speculation	-	-	6
corporation	-	-	6
commercial	-	-	5
protectionism	-	-	5
finish business	-	-	4
businessman	-	-	4
weaving business	-	-	3

INFLATION,RECESSION	US	PRC	TW
	264	16	58
inflation	108	-	15
recession	101	-	2
depression	49	16	25
repression	6	-	-
deficit	-	-	16

GOVERNMENT, POLITICS	US	PRC	TW
	118	142	60
politics	31	36	16
Carter	29	-	-
government	27	-	8
GNP	13	-	-
policy	9	-	16
Congress	5	-	-
political economics	4	81	-
national defense	-	10	-
military affairs	-	6	4
war	-	6	-
law	-	3	5
diplomatic negotiation	-	-	8
authority	-	-	3

SOCIETY, COUNTRY	US	PRC	TW
	32	73	60
ours	9	-	-
country	8	15	4
U.S.A.	8	-	14
nation	7	-	-
China	-	13	-
relationship	-	13	-
national	-	12	-
culture	-	9	-
Japan	-	6	4
society	-	5	12
Taiwan	-	-	16
super country	-	-	5
building (a country)	-	-	5

LIVELIHOOD,JOBS	US	PRC	TW
	47	94	100
job,s	20	2	11
employment,work	14	-	-
people	7	9	-
family	6	-	-
living,livelihood	-	39	-
living standard	-	22	3
income	-	16	-
labor	-	3	5
wages	-	3	-
living life	-	-	23
people's livelihood	-	-	17
earn money	-	-	16
worker	-	-	11
life	-	-	8
per capita income	-	-	6

POOR,BAD,CRISIS	US	PRC	TW
	216	66	63
poor	39	-	8
bad	38	-	-
downhill	17	-	-
unemployment	16	-	-
problem	16	-	-
tight	13	-	-
failing	11	-	-
falling	8	-	-
rough	7	-	-
messed up	7	-	-
weak	7	-	-
worsening	7	-	-
slump	7	-	-
welfare	7	-	-
unstable	6	-	-
poverty	5	-	-
crash	5	-	-
crisis	-	29	23
backward	-	27	-
undeveloped	-	10	-
exploit	-	-	13
fragile economy	-	-	6
shrink	-	-	5
depreciation	-	-	4
losing job	-	-	4

ECONOMICS,SYSTEMS,THEORY	US	PRC	TW
	91	54	115
economics	24	38	-
system	18	-	-
capitalist	12	-	-
demand	12	-	-
books	7	-	2
course,s	7	-	-
graphs	7	-	-
supply and demand	4	-	8
information	-	12	-
study,ing	-	4	-
theory	-	-	31
economy system	-	-	27
economist	-	-	18
capitalism	-	-	14
knowledge	-	-	8
mathematics	-	-	7

PROSPEROUS,LIFEBLOOD	US	PRC	TW
	49	184	110
sound	10	-	-
growth	9	-	4
rich	8	-	34
help	8	-	-
rising	6	-	-
freedom	4	-	4
size	4	-	-
prosperous	-	57	33
lifeblood of country	-	42	-
beneficial result	-	20	-
lifeblood	-	15	-
important	-	12	15
lifeline of society	-	12	-
proportion	-	6	-
growth rate	-	6	-
benefit	-	6	-
unite	-	5	-
great	-	3	-
stable	-	-	10
necessary	-	-	6
good future	-	-	4

MANAGEMENT,BUDGET	US	PRC	TW
	81	136	59
budget	30	-	-
taxes	17	-	-
plan,ning	14	19	1
balance	11	-	-
complex	9	-	10
management	-	71	6
reform	-	16	1
four modernizations	-	10	-
make efforts	-	9	-
adjust	-	6	-
managment of economy	-	3	-
utilize	-	2	-
making improvement	-	-	13
use it smartly	-	-	7
to use	-	-	5
utilitarianism	-	-	3
control	-	-	5
influence	-	-	5
negotiation meeting	-	-	3

CHEAP	US	PRC	TW
	13	4	12
frugal	-	-	12
thrift	7	-	-
thrifty	3	-	-
miser	3	-	-
cheap	-	4	-

MISCELLANEOUS	US	PRC	TW
	19	8	24
talent person	-	2	-
traffic (communicate)	-	-	9
miracle	-	-	7
arabic numbers	-	-	7
sordid merchant	-	-	1
news	7	-	-
boring	7	-	-
expensive	5	-	-
manner	-	6	-

SUMMARY

Main Components	Percentage of Total Score		
	US	PRC	TW
MONEY,TRADING,BANKING	21	11	31
DEVELOPMENT,SCIENCE	1	18	4
INDUSTRY,AGRIC,COMMERCE	9	18	14
INFLATION,RECESSION	19	1	4
GOVERNMENT,POLITICS	9	10	5
SOCIETY,COUNTRY	2	5	5
LIVELIHOOD,JOBS	3	6	8
POOR,BAD,CRISIS	16	5	5
PROSPEROUS,LIFEBLOOD	4	13	8
ECONOMICS,SYSTEMS,THEORY	7	4	9
MANAGEMENT,BUDGET	6	9	5
CHEAP	1	0	1
MISCELLANEOUS	1	1	2
Total Scores	1357	1464	1310

DEVELOPMENT
MAIN COMPONENTS AND RESPONSES

ADVANCE,GROWTH,CHANGE	US	PRC	TW
	290	363	317
growth,grow	128	-	42
advance,d,advancement	30	202	157
change	23	12	-
improve,improvement	21	11	-
better	20	-	-
new	18	-	-
progress	17	-	12
expand,expansion	12	-	-
increase	11	6	-
occurrence	7	-	-
plan	3	-	26
developed,development	-	28	38
movement	-	16	-
enhance	-	14	-
take place	-	14	-
open up	-	12	-
Four modernizations	-	10	-
modernization	-	10	-
raise interest	-	9	-
reform	-	8	-
condition	-	6	-
in process	-	5	-
become larger,enlarge	-	-	28
new life	-	-	8
exciting	-	-	6

INDUSTRY,COMMERCE	US	PRC	TW
	30	128	67
land	25	-	-
industry	5	21	31
develop industry	-	29	-
agriculture	-	28	5
develop agriculture	-	23	-
production	-	13	-
factory	-	8	2
farmer	-	6	-
industry and commerce	-	-	16
management	-	-	5
man power	-	-	5
trading	-	-	3

ECONOMY	US	PRC	TW
	24	44	64
economy,economic	6	44	46
career	9	-	-
money	6	-	4
work	3	-	12
investment	-	-	2

COUNTRY,SOCIETY	US	PRC	TW
	117	180	101
country,s	48	32	15
city,s	24	-	-
community	17	-	-
Third World	16	-	-
society	5	42	25
civilization	5	14	5
government	2	-	1
how society developed	-	15	-
China	-	14	2
world	-	13	-
national defense	-	13	-
culture	-	8	3
motherland	-	8	-
peace	-	8	-
history	-	5	-
coastal city	-	5	-
mankind	-	3	-
human life	-	-	8
world system	-	-	6
national	-	-	6
Western World	-	-	5
military power	-	-	5
hegemony	-	-	5
bomb	-	-	5
war	-	-	4
U.S.A.	-	-	3
political	-	-	3

TECHNOLOGY,SCIENCE	US	PRC	TW
	30	75	35
technology	12	9	10
computers	5	-	-
research	5	-	-
machines	5	-	-
space	3	-	4
science	-	48	-
science and technology	-	13	13
rocket	-	5	-
scientist	-	-	5
airplane	-	-	3

LEARNING,KNOWLEDGE	US	PRC	TW
	128	35	52
learn,ing	31	-	-
mind	25	-	-
mental,intellectual	24	-	-
knowledge	14	5	25
experience	11	-	-
brain	11	-	-
school	5	-	-
creative	5	-	-
thought	2	5	-
education	-	12	-
literature and art	-	9	-
idea	-	4	-
I.Q.	-	-	12
school work	-	-	8
study	-	-	5
ability	-	-	2

FORGE AHEAD,UNDERTAKING	US	PRC	TW
	68	171	122
help	19	-	-
make	18	-	-
create	17	-	14
mold	5	-	-
courage	5	-	-
nurture	4	-	-
forge ahead	-	77	-
forward,push forward	-	19	-
direction	-	15	6
course	-	15	-
undertakings	-	9	19
motive force	-	9	-
extent	-	8	-
strive	-	6	-
level	-	6	-
make efforts	-	5	-
method	-	2	-
struggle	-	-	30
breakthrough	-	-	14
establish	-	-	8
opportunity	-	-	8
rising	-	-	7
desire	-	-	5
difficulty	-	-	4
pursuit	-	-	4
push	-	-	3

PROSPECT,FUTURE	US	PRC	TW
	25	59	74
future	9	16	27
people	9	11	-
necessity	7	-	-
prospect	-	21	12
interim	-	6	-
past	-	5	-
Communism	-	-	25
hope	-	-	10

SUCCESS,ACHIEVEMENT	US	PRC	TW
	26	51	79
important	11	-	-
achievement	8	6	23
good	7	5	-
prosperous	-	14	6
great	-	8	-
fine	-	8	-
wealthy,wealth	-	6	5
result	-	4	4
success	-	-	25
great nature	-	-	7
healthy	-	-	6
promote (reward)	-	-	3

PACE: SPEED,SLOW	US	PRC	TW
	25	161	74
poor	16	-	-
regression	7	-	-
control	2	-	-
speed	-	34	7
quick	-	20	-
backward	-	19	13
stop	-	15	-
prompt	-	15	-
slow	-	11	-
considerable	-	11	-
measure	-	9	-
stagnate	-	8	-
fall back	-	7	-
go backward	-	7	-
accelerate	-	5	-
exploitation,exploit	-	-	16
slowly	-	-	11
promptly	-	-	8
balance	-	-	8
frustration (setback)	-	-	4
defeat	-	-	4
limit	-	-	3

PHYSICAL, MATURITY	US	PRC	TW
	212	10	10
children	39	-	-
breast,s,bust	27	-	-
mature,maturity	27	-	-
physical	20	-	-
age	19	-	-
body	18	-	-
personal	17	-	-
sex	7	-	-
nature	7	-	-
chest	7	-	-
adult	6	-	-
old	5	-	-
muscles	4	-	-
hair	3	-	-
fetus	3	-	-
strength	3	-	-
grow up	-	10	-
mother	-	-	10

BUILDING,CONSTRUCTION	US	PRC	TW
	205	3	10
building,s	43	-	-
housing	39	-	-
house,s	32	-	-
build	30	-	-
apartments	13	-	-
homes	10	-	-
neighborhood	6	-	-
construction	8	3	-
project	8	-	-
build up	7	-	-
construct	6	-	-
concrete	3	-	-
urban area	-	-	10

PERSONAL DEVELOPMENT	US	PRC	TW
	7	41	76
live	4	-	-
trust	3	-	-
develop relationships	-	12	-
relationship	-	11	-
happy,ness	-	6	5
daily life	-	6	-
friendship	-	6	-
latent energy	-	-	18
person	-	-	18
love betw man and woman	-	-	17
character	-	-	10
moral	-	-	8

MISCELLANEOUS	US	PRC	TW
	33	21	27
film	20	-	-
event	7	-	-
news	6	-	-
sports	-	15	-
different colors	-	6	-
fresh	-	-	10
test	-	-	6
traffic	-	-	4
pollution	-	-	4
agree	-	-	3

SUMMARY

Main Components	Percentage of Total Score		
	US	PRC	TW
ADVANCE,GROWTH,CHANGE	24	27	29
INDUSTRY,COMMERCE	2	10	6
ECONOMY	2	3	6
COUNTRY,SOCIETY	10	13	9
TECHNOLOGY,SCIENCE	2	6	3
LEARNING,KNOWLEDGE	10	3	5
FORGE AHEAD,UNDERTAKING	6	13	11
PROSPECT,FUTURE	2	4	7
SUCCESS,ACHIEVEMENT	2	4	7
PACE: SPEED,SLOW	2	12	7
PHYSICAL, MATURITY	17	1	1
BUILDING,CONSTRUCTION	17	0	1
PERSONAL DEVELOPMENT	1	3	7
MISCELLANEOUS	3	2	2
Total Scores	1220	1342	1108

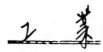

INDUSTRY
MAIN COMPONENTS AND RESPONSES

DEVELOPMENT	US	PRC	TW
	24	174	104
revolution	24	-	7
industrial revolution	-	6	25
development	-	70	28
developed	-	67	18
develop quickly	-	8	-
industry	-	8	-
four modernizations	-	7	-
position	-	5	-
development of society	-	3	-
construction	-	-	6
civilization	-	-	6
industrious	-	-	5
invention	-	-	5
industrialization	-	-	4

FACTORIES,MACHINERY	US	PRC	TW
	187	292	166
factory,s	151	132	77
machine,s,machinery	27	83	64
material	7	-	11
plant	2	-	-
factory building	-	30	-
metallurgy	-	13	-
working shop	-	12	-
raw material	-	11	-
equipment	-	8	-
tools	-	3	-
metal	-	-	7
water resources	-	-	7

LIFELINE,IMPORTANT	US	PRC	TW
	24	58	12
necessity,necessary	12	-	-
important	10	28	-
need	2	-	-
lifeline of the country	-	21	-
foundation	-	9	-
importance	-	-	10
backbone	-	-	2

PRODUCTION	US	PRC	TW
	169	91	92
manufacture	30	12	-
production	29	32	-
product,s	25	43	33
produce,productivity	11	-	-
assembly,line,s	18	-	-
mass production	15	-	-
markets	9	-	-
industrial	7	-	-
goods	7	-	-
make	7	-	-
build	4	-	-
marketing	7	-	-
annual total industry prod	-	4	-
manufacturer	-	-	28
man-day	-	-	27
production power	-	-	4

MONEY,ECONOMY,JOBS	US	PRC	TW
	192	53	91
money	71	-	12
job,s	53	-	4
economy	33	22	42
economics	12	-	-
capitalism	6	-	4
finance	4	-	-
profitable	4	-	-
profit	3	11	-
capital	3	-	-
government	3	-	-
backward	-	18	5
competition	-	2	-
capitalist	-	-	17
earn money	-	-	7

POLLUTION	US	PRC	TW
	72	24	250
pollution	48	20	132
smoke	19	-	3
dirty	5	-	-
noise	-	4	12
ecological prevention	-	-	29
chimney	-	-	24
air pollution	-	-	23
black smoke	-	-	12
public toxicants	-	-	6
waste material	-	-	3
smokeless industry	-	-	3
waste gas	-	-	3

WORK,WORKERS	US	PRC	TW
	168	181	139
union,s	34	-	-
labor	26	8	-
work	26	3	-
strike,s	12	-	-
people	11	-	-
worker,s	10	124	70
wage,s	10	10	-
blue collar	10	-	-
management	7	17	2
life	5	-	-
employees	5	-	-
toil	5	-	-
manager	4	-	-
man	3	-	-
factory director	-	7	-
leader	-	5	-
engineer	-	4	-
person	-	3	-
exploit	-	-	18
rel betw laborer & capital	-	-	11
boss	-	-	10
demonstration	-	-	8
protection of laborers	-	-	6
laborer's insurance	-	-	5
population	-	-	4
living	-	-	3
labor cost	-	-	2

AGRICULTURE	US	PRC	TW
	6	111	19
agriculture	6	104	19
relations to agriculture	-	7	-

PROGRESS	US	PRC	TW
	58	154	186
technology	21	3	4
progress	9	14	78
growth	9	-	4
future	7	7	-
rich	7	-	-
power	5	-	-
science and technology	-	26	49
modernization	-	26	16
advanced	-	23	-
reform	-	13	-
science	-	11	9
achievement	-	11	-
progress of society	-	8	-
present situation	-	7	-
great	-	4	-
property	-	1	-
wealth	-	-	10
upgrade	-	-	5
improving one's life	-	-	4
prosperous	-	-	4
research	-	-	3

TYPE OF INDUSTRY	US	PRC	TW
	234	335	106
car,s	51	-	-
automobile,auto	7	21	11
steel,industry	36	7	36
heavy,industry	25	56	-
clothes	18	-	-
coal	17	22	4
food	17	-	-
textile,industry	11	3	-
oil	10	-	5
cotton	8	-	-
computer,s	7	8	5
tobacco	7	-	-
music	7	-	-
time	6	-	-
iron	5	9	-
drugs	2	-	-
iron and steel,company	-	59	-
light industry	-	51	8
national defense	-	34	6
light and heavy industries	-	16	-
petroleum	-	15	-
modern industry	-	12	-
information	-	12	-
handicraft industry	-	10	-
petrochemical	-	-	10
weaving industry	-	-	5
ship building	-	-	5
knowledge	-	-	4
substance	-	-	4
electronics	-	-	3

BUSINESS,TRADE	US	PRC	TW
	103	14	56
business	71	-	-
company,s	13	-	-
trade	10	-	6
monopoly	5	-	-
export	4	-	13
enterprises	-	14	-
commerce	-	-	17
tycoon	-	-	8
businessman	-	-	5
import	-	-	4
international trade	-	-	3

CITIES,COUNTRIES,PLACES	US	PRC	TW
	56	48	48
city,s	17	10	4
Detroit	7	-	-
international	7	-	-
north	6	-	-
New Jersey	6	-	-
Pittsburgh	6	-	-
America	5	-	-
Japan	2	7	6
country	-	13	-
Shanghai	-	8	-
United States	-	4	-
society	-	3	10
motherland	-	3	-
nation	-	-	11
U.S.A.	-	-	9
England	-	-	6
industrial area	-	-	2

TRANSPORTATION	US	PRC	TW
	0	11	16
train	-	7	2
railway	-	4	-
transportation	-	-	5
river	-	-	4
shipment	-	-	3
truck	-	-	2

SIZE AND CONDITION	US	PRC	TW
	63	35	16
big	22	-	-
large	14	-	-
firm	10	-	-
hard	9	-	-
good	6	-	-
fast	2	-	-
undeveloped	-	10	-
huge	-	10	-
past	-	9	-
surprising	-	6	-
stronger	-	-	7
busy	-	-	5
boring	-	-	4

MISCELLANEOUS	US	PRC	TW
	10	16	3
Carnegie	10	-	-
third tide	-	9	-
mine	-	7	-
conflict	-	-	3

SUMMARY

Main Components	Percentage of Total Score		
	US	PRC	TW
DEVELOPMENT	2	11	8
FACTORIES,MACHINERY	14	18	13
LIFELINE,IMPORTANT	2	4	1
PRODUCTION	12	6	7
MONEY,ECONOMY,JOBS	14	3	7
POLLUTION	5	2	19
WORK,WORKERS	12	11	11
AGRICULTURE	0	7	1
BUSINESS,TRADE	8	1	4
PROGRESS	4	10	14
TYPE OF INDUSTRY	17	21	8
CITIES,COUNTRIES,PLACES	4	3	4
TRANSPORTATION	0	1	1
SIZE AND CONDITION	5	2	1
MISCELLANEOUS	1	1	0
Total Scores	1366	1597	1304

AGRICULTURE
MAIN COMPONENTS AND RESPONSES

FARM, LAND, FIELD	US 399	PRC 151	TW 84
farm,s farmland	250	-	-
land	52	-	23
field	30	34	26
country	19	7	-
soil	18	-	9
dirt	11	-	-
nature	10	-	-
environment	5	-	-
plain,s	4	-	3
earth	-	77	-
countryside	-	33	3
natural world	-	-	13
tillable land	-	-	5
flatland	-	-	2

PLANT,GROW,PLOW	203	152	196
farming	58	28	9
plow,ing	39	8	51
grow,growth,growing	59	-	-
harvest	19	9	20
planting	7	-	-
till	5	-	-
irrigation	5	-	-
hot	5	-	-
maintain	4	-	-
labor	2	17	15
good harvest	-	16	-
toil	-	11	66
sow	-	10	18
reap	-	9	-
cultivation	-	8	-
work	-	8	-
weeding	-	7	-
develop agricultural products	-	7	-
sweat	-	6	-
toilsome	-	4	-
develop agriculture	-	3	-
irrigation works	-	1	-
perspiration	-	-	12
hard-working	-	-	5

CROPS,GRAIN,PRODUCE	490	454	287
food	107	7	62
crop,s	100	67	27
corn	68	21	-
plant,s	39	-	2
grain	26	156	4
wheat	25	28	-
green	25	-	-
grass	23	-	-
produce	20	-	20
hay	15	-	-
flowers	10	-	-
rice	8	47	25
carrots	7	-	-
potatoes	6	-	-
tomatoes	5	-	-
vegetable,s	4	9	3
strawberries	2	-	-
eat	-	29	18
agriculture	-	14	11
Chinese sorghum	-	12	-
grains and oil crops	-	12	-
oil bean	-	10	-
cotton	-	9	-
peanut	-	8	-
grain ration	-	7	-
non stable food	-	6	-
meal	-	6	-
oil	-	4	-
fruit	-	2	-
wheat and rice	-	-	41
rice farm	-	-	24
vegetable and fruit	-	-	21
farm products	-	-	19
green color	-	-	10

TRACTOR,MACHINERY	11	124	43
tractor	11	35	-
machinization	-	27	28
machine	-	19	4
farming tools	-	8	-
farming machine	-	8	-
hoe	-	7	7
tools	-	7	-
machinery	-	5	-
automobile	-	5	-
factory	-	3	-
farming instrument	-	-	4

INDUSTRY	US 32	PRC 131	TW 72
department	11	-	-
industry	8	93	34
surplus	5	-	-
export	4	-	3
trade	2	-	-
business	2	-	-
production	-	14	-
commerce	-	10	-
contract	-	6	-
aircraft	-	6	-
traffic	-	2	-
Dept of Agriculture office	-	-	16
products and sales system	-	-	9
industrious	-	-	4
import	-	-	3
transportation	-	-	3

DEVELOPMENT,TECHNOLOGY	41	187	91
study	23	-	-
school	11	-	-
science	7	1	-
development	-	45	6
science and technology	-	27	17
modernization	-	27	3
developed	-	25	-
raw material	-	17	-
develop quickly	-	11	-
universal education	-	10	-
reform	-	10	-
responsibility	-	7	-
modern agriculture	-	4	-
knowledge	-	3	-
demonstration	-	-	17
improvement	-	-	14
over production	-	-	10
develop	-	-	8
help and advise	-	-	7
pursuit of progress	-	-	7
scientific	-	-	2

CHINA,COUNTRIES	83	13	62
rural	23	-	-
Midwest	19	-	-
Beltsville	15	-	-
west	7	-	-
Iowa	6	-	-
Africa	5	-	-
U.S.	4	-	-
Nebraska	4	-	-
village	-	10	33
nation	-	3	-
China	-	-	13
culture	-	-	7
society	-	-	4
government	-	-	3
Third World	-	-	2

ANIMALS	195	47	10
cow,s	72	20	-
animals	30	-	-
barn,s	25	-	-
horses	20	-	-
milk	16	-	-
pig,s	10	5	3
livestock	7	11	-
smell	7	-	-
sheep	5	3	-
chickens	3	-	-
meat	-	8	-
fowl (chicken, duck)	-	-	7

BACKWARD,POOR,EXPLOITED	24	23	136
poor	11	-	12
dirty	7	-	-
famine	2	-	3
foreclosure	2	-	-
boring	2	-	-
backward	-	23	33
exploited	-	-	27
low	-	-	16
victim	-	-	10
pollution	-	-	6
brain drain	-	-	6
little profit	-	-	6
pity	-	-	5
survive	-	-	5
underprivileged	-	-	4
hopeless	-	-	3

PEASANTS,FARMERS	US 96	PRC 186	TW 198
farmer,s	85	176	93
hicks	6	-	-
living	5	-	-
children	-	6	-
population	-	3	4
worker	-	1	-
peasants	-	-	76
human life (living)	-	-	20
people	-	-	5

BASE OF ECONOMY	41	99	190
need,ed	11	-	-
economy	8	-	16
necessary,ity	8	-	-
important	7	-	12
money	4	-	-
aid	3	-	-
base	-	30	-
national defense	-	28	-
fundamental	-	12	-
daily life	-	9	-
wealthy	-	9	-
prosperous	-	7	-
income	-	4	-
basis of founding nation	-	-	69
policy (land distribution)	-	-	21
important industry	-	-	16
tradition	-	-	10
old	-	-	8
protect	-	-	7
issue of livelihood	-	-	7
memory	-	-	6
rich	-	-	5
early history and Taiwan	-	-	5
history	-	-	5
revolution	-	-	3

WATER,SEEDS,FERTILIZER	53	26	45
water	15	-	3
seeds	10	-	-
manure	9	-	-
rain	7	-	4
fertilizer	6	6	4
weather	3	6	4
pests	3	-	-
chemical fertilizer	-	12	-
waterpower	-	2	-
liquid insecticide	-	-	10
resources	-	-	7
little stream	-	-	7
sun,light	-	-	4
dam	-	-	2

MISCELLANEOUS	2	14	16
4H	2	-	-
taking off of the agriculture	-	7	-
position	-	7	-
good heart	-	-	6
free	-	-	5
subtle	-	-	5

SUMMARY

Main Components	Percentage of Total Score		
	US	PRC	TW
FARM, LAND, FIELD	24	9	6
PLANT,GROW,PLOW	12	9	14
CROPS,GRAIN,PRODUCE	29	28	20
TRACTOR,MACHINERY	1	8	3
INDUSTRY	2	8	5
DEVELOPMENT,TECHNOLOGY	2	12	6
PEASANTS,FARMERS	6	12	14
CHINA,COUNTRIES	5	1	4
ANIMALS	12	3	1
BACKWARD,POOR,EXPLOITED	1	1	10
BASE OF ECONOMY	2	6	13
WATER,SEEDS,FERTILIZER	3	2	3
MISCELLANEOUS	0	1	1
Total Scores	1670	1607	1430

FOOD
MAIN COMPONENTS AND RESPONSES

TASTY,TASTE,SMELL	US	PRC	TW
	188	148	261
good	64	9	6
tasty,delicious	31	30	160
taste	15	-	-
hot	11	6	8
great	11	-	-
favorite	11	-	-
love	11	-	-
smell	8	-	-
gourmet	7	-	-
yum	6	-	-
happy	5	-	3
enjoy,enjoyable	6	-	-
exciting	2	-	-
appetizing	-	23	-
fragrant and sweet	-	20	-
sweet	-	15	7
sour	-	14	4
bitter	-	11	2
color	-	7	-
not delicious	-	7	-
color,taste,smell	-	6	16
enjoyment	-	-	14
delicate (beautiful)	-	-	11
wonderful	-	-	8
fragrance	-	-	7
desire	-	-	5
hard to resist	-	-	5
tasteless	-	-	5

HUNGER,DISEASE	US	PRC	TW
	168	49	117
hungry	102	12	24
hunger	32	16	19
starving,starvation	11	5	19
Ethiopia,Africa	7	-	11
distribution	7	-	-
disease	6	-	1
famine	3	-	12
go bad	-	8	-
rotten	-	8	-
refugee,famine refugee	-	-	13
waste	-	-	8
death	-	-	7
pains	-	-	3

FULL,SATISFIED	US	PRC	TW
	60	110	120
energy	16	10	18
lots,a lot	15	-	-
filling,full,be full	12	45	45
satisfaction,satisfying	7	-	31
always	5	-	-
intake	3	-	-
enough	2	-	-
allay one's hunger	-	31	5
digest	-	11	-
sufficient	-	7	-
absorb	-	6	-
abundant	-	-	17
picky about food	-	-	4

PREPARATION,COOKING	US	PRC	TW
	53	55	75
cook,-ed,-ing,-er	31	11	23
refrigerator	8	-	16
home	5	-	-
cold,cold dish	4	6	-
serve	3	-	-
microwave	2	-	-
oil	-	14	-
uncooked	-	11	-
process	-	9	-
person	-	4	-
ice	-	-	9
kitchen	-	-	7
fire	-	-	7
mother	-	-	7
return home	-	-	3
seasoning	-	-	3

FAT,DIET	US	PRC	TW
	105	0	90
fat	39	-	47
diet	28	-	20
calories	13	-	5
carbohydrates	7	-	-
skinny	5	-	-
excess	5	-	-
overweight	4	-	-
pig out	4	-	-
over eater	-	-	8
exercise	-	-	7
thin	-	-	3

FOODS	US	PRC	TW
	407	458	150
Chinese,Chinese food	71	-	6
pizza	57	-	-
fruit,s	34	44	27
Italian	24	-	-
ice cream	22	-	-
fast,fast food	19	-	7
junk,junk food	16	-	-
drink,beverage	14	20	8
spaghetti,lasagna,pasta	20	-	-
Mexican,tacos	14	-	-
bread	10	42	22
salad	10	-	-
sandwich	9	9	-
potatoes	9	-	-
rice,cooked rice	7	69	16
eggs	7	13	-
french fries	7	-	-
corn,popcorn	13	-	-
pretzels	6	-	-
sauce	6	-	-
cheese	5	-	-
cereal	5	-	-
milk	4	10	-
French	4	-	-
banana	4	-	-
vegetable,s	3	23	14
varied,variety	2	-	10
beer,wine	2	10	-
snack,food	3	5	7
grain	-	42	12
steamed bread	-	37	-
food	-	26	-
cake	-	23	1
flour	-	22	-
non-staple food	-	14	-
biscuit	-	9	-
candy	-	8	-
staple food	-	7	-
apple	-	7	-
melon seeds	-	6	-
western meal	-	6	-
sugar	-	6	-
chocolate	-	-	8
7-up	-	-	4
fluid	-	-	4
cookies	-	-	3
soup	-	-	1

NUTRITION,HEALTH	US	PRC	TW
	103	38	87
nutrition,nutrients	55	32	62
health,healthy	41	6	20
protein	7	-	-
vitamin	-	-	5

PLACES,SOURCES	US	PRC	TW
	66	25	49
restaurant,s	33	-	-
dining hall	9	7	14
grocery store	6	4	-
Safeway	5	-	-
co-op	5	-	-
market	4	-	-
shop,food shop	3	8	-
McDonald,'s	1	-	3
canteen	-	6	-
supermarket,night market	-	-	23
vendor	-	-	9

MEALS,EATING,UTENSILS	US	PRC	TW
	228	250	183
eat	128	145	111
dinner	35	-	4
lunch	24	-	8
breakfast	20	-	2
consume	7	-	-
plate	5	-	-
spoon,fork,knife	9	-	-
meal,eat a meal	-	68	-
dishes,bowl,s	-	35	3
chopstick	-	2	-
3 meals	-	-	11
eat rich	-	-	10
self-serve dinner	-	-	10
eat one's supper	-	-	9
moderate	-	-	8
food eaten betw meals	-	-	7

MEAT,FISH	US	PRC	TW
	108	91	23
meat	27	42	8
hamburger,burgers	21	-	-
steak ,beef	25	12	-
lobster,shrimp	11	-	-
chicken,leg	9	-	9
hot dog	7	-	-
ribs	6	-	-
fish,seafood	2	18	4
pork	-	10	-
aquatic,marine products	-	9	2

LIFE,NECESSITY	US	PRC	TW
	105	73	137
necessity,need,necessary	53	23	50
clothing	15	-	-
life,keep living	9	22	64
important	7	-	10
shelter	7	-	-
sustenance	7	-	-
survival	7	-	-
subsist	-	25	6
level	-	3	-
population	-	-	7

MONEY	US	PRC	TW
	47	11	22
money	25	8	12
stamps	8	-	-
buy	5	-	-
card	5	-	-
poverty,poor	4	3	6
price	-	-	4

FOOD PRODUCTION	US	PRC	TW
	28	103	36
farm,s,farmer	14	15	11
water	7	6	17
grow	7	-	-
production	-	17	-
animal	-	11	-
labor	-	8	-
work,worker	-	14	4
study	-	7	-
plant	-	6	-
source	-	5	-
man-made	-	5	-
country	-	5	-
tools	-	4	-
economize	-	-	4

MISCELLANEOUS	US	PRC	TW
	24	23	18
me	7	-	-
now	7	-	-
for thought	7	-	-
fight	3	-	-
save	-	8	-
poisoning	-	8	-
movement	-	7	-
stomach	-	-	6
God's gifts	-	-	5
clean the bowels	-	-	4
troublesome	-	-	3

SUMMARY

Main Components	Percentage of Total Score		
	US	PRC	TW
TASTY,TASTE,SMELL	11	10	19
HUNGER,DISEASE	10	3	9
FULL,SATISFIED	4	8	9
FOODS	24	32	11
PREPARATION,COOKING	3	4	5
FAT,DIET	6	0	7
NUTRITION,HEALTH	6	3	6
PLACES,SOURCES	4	2	4
MEALS,EATING,UTENSILS	13	17	13
MEAT,FISH	6	6	2
LIFE,NECESSITY	6	5	10
MONEY	3	1	2
FOOD PRODUCTION	2	7	3
MISCELLANEOUS	1	2	1
Total Scores	1690	1434	1368

HOUSING
MAIN COMPONENTS AND RESPONSES

LIVING QUARTERS	US	PRC	TW
	382	193	252
dorm,s,dormitory	114	-	-
apartment,s	81	-	10
home	65	3	55
house	25	46	7
project,s	20	-	-
condo,s	20	-	-
public	10	-	-
subsidized	8	-	-
building	7	-	10
dwelling	6	-	84
mansion	5	25	10
private	5	-	-
quarters	5	-	-
townhouse	3	-	-
temporary	3	-	-
tenement	3	-	-
cave	2	-	-
storied building	-	57	-
storied bldg,one-story	-	29	-
thatched cottage	-	9	-
hostel	-	9	-
tile-roofed house	-	6	-
hotel	-	5	-
level	-	4	-
villa	-	-	59
flat houses	-	-	9
log cabin	-	-	8

HOUSING DEVELOPMENT	US	PRC	TW
	75	45	98
development	32	-	-
government	12	-	-
build	8	9	-
HUD	7	-	-
brick	6	7	10
construction	5	-	-
structure	3	-	-
land	2	-	6
modernization	-	10	-
cement	-	8	11
reform	-	6	-
builder	-	5	-
building (construction)	-	-	30
properties	-	-	15
design	-	-	7
wall	-	-	6
steel	-	-	5
land speculation	-	-	5
repair	-	-	3

BRIGHT,BEAUTIFUL	US	PRC	TW
	23	140	57
clean	16	12	11
fun	7	-	-
bright	-	55	-
beautiful	-	26	12
commodious and bright	-	26	-
good	-	15	-
high class	-	6	-
fancy	-	-	12
neat	-	-	10
enjoy	-	-	8
happiness	-	-	4

PARTS OF HOUSE	US	PRC	TW
	47	84	70
room	16	10	8
roof	14	-	5
bathroom	5	6	-
suite	5	-	-
bedroom	4	18	-
utilities	3	-	-
kitchen	-	14	8
one room	-	10	-
drawing room	-	9	-
car	-	8	17
lavatory	-	6	-
tile	-	3	-
door and window	-	-	14
living room	-	-	4
balcony	-	-	4
window	-	-	4
chimney	-	-	4
toilet	-	-	2

LIVE, SLEEP	US	PRC	TW
	82	52	30
live,living	67	-	5
sleeping	15	4	10
daily life	-	21	-
dwell,live in	-	10	-
rest	-	5	8
study	-	5	4
settle	-	4	-
eat	-	3	-
live solitary existence	-	-	3

MONEY,COST,RENT	US	PRC	TW
	224	28	84
expensive	84	-	14
money	51	-	33
rent,house rent	29	15	16
low income	14	-	-
cheap	11	-	-
mortgage	7	-	-
lease	7	-	-
free	7	-	-
costs	6	-	-
own	5	-	-
loan	3	-	-
job	-	13	-
buy	-	-	7
real estate tax	-	-	5
insure	-	-	5
value	-	-	4

FAMILY,PEOPLE	US	PRC	TW
	87	79	130
people	15	-	-
friend,s	14	-	3
family	11	37	61
student	11	-	-
roommates	9	-	-
parents	7	-	12
landlord	7	-	-
girls	7	-	-
group	6	-	-
person	-	17	22
population	-	17	-
neighbor	-	8	2
wife,mother	-	-	12
children	-	-	10
me	-	-	5
dog	-	-	3

FURNITURE,DECORATE	US	PRC	TW
	7	49	99
furniture	4	11	19
decoration,decorate	3	-	19
bed	-	12	10
furnish and decorate	-	9	18
bed,table,chair	-	9	-
table	-	8	2
flowers	-	-	11
lights (lamps)	-	-	7
plants	-	-	6
chair	-	-	4
hi-fi stereo	-	-	3

PROBLEMS	US	PRC	TW
	151	152	10
problem,s	27	5	-
poor,poverty	25	-	-
homeless	21	-	-
in short supply,shortage	18	65	-
roaches,rats	12	-	-
bad	11	6	-
not enough	9	-	-
welfare	7	-	-
old	7	-	-
ugly	6	-	-
difficulty	4	10	-
asbestos	2	-	-
discrimination	2	-	-
worn,worn out	-	14	-
degree (quality)	-	13	-
living standard	-	8	-
dark	-	6	-
many	-	6	-
dirty	-	5	-
status	-	3	-
struggle	-	-	5
leaking	-	-	4
quarrel	-	-	1

SHELTER,WARMTH,SECURITY	US	PRC	TW
	124	96	244
shelter	35	-	59
protection	19	-	16
comfortable,comfort	15	50	42
necessary,need	15	-	-
warm,warmth	8	11	38
close	8	-	-
important	7	-	10
necessity	7	-	8
security	7	-	-
food	3	-	-
good cooking	-	12	-
advantageous	-	10	-
may keep out cold	-	7	-
dry	-	6	-
sense of security	-	-	23
safety	-	-	16
solid	-	-	15
lukewarm	-	-	13
convenient	-	-	4

SPACE,CROWDED,SIZE	US	PRC	TW
	41	403	64
crowded	11	96	4
big and tall	10	36	-
small	10	28	-
limited	7	-	-
spacious,space	3	98	42
large	-	53	-
size	-	28	18
narrow	-	27	-
broad	-	17	-
short	-	8	-
how many people	-	6	-
tiny	-	5	-
simple & crude	-	1	-

ENVIRONMENT	US	PRC	TW
	158	85	108
campus	48	-	-
off-campus	20	-	-
college	17	-	-
urban	14	-	-
on campus	13	-	-
new	10	7	-
slum,ghetto	10	-	-
school	9	-	-
environment	6	17	7
place	6	-	-
city	3	18	-
neighborhood	2	-	-
classroom	-	12	-
quiet	-	10	-
countryside	-	8	-
noise,and exciting	-	7	1
lawn	-	3	-
society	-	3	-
yard and garden	-	-	36
tree (maple)	-	-	12
shady	-	-	11
breezy	-	-	8
swimming pool	-	-	7
blocks	-	-	6
village	-	-	5
rocks	-	-	5
stream	-	-	4
geography and location	-	-	4
sea	-	-	2

MISCELLANEOUS	US	PRC	TW
	20	4	18
party,s	11	-	-
love	5	-	-
help	4	-	-
future	-	4	-
TV programs	-	-	11
dignity	-	-	7

SUMMARY

Main Components	Percentage of Total Score		
	US	PRC	TW
LIVING QUARTERS	27	14	20
HOUSING DEVELOPMENT	5	3	8
BRIGHT,BEAUTIFUL	2	10	5
PARTS OF HOUSE	3	6	6
LIVE, SLEEP	6	4	2
MONEY,COST,RENT	16	2	7
FAMILY,PEOPLE	6	6	10
FURNITURE,DECORATE	0	3	8
PROBLEMS	11	11	1
SHELTER,WARMTH,SECURITY	9	7	19
SPACE,CROWDED,SIZE	3	29	5
ENVIRONMENT	11	6	9
MISCELLANEOUS	1	0	1
Total Scores	1421	1410	1264

RENT
MAIN COMPONENTS AND RESPONSES

HOUSING	US	PRC	TW
HOUSING	340	28	150
apartment	184	-	4
house	88	15	37
housing	18	-	-
room	16	-	9
home	11	-	-
live	9	-	-
condo	5	-	-
space	5	-	-
move	4	-	-
rent a house	-	13	4
big or small (size)	-	-	21
facilities	-	-	18
campus	-	-	14
living,lived	-	-	14
moving to a new house	-	-	13
temporary residence	-	-	11
place	-	-	5

EXPENSIVE,CHEAP	US	PRC	TW
EXPENSIVE,CHEAP	182	0	216
expensive	88	-	143
high	30	-	-
cost	16	-	-
cheap	11	-	21
free	11	-	-
control	9	-	-
expense	7	-	-
rising	6	-	-
low	4	-	-
reasonable	-	-	21
price hike	-	-	10
bargaining	-	-	8
how much (money)	-	-	7
reducing the price	-	-	3
price	-	-	3

MONEY,CASH	US	PRC	TW
MONEY,CASH	258	212	159
money	187	86	115
borrow	36	67	2
check,s	16	-	-
loan	10	-	-
bank	5	-	7
credit	4	-	-
spend money	-	18	-
interest	-	14	4
repay	-	11	-
need money	-	10	-
cash	-	6	-
investment	-	-	12
profitable	-	-	11
rent (money)	-	-	8

MONTHLY BILL	US	PRC	TW
MONTHLY BILL	239	0	105
monthly	61	-	-
pay	57	-	-
payment,s	31	-	-
due	30	-	-
bill,s	18	-	-
utilities	8	-	8
late	8	-	-
overdue	7	-	-
fee	6	-	-
deposit	5	-	-
heat	4	-	-
reality	4	-	-
monthly payment	-	-	36
pay money	-	-	19
part of expense	-	-	16
month	-	-	8
tax	-	-	8
pay late	-	-	6
tax evasion	-	-	4

LEASE,LET	US	PRC	TW
LEASE,LET	69	102	18
lease	61	27	-
not owned	5	-	-
limited	3	-	-
rent	-	40	-
let	-	29	-
rent out	-	6	2
agreement	-	-	16

ITEMS: CAR,BIKE	US	PRC	TW
ITEMS: CAR,BIKE	74	74	11
car,s	39	8	-
furniture	9	-	7
boat	6	-	-
movies	5	-	-
appliances	5	-	-
bicycle,bike	4	9	-
T.V.	4	-	-
truck	2	-	-
things	-	17	-
camera	-	15	-
goods	-	10	-
use	-	8	-
grain	-	7	-
transportation	-	-	4

PEOPLE: LANDLORD,TENANT	US	PRC	TW
PEOPLE: LANDLORD,TENANT	126	74	235
landlord,s	83	48	129
tenant,s	10	-	16
roommate,s	10	-	12
fraternity	7	-	-
pets	5	-	-
landlady	5	-	-
friend,s	4	-	10
parent,s	2	-	9
farmer	-	18	12
person	-	8	8
students from other areas	-	-	14
family	-	-	12
group of three people	-	-	5
woman	-	-	4
landlord's daughter	-	-	4

DIFFICULTIES	US	PRC	TW
DIFFICULTIES	30	48	158
problems	7	-	-
eviction	7	-	-
roach	6	-	-
poor	5	-	14
dumb	5	-	-
debt	-	17	-
exploit	-	14	-
no money	-	10	-
detestable	-	7	7
burden	-	-	27
bad landlord	-	-	15
trouble	-	-	14
irrational	-	-	13
exploitation	-	-	10
pitiable	-	-	10
dislike	-	-	8
to have a headache	-	-	8
difficult	-	-	6
shabby	-	-	6
pressure	-	-	6
inconvenient	-	-	5
leaking (of a house)	-	-	5
short of money	-	-	4

OLD SOCIETY	US	PRC	TW
OLD SOCIETY	0	26	0
old society	-	17	-
capitalist	-	5	-
society	-	4	-

BUY,OWN	US	PRC	TW
BUY,OWN	88	8	29
own	28	-	-
buy	20	-	-
no	17	-	-
mortgage	12	-	-
owner	5	-	-
ownership	3	-	-
temporary	3	-	-
buy or sell on credit	-	8	18
buying a house	-	-	11

JOB	US	PRC	TW
JOB	38	0	35
job	32	-	21
work	4	-	-
employment	2	-	-
salary	-	-	14

LAND,PROPERTY	US	PRC	TW
LAND,PROPERTY	4	66	6
property	4	-	-
land rent	-	40	3
rent land	-	18	-
land	-	8	3

ENVIRONMENT	US	PRC	TW
ENVIRONMENT	13	0	26
food	8	-	-
window	3	-	-
security	2	-	-
comfortable	-	-	9
independent life	-	-	6
environment	-	-	5
tolerant	-	-	3
peaceful	-	-	3

MISCELLANEOUS	US	PRC	TW
MISCELLANEOUS	15	9	25
company	7	-	-
time	5	9	-
service	3	-	-
advertisement	-	-	9
post office	-	-	7
future	-	-	5
government	-	-	4

SUMMARY

Main Components	Percentage of Total Score		
	US	PRC	TW
HOUSING	23	4	13
EXPENSIVE,CHEAP	12	0	18
MONEY,CASH	17	33	14
MONTHLY BILL	16	0	9
LEASE,LET	5	16	2
ITEMS: CAR,BIKE	5	11	1
PEOPLE: LANDLORD,TENANT	9	11	20
DIFFICULTIES	2	7	13
OLD SOCIETY	0	4	0
BUY,OWN	6	1	2
JOB	3	0	3
LAND,PROPERTY	0	10	1
ENVIRONMENT	1	0	2
MISCELLANEOUS	1	1	2
Total Scores	1476	647	1173

CLOTHING
MAIN COMPONENTS AND RESPONSES

APPEARANCE,BEAUTIFUL	US	PRC	TW
	107	372	321
nice,pretty	25	-	-
appearance,looks	20	-	-
new	19	12	-
casual,sporty	13	-	-
matching	9	-	-
different	6	-	-
image	6	-	-
plain	5	-	6
beautiful,lovely	4	152	90
tasteful	-	34	30
grace	-	34	-
simple	-	29	2
nice looking,good looking	-	24	103
beauty	-	24	-
neat	-	20	8
good	-	17	-
magnificent	-	12	12
demeanor	-	7	-
beautiful and tasteful	-	7	-
dignity	-	-	24
attractive	-	-	19
refined,high class	-	-	12
taste (food)	-	-	11
special	-	-	4

PANTS,SHIRT,DRESSES	US	PRC	TW
	384	253	156
shirt,s	82	15	5
pants,trousers	66	42	7
shoes	42	-	-
jeans	33	-	5
dress,es	24	-	-
sweater,s	20	-	-
socks	17	-	-
underwear	16	8	-
overcoat,coat,s	14	25	3
jacket	9	49	-
shorts	9	-	-
t-shirt,s	8	-	4
sweats	7	-	-
garments	7	-	-
skirt,s	5	-	10
tie	5	-	2
suit	4	-	13
belts	4	-	-
hat	3	16	-
bra	3	-	-
accessories	3	-	-
glasses	3	-	-
clothes	-	23	46
outer garment	-	20	-
skin shoes	-	13	9
sportswear	-	9	-
summer clothes	-	7	-
woolen sweater	-	6	-
student clothes	-	6	-
short clothes	-	5	-
fur clothes	-	5	-
school uniform	-	4	-
jewelry	-	-	23
button	-	-	10
outfit	-	-	10
women's make up	-	-	3
swim suit	-	-	3
mini skirt	-	-	3

FUNCTION	US	PRC	TW
	127	339	221
warm,warmth	51	13	66
wear,for wearing	45	46	-
cover the body,cover	16	15	-
keep off cold,cold	9	55	12
protect,protection	6	-	7
heat preservation	-	84	37
warm oneself	-	30	3
dressing	-	26	28
decoration,decorate people	-	32	-
winter,winter clothes	-	20	6
period of wearing	-	12	-
change in temperature	-	6	-
cover, screen	-	-	48
season	-	-	8
environment	-	-	4
weather	-	-	2

MONEY,COST	US	PRC	TW
	149	28	82
expensive,expense	75	11	29
money	65	17	29
rich	5	-	-
cheap	4	-	3
waste	-	-	8
on sale	-	-	7
price	-	-	6

CLOTH,MATERIAL	US	PRC	TW
	66	73	37
cotton	15	19	5
quality	14	-	-
leather	12	-	-
cloth	9	26	-
material,cloth material	6	6	8
durable	5	7	12
denim	5	-	-
string	-	7	-
cotton padded clothes	-	4	-
dacron	-	4	-
texture	-	-	7
velour	-	-	5

COLOR,SIZE,CONDITION	US	PRC	TW
	79	71	110
color,s	25	53	43
blue	15	-	-
colorful	14	-	9
ugly	8	4	-
old	8	-	-
black,black color	7	-	1
borrow	2	-	-
used	-	7	-
flower	-	7	-
shape	-	-	29
favorite	-	-	7
torn	-	-	6
few	-	-	5
white	-	-	5
bright	-	-	5

PEOPLE	US	PRC	TW
	37	124	73
personality	11	-	12
girl,s	8	9	4
friends	7	-	-
model,s	6	41	2
woman,en	5	-	6
person,people	-	28	-
worker	-	13	-
male and female	-	10	-
labor	-	9	-
work	-	9	-
female	-	5	-
mother	-	-	11
show	-	-	10
me	-	-	8
human being	-	-	7
women's taste	-	-	5
salesman	-	-	4
job	-	-	4

WASH,SEW	US	PRC	TW
	36	58	27
clean	15	22	-
dirty	8	7	-
laundry	7	-	-
wash,wash clothes	4	3	15
sew	2	-	7
machine	-	11	-
spinning and weaving	-	9	-
washing machine	-	6	5

AMOUNT,NEED,BUY	US	PRC	TW
	108	11	65
need,needs,necessity	44	-	23
buy	22	-	-
many	14	8	16
important	11	-	-
not enough	7	-	10
sell	6	-	-
lots	4	-	-
daily life	-	3	-
burden	-	-	6
purchasing desire	-	-	5
poor	-	-	5

STORE,BOUTIQUE	US	PRC	TW
	98	17	50
store,s	30	6	-
shop,shopping	46	-	13
closet	19	-	8
malls	3	-	-
clothing store	-	11	-
boutique	-	-	16
department store	-	-	13

FASHION,STYLE	US	PRC	TW
	245	141	92
fashion,fashions	76	-	-
fashionable,style	8	10	35
style,s, stylish	53	-	4
designer	24	-	-
fun,trendy	23	-	-
Polo	11	-	-
Levis	11	-	-
statement	9	-	-
Guess	7	-	-
conservative	7	-	-
Adidas	5	-	-
sexy	5	-	-
line	4	-	-
design	2	-	3
western clothes	-	52	-
Chinese style clothes	-	38	-
in vogue	-	21	-
pattern	-	13	-
should be varied	-	7	-
modern	-	-	22
brand,famous brand	-	-	17
Paris	-	-	7
Japan	-	-	4

FIT	US	PRC	TW
	50	113	97
comfortable,comfort	19	14	45
cool	9	-	4
fit	8	36	18
loose	7	-	-
tight	7	-	-
size	-	22	10
large	-	15	-
small	-	12	-
natural and unrestrained	-	12	-
convenient	-	2	-
big size	-	-	5
bind up	-	-	5
hot	-	-	5
enjoyable	-	-	5

NUDITY,NO CLOTHES	US	PRC	TW
	39	9	32
nudity,nude,naked	19	-	-
body	6	-	11
sex	6	-	3
no	6	-	-
remove	2	-	-
cover embarrassment	-	9	-
hush up scandal	-	-	9
ashamed	-	-	5
pornographic	-	-	4

MISCELLANEOUS	US	PRC	TW
	8	9	16
acceptance	5	-	-
symbolic	3	-	-
development	-	5	-
study	-	4	-
feel distressed	-	-	5
sensitive	-	-	5
disgusted	-	-	3
coat hanger	-	-	3

SUMMARY

Main Components	Percentage of Total Score		
	US	PRC	TW
APPEARANCE,BEAUTIFUL	7	23	23
PANTS,SHIRT,DRESSES	25	16	11
FUNCTION	8	21	16
CLOTH,MATERIAL	4	5	3
COLOR,SIZE,CONDITION	5	4	8
MONEY,COST	10	2	6
PEOPLE	2	8	5
WASH,SEW	2	4	2
AMOUNT,NEED,BUY	7	1	5
FASHION,STYLE	16	9	7
FIT	3	7	7
STORE,BOUTIQUE	6	1	4
NUDITY,NO CLOTHES	3	1	2
MISCELLANEOUS	1	1	1
Total Scores	1533	1618	1379

195

SUMMARY OF TRENDS IN THE DOMAIN OF ECONOMY

Contrasting Views of Economy, Development, Industry, and Agriculture

The following trends were observed in the context of the four economic concepts of higher level abstraction and reflect how the three different systems affect the perceptions and attitudes of the American and Chinese student groups.

Needs and Products versus Means of Production. In response to the word "industry," the American focus on consumer needs and products emerges in sharp contrast to Mainlander focus on means of production. Americans think of cars and clothes, while Mainlanders think of heavy industry, light industry, and iron and steel. In response to agriculture, Americans focus on food and farms, while Mainlanders think of grain and land. When it comes to development, Americans think of apartments, career, and money, while Mainlanders think of developing agriculture, industry and the economy. In response to economy, Americans think of business, supply, oil, and cars, while Mainlanders think of industry and agriculture.

The Taiwanese responses at times more closely resemble those of Americans and at other times those of the Mainlanders. Very often they share characteristics of both, or are intermediate in terms of frequency of a given response. An interesting Taiwanese response to the word economy is "people's livelihood." This is one of the "Three Principles of the People" which served as a political and economic blueprint for Sun Yat-sen, the founder of the Chinese Republic (1911) whose words and memory are revered by both Mainlanders and Taiwanese. The principle of "people's livelihood" obligates the government to ensure full employment at a fair wage.

Business and Finance versus Agriculture, Industry, and Commerce. Perhaps the most fundamental difference observable in the context of all four economic themes examined is a dichotomy between a predominantly financial and business activity based conceptualization characteristic of Americans and the characteristic Chinese view of economy as built on three main pillars: agriculture, industry and commerce. Americans do not ignore agriculture and industry but they do not see them as the two main elements of economy as the Mainlanders do. The Americans think primarily in terms of productive, lucrative activities centered around money as the primary goal as well as the critical driving force. The American concern is with these financially driven business activities, their dynamism and success, as well as their problems and crises. Since money is seen by Americans as the main driving force, the financial conditions and problems, inflation, and recession are very much in the center of interest.

Compared to the American view of a complex tangle of interdependent business activities, the Mainland Chinese view economy as dependent on three main sectors: agricultural production, industrial production and commerce, and their special problems dominate in their minds. What these problems are in the mind of the Mainland student becomes apparent with considerable consistency not only in the context of economy but in the context of agriculture, industry and development as well. Compared to the American focus on money, supply and demand, and their dynamic balance, the Mainlanders see the problems of economy in the low status of development, low performance of agriculture and industry.

The Taiwanese occupy an intermediary position between the American and the PRC views. They show a particularly heavy emphasis on money, on financial policies and management exceeding even the Americans. They also show a strong propensity to recognize agriculture and industry as vital spheres of economy as well, yet they don't emphasize their independent role to the same extent as do the Mainlanders.

Cyclical Economy versus Modernizing to Overcome Backwardness. In the context of almost every economic theme, Americans express concern about uncertainties and downhill trends in the economy. Frequent responses to "economy" are poor, bad, inflation, recession and depression.

In contrast, the Chinese, especially the Mainlanders, think more about development as a more or less linear upward movement in the economic sphere. They picture their country moving from a state of backwardness and poverty toward a state of modernity and prosperity. This model does not preclude problems. Shortages and crises occurring in the economy are viewed as occasional and temporary. The expectation built into this model is progress toward a materially better future. Science, technology and the introduction of machinery, especially in the fields of agriculture and industry, are seen as steps toward achieving the goal of economic development. These trends emerge consistently in the context of the themes economy, development, industry, and agriculture.

The American perspectives reflect historic experiences. For more than a century, with the exception of the 30-year period following American entry into World War II, Americans have been accustomed to prosperity and recession or depression, alternately. As the American responses show, Americans are prepared to expect that economy and all related activities can expand as well as shrink, economic activities and business go up and down. There is a great concern with instability and unpredictability and anxiety about downturn, negative trends, inflation, and depression. American responses throughout the economic domain indicate that a downturn is a dominant expectation, in moderate contrast to the expectations of the Taiwanese, and in very sharp contrast to what the Mainlanders expect. The dominant PRC preoccupation is with the development of economy, industry, and agriculture from a presently low level of functioning, backwardness, poverty, and shortages along a line of rise and progression, advances and expansion.

The Chinese, predominantly the PRC, emphasis on development ties in closely with expectations attached to modernization, the adoption of technology, scientific achievements, the use of machinery, the building of factories. In the subjective world of the Americans, these means of production receive little attention; apparently, they are taken for granted. From the Chinese perspective these are viewed as essential prerequisites of overcoming backwardness, and of improving material existence. These convergent response trends show how dominant are the perspectives of a development model in the mind of the PRC students. Again, in this respect the Taiwanese students show perceptions and attitudes which occupy an intermediary position between the post-industrial American and the pre-industrial PRC perspectives.

Individual Needs versus National Goals. The American students view economy more as an aggregate of business and financial operations focusing on marketing of products designed to meet individual needs. Since the balance between demand and supply is delicate, and success depends on sharp and unpredictable competition, the American view of economy is replete with uncertainties and anxieties.

Along with their financial focus, the American students gave more considerations to budgeting and taxes as instruments of directing and managing the economy. The PRC students think more of planning and management.

From the PRC Chinese perspective, the problem is lack of goods, that is a failure of agriculture and industrial production that follows from backwardness. The low level of development affects all other areas. The PRC students think in the context of all economic issues more of the problems: industrial, agricultural and production, heavy industry and light industry, factories and machinery. Since these issues involve broad national problems that hinge on economic development, there is a strong indication to view economy as a broad collective issue of national development. The American students think more of business, financial transactions, and marketable products.

It may be noted that management is a thoroughly American concept that is usually untranslatable with its American meaning into foreign languages. In most third world countries, it implies centralized administration and planning.

The different perspectives registered reflect a predominantly individualistic American outlook on the world that emphasizes human existence and performance as driven by individual needs. In comparison, the PRC students show a stronger inclination to view economic as well as other human problems, more as collective, national issues dependent on such broad collective problems as the backwardness of the country, the scarcity of resources, the low level of economic development. The same is true of all Communist countries.

From the PRC perspective, all four economic concepts have stronger political and societal connotations. Also there is more explicit concern with people: workers, farmers, their own country and society. The American students think more of jobs, wages and trade unions. While the development could be viewed as an exception, since in this context Americans make more direct references to people, this is a consequence that development means to Americans beyond economic and social development, human development as well, implying physical growth and maturation that is an individual human process.

Most of the above trends support some generic contrasts in perspectives. The perceptual and attitudinal trends shown by the Americans reflect a frame of reference with focus on individual needs, materialistic orientation of an affluent, highly developed industrial society used to the worries caused by the ups and downs characteristic of their advanced economy.

The PRC trends reflect the world of people living in a relatively poor country of a low level of industrial development under a command economy that follows the Marxist principles of economic development, and that is mobilized along the blueprints of economic modernization. Although explicit references to Marxism or Communism are relatively few, the basic response trends show that the PRC students look at the world from a perspective of collectivism and nationalism. They convey the implicit conclusion that the fate of the individual depends on large national objective, its level of development and modernization.

The Taiwanese students show trends and perspectives that in several respects are similar to the American perspectives -- intensive preoccupation with financial and business matters, preoccupation with industrial problems like pollution, labor problems, and attention given to agricultural products; however, on other dimensions they stand closer to the PRC students' views of economic and developmental problems.

Necessities: Food, Clothing and Housing

These necessities are concrete and universal, and as such it is rather compelling to assume that on these fundamentals like food or clothing, the differences among the three culture groups would be negligible. Yet there were several dimensions reflected in the response trends which do show some interesting contrasts.

Consumption versus Production. There is usually a stronger American focus on the use and consumption of these necessities. In relationship to food, there is more American emphasis on eating and on meals. The PRC Chinese, compared to the other two groups, think more about the preparation of food as well as food production. With regard to clothing, Americans pay the most attention to fashion and style and other factors affecting purchase and consumption. The PRC students, on the other hand, consider more whether the clothing is proper in fit, size and shape. With regard to housing, Americans focus on the living quarters, their use for living and sleeping. The PRC students are more preoccupied with the availability of space and the use of space; they speak of crowding and limited space. The Taiwanese most of all consider the family situation with regard to housing. They consider family use and furniture. These trends fit well with the logic of the next major dimension regarding choice and limitations.

Choice and Diversity versus Problems of Shortage. With regard to food, Americans think of a greater diversity of food items and few food types. Apparently, they are used to having a wide variety of choices. The PRC choices involve such fundamentals as rice, bread, and vegetables, compared to the Americans who are interested in ethnic food such as Chinese, Mexican, western style and other types. Americans consider food as instrumental in meeting their needs, satisfying their hunger at mealtime. The Chinese, particularly the Taiwanese, think more of food as instrumental to existence, as well as instrumental to reach satisfaction and fulfillment. At the same time, both the Americans and the Taiwanese express concern with diets, fat, fear of overeating and being overweight, and they think more of nutrition and health. The Mainland group makes no references to diet or fat. The Taiwanese characterize food more as a basic necessity, essential for maintaining life.

With regard to clothing, the Americans show the most interest in the diversity of clothing items, including their different colors and shapes. The PRC Chinese think to a lesser extent in terms of diversity but consider the function of clothes, like heat preservation, warmth, keeping off cold, etc. At the same time, they express considerable interest in the aesthetic quality of clothing as pretty, nice, neat in appearance, also simplicity and taste. In this respect, both the Taiwanese and PRC Chinese show similarity. The American interest in diversity of clothing is expressed by their heavy emphasis on fashion and style, describing different types of style and different trademarks, makes and designs. The PRC Chinese reactions do not refer directly to shortage of clothing, but their emphasis on beauty and appearance shows a certain degree of appreciation and desire to have nice, good-looking clothing available.

In connection with housing, the Americans make the most references to diverse housing facilities and living quarters, reflecting again a broad variety of choice and interest in diversity. With regard to shortage of housing, the Americans make reference to special disadvantaged groups, e.g., the homeless and poor. The Taiwanese think more of the functional features of housing as providing shelter, providing warmth and protection and security.

Quality versus Utility and Function. As already observed in connection with food, clothing and housing, basic human needs, the Americans think increasingly in terms of diversity of available products and facilities. They are more interested in fashion, make and quality. The Chinese have been referred to as a "practical" people. The Chinese groups show more preoccupation with the function of the product: in the case of food, it provides nourishment; in the case of shelter, it provides warmth and security. In connection with clothing, Americans indicate diverse makes and fashions, while the Chinese think more of fundamental needs such as fit, keeping warm, providing protection against cold.

Money, Buying versus Existential Utility. In the context of all these basic necessities, the Americans make more references to prices, costs, purchasing, buying and acquisition of the items. On the part of the Chinese, they pay little attention to price and purchasing; apparently, in the PRC context, the problem is more a question of availability. Their focus is more on production and keeping in shape and usable what is available. The PRC Chinese make more references to food production, agriculture and farming, the fundamental problem of the PRC economy. The Taiwanese references are usually between the American and PRC. They are less diversified and less choice oriented than the American, but same time much more so than the Mainland Chinese.

These differences in perspectives reflect the role played by environmental conditions and culture on even basic necessities of life, like food and clothing. They show how items involving the satisfaction of basic needs can develop somewhat different meanings for people who live under different social and economic conditions. These differences in perspectives become explicable when one is familiar with the different living condition characteristic of the three populations. The Mainland Chinese reactions are interesting because they reflect views of people living in a controlled egalitarian environment which is well known for its shortages and lack of high quality products. Nonetheless, interestingly, the PRC responses do not show any particular disappointment or fundamental dissatisfaction or complaints about shortages and poor quality of products. The desires for higher quality products are expressed mainly by the references to beauty, to nice appearance, to good looks, which are frequent both in the PRC and Taiwanese groups. From the part of the PRC Chinese, however, references to fashion and style are relatively rare. The drab monotony of the Chinese social scene with the blue working jackets and uniforms is apparently more a reflection of the frame of reference of the Western observer or visitor. The response trends give little indication that monotony would dominate the PRC views with regard to their uniform appearance, their style of dressing. From their angle, what seems to be important is that the clothing fits well, neither too large or too small, that it provides warmth, and protection, and that it lasts long.

Chapter 6

EDUCATION

American and Chinese perspectives on education are a particularly fascinating and timely subject. The Taiwanese Republic is frequently characterized as the fastest developing country that combines the highest rate of economic progress with relative social and political stability. It is operating an educational system which subscribes to the democratic principles but under conditions of governmental support, which involves naturally a certain degree of central control, at least by Western standards.

The People's Republic of China, the most populous country in the world, maintains an essentially socialistic political system and operates an educational system that is highly centralized, state controlled, and has an essentially Marxist ideological foundation.

Both Chinese groups build on an educational tradition of thousands of years of experience. The Chinese culture is famous for its emphasis on education, for its educational examination and reward system. This educational tradition is frequently said to be at the core of the Chinese culture and to be a potent factor behind the exceptional Chinese coping skills and achievements.

The United States has a free democratic educational system most advanced in educational technology as well as promoting the principles of freedom and pluralism. At the same time there is a widespread malaise and dissatisfaction. The heated contemporary debate on the crisis of the American educational system is driven not only by alarming indicators of declining academic achievement (SAT scores, rate of functional literacy at graduation), but by indicators showing parallel increases in drop-out rates, crime statistics, suicide rates suggest an intimate relationship between academic achievement and those invisible psychological effects of the school environment variously identified as factors of socialization or motivation.

The comparison of the American, Taiwanese, and PRC Chinese students on their educational perspectives has been organized to gain insights into this interface of educational achievement and psychocultural dispositions in different environments that represent three particularly interesting combinations of educational settings and philosophies.

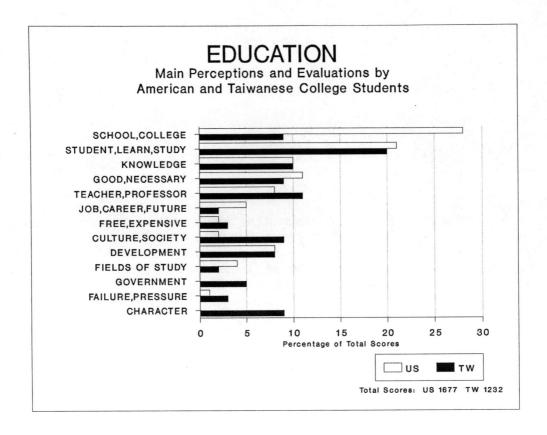

EDUCATION
Main Perceptions and Evaluations by
American and Taiwanese College Students

Percentage of Total Scores

US   TW

Total Scores: US 1677 TW 1232

American View: College, Learning, Books. For the American students tested, education is seen in the college setting and involves obtaining knowledge from books. For this group, focus is on students, learning and studying. Education means acquiring knowledge. Americans connect education to jobs and career and their future more than the other groups. Far more than the other groups, the Americans are concerned about diplomas and graduating. While fields of study do not receive great emphasis from Americans, the subjects comprising this component are very different for Americans compared to the Chinese groups. The greatest emphasis for Americans is on the fields of life, sex, health, and sports.

Taiwanese View: Family, Government. Teacher is the first thing the Taiwanese think of when education is mentioned. Students learning and studying is the most important component. This is followed by the importance of progress and advancement. Knowledge is about as important to the Taiwanese as to the others, but for them it carries the connotation of enlightenment. As it is for Mainlanders, education for the Taiwanese is closely related to culture and society. They also tie it more closely to family and children. This reflects a cultural trend among the Chinese to emphasize the teacher-student as well as parent-child relationship. The government, especially the Ministry of Education, plays a significant role for the Taiwanese, as does the government-generated joint entrance exam, which screens high-school students for college eligibility. They emphasize the cramming method of learning.

American and Taiwanese Contrasts: Book Learning versus Enlightenment and Cultivation.
Learning receives strong emphasis from Americans, but is hardly mentioned by the Taiwanese. Books are much more prominent in the American view of education, while teachers are mentioned, somewhat more by the Taiwanese. In regard to educational advancement, Americans focus on getting a degree, while the Taiwanese focus on character development, change in social manners and personality. This is not to say that the Taiwanese do not also prize the diploma; to them a college diploma is a "lifelong coupon" for rice. Enlightenment, important to the Taiwanese, is not mentioned by Americans. The American interest in the related subjects of life, sex, health, and sports finds no counterpart among the Taiwanese. Americans make almost no mention of government in the context of education.

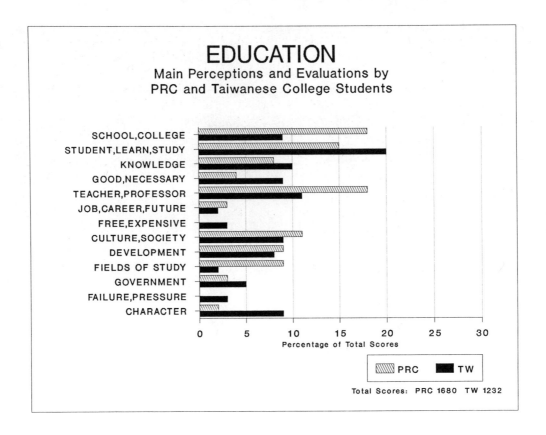

EDUCATION
Main Perceptions and Evaluations by
PRC and Taiwanese College Students

Percentage of Total Scores

PRC   TW

Total Scores: PRC 1680   TW 1232

PRC Chinese View: Teachers and Students. For the Mainland Chinese, education depends upon teachers and professors, significantly more than for the other groups. Students, also, have greater significance for Mainland Chinese, reflecting stronger self identification with their student status. Beyond the importance of the traditional student-teacher relationship, the PRC Chinese indicate that they value education as a means toward progress and development, which they view collectively rather than in terms of personal advancement. As for the good of the society and country, they specifically stress the importance of a scientific education.

Taiwanese View: Family, Government. Teacher is the first thing the Taiwanese think of when education is mentioned. Students learning and studying is the most important component. This is followed by the importance of progress and advancement. Knowledge is about as important to the Taiwanese as to the others, but for them it carries the connotation of enlightenment. As it is for Mainlanders, education for the Taiwanese is closely related to culture and society. They also tie it more closely to family and children. This reflects a cultural trend among the Chinese to emphasize the teacher-student as well as parent-child relationship. The government, especially the Ministry of Education, plays a significant role for the Taiwanese, as does the government-generated joint entrance exam, which screens high-school students for college eligibility. They emphasize the cramming method of learning.

PRC and Taiwanese Contrasts: Scientific Development versus Character Development. The Mainland Chinese place much greater emphasis on the student-teacher relationship than do the Taiwanese. The role of education in national development is somewhat stronger for the PRC Chinese. The Taiwanese are more explicit in their positive attitudes toward education as very important and valuable. Education's place in society is emphasized by both Mainlanders and Taiwanese, however the Mainlander's emphasis on culture and literature is much stronger. The Mainland Chinese show greater interest in the fields of study, particularly science, than do the other groups. Science is not mentioned by the Taiwanese or Americans. The development of moral character is seen as an important aspect of education among both Chinese groups, in contrast to the Americans. The Taiwanese express more concern about exams, particularly the joint entrance exam. To be admitted to an ideal college, a student has to pass the highly competitive joint entrance college exam. The exam is a life-and-death struggle in their life, so to speak.

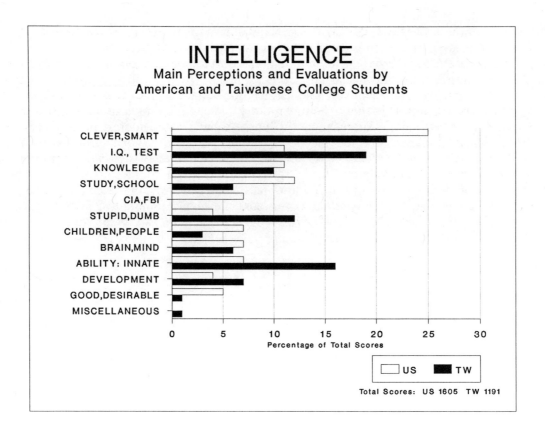

INTELLIGENCE
Main Perceptions and Evaluations by
American and Taiwanese College Students

Percentage of Total Scores

US   TW

Total Scores: US 1605   TW 1191

American View: Smart, Knowledgeable. Americans place great emphasis on being smart or clever, as do the Chinese groups. They distinguish themselves from the Chinese by identifying intelligence more closely with learning and schools, and least with inborn ability. The notion of measuring intelligence, or I.Q., is very strong. The ability to learn and acquire knowledge is an important indication of intelligence for Americans. Nevertheless, more than the others, Americans consider intelligence desirable and valuable. Unique to the Americans is the concept of gathering information in the sense of spying, secrecy, and identified with two federal agencies -- the FBI and CIA. In Chinese or Taiwanese there is no such double meaning.

Taiwanese View: Clever, Dull, Congenital. The Taiwanese, far more than the others, place great stress on genius, congenital ability, and heritage. They believe that intelligence varies greatly among different peoples. No other group places such great stress on IQ test scores. (Gifted children in Taiwan do not have to attend an exam to be admitted to an ideal college.) The Taiwanese are also the ones most preoccupied with idiocy, dullness, and mental retardation.

American and Taiwanese Contrasts: Learning versus Cleverness. While cleverness is seen as intelligence by both groups, the connection is much stronger among the Taiwanese. The latter view intelligence as a largely innate, inborn quality that varies among people and can be compared through I.Q. scores. The American stress on I.Q. and testing is lower than that of the Taiwanese, but much higher than the PRC Chinese. The disparity on viewing intelligence as inborn is even greater. The Taiwanese also emphasize academic degrees as a measure or validation of one's level of intelligence. Americans place greater stress on knowledge than the Taiwanese, while the latter place more stress on wisdom than do the Americans. Child prodigies enter Taiwanese thinking, but not American, while government intelligence agencies occur to Americans, but not to Taiwanese. Perhaps the greatest contrast between Americans and the Chinese groups is the great emphasis the latter place on the role of intelligence in progress, development, and success.

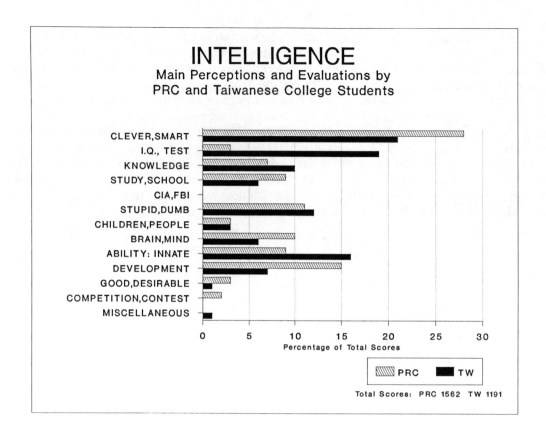

PRC Chinese View: Cleverness, Development. The Mainland Chinese see being clever as the most important manifestation of intelligence. Well over one fourth of all the responses fall into this general component. Interestingly, even though they place less emphasis on education and learning compared to the other two groups, the Mainlanders stress studying more. On the issue of the role of inborn ability or heredity, this group is intermediate between the Americans and the Taiwanese. They pay little attention to I.Q., or any other kind of tests. More than the other groups, they connect intelligence to the brain or mind: memory, thinking, mental capacity, and imaginative power. They value intelligence for its role not only in personal development but also in the development of their nation. They are the only group to mention intellectual competition in the form of tournaments.

Taiwanese View: Clever, Dull, Congenital. The Taiwanese, far more than the others, place great stress on genius, congenital ability, and heritage. They believe that intelligence varies greatly among different peoples. No other group places such great stress on IQ test scores. (Gifted children in Taiwan do not have to attend an exam to be admitted to an ideal college.) The Taiwanese are also the ones most preoccupied with idiocy, dullness, and mental retardation.

PRC and Taiwanese Contrasts: Brain/Mind Development versus Congenital Heritage. A major contrast is that the Mainlanders focus on development, as usual, but in this context it is juxtaposed to the idea of innate ability, which is more characteristic of the Taiwanese. Cleverness receives much more emphasis from the PRC group. Academic degrees have far more importance to the Taiwanese. Intelligence in the context of school and study receives about the same attention from both. Emphasis on innate intelligence is twice as strong among the Taiwanese, while concern with stupidity is roughly equal. Where the groups are at polar opposites is in the dependence upon intelligence testing which is very much in vogue on Taiwan, and not at all on the Mainland. Focus on the brain, mind, and thinking is more characteristic of the Mainlander group. A curious cluster in the knowledge component for both groups is wise merchant-wisdom-knowledge. A fair guess might be that this could involve elements of a popular Chinese folk tale. According to a Chinese saying, "No merchant is not shrewd."

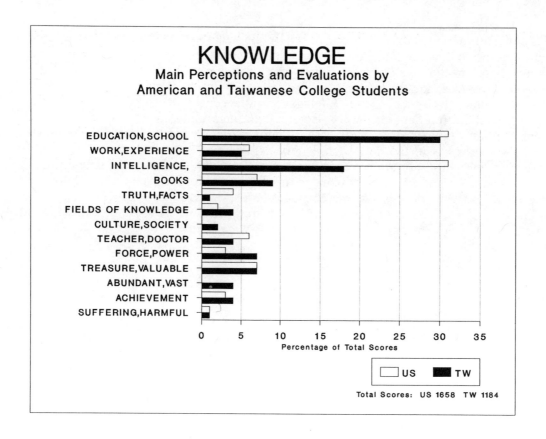

KNOWLEDGE
Main Perceptions and Evaluations by American and Taiwanese College Students

EDUCATION, SCHOOL
WORK, EXPERIENCE
INTELLIGENCE,
BOOKS
TRUTH, FACTS
FIELDS OF KNOWLEDGE
CULTURE, SOCIETY
TEACHER, DOCTOR
FORCE, POWER
TREASURE, VALUABLE
ABUNDANT, VAST
ACHIEVEMENT
SUFFERING, HARMFUL

0   5   10   15   20   25   30   35
Percentage of Total Scores

☐ US   ■ TW

Total Scores: US 1658 TW 1184

American View: Education, Intelligence. For Americans, more than for either Chinese group, knowledge results from a combination of intelligence and education. No other factors come near in importance or emphasis. Also with more emphasis than among the Chinese, knowledge is acquired by learning in school and college. In contrast to the Chinese, Americans emphasize the mental ability to acquire knowledge -- intelligent, smart, brains. Books and reading are less emphasized by Americans in the acquisition of knowledge than by either Chinese group. Americans are less inclined than the Chinese to see knowledge as a source of power or force. The various fields of knowledge receive the least attention from Americans. Science and literature are the only disciplines mentioned - and just barely. Learning the truth and the facts is especially important to Americans.

Taiwanese View: Wisdom, Books. Study and learning are the chief avenues of acquiring knowledge for the Taiwanese, and they place less stress on study than the Mainland Chinese and less emphasis on learning than the Americans. Books and other reading matter are more important to them than to the other groups, and they stress combining knowledge with wisdom. They consider the accumulation of knowledge a great strength and a precious resource which enriches oneself. Only the Taiwanese think of death in relation to knowledge. This reflects the popular wisdom frequently quoted: "A person without knowledge is no more than a beast -- he may be alive, but his is virtually dead."

American and Taiwanese Contrasts: Learning in School Versus Acquiring Wisdom.
Learning in school is important to both groups, but much more so to Americans. Relatively less important to both groups is the gaining of wisdom, but here the Taiwanese emphasis is proportionately much stronger than that in the American view of knowledge. Acquiring understanding receives more attention from Americans than from the Taiwanese. Knowledge as force or instrument of power receives comparative little emphasis from the Americans. Both groups acknowledge the importance of science, but only the Taiwanese mention philosophy. Neither group makes much mention of parents as a source of knowledge. Both groups consider knowledge important, useful, and necessary. Experience as an important source of knowledge is stressed more by Americans.

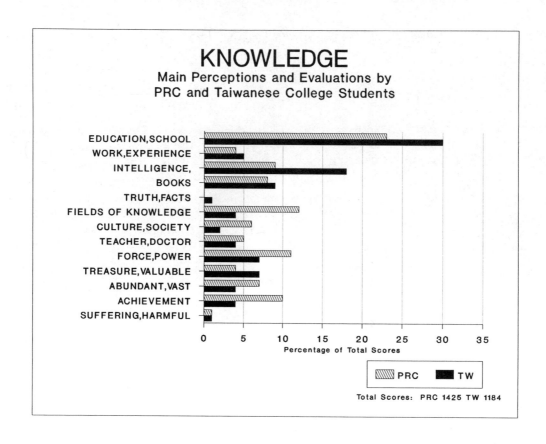

KNOWLEDGE
Main Perceptions and Evaluations by
PRC and Taiwanese College Students

Total Scores: PRC 1425 TW 1184

PRC Chinese View: Force, Study, Science. Knowledge as a force or power is what occurs most frequently to a Mainlander. Books are an important source. As with the other two groups, the component of education and schools receives the most emphasis. Within this, study, students, and learning receive the most attention. School receives less emphasis among the Mainland Chinese than among the other groups, while study receives far more. Compared to the other groups, talent and ability are more important to the Mainlanders (who view themselves as an elite of 3% of their age cohort chosen theoretically on this basis). Books themselves are given great emphasis by Mainlanders, and libraries the least, compared to the other two groups. This can probably be explained by their scarcity, inefficiency, and poor collections of libraries in the PRC. Knowledge is seen as a source of force and energy far more by the PRC Chinese than by the other groups. It is also seen as an abundant accumulated treasure. Individual fields of knowledge are very important to the Mainlanders. Chief among them are science, rocket technology, literature, mathematics, social science knowledge, and history -- in that order. With three times the emphasis of the other groups, Mainland Chinese see knowledge as the basis for social progress and development. They also stress its role in work and production.

Taiwanese View: Wisdom, Books. Study and learning are the chief avenues of acquiring knowledge for the Taiwanese, and they place less stress on study than the Mainland Chinese and less emphasis on learning than the Americans. Books and other reading matter are more important to them than to the other groups, and they stress combining knowledge with wisdom. They consider the accumulation of knowledge a great strength and a precious resource which enriches oneself. Only the Taiwanese think of death in relation to knowledge. This reflects the popular wisdom frequently quoted: "A person without knowledge is no more than a beast -- he may be alive, but his is virtually dead."

PRC and Taiwanese Contrasts: Talent Versus Wisdom. Both groups stress the importance of studying and school, with a little more emphasis on studying among the Mainlanders. The component of intelligence and wisdom receives greater emphasis from the Taiwanese, compared to the Mainlanders. Wisdom is greatly stressed by the Taiwanese, while the Mainland Chinese stress intellectual ability and talent. While the latter consider knowledge precious, the Mainlanders call it a treasure and wealth. Both groups consider knowledge important and useful, but the Taiwanese stress that it is necessary. The Mainlander stress science much more than do the Taiwanese, who mention philosophy, which the former do not. Teachers are far more important on the Mainland. The Mainlanders are more impressed with the vast abundance of knowledge than the Taiwanese, possibly because of the PRC's emphasis on China's long history, or because knowledge is so poorly organized on the Mainland. The Mainlanders place far more stress on the connection between knowledge on the one hand and culture and society on the other.

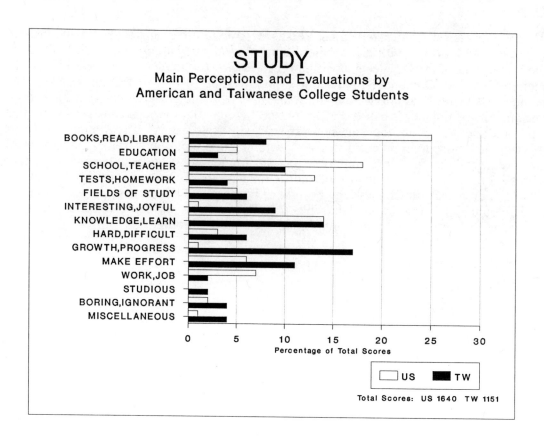

STUDY

Main Perceptions and Evaluations by
American and Taiwanese College Students

Percentage of Total Scores

US TW

Total Scores: US 1640 TW 1151

American View: Books, School. Americans, far more than for the other groups, emphasize book learning: Studying is done with books in school and college. In great contrast to the others, study is the primary means of learning and may involve library work. History and math are the only fields of study specified. Making great efforts and intense concentration is less of a factor for Americans studying than for the others. Unlike the Chinese, Americans study mainly for tests, and to a lesser extent for exams. Americans do not see studying as a means of acquiring knowledge to nearly the extent that Chinese do. Americans are also the least likely to see studying as a source of joy or a following-up of interest, but see it as hard, sometimes boring, work necessary to prepare for a profession.

Taiwanese View: Learn, Grow. The Taiwanese see studying as a process of learning, growth, and progress -- and more than the other groups -- as a means of acquiring knowledge. By them, studying is done cheerfully, out of interest, and can become a source of joy. It is a means of understanding life and being able to grasp technology. The Taiwanese are the least likely to consider studying as work.

American and Taiwanese Contrasts: Work Versus Joy and Interest. While Americans see studying as a necessary unpleasant work by which they can prepare for a profession or career, the Taiwanese view it as an interesting opportunity for growth and progress. Such professionals as intellectuals who are related to books and studying are traditionally respected, because they are imparters of knowledge and edifiers of people in general. Studying is fun to the Taiwanese. The school, college, or library setting is very important for Americans and not at all for the Taiwanese.

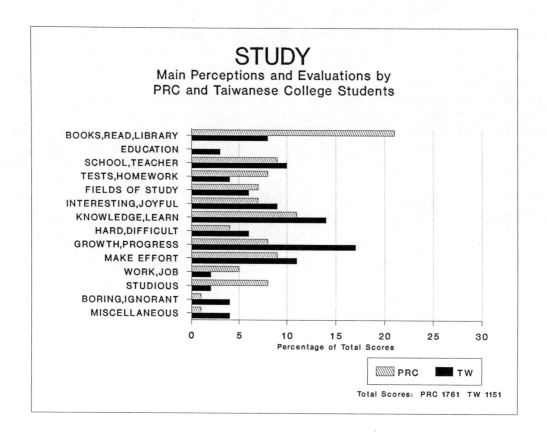

STUDY

Main Perceptions and Evaluations by
PRC and Taiwanese College Students

Percentage of Total Scores

PRC   TW

Total Scores: PRC 1761   TW 1151

PRC Chinese View: Assiduous Students. For Mainland Chinese, studying is what students do, but neither books nor libraries are as important to them as to Americans. Although they show a significantly greater interest in studying than the other two groups, for them it is, oddly enough, not associated with learning, but with acquiring knowledge as a means of bringing about the country's progress in the future, at the cost of great effort. In practical terms, studying means doing research papers and requires assiduous dedication and earnest industriousness. The focus is on science and technology. The PRC students are the group least likely to complain about studying. There is great symbolic significance for them in the writing pen. Formerly it was carried as a badge identifying a person as a cadre or a student -- in either case a member of a privileged elite.

Taiwanese View: Learn, Grow. The Taiwanese see studying as a process of learning, growth, and progress -- and more than the other groups -- as a means of acquiring knowledge. By them, studying is done cheerfully, out of interest, and can become a source of joy. It is a means of understanding life and being able to grasp technology. The Taiwanese are the least likely to consider studying as work.

PRC and Taiwanese Contrasts: Scientific Research Versus Understanding Life. Reading books is a far more important aspect of studying for Mainlanders than for the Taiwanese. While the former focus on studying as a means of acquiring knowledge and ability, the latter see it as a means of personal growth in the direction of wisdom and enlightenment. While the Mainlanders stress great efforts, and methods of study, the Taiwanese view study as a process of concentrated recollection. This may be partially the result of focus on science and the humanities respectively. The Taiwanese are more likely than the Mainlanders to consider studying a joyful and happy means of spending their time. In contrast to American students, the Chinese students largely forgo social life because it would interfere with their studying. The Mainlanders' stress on research papers is absent among the Taiwanese. Oral and written exams are more popular than paper-writing. The Taiwanese are somewhat more critical in finding fault with studying or showing concern about ignorant errors.

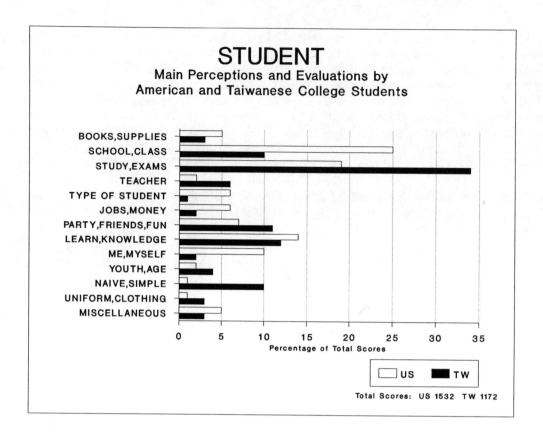

American View: Learn in Class. Americans express a strong sense of self-identification as students. With far more emphasis than for the Chinese groups, American students' perception is that they learn in class and from books. Americans do not sharply distinguish between students at various levels, nor do they ascribe traits to themselves which would set them apart from other people, other than considering themselves smart and intelligent. The acquisition of knowledge is less important to American than to Chinese students. More than the Chinese, they are concerned about work (in school or jobs) and money. American students generally have to pay their own tuition. In contrast, the Taiwanese students depend on their parents for living expenses and tuition.

Taiwanese View: Study Hard for Exams. Taiwanese students visualize themselves as studying hard and often, and especially in preparation for examinations. The acquisition of knowledge is far more important to them than to the other two groups. On the other hand, Taiwanese, apparently to a significantly greater extent than the other groups, see student life as a carefree, happy, time of pleasure seeking -- not all of it innocent, in their view. Fooling around, being naughty, and drinking wine all receive mention by them but not by the other groups. Books and supplies are less of a concern to them than to the others: probably because these things are paid for their parents. For the same reason, most probably, the Taiwanese have less concern about work and money than the other two groups. The Taiwanese are more aware of their youth than the others, and they are the only ones to make mention of their uniforms.

American and Taiwanese Contrasts: School and Degree Versus Knowledge and Pleasure. American and Taiwanese students both mention schools, degrees, and libraries; however, schools and degrees are far more important to the Americans. Learning and education are emphasized by Americans, while studying and obtaining knowledge receive more attention from the Taiwanese. Friends are far more important to Americans, while the Taiwanese think in terms of classmates. Parties receive significant emphasis from Americans but are not even mentioned by the Taiwanese. The Taiwanese are four times as likely as the American students to consider themselves happy or cheerful. The Taiwanese students also describe themselves as carefree -- a term which does not occur to the Americans. The Taiwanese emphasis of physical activities and exercise is not reflected among American responses. The link between student and teacher is more than twice as strong for the Taiwanese as for the Americans, while books are more important to American students. The Taiwanese concern with work and money is lesser than that among Americans.

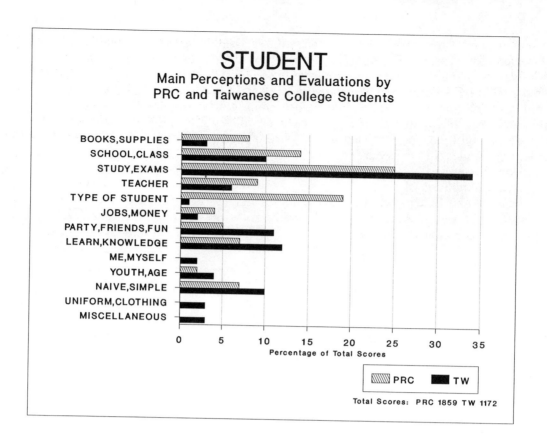

PRC Chinese View: University Student, Teacher. Neither of the other groups puts so much emphasis on studying, and to neither of them is the status of student nearly so important. They view themselves as scholar-intellectuals. Several responses, including study hard, make efforts, and hard work, emphasize exertion. Mainlanders are the only group to express concern about their school record -- and they place the greatest emphasis on being university students. There is some emphasis on gender -- more on male than on female. While there is some stress on physical exercise and sports, there is much greater emphasis on obtaining knowledge from teachers. To a considerable extent PRC students identify themselves as workers and also as naive, simple, and pure.

Taiwanese View: Study Hard for Exams. Taiwanese students visualize themselves as studying hard and often, and especially in preparation for examinations. The acquisition of knowledge is far more important to them than to the other two groups. On the other hand, Taiwanese, apparently to a significantly greater extent than the other groups, see student life as a carefree, happy, time of pleasure seeking -- not all of it innocent, in their view. Fooling around, being naughty, and drinking wine all receive mention by them but not by the other groups. Books and supplies are less of a concern to them than to the others: probably because these things are paid for their parents. For the same reason, most probably, the Taiwanese have less concern about work and money than the other two groups. The Taiwanese are more aware of their youth than the others, and they are the only ones to make mention of their uniforms.

PRC and Taiwanese Contrasts: School Versus Examination. The Mainlanders lay far greater stress on schools, while the Taiwanese emphasis is on examinations. Unlike Americans, both groups of Chinese consider classmates important. Students generally make lasting friendships with their fellow students in both Mainland China and Taiwan. Both exercise and books are far more important to the Mainlanders. For the Taiwanese the pen does not have the Mainlanders' great symbolic significance. Similar to the Mainlanders' characterization of students as simple and pure, the Taiwanese view students as clean and honest -- and, uniquely, obedient.

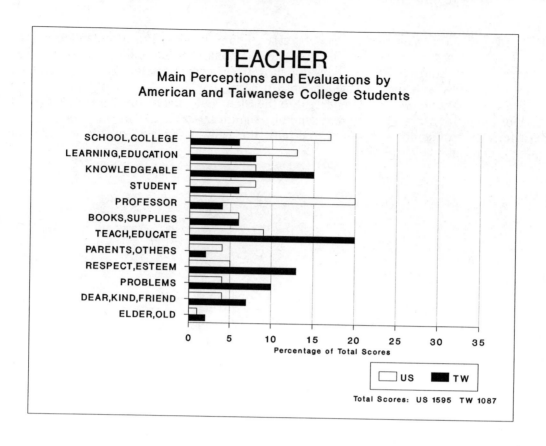

TEACHER
Main Perceptions and Evaluations by
American and Taiwanese College Students

Percentage of Total Scores

US ☐ TW ■

Total Scores: US 1595 TW 1087

American View: Knowledge, Books. Americans are the least likely to consider their teacher a dear kind friend, which is the predominant image of teacher among the Chinese, especially the Mainlanders. Americans view the role of their teacher as one who teaches, guides, lectures, and gives help -- in that order. They view a teacher as a person who has knowledge, understanding, wisdom, experience, and intelligence -- in that order. Much more than the other groups, Americans see a teacher as a professor or instructor, but far more than the other groups, they place the teacher in a school, as an authority. They view their mother as teacher.

Taiwanese View: Good Friends and Stern Teachers. The Taiwanese are the most emphatic of the three groups in the view that teachers teach. They view teachers as fond of teaching and solving problems and as good, kindly friends, with loving, tender, forgiving hearts. The Taiwanese express a great amount of respect and esteem for teachers and their authority. Nevertheless, they also mention brutal punishment by stern teachers. As Taiwanese experts observe, it was so in the past, but in recent years the situation has been drastically changed under the influence of the American educational system. The Taiwanese students consider Confucius to be their teacher as well.

American and Taiwanese Contrasts: Authority Versus Respect and Loving Kindness. In almost every component regarding teachers, Americans are at the opposite position of the Taiwanese. The Taiwanese are far more impressed with their teachers' knowledge than the Americans. However, the latter give teachers more credit for experience and wisdom. Lectures are relatively unimportant for both groups. The teacher's role in learning and education is far greater for Americans, their emphasis on learning rather than teaching reflects American individualism. However, the level of respect for teachers is nearly three times higher among the Taiwanese. In terms of the "greatness," the teacher is placed next only to the Heaven, the Earth, the Emperor and the Parents. The latter are also more likely to consider their teacher a good friend who always helps people. Americans are more likely to view their parents, especially their mother, as teachers. The main American complaint against teachers is their having a teacher's pet, while the Taiwanese object to brutal, stern teachers.

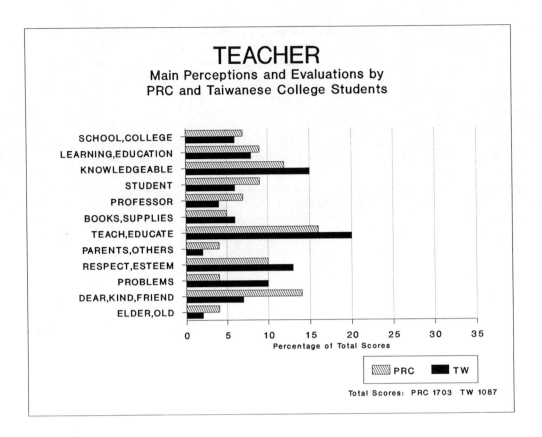

TEACHER
Main Perceptions and Evaluations by
PRC and Taiwanese College Students

Total Scores: PRC 1703   TW 1087

PRC Chinese View: Lectures and Respect. Mainland Chinese mention lectures about five times as often as either of the other groups. They give teachers credit for solving difficult questions, but especially for having a great deal of knowledge. With emphasis similar to that of Americans, they place teachers in classrooms. Of the three groups, the Mainlanders most frequently mention respect and esteem, and they are the most enthusiastic, by far, about cherishing their teachers. They describe them as great, kindly, dear, selfless, lovable persons, for whom they have friendly affection and deep love, and of whom they "want to take every care." They also express concern about the hardships which teachers undergo. From the high frequency with which old age was mentioned, it is likely that there is a high proportion of elderly teachers and that the elderly are often viewed as teachers. Old age is a symbol of wisdom, more so in the Mainland than in Taiwan. More than the other groups, the Mainlanders consider their parents as teachers.

Taiwanese View: Good Friends and Stern Teachers. The Taiwanese are the most emphatic of the three groups in the view that teachers teach. They view teachers as fond of teaching and solving problems and as good, kindly friends, with loving, tender, forgiving hearts. The Taiwanese express a great amount of respect and esteem for teachers and their authority. Nevertheless, they also mention brutal punishment by stern teachers. As Taiwanese experts observe, it was so in the past, but in recent years the situation has been drastically changed under the influence of the American educational system. The Taiwanese students consider Confucius to be their teacher as well.

PRC and Taiwanese Contrasts: Diligent Lecturer Versus Erudite Imparter of Principles.
Mainland Chinese see their teachers primarily as persons who give lectures, while the Taiwanese stress teaching, including the imparting of great principles. Knowledge is stressed by both groups. While a PRC teacher is viewed as diligent and industrious, the one on Taiwan is more likely to be seen as dignified and erudite. The classroom receives far greater importance on the Mainland. Gender is mentioned by Mainlanders (slightly more male than female) but not by the Taiwanese. Responses related to respect and esteem are more frequent among the latter, while the Mainlanders are more likely to consider their teacher a good, kind friend. The Taiwanese, more than the Mainlanders, complain of teachers who are brutal, stern, strict, or severe, while the Mainland Chinese express more concern about the hardships their mentors undergo. The Mainlanders more frequently view teachers as old.

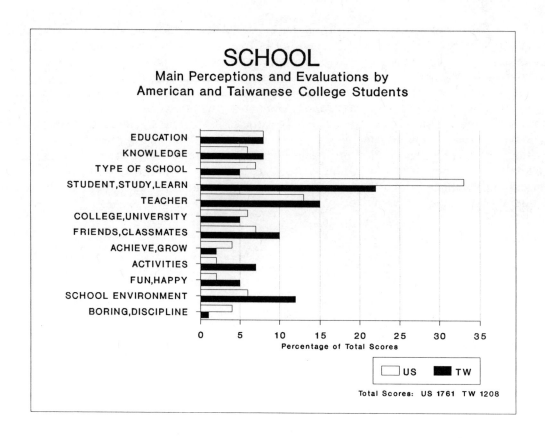

SCHOOL
Main Perceptions and Evaluations by
American and Taiwanese College Students

Percentage of Total Scores

US   TW

Total Scores: US 1761 TW 1208

American View: Books, Boring. For Americans schools consist mainly of teachers, learning, education, studying, books, grades, friends, students, and knowledge. By contrast, learning and schoolbooks hardly appear among the responses of the Chinese. Grades do not appear at all. Studying and learning are the most frequent images for Americans. Teaching and teachers are next in importance, followed by education. More than the other groups, American students complain about problems with boredom, discipline, and money. However, more than the other groups, they expect schools to help them achieve success. Only Americans mention school vacation.

Taiwanese View: Happy, Studying. For the Taiwanese, too, teachers come first to mind when schools are mentioned. Students studying are next in importance. There is a very strong stress on friends, and classmates -- which may explain why the Taiwanese, far more than the others, are happy to be in school. They have none of the complaints that appear among American responses. The only complaint of significance is competition. Far more than the others, the Taiwanese see schools as sources of knowledge. They express far more concern about examinations than do the other groups. The Taiwanese are the only ones to mention a history primary school, or military teachers.

American and Taiwanese Contrasts: Grades and Success Versus Examinations and Friendship. Studying is of very nearly the same importance among both groups, but the general component of student, study, and learning is of far greater importance to Americans. Grades have a very high importance to Americans, but are not mentioned by the Taiwanese. As experts observe, grades are very important to the Taiwanese, as well. In the present case, the Taiwanese have taken the grade for granted. On the other hand, the latter have a great concern about examinations, while this response hardly appears among Americans. The principal is more prominent in the Taiwanese image of school. The Taiwanese give greater importance to friends and classmates than do Americans. They also place much more stress on acquiring knowledge in school. American mention of good schools and fun is exceeded by Taiwanese responses celebrating liberty and happiness. American emphasis on achievement and success is little reflected in the Taiwanese view of school. American complaints about boredom, discipline and money are also not shared by the Taiwanese.

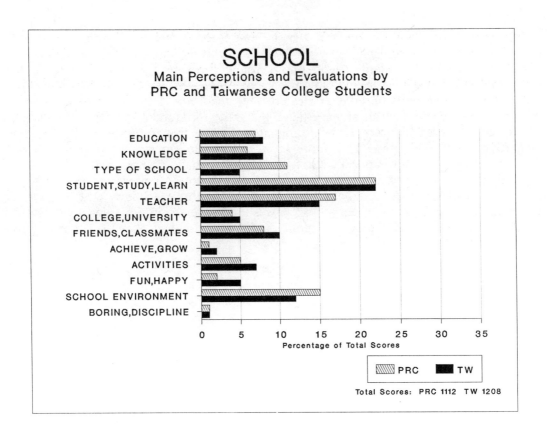

SCHOOL
Main Perceptions and Evaluations by
PRC and Taiwanese College Students

PRC Chinese View: Teacher, Classroom. Like the other groups, Mainlanders stress teachers and students, but they hardly mention books -- and, unlike the others, they don't mention libraries at all. On the other hand, more than the other groups, they stress the school environment, especially the classroom and the school building. Classmates are a more important part of their image of school than to the others, as is distinguishing between types of schools. Their greatest stress is on primary schools and universities. They have fewer complaints about school than the others.

Taiwanese View: Happy, Studying. For the Taiwanese, too, teachers come first to mind when schools are mentioned. Students studying are next in importance. There is a very strong stress on friends, and classmates -- which may explain why the Taiwanese, far more than the others, are happy to be in school. They have none of the complaints that appear among American responses. The only complaint of significance is competition. Far more than the others, the Taiwanese see schools as sources of knowledge. They express far more concern about examinations than do the other groups. The Taiwanese are the only ones to mention a history primary school, or military teachers.

PRC and Taiwanese Contrasts: Stoicism Versus Happiness. Examinations play a stronger role in the Taiwanese school experience than in the Mainlanders'. The Taiwanese, more than the Mainlanders, view schools as sources of education and knowledge. Distinguishing between different universities is more important to the Taiwanese than to Mainlanders. Physical activities, especially those on the sporting field, are of moderate interest to both groups [in contrast to the American group whose only significant activity is vacation]. The Mainland Chinese express less happiness about being in school than the Taiwanese, but they also have fewer complaints.

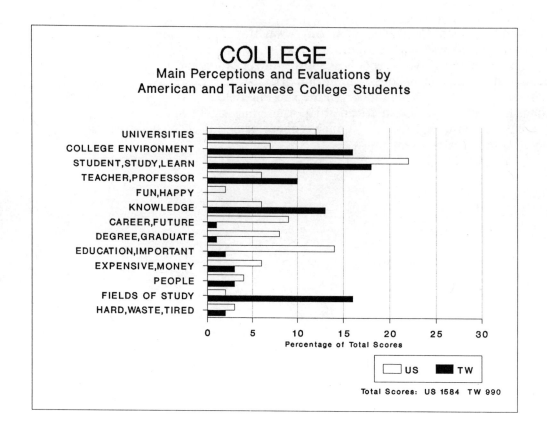

COLLEGE
Main Perceptions and Evaluations by American and Taiwanese College Students

American View: Books, Education, Degree. For Americans a college is a school where students study and learn from books and prepare for exams. Fraternities are an important part of campus life, as are sports, especially football. To Americans, much more than to the Chinese groups, a college is a place of education, a degree from which will help with career and job prospects. Money is a major obstacle, since colleges are expensive. To some Americans colleges are hard or tiring.

Taiwanese View: Knowledge, Literature, Freedom. Knowledge and its imparting and pursuit are of major importance in the Taiwanese view of college. More than for the other groups, fields of study capture their attention, led by literature, interdepartmental studies, and sociology. Friends and classmates are less important in college than in the context of school for the Taiwanese, and than they are to the other two groups in this setting. The freedom of the college environment has great appeal to the Taiwanese students.

American and Taiwanese Contrasts: Education and Friends Versus Freedom and Library.
The Taiwanese are more inclined than Americans to name specific universities: Soochow University, Harvard, Cambridge. They also place greater stress than Americans on students, but much less on study and books, and about the same amount on exams. The college environment is more important to the Taiwanese and of that, freedom receives the greatest emphasis. The important aspects of American campus life, such as fraternities, sports, football, and sororities, are not mentioned by the Taiwanese. Unlike the Americans, the Taiwanese mention classrooms. Professors get about the same amount of attention from both groups, but other teaching personnel get more mention from the Taiwanese. Knowledge is emphasized by the Taiwanese, while education is emphasized by Americans as a major contrast in their views of college. Unlike the Taiwanese, the Americans do not mention specific courses or subjects. The American emphasis on degrees and career is totally absent among the Taiwanese. Experts believe that the Taiwanese may have taken these for granted.

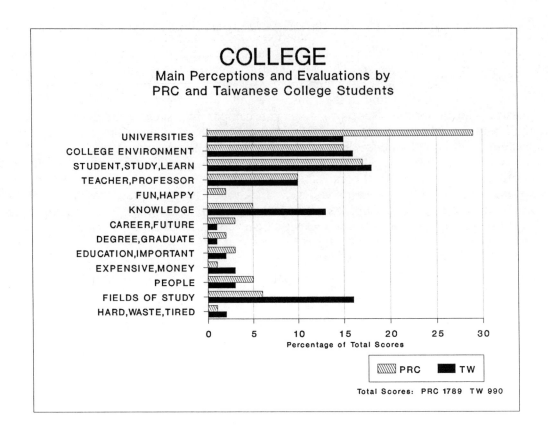

COLLEGE
Main Perceptions and Evaluations by PRC and Taiwanese College Students

PRC Chinese View: University, Classroom. Nothing exceeds the importance of a university for Mainlanders. They mention several institutions by name: Northeast University of Technology, Beijing University, Quing Hua University. For them a university is a beautiful place for students to study and for graduate students to do experiments and pursue advanced studies. The college environment holds more interest for them than for Americans and, again, as at secondary level, the classroom assumes great significance. Professors play a bigger role for the Mainlanders than for the others. Classmates are still very important to the PRC students at this level -- but less than they were in the context of school.

Taiwanese View: Knowledge, Literature, Freedom. Knowledge and its imparting and pursuit are of major importance in the Taiwanese view of college. More than for the other groups, fields of study capture their attention, led by literature, interdepartmental studies, and sociology. Friends and classmates are less important in college than in the context of school for the Taiwanese, and than they are to the other two groups in this setting. The freedom of the college environment has great appeal to the Taiwanese students.

232

PRC and Taiwanese Contrasts: Experiments in Advanced Studies Versus Literature. The university is about twice as important for the Mainlanders, compared to the Taiwanese. In regard to fields of study, the Taiwanese emphasize literature and interdepartmental studies, while the Mainlanders emphasize science and technology. Knowledge in general is stressed much more by the Taiwanese. Classmates are still quite important to the Mainlanders at this level, but are not mentioned by the Taiwanese.

EDUCATION
MAIN COMPONENTS AND RESPONSES

SCHOOL, COLLEGE	US	PRC	TW
	476	302	112
school,s	199	206	74
college	151	8	-
high school	19	-	-
university	16	33	3
secondary	15	-	-
elementary,primary	14	5	-
institution	11	-	-
Maryland	9	-	-
higher	7	-	-
schooling	7	-	-
building	7	-	-
private	6	-	-
continuing	5	-	-
library	5	-	-
public	5	-	-
education	-	12	-
system	-	10	15
level	-	10	-
school and college	-	9	-
middle school	-	9	-
crammed school	-	-	11
belief in form	-	-	5
facilities	-	-	4

STUDENT,LEARN,STUDY	US	PRC	TW
	349	249	247
learning,learn	138	-	2
book,s,textbooks	68	26	29
read,reading	28	-	-
study,studying	27	64	50
grades	13	-	-
student,s	11	122	55
training	11	-	-
test,s	8	-	-
academic	7	-	-
examination,exam,s	6	8	20
college paper	6	-	-
write	6	-	-
life long	6	-	-
preparation	4	-	-
listen	4	-	-
practice	4	-	-
notes	2	-	-
schoolwork	-	12	-
exercise	-	8	-
classroom	-	5	-
university student	-	4	-
long-standing project	-	-	40
entrance exam for college	-	-	32
classmates	-	-	6
cram	-	-	5
class	-	-	4
discipline	-	-	4

KNOWLEDGE,ENLIGHTENMENT	US	PRC	TW
	170	128	125
knowledge	89	67	57
intelligent,ce	27	8	-
smart	20	-	-
wisdom,wise	18	-	4
knowing	7	-	-
understand	5	-	-
explore	4	-	-
thought	-	33	8
intellectual	-	11	-
learn knowledge	-	9	-
enlightenment	-	-	22
imparting knowledge	-	-	14
knowledge seeking	-	-	10
I.Q.	-	-	7
theory	-	-	3

GOOD,NECESSARY	US	PRC	TW
	177	62	114
necessary,needed,need	62	-	4
good	30	13	-
important	29	14	-
help,helpful	13	6	-
mandatory	7	-	-
challenge	6	-	-
fun	6	-	-
success	5	-	-
valuable	5	-	-
love	4	-	18
want	4	-	-
useful,become useful	3	11	-
required	3	-	-
great	-	6	-
spirit	-	6	-
ideal	-	6	-
very important	-	-	53
holy	-	-	12
bel.in further studies	-	-	11
leading	-	-	10
duty	-	-	6

TEACHER,PROFESSOR	US	PRC	TW
	128	303	136
teacher,s	100	172	106
teach,teaching	18	27	7
professor,s	6	21	17
principal	4	-	-
teach and learn	-	49	-
foster	-	18	-
guide	-	16	-
cramming meth of teaching	-	-	6

JOB,CAREER,FUTURE	US	PRC	TW
	85	54	27
job,s	30	-	10
work	21	11	-
experience	13	-	-
career	13	-	-
goals	4	-	-
business	4	-	-
for the future	-	11	-
future	-	10	9
purpose	-	9	-
worker	-	6	-
faith	-	5	-
hopes	-	2	-
tool	-	-	8

COST: FREE,EXPENSIVE	US	PRC	TW
	38	5	43
expensive	18	-	-
money	13	-	8
grant	7	-	-
material	-	5	-
nine-year free education	-	-	22
tuition	-	-	8
pay out something	-	-	5

CULTURE,SOCIETY,PEOPLE	US	PRC	TW
	27	184	107
society	7	18	19
people	7	2	-
friend,s	6	-	-
me	4	-	-
children	3	-	23
culture, literature	-	74	-
civilization	-	25	-
human resource	-	14	-
educate people	-	12	-
parents	-	8	10
farmer	-	7	-
country	-	6	14
China	-	6	-
person	-	4	-
youth	-	4	-
motherland	-	4	-
culture	-	-	16
family	-	-	9
Confucius	-	-	7
authority	-	-	5
background	-	-	4

DEVELOPMENT	US	PRC	TW
	129	155	94
degree	35	-	10
achieve,achievement	11	-	-
B.S.	10	-	-
power	10	-	-
diploma	9	-	-
freedom	8	-	-
opportunity	8	-	-
development	7	36	14
advanced,advancement	7	28	-
graduation	7	-	-
B.A.	7	-	-
ability	5	-	4
improvement	5	-	-
reform	-	24	-
undertaking	-	21	-
for the world	-	10	-
skill, ability	-	9	-
backward	-	9	-
for the modernization	-	9	-
educational undertaking	-	9	-
progress	-	-	19
tree	-	-	14
growth	-	-	13
times	-	-	8
communication	-	-	4
to upgrade one's status	-	-	4
equality	-	-	4

FIELDS OF STUDY	US	PRC	TW
	75	151	19
life	19	5	-
sex	11	-	-
Math	10	-	-
courses	7	-	-
health	7	-	-
Law	7	-	-
special	6	-	-
English	5	6	-
sports	3	-	-
science	-	53	-
moral character	-	23	3
scientific education	-	17	-
development of science	-	9	-
science and technology	-	8	-
physical training	-	13	-
sanitation	-	7	-
environment	-	5	-
revolution	-	3	-
construction	-	2	-
liberal	-	-	6
Psychology	-	-	6
Art	-	-	4

GOVERNMENT	US	PRC	TW
	7	45	63
Board of	7	-	-
Ministry of Education	-	19	20
politics	-	15	-
economy	-	8	-
policy	-	3	12
educational department	-	-	12
measures	-	-	7
project of the nation	-	-	7
Minister of Education	-	-	5

FAILURE,PRESSURE	US	PRC	TW
	16	6	39
hard	6	-	-
bad	5	6	-
long	5	-	-
failure	-	-	13
fossified	-	-	10
repression	-	-	8
toilsome	-	-	4
illiterate person	-	-	4
burden	-	-	-

CHARACTER,PERSONALITY	US	PRC	TW
	0	36	106
cultivation	-	16	-
talented person	-	16	-
manner	-	4	-
cultivating good talents	-	-	25
reform of personality	-	-	18
change the social manners	-	-	17
conscience (-related)	-	-	10
patient	-	-	9
personality	-	-	7
set a good example	-	-	6
bearing	-	-	5
morality	-	-	5
how to live	-	-	4

SUMMARY

Main Components	Percentage of Total Score		
	US	PRC	TW
SCHOOL, COLLEGE	28	18	9
STUDENT,LEARN,STUDY	21	15	20
KNOWLEDGE,ENLIGHTENMENT	10	8	10
GOOD,NECESSARY	11	4	9
TEACHER,PROFESSOR	8	18	11
JOB,CAREER,FUTURE	5	3	2
COST: FREE,EXPENSIVE	2	0	3
CULTURE,SOCIETY,PEOPLE	2	11	9
DEVELOPMENT	8	9	8
FIELDS OF STUDY	4	9	2
GOVERNMENT	0	3	5
FAILURE,PRESSURE	1	0	3
CHARACTER,PERSONALITY	0	2	9
Total Scores	1677	1680	1232

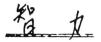

INTELLIGENCE
MAIN COMPONENTS AND RESPONSES

CLEVER,SMART	US	PRC	TW
	400	433	247
smarts	207	-	-
educated	48	-	-
common sense	27	-	-
genius	18	29	68
brilliant	16	5	-
bright	15	10	-
intelligent	13	-	-
gifted	11	-	-
clever	9	213	120
sensitive	9	-	-
perceptive	6	-	-
sense	5	-	-
quick	4	5	-
crafty	4	-	-
sharp	4	-	-
patience	4	-	-
brisk	-	34	-
high	-	33	39
shrewd	-	22	-
hardworking	-	13	2
strong	-	12	-
intelligence	-	11	-
quick-witted	-	11	-
acute	-	9	-
speed	-	8	-
abundant	-	7	-
tricky	-	6	-
smart	-	5	-
proud	-	-	6
clear	-	-	4
wit	-	-	4
class for geniuses	-	-	4

I.Q., TEST	US	PRC	TW
	179	42	224
I.Q	102	-	72
test,s	30	31	32
quotient	16	-	-
measures	8	-	-
degree	7	-	34
report card	7	-	-
S.A.T.	6	-	-
135-140	3	-	-
I.Q. test	-	11	46
I.Q. score	-	-	23
examination	-	-	17

KNOWLEDGE	US	PRC	TW
	176	105	114
knowledge	98	26	10
wisdom	21	39	31
understand,-ing	16	-	7
experience	13	-	-
insight	10	-	-
life	10	-	-
know	6	-	-
openness	2	-	-
wise merchant	-	40	62
insight(observation)	-	-	4

STUDY,SCHOOL	US	PRC	TW
	194	133	72
learn,learning	58	-	2
school	35	-	3
book,s	22	7	-
college	18	-	-
read,reading	14	-	-
study	10	42	-
student	10	-	-
grades	10	-	-
teacher	7	-	-
math	5	-	-
speech	5	-	-
cultivate	-	22	-
studious	-	22	-
priority, degree	-	15	-
intellectual education	-	9	-
study hard	-	7	-
university	-	5	-
science	-	4	7
study, learn	-	-	31
mathematics	-	-	7
education	-	-	6
cultivation	-	-	4
lessons	-	-	4
music	-	-	4
computer	-	-	2
efforts	-	-	2

CIA,FBI	US	PRC	TW
	112	0	0
CIA	47	-	-
FBI	20	-	-
spy,s	20	-	-
world	7	-	-
military	6	-	-
navy	5	-	-
foreign	5	-	-
secret	2	-	-

STUPID,DUMB	US	PRC	TW
	59	172	141
stupid	24	-	2
dumb	16	24	-
ignorance	7	-	-
problem,s	6	-	-
lack	6	-	-
dull	-	51	31
ignorant	-	13	-
inferior	-	13	-
low-grade	-	12	-
bad	-	12	-
awkward	-	10	-
not up to standard	-	9	-
low	-	9	-
fool	-	7	-
simple	-	6	-
slow	-	6	-
idiocy	-	-	47
retarded child	-	-	23
inequality	-	-	21
unfair	-	-	5
inferiority complex	-	-	4
useless effort	-	-	4
pitiable	-	-	4

CHILDREN,PEOPLE	US	PRC	TW
	115	48	36
me	22	1	-
myself,oneself	10	6	-
people	12	-	-
Einstein	9	-	4
parent	8	-	-
professor	7	-	-
childhood	7	-	-
man	7	-	-
father	6	-	-
sisters	5	-	-
politician	5	-	-
friend	5	-	-
Joe	5	-	-
Superfly	4	-	-
dad	3	-	-
person	-	14	-
child prodigy	-	10	20
child,-ren	-	8	4
scientist	-	6	-
civilization	-	3	-
Edison	-	-	3
great man	-	-	3
Superman	-	-	2

BRAIN,MIND,THINKING	US	PRC	TW
	113	164	70
brain	58	44	12
brain, mind	-	20	-
mind	22	-	-
thinking	14	17	11
logical,logic	7	-	5
thoughts	6	-	-
feelings	6	-	-
memory (recollection)	-	22	-
creation	-	18	-
mental capacity	-	16	-
imaginative power	-	13	-
faculty of understanding	-	8	-
exercise	-	6	-
judgment	-	-	9
creativity	-	-	8
imagination	-	-	7
analysis	-	-	7
exercise one's faculty	-	-	5
head	-	-	4
recollection	-	-	2

COMPETITION,CONTEST	US	PRC	TW
	0	27	5
competition, contest	-	24	-
intellectual tournament	-	3	-
superiority in competition	-	-	5

ABILITY: INNATE,INBORN	US	PRC	TW
	111	146	187
ability	31	55	40
innate	13	-	-
power	13	-	-
inherent	11	-	-
potential	11	-	-
native	10	-	-
age	8	-	-
natural	7	-	-
genetic	4	-	-
born	3	-	-
responsive ability	-	38	-
inborn	-	23	-
difference	-	9	-
analytical capacity	-	9	-
heredity	-	7	-
factor	-	5	-
congenital	-	-	79
depend on one's efforts	-	-	36
heritage	-	-	20
different among people	-	-	12

DEVELOPMENT	US	PRC	TW
	62	241	78
work	15	8	-
maturity	9	-	-
developed	7	49	-
achievement	7	6	29
communicate	7	-	-
success	6	11	9
goals	4	-	-
planning	4	-	-
growing,growth	3	7	-
development	-	116	8
invention	-	23	8
mobility	-	9	-
intellect development	-	7	-
future	-	5	6
attainment	-	-	10
progress	-	-	5
cooperative	-	-	3

GOOD,DESIRABLE	US	PRC	TW
	79	51	10
good	23	47	2
desirable	11	-	-
valuable	9	-	-
useful	7	-	-
admire	7	-	-
respected	6	-	-
necessary	6	-	-
want	5	-	-
helpful	5	-	-
great	-	4	-
confidence	-	-	4
beautiful	-	-	4

MISCELLANEOUS	US	PRC	TW
	5	0	7
money	5	-	-
class for handicapped	-	-	4
animals	-	-	3

SUMMARY

Main Components	Percentage of Total Score		
	US	PRC	TW
CLEVER,SMART	25	28	21
I.Q., TEST	11	3	19
KNOWLEDGE	11	7	10
STUDY,SCHOOL	12	9	6
CIA,FBI	7	0	0
STUPID,DUMB	4	11	12
CHILDREN,PEOPLE	7	3	3
BRAIN,MIND,THINKING	7	10	6
ABILITY: INNATE,INBORN	7	9	16
DEVELOPMENT	4	15	7
GOOD,DESIRABLE	5	3	1
COMPETITION,CONTEST	0	2	0
MISCELLANEOUS	0	0	1
Total Scores	1605	1562	1191

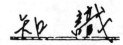

KNOWLEDGE
MAIN COMPONENTS AND RESPONSES

EDUCATION,SCHOOL	US	PRC	TW
	513	321	352
education	149	13	25
learning	80	27	37
school	67	16	32
college	66	-	-
learned	57	-	-
study,studying	37	108	56
study hard	-	10	-
study in school	-	-	16
degree	11	-	-
listen,listening	9	-	-
idea,s	8	-	8
relate	8	-	-
willing to	7	-	-
university	5	-	4
question	4	-	-
acquired	3	-	-
student,s	2	31	-
practice	-	15	-
level	-	12	8
erudite	-	11	18
research	-	10	9
have class	-	9	-
learn	-	8	-
creation	-	8	-
hunt for	-	8	-
sports	-	8	-
university students	-	7	4
exercise	-	6	-
studious	-	5	-
pursue	-	3	25
content	-	3	-
regular pattern	-	3	-
cultivate the essentials	-	-	31
tool	-	-	15
special skills	-	-	11
self-cultivation	-	-	10
attended class	-	-	7
basic education	-	-	6
creativity	-	-	6
cope with problems	-	-	6
self-pursuing	-	-	5
travel	-	-	5
vending	-	-	4
thirsty for	-	-	2
examination	-	-	2

WORK,EXPERIENCE	US	PRC	TW
	100	58	62
experience	49	-	27
life	14	7	-
work	11	22	4
streets	10	-	-
living	7	-	12
money	5	-	-
job	4	-	-
production	-	9	-
labor	-	7	-
machinery	-	5	-
worker	-	5	-
factory	-	3	-
have a job	-	-	10
profession	-	-	4
making money	-	-	3
require	-	-	2

INTELLIGENCE,WISDOM	US	PRC	TW
	509	134	219
intelligent,ce	118	3	-
smart	97	-	-
understand	71	-	-
wisdom,wise	77	9	47
know how	36	-	-
brain,s	26	-	5
think	14	-	-
knowing	11	-	-
insight	10	-	-
sense	10	-	-
wonder	10	-	-
awareness	9	-	-
mind	8	-	-
common sense	7	-	20
perception	5	-	-
intellectual	-	36	15
know well	-	20	-
ability	-	19	5
talent	-	16	-
clever	-	13	-
talent and ability	-	9	-
realize	-	7	-
talent & capacity	-	2	2
knowledge	-	-	81
judgment	-	-	13
thought	-	-	10
recognition	-	-	9
inward bearing	-	-	7
understanding	-	-	5

BOOKS	US	PRC	TW
	123	119	112
books	82	110	81
library	17	6	12
reading,read	24	-	-
reading cursorily	-	3	-
words	-	-	8
information	-	-	7
newspaper	-	-	4

FIELDS OF KNOWLEDGE	US	PRC	TW
	27	169	43
science	13	67	12
literature	7	13	-
discipline	7	-	-
type	-	11	-
mathematics	-	11	-
rocket	-	9	-
technology	-	8	-
history	-	7	-
chemistry	-	6	-
apply	-	6	-
element	-	6	-
social knowledge	-	6	-
development of science	-	5	-
physics	-	5	-
invent	-	4	-
social science	-	3	-
language	-	2	4
philosophy	-	-	8
application	-	-	7
humanistic fields	-	-	6
new discovery	-	-	4
ocean	-	-	2

CULTURE,SOCIETY	US	PRC	TW
	0	82	24
culture	-	42	13
society	-	26	-
service	-	7	-
motherland	-	5	-
civilization	-	2	5
facts of society	-	-	4
television	-	-	2

TEACHER,DOCTOR	US	PRC	TW
	98	78	43
teacher	-	51	18
teaching,teach	40	-	-
professor,s	11	5	2
people	11	-	-
scholars	10	-	11
oneself,self	6	4	-
giving	5	-	-
parent,s	4	-	3
Einstein	4	-	-
leaders	4	-	-
me	3	-	-
scientist	-	7	-
doctor	-	5	2
human being	-	3	-
give a lecture	-	3	-
friends	-	-	7

FORCE,POWER	US	PRC	TW
	46	155	79
force	-	146	74
power	39	-	-
God	7	-	-
knowledge is energy	-	9	-
from the natural	-	-	5

TREASURE,GOOD,VALUABLE	US	PRC	TW
	112	55	81
good	35	-	-
important	17	6	11
useful	17	6	1
helpful	10	-	-
necessary,need	14	-	12
want	7	-	-
key	7	-	-
respected,respect	5	-	3
treasure, wealth	-	21	-
happiness	-	8	-
interest,-ing	-	8	-
foundation	-	4	-
utilize	-	2	-
precious	-	-	22
attractive (magnetic)	-	-	10
help the world	-	-	7
ideal	-	-	6
essential	-	-	5
good (n.)	-	-	4

TRUTH,FACTS	US	PRC	TW
	60	0	8
truth	37	-	4
common	13	-	-
facts	10	-	-
faith	-	-	4

ABUNDANT,VAST	US	PRC	TW
	2	96	47
abundant	-	33	-
profound	-	15	2
accumulate	-	10	21
wide range	-	10	-
plenty	-	9	-
vast	-	6	-
wide	-	5	-
amount	-	5	-
flourishing	-	3	-
endless	-	-	16
the more, the better	-	-	5
no limit	-	-	3
depth	2	-	-

ACHIEVEMENT	US	PRC	TW
	46	136	46
expanding	11	-	-
successful	9	-	-
growth	8	-	-
tree	7	-	-
achieve,achievement	6	14	4
independence	5	-	-
construction	-	15	-
remake the world	-	13	-
development,developed	-	22	-
make great efforts	-	11	-
modernization	-	10	-
make progress	-	10	4
accept	-	9	-
future	-	8	5
contribution	-	8	-
social progress	-	8	-
hobby	-	5	-
reform	-	3	-
enrich oneself	-	-	19
enlarge one's horizon	-	-	14

SUFFERING, HARMFUL	US	PRC	TW
	14	12	15
ignorance	7	9	-
stupidity	7	-	-
backward	-	3	-
sins	-	-	6
suffering	-	-	5
harmful to people	-	-	4

MISCELLANEOUS	US	PRC	TW
	8	10	53
foods	8	-	-
battle outfit	-	8	-
major	-	2	-
death	-	-	29
bearing	-	-	12
very	-	-	8
an expression	-	-	4

SUMMARY

Main Components	Percentage of Total Score		
	US	PRC	TW
EDUCATION,SCHOOL	31	23	30
WORK,EXPERIENCE	6	4	5
INTELLIGENCE,WISDOM	31	9	18
BOOKS	7	8	9
TRUTH,FACTS	4	0	1
FIELDS OF KNOWLEDGE	2	12	4
CULTURE,SOCIETY	0	6	2
TEACHER,DOCTOR	6	5	4
FORCE,POWER	3	11	7
TREASURE,GOOD,VALUABLE	7	4	7
ABUNDANT,VAST	0	7	4
ACHIEVEMENT	3	10	4
SUFFERING, HARMFUL	1	1	1
MISCELLANEOUS	0	1	4
Total Scores	1658	1425	1184

STUDY
MAIN COMPONENTS AND RESPONSES

BOOKS,READ,LIBRARY	US	PRC	TW
	410	371	89
book,s	166	96	25
reading,read books	45	52	16
library	42	6	-
room,hall,den	50	-	-
time	22	13	12
desk,chair	14	39	-
note,s,notebook	12	17	2
writing,write	11	14	6
quiet	11	-	-
pen,ink	7	79	5
hours,night	12	-	-
habits	7	-	-
light,lamp	6	9	4
words	5	-	7
classroom	-	23	6
textbook	-	13	4
study facility	-	10	-
computer	-	-	2

EDUCATION	US	PRC	TW
	76	5	35
education	43	5	20
educate,teach	26	-	-
schooling	7	-	-
teach a lesson	-	-	10
instruct	-	-	5

SCHOOL,TEACHER,STUDENT	US	PRC	TW
	299	164	115
school	164	27	28
teacher,s	49	42	36
student,s	34	50	14
college	25	-	-
people,person	11	4	-
university	9	16	-
scholar	7	-	-
classmates	-	10	4
scientists	-	8	-
relationship	-	4	-
society	-	3	8
socialization	-	-	15
association with others	-	-	6
friend	-	-	4

TESTS,HOMEWORK	US	PRC	TW
	215	146	45
test,s	65	-	-
homework	34	18	6
exam,s	29	11	2
paper,s	22	21	-
grades	20	-	-
research	16	18	-
examine	8	-	-
class	8	-	-
graduate	5	-	-
type	5	-	-
report	3	-	-
school records	-	33	-
attend class,school	-	29	20
listen to a lecture	-	16	-
review	-	-	9
grade (g.p.a.)	-	-	4
discussion	-	-	2
ask questions	-	-	2

FIELDS OF STUDY	US	PRC	TW
	76	118	67
history	16	-	-
subjects,courses	24	-	-
math	11	10	-
life,daily life	11	31	-
English	7	-	-
foreign,language	4	15	7
music	3	-	-
science	-	16	-
technology	-	14	18
sports	-	10	-
play balls	-	9	-
major	-	8	-
literature	-	5	-
human life	-	-	25
speaking English	-	-	13
unlimited	-	-	4

HARD,DIFFICULT	US	PRC	TW
	57	70	67
hard,hardship	47	21	-
difficult,difficulty	10	11	10
laborious, toilsome	-	28	20
arduous	-	10	-
struggle	-	-	29
suffering	-	-	8

INTERESTING,JOYFUL	US	PRC	TW
	23	126	104
enjoy,joy,joyful	6	32	25
fun	6	-	-
must	6	-	-
important	5	-	7
interesting,interest	-	48	19
cultural recreation	-	12	-
good	-	9	-
good & bad	-	8	-
recreation	-	8	-
happy,happiness	-	6	10
replenish	-	3	-
cheerful	-	-	16
necessary	-	-	6
independent	-	-	6
attitude	-	-	4
desire	-	-	4
active	-	-	4
new	-	-	3

KNOWLEDGE,LEARN	US	PRC	TW
	223	191	164
learn,learning	139	-	-
knowledge,gain knowledge	37	128	73
thinking,think	14	-	2
understand,understanding	10	-	7
intellect	8	-	-
brains	7	-	-
know	4	-	-
mind	4	-	-
literature & knowledge	-	54	-
competence	-	5	-
clever	-	3	-
innovation	-	1	-
pursue new knowledge	-	-	43
wisdom	-	-	8
learn new things	-	-	7
increase in knowledge	-	-	7
enlightenment	-	-	7
genius	-	-	6
pondering	-	-	4

GROWTH,PROGRESS	US	PRC	TW
	10	134	192
grow,growth	7	-	27
observe	3	-	-
for the country	-	16	-
ability	-	15	-
target	-	14	-
achievement	-	11	7
progress, advance	-	11	-
future	-	10	4
purposes	-	9	-
talent and ability	-	8	-
service	-	7	-
behave as a person	-	6	-
reform	-	5	-
skill and ability	-	5	-
contribution	-	5	-
become useful person	-	4	-
prospect	-	3	-
forge ahead	-	3	-
status	-	2	-
live and learn	-	-	33
seek for progress	-	-	26
experience	-	-	21
behave	-	-	14
capability	-	-	13
success	-	-	9
many-sided	-	-	7
not too proud to question	-	-	7
curious	-	-	6
every place	-	-	5
potential	-	-	5
model	-	-	4
undertaking	-	-	4

STUDIOUS,DEDICATED	US	PRC	TW
	0	141	24
assiduous	-	88	-
earnest	-	19	4
studious, industrious	-	16	-
firm	-	8	-
faith	-	7	-
indomitable	-	3	-
far-sighted	-	-	6
pay out	-	-	5
encouragement	-	-	5
price paid	-	-	4

MAKE EFFORT,CONCENTRATE	US	PRC	TW
	93	166	129
concentrate,-ed	19	-	8
absorb	15	-	-
apply	14	-	-
memorize	11	-	-
cram	10	-	-
discipline	9	-	4
training	7	-	-
goal	5	-	-
long	3	-	-
study by self	-	32	12
make efforts	-	48	-
study hard,study	-	30	-
study intensively,intense	-	23	5
method,s	-	19	6
constancy of purpose	-	9	-
strive,striving	-	5	6
process	-	-	21
recollection	-	-	11
recognize	-	-	9
perseverance	-	-	9
challenge	-	-	8
take pains	-	-	8
hard-working	-	-	6
continuous	-	-	4
self-requiring	-	-	4
efforts	-	-	4
try	-	-	4

WORK,JOB	US	PRC	TW
	120	94	28
work	97	-	10
profession	13	-	-
job,s, work	5	85	5
career	5	2	-
climb	-	7	-
working place	-	-	7
modest (working hard)	-	-	6

BORING,IGNORANT,ERROR	US	PRC	TW
	29	14	50
boring	16	-	-
money	5	-	8
forget	5	-	7
passing	3	-	-
senseless	-	5	-
force	-	5	-
short-sightedness	-	4	-
error	-	-	12
ignorant	-	-	8
crammed school	-	-	7
failure	-	-	4
bondage	-	-	4

MISCELLANEOUS	US	PRC	TW
	9	21	42
look	5	-	-
pencil	4	-	-
rest	-	9	-
movement	-	5	-
eating	-	4	-
condition	-	3	-
practice	-	-	10
baby,child	-	-	14
parent,relatives	-	-	7
level	-	-	4
t.v.	-	-	4
bookbag	-	-	3

SUMMARY

Main Components	Percentage of Total Score		
	US	PRC	TW
BOOKS,READ,LIBRARY	25	21	8
EDUCATION	5	0	3
SCHOOL,TEACHER,STUDENT	18	9	10
TESTS,HOMEWORK	13	8	4
FIELDS OF STUDY	5	7	6
INTERESTING,JOYFUL	1	7	9
KNOWLEDGE,LEARN	14	11	14
HARD,DIFFICULT	3	4	6
GROWTH,PROGRESS	1	8	17
MAKE EFFORT,CONCENTRATE	6	9	11
WORK,JOB	7	5	2
STUDIOUS,DEDICATED	0	8	2
BORING,IGNORANT,ERROR	2	1	4
MISCELLANEOUS	1	1	4
Total Scores	1640	1761	1151

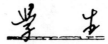

STUDENT
MAIN COMPONENTS AND RESPONSES

	US	PRC	TW
BOOKS,SUPPLIES	77	145	41
book,s	60	49	12
pencil	8	-	-
handbook	7	-	-
pen	2	29	2
bookbag,schoolbag	-	33	19
table	-	10	-
glasses	-	7	5
chalk,blackboard	-	12	-
desk	-	4	-
textbook	-	1	3

	US	PRC	TW
SCHOOL,CLASS	376	261	114
school	141	176	42
college	93	-	-
class,es,go to class	77	19	5
University of Maryland	20	-	-
high school	17	-	-
dorms,hostel,housing	12	2	-
tuition	10	-	-
elementary	6	-	-
daily life	-	30	-
classroom	-	24	-
spirit	-	6	-
campus	-	4	4
go to school	-	-	20
attend classes,school	-	-	20
cut class	-	-	14
school bus	-	-	5
travel	-	-	4

	US	PRC	TW
STUDY,EXAMS	286	463	393
study	122	318	92
grades	38	-	-
homework,do homework	17	16	-
graduate,graduation	16	-	-
test,s	15	-	-
degree	14	-	5
library	9	3	10
paper,s	9	-	-
write	8	-	-
examination,exams	6	13	82
lecture	5	-	-
difficult	5	-	-
easy	5	-	-
pass	4	-	-
time consuming,time	7	-	-
research	2	5	-
notes	2	-	-
pressure	2	-	-
study knowledge	-	21	-
school record	-	18	-
science	-	11	-
curious and studious	-	9	-
study hard	-	8	12
make efforts, hard-working	-	8	-
hard-working	-	7	-
literature	-	6	2
study by self	-	6	-
health	-	6	-
studious	-	4	-
assignment	-	4	-
reading	-	-	79
hand in the homework	-	-	20
struggle	-	-	12
doing one's obligation	-	-	11
lessons	-	-	9
lucky times	-	-	8
cramming	-	-	7
crammed school (cramming)	-	-	6
report	-	-	5
pressure-free	-	-	5
not studying hard	-	-	5
academic transcript	-	-	4
burn the midnight oil	-	-	4
pressure from exams	-	-	4
conflict	-	-	4
discussion	-	-	4
recollection	-	-	3

	US	PRC	TW
TEACHER	31	161	65
teacher,s	28	154	65
professor	3	7	-

	US	PRC	TW
YOUTH,AGE	25	38	42
future	11	3	8
young,youths	9	4	20
kids	5	-	-
age	-	21	-
parent,s	-	10	4
immature	-	-	6
still very young	-	-	4

	US	PRC	TW
TYPE OF STUDENT	87	362	6
university	22	1	2
pupil	16	-	-
person	11	-	-
forever	7	-	-
people	7	-	-
group	7	-	-
freshman	7	-	-
co-ed	7	-	-
medical	3	-	-
university student	-	97	-
middle sch. student	-	56	-
elementary sch. students	-	35	-
male	-	32	-
primary sch. student	-	31	-
female student,female	-	30	-
student	-	10	-
leader	-	9	-
student studying abroad	-	9	-
graduate student	-	9	-
beautiful	-	9	-
doctor	-	8	-
cadre	-	8	-
student(univ,mid&primary)	-	7	-
boy student	-	5	-
boy classmates	-	3	-
male and female	-	3	-
pillars (of a nation)	-	-	4

	US	PRC	TW
JOBS,MONEY	86	69	24
work,worker	32	45	-
money	15	-	9
government	15	-	-
poor	11	-	-
loan	9	-	-
expensive	4	-	-
labor	-	10	-
farmer	-	8	-
friendship	-	6	-
find and do a job	-	-	5
profession	-	-	5
working parttime	-	-	5

	US	PRC	TW
PARTY,FRIENDS,FUN	101	101	133
party,s	36	-	-
friend,s,making friends	29	-	11
fun	12	-	-
drink	9	-	-
happy	6	7	16
play,play games	5	-	5
social life	4	-	-
classmate	-	28	12
exercise	-	21	6
relationship	-	9	-
sports	-	8	-
physical training	-	6	-
evening party	-	6	-
sing (a song)	-	6	-
dance	-	6	-
play balls	-	4	-
carefree	-	-	20
pleasure-seeking	-	-	20
cheerful in life	-	-	12
fooling around	-	-	12
activities,active	-	-	12
movies	-	-	4
drink wine	-	-	3

	US	PRC	TW
LEARN,KNOWLEDGE	213	129	146
learn,s,learning,learner	103	-	-
education,educated	35	18	16
smart	23	-	-
knowledge,-able	17	54	42
responsibility	8	-	8
intelligent	8	-	-
growth	7	-	4
important	5	-	-
fast	4	-	-
educate	3	-	-
intellectual	-	9	-
thinking,thought	-	16	12
scholar	-	7	-
achievement	-	5	7
ability	-	5	-
interest	-	5	-
clever	-	5	-
win honor for country	-	5	-
obtain knowledge	-	-	41
care for society	-	-	4
ask questions	-	-	4
learn while teaching	-	-	4
cram student w/ knowledge	-	-	4

	US	PRC	TW
ME,MYSELF	151	0	18
me	134	-	-
oneself,myself	17	-	18

	US	PRC	TW
NAIVE,SIMPLE	11	122	123
good	8	15	-
hope	3	-	-
naive	-	27	-
simple and pure	-	22	-
be polite	-	11	-
ask for advice	-	10	-
simple	-	8	-
lovable	-	6	-
moral character	-	6	-
want to learn	-	6	-
vivid, lively	-	5	-
yearn for	-	4	-
ideal	-	2	-
clean and honest	-	-	20
obedient,obey	-	-	19
pitiable person	-	-	9
ignorant	-	-	9
dull	-	-	8
rebel	-	-	8
naughty	-	-	8
passive	-	-	7
wish	-	-	7
limited	-	-	5
stupid	-	-	5
good-hearted	-	-	5
easy-going	-	-	5
respect for teachers	-	-	4
open	-	-	4

	US	PRC	TW
UNIFORM,CLOTHING	9	0	31
skirt	7	-	-
clothes	2	-	-
uniforms	-	-	31

	US	PRC	TW
MISCELLANEOUS	79	8	36
life	19	-	-
union	18	-	-
body	11	-	-
car	8	-	-
rates	5	-	-
apple	5	-	-
drugs	5	-	-
discount	4	-	-
unite	-	6	-
May 4th movement of 1919	-	2	-
community	-	-	14
unwilling to go up in soc	-	-	7
pitiful	-	-	6
repression	-	-	5
not free	-	-	4
I.D.	4	-	-

SUMMARY

Main Components	Percentage of Total Score		
	US	PRC	TW
BOOKS,SUPPLIES	5	8	3
SCHOOL,CLASS	25	14	10
STUDY,EXAMS	19	25	34
TEACHER	2	9	6
TYPE OF STUDENT	6	19	1
JOBS,MONEY	6	4	2
PARTY,FRIENDS,FUN	7	5	11
LEARN,KNOWLEDGE	14	7	12
ME,MYSELF	10	0	2
YOUTH,AGE	2	2	4
NAIVE,SIMPLE	1	7	10
UNIFORM,CLOTHING	1	0	3
MISCELLANEOUS	5	0	3
Total Scores	1532	1859	1172

TEACHER
MAIN COMPONENTS AND RESPONSES

	US	PRC	TW
SCHOOL,COLLEGE,CLASS	276	112	67
school	162	26	21
classes	40	-	-
college	33	-	-
university	14	13	-
high school	13	2	-
elementary,primary	11	-	8
field	3	-	-
classroom	-	46	10
house	-	10	-
office	-	10	-
platform	-	5	8
corridor	-	-	9
crammed school	-	-	7
after class	-	-	4
LEARNING,EDUCATION	213	153	89
learning	97	13	4
education	66	53	23
test,s	16	-	-
homework	13	-	-
papers	7	-	-
notes	5	-	-
life long	5	-	-
degree	4	-	-
study	-	34	-
assignment	-	15	4
correct students'homework	-	13	-
prepare lessons	-	11	-
reading, study in school	-	5	-
home	-	5	-
study abroad	-	4	-
exam	-	-	29
roll-calling	-	-	11
transcript	-	-	8
lower the grades	-	-	6
book learning	-	-	4
KNOWLEDGEABLE	134	198	161
knowledge,knowledgeable	64	72	23
wisdom,wise	18	4	4
understand	18	-	-
experience	16	-	5
intelligent	11	-	-
smart	7	-	-
diligent	-	21	-
spiritual engineer	-	33	-
propagate knowledge	-	12	-
industrious	-	12	-
industrious gardener	-	10	-
source of knowledge	-	10	-
teach knowledge	-	9	-
learned	-	8	-
earnest	-	4	2
advanced	-	3	-
treasure of knowledge	-	-	47
sower of knowledge	-	-	23
dignified	-	-	20
erudite	-	-	15
conscientious	-	-	6
hard-working	-	-	6
truth	-	-	5
dutiful	-	-	5
PROFESSOR,INSTRUCTOR	322	117	45
professor	94	21	19
instructor	72	-	-
woman,en, lady	25	-	-
grader	24	-	-
helper	24	-	-
job	12	-	-
leader	11	-	-
mind reader	10	-	-
principal	9	-	-
man,male	7	12	-
trainer	7	-	-
aide	7	-	-
female,teacher	6	9	-
developer	5	-	-
educator	4	-	-
counselor	3	-	-
work	2	15	-
lecturers	-	13	-
act as a teacher	-	13	-
person	-	12	8
teacher	-	10	-
human resource	-	7	-
occupation	-	5	-
work on job	-	-	5
tutor	-	-	5
thankful teacher	-	-	5
assistant	-	-	3

	US	PRC	TW
STUDENT	121	151	66
student,s	102	121	59
pupil	19	-	-
classmates	-	30	-
relationship w/teacher	-	-	7
BOOKS,SUPPLIES	99	89	69
book,s	52	11	2
chalk	11	26	13
blackboard	11	25	20
desk	11	9	-
ruler	11	-	-
pointer	3	-	21
candle	-	18	-
textbook	-	-	13
TEACH,EDUCATE	151	269	214
teach without discriminat ion	-	-	5
teach,-ing	40	35	62
guide	24	-	4
lecture,give lectures	18	-	15
helping,help	16	6	-
math	16	-	-
give	9	-	-
impart	8	9	-
subject	8	-	-
English	7	-	-
language	5	-	-
talk in class,give lecture	-	58	-
have classes,give lectures	-	49	-
instruct, educate	-	24	-
solve difficult question	-	16	-
cultivate	-	15	-
daily life	-	13	-
educate people	-	10	-
teach students	-	9	-
ability	-	9	-
help straighten wrong	-	5	-
explain	-	5	-
teach people	-	3	-
spirit	-	3	-
solves confusing problems	-	-	31
impart great prin. of sage	-	-	25
teach lessons	-	-	21
to be fond of teaching	-	-	13
indicator	-	-	11
educate	-	-	10
character	-	-	8
edifying	-	-	5
speaking	-	-	4
ELDER,OLD	10	66	17
old,older generation	10	20	-
teacher, older people	-	19	-
elder,senior,elders	-	14	17
age	-	13	-
PARENTS,OTHER PEOPLE	57	69	25
mother	17	4	-
me	10	-	-
parents	9	34	4
father	9	-	-
preacher	7	-	-
people	5	-	-
gardener	-	12	-
mankind	-	11	-
doctor	-	8	-
Confucius	-	-	15
myself (me)	-	-	6
RESPECT,ESTEEM	78	172	145
apple	32	-	-
authority	30	-	36
respect	14	76	-
respectable	-	35	-
be respected	-	16	-
respectful	-	-	44
influential	2	-	10
esteem	-	24	-
status	-	6	4
morals	-	6	-
glory	-	5	-
revere	-	4	-
example	-	-	10
worshipped	-	-	9
set an example	-	-	8
serious	-	-	7
respect the teacher	-	-	5
obey	-	-	4
to be held highly	-	-	4
Teachers' Day	-	-	4

	US	PRC	TW
PROBLEMS	62	66	104
pet	15	-	-
bad	8	-	-
lover	8	-	-
show-offs	7	-	-
over bearing	5	-	-
mean	5	-	-
transfer	5	-	-
substitute	5	-	-
strike	4	-	-
hardship	-	32	-
glasses	-	15	8
some are good,some bad	-	10	-
strict, severe	-	6	-
force	-	3	-
brutal	-	-	20
punishment	-	-	10
stern	-	-	8
doctrinaire	-	-	8
beating others	-	-	8
dull	-	-	5
boring	-	-	5
teachers are very poor	-	-	5
old hand-outs	-	-	5
on leave	-	-	4
pressure	-	-	4
play truant	-	-	4
hard to be close to	-	-	4
mislead students	-	-	3
scold students	-	-	3
DEAR,KIND,FRIEND	69	234	81
good	18	-	-
friendly	13	-	-
patient	12	13	4
important	7	-	-
interested	5	-	-
helpful	5	-	-
advice	5	-	-
discipline	4	-	-
kind,-ly,kindness	-	43	12
dear,dear person	-	49	-
great	-	19	10
lovable	-	19	-
selfless	-	17	-
take every care for	-	14	-
cherish	-	10	-
graceful	-	9	-
friendly affection	-	8	-
amiable & easy to approach	-	8	-
careful	-	8	-
willingly bear burden	-	6	-
have deep love in	-	5	-
beautiful	-	3	-
courtesy	-	3	-
good friend	-	-	25
loving heart	-	-	12
always help people	-	-	8
tender	-	-	5
forgiving	-	-	5
MISCELLANEOUS	3	7	4
Smith	3	-	-
abundant	-	4	-
vidgepole & beam	-	3	-
vacation	-	-	4

SUMMARY

Main Components	Percentage of Total Score		
	US	PRC	TW
SCHOOL,COLLEGE,CLASS	17	7	6
LEARNING,EDUCATION	13	9	8
KNOWLEDGEABLE	8	12	15
STUDENT	8	9	6
PROFESSOR,INSTRUCTOR	20	7	4
BOOKS,SUPPLIES	6	5	6
TEACH,EDUCATE	9	16	20
PARENTS,OTHER PEOPLE	4	4	2
RESPECT,ESTEEM	5	10	13
PROBLEMS	4	4	10
DEAR,KIND,FRIEND	4	14	7
ELDER,OLD	1	4	2
MISCELLANEOUS	0	0	0
Total Scores	1595	1703	1087

SCHOOL
MAIN COMPONENTS AND RESPONSES

EDUCATION	US	PRC	TW
EDUCATION	147	76	95
education	136	57	82
educate	11	-	-
cultivate human resource	-	16	8
culture	-	3	-
socialization	-	-	5

KNOWLEDGE	US	PRC	TW
KNOWLEDGE	105	63	96
knowledge	34	43	46
intellect	12	-	-
courses	8	-	-
language	8	-	-
scholar,s	6	-	-
subjects	6	-	-
art	6	-	-
math	5	-	-
English	5	-	-
thought	4	-	5
science	3	3	-
lessons	3	-	8
religion	3	-	-
understand	2	-	-
foster	-	10	-
ability	-	7	2
knowledge-seeking	-	-	13
imparting of knowledge	-	-	12
pondering	-	-	6
wisdom	-	-	4

TYPE OF SCHOOL	US	PRC	TW
TYPE OF SCHOOL	124	125	65
high,high school	46	49	23
Catholic	24	-	-
institute	13	-	-
grammar	11	-	-
elementary	11	-	-
public	6	-	-
higher	5	-	-
private	5	-	-
nursery	3	-	-
primary school	-	50	-
beautiful	-	10	-
big	-	9	-
country	-	4	-
one's old school	-	3	-
history primary school	-	-	27
kindergarten	-	-	10
organization	-	-	5

STUDENT,STUDY,LEARN	US	PRC	TW
STUDENT,STUDY,LEARN	583	250	261
book,s	87	8	8
learn	79	-	-
learning	69	-	-
study,studying,studies	67	69	75
grade,s	49	-	-
work	47	7	-
class,es	37	-	-
student,s	35	95	92
homework	34	-	-
reading,read,read books	19	9	-
pencil,s	11	-	-
tests	11	-	-
writing	9	-	-
exams	7	-	-
attend	7	-	-
challenge	7	-	-
hard	6	-	-
spelling	2	-	-
in class	-	27	-
have class	-	18	-
pen	-	7	2
examination	-	5	35
school record	-	5	-
on the class	-	-	29
ways to behave oneself	-	-	7
class attendent	-	-	5
recollection	-	-	4
research	-	-	4

TEACHER	US	PRC	TW
TEACHER	224	185	179
teacher,s	180	150	135
teach	16	-	-
principal	11	18	26
teaching	9	10	2
teaches,taught	8	-	-
professor	-	4	2
scientist	-	3	-
military teacher	-	-	10
technique	-	-	4

FRIENDS,CLASSMATES	US	PRC	TW
FRIENDS,CLASSMATES	119	89	124
children,kids	50	-	-
friend,s	36	-	27
people	12	-	-
-classmate,s	8	60	41
youth	7	-	-
young	6	-	-
human resource	-	13	-
unite	-	12	-
mankind	-	2	-
male and female	-	2	-
make friends,friendship	-	-	18
groups	-	-	10
human group	-	-	10
family	-	-	7
pure	-	-	6
interrelationship	-	-	5

ACHIEVE,GROW	US	PRC	TW
ACHIEVE,GROW	70	14	22
achieve	16	-	-
success	13	-	-
future	8	1	-
progress	7	-	-
years	7	-	-
advance	5	-	-
growth	4	-	-
time	4	-	-
graduate	4	-	-
diploma	2	-	6
grow up	-	7	6
cradle	-	6	-
further one's studies	-	-	10

ACTIVITIES	US	PRC	TW
ACTIVITIES	32	54	83
vacation	11	-	-
training	7	-	-
play	6	-	7
sports	5	-	-
gym	3	-	-
sporting field	-	27	30
physical exercise	-	14	-
life	-	11	-
ball	-	2	-
competition	-	-	10
take a stroll	-	-	8
playground	-	-	6
club activities	-	-	5
substantial life	-	-	5
be on leave	-	-	4
activities	-	-	4
race	-	-	4

FUN,HAPPY	US	PRC	TW
FUN,HAPPY	38	21	61
good	11	5	2
fun	10	-	-
opportune	7	-	-
enjoy	4	-	-
important	3	-	-
exciting	3	-	-
lively	-	8	3
lovable	-	5	5
cheer	-	3	-
liberty	-	-	21
happy	-	-	20
style	-	-	5
open	-	-	5

SCHOOL ENVIRONMENT	US	PRC	TW
SCHOOL ENVIRONMENT	106	163	142
building	25	-	-
school building	-	23	-
teaching building	-	10	-
house	16	-	-
bus,school bus	11	-	6
lunch	9	-	-
blackboard	8	12	7
desk	8	8	-
library	7	-	11
place	5	-	-
yard	5	-	-
chairs	5	-	-
cafeteria	4	-	8
flag	3	-	-
classroom	-	57	31
environment,s	-	16	9
gate of school	-	12	-
campus	-	12	-
school worker	-	6	4
table and chair	-	4	10
table	-	3	-
tree	-	-	13
bell	-	-	10
community	-	-	9
meal box	-	-	8
green grass	-	-	8
school uniforms	-	-	8

COLLEGE,UNIVERSITY	US	PRC	TW
COLLEGE,UNIVERSITY	102	49	59
college	90	-	-
university	12	49	21
Soochow university	-	-	23
Taiwan University	-	-	9
system	-	-	6

BORING,DISCIPLINE,FORCE	US	PRC	TW
BORING,DISCIPLINE,FORCE	68	12	16
boring	18	-	-
discipline	16	-	-
control	7	-	-
discriminate	6	-	-
rules	6	-	-
power	4	-	-
strict	4	-	-
indoctrine	4	-	-
absent	3	-	-
force	-	7	2
stress	-	5	-
education of punishing	-	-	5
bureaucracy	-	-	5
play truant	-	-	4

MISCELLANEOUS	US	PRC	TW
MISCELLANEOUS	43	11	5
days	18	-	-
money	14	-	-
tuition	8	-	-
fish	3	-	-
apparatus	-	7	-
modernization	-	2	-
means	-	2	-
dog	-	-	5

SUMMARY

Main Components	Percentage of Total Score		
	US	PRC	TW
EDUCATION	8	7	8
KNOWLEDGE	6	6	8
TYPE OF SCHOOL	7	11	5
STUDENT,STUDY,LEARN	33	22	22
TEACHER	13	17	15
COLLEGE,UNIVERSITY	6	4	5
FRIENDS,CLASSMATES	7	8	10
ACHIEVE,GROW	4	1	2
ACTIVITIES	2	5	7
FUN,HAPPY	2	2	5
SCHOOL ENVIRONMENT	6	15	12
BORING,DISCIPLINE,FORCE	4	1	1
MISCELLANEOUS	2	1	0
Total Scores	1761	1112	1208

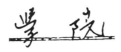

COLLEGE
MAIN COMPONENTS AND RESPONSES

SCHOOLS,UNIVERSITIES	US	PRC	TW
	190	519	146
school	121	32	36
university	53	155	47
institute,s	11	-	-
many	5	-	-
Northeast Univ. of Tech.	-	136	-
teaching building	-	28	-
institutions of higher ed.	-	25	4
college & universities	-	23	-
place for study	-	37	-
Beijing University	-	16	2
high school	-	14	-
my school	-	11	-
Qing Hua University	-	10	-
primary school	-	9	-
research institute	-	8	-
famous university	-	6	-
place for educating peopl	e	5	10
there are various univs.	-	4	14
college branch	-	-	15
Soochow University	-	-	10
Cambridge University	-	-	4
Harvard University	-	-	4

COLLEGE ENVIRONMENT	US	PRC	TW
	117	262	156
fraternity	16	-	-
campus	14	16	11
life	13	15	-
big	11	-	-
sports	8	3	-
football	8	3	-
building,s,high bldgs	8	20	8
dormitory,dorms	8	-	7
sorority	7	-	-
freedom	6	-	21
activities	6	-	-
quad	5	-	-
library	4	24	11
vacation	3	-	-
classroom	-	53	21
hostel	-	21	-
beautiful	-	17	-
dining room	-	14	-
physical exercise	-	10	-
quiet	-	9	4
sports field	-	9	-
exercise	-	8	5
desk	-	8	-
volleyball	-	6	-
environment	-	6	-
house	-	5	-
basketball	-	5	-
construction	-	4	-
on campus	-	3	-
reading room	-	3	-
bell	-	-	9
tradition	-	-	8
culture	-	-	7
university life	-	-	7
community	-	-	6
beautiful building	-	-	5
edification	-	-	5
bicycle	-	-	5
playground	-	-	4
small	-	-	4
old	-	-	4
gymnasium	-	-	4

STUDENT,STUDY,LEARN	US	PRC	TW
	354	310	177
learn,learning	103	2	-
study,studying,studious	84	98	25
book,s	56	-	18
student,s	30	86	70
exam,s,examination	18	7	12
class,es	15	-	-
paper,s	10	-	-
prepare	9	-	-
challenge	7	-	-
research	6	7	4
read	5	-	-
grades	4	-	-
interest	4	-	-
tests	3	-	-
university student	-	32	-
booklearning	-	23	-
experiment	-	15	-
graduate student	-	14	-
in class,class attendance	-	8	20
go to school	-	5	-
go to practice	-	3	-
laboratory	-	5	5
reading	-	5	-
style of study	-	-	16
technology	-	-	5
computer	-	-	2

TEACHER,PROFESSOR	US	PRC	TW
	91	176	103
professor,s	58	71	53
teacher,s,teach	30	74	33
lecturer,s,lecture	3	31	3
specialist	-	-	8
teachable/cultivatable	-	-	6

FUN,HAPPY	US	PRC	TW
	32	28	4
fun	21	-	-
like	8	-	-
sex	3	-	-
happy	-	14	-
lovable	-	8	-
entertainment	-	6	-
kindly	-	-	4

KNOWLEDGE	US	PRC	TW
	90	90	124
knowledge	40	53	49
experience	13	-	-
smart	11	-	-
brains	7	-	-
intellect,intellectuals	6	-	6
opportune,opportunity	9	-	-
think	4	-	-
master	-	11	-
ability	-	6	-
discretion	-	6	-
leadership	-	5	-
fruit	-	4	-
bring forth new ideas	-	3	-
wisdom	-	2	5
pursue knowledge	-	-	44
imparting knowledge	-	-	10
talents	-	-	6
to be well-read	-	-	4

CAREER,FUTURE	US	PRC	TW
	142	46	13
work	49	11	-
career	37	-	-
job,s	17	-	4
doctor	11	12	-
future	11	6	-
profession	10	-	-
goals	7	-	-
country	-	7	3
stairs of career	-	6	-
prospects	-	4	6

DEGREE,GRADUATE	US	PRC	TW
	127	36	8
degree	76	7	-
graduate,graduation	19	-	-
advancement,advanced	7	2	-
success	6	-	-
diploma	5	-	2
B.A.	5	-	-
thesis	5	-	-
achieve	4	-	-
graduate school	-	13	-
pursue advanced studies	-	10	2
status	-	3	-
make efforts	-	1	-
advanced knowledge	-	-	4

EDUCATION,IMPORTANT	US	PRC	TW
	218	59	19
education,educate	154	12	10
good	15	-	-
need,necessary	23	-	-
higher	11	-	-
important,importance	7	6	-
helpful	5	-	-
academic	3	-	-
educate people	-	20	-
cultivate	-	13	-
desire	-	8	-
quality	-	-	5
higher education	-	-	4

EXPENSIVE,MONEY	US	PRC	TW
	92	14	31
money	37	-	-
expensive,expense	44	-	-
tuition	11	-	-
full of people	-	9	-
highly paid	-	5	-
scholarship	-	-	31

PEOPLE	US	PRC	TW
	56	89	32
friend,s	19	-	7
people	13	-	-
youth	12	-	-
girl	6	-	-
adult	3	-	-
social	3	-	-
classmates	-	28	-
human resources	-	24	-
scholar	-	11	-
president of college	-	10	-
school workers	-	6	-
family	-	4	-
society	-	3	4
female & male	-	3	-
dean	-	-	9
principal	-	-	6
girlfriend	-	-	6

FIELDS OF STUDY	US	PRC	TW
	27	103	159
course,s	12	-	-
credit,s	9	-	-
major	6	-	-
science	-	35	5
college of technology	-	19	-
scientific research	-	12	-
business school	-	10	-
college of agriculture	-	10	-
school of literature	-	6	42
medical school	-	6	-
college of science	-	5	-
interdepartmental	-	-	39
sociology	-	-	12
business administration	-	-	10
school of science	-	-	10
department	-	-	8
law school	-	-	8
art	-	-	8
Chinese department	-	-	7
literature	-	-	6
departmental bldg (anthro)	-	-	4

HARD,WASTE,TIRED	US	PRC	TW
	48	13	16
hard	18	-	-
time	10	-	-
waste	7	-	-
tired, of studying	6	-	6
drugs	4	-	-
years	3	-	-
factory	-	6	-
overwork	-	4	-
reform	-	3	-
conservative	-	-	10

MISCELLANEOUS	US	PRC	TW
	0	44	2
scale	-	15	-
movement	-	9	2
base	-	9	-
bring up	-	8	-
condition	-	3	-

SUMMARY

Main Components	Percentage of Total Score		
	US	PRC	TW
SCHOOLS,UNIVERSITIES	12	29	15
COLLEGE ENVIRONMENT	7	15	16
STUDENT,STUDY,LEARN	22	17	18
TEACHER,PROFESSOR	6	10	10
FUN,HAPPY	2	2	0
KNOWLEDGE	6	5	13
CAREER,FUTURE	9	3	1
DEGREE,GRADUATE	8	2	1
EDUCATION,IMPORTANT	14	3	2
EXPENSIVE,MONEY	6	1	3
PEOPLE	4	5	3
FIELDS OF STUDY	2	6	16
HARD,WASTE,TIRED	3	1	2
MISCELLANEOUS	0	2	0
Total Scores	1584	1789	990

SUMMARY OF TRENDS IN THE DOMAIN OF EDUCATION

Our attempt to reconstruct the American and Chinese views on education follows two strategies. One is based on the analysis of reactions elicited by the word "Education." The second strategy involves the analysis of response trends observed across the eight themes used in the representation of the domain of education.

The findings on the word education indicate that the Chinese think more of proper behavior, the promotion of desirable personality traits, which in the American culture fit more with the objective of "upbringing" rather than "education." One may suspect, then, that the differences result from selecting a Chinese word that introduces semantic differences which may or may not have deeper cultural foundation. Since our main interest is in deeper, culturally based psychological dispositions, the use of the second strategy becomes informative and useful. By looking at the differences across several themes, we can be sure that if consistent differences emerge, these are not influenced merely by the choice of the particular word.

In the representation of this domain, we used three clusters of stimulus words. The first cluster -- education, college, and school -- we may identify as representing the academic dimension. The second cluster -- knowledge, study, intelligence -- may be characterized as representing the performance or achievement dimension. The third cluster -- teacher and student -- represents a personal dimension.

College, School -- The Academic Dimension

In the context of school, college, and education we find in a very close relationship for the Americans between education and the academic, school context. College and school elicit more references to education and education elicits more references to college and school from the American than from the Chinese groups. The response trends observed across these themes show that education and school attendance are essentially synonymous for Americans. At the same time, the Chinese responses suggest that education includes a broader diversity of subjects for the Chinese that are not considered by the Americans. Also, school brings in a somewhat different focus of attention. To the Chinese, a university is not the only place to acquire knowledge.

On the other hand, a second major focus of Americans is on knowledge and learning. Whether in the context of education, school or college, Americans place consistently greater emphasis on knowledge and make more references to the process of learning, the acquisition of knowledge. The Chinese groups' fewer references to knowledge and the learning process do not exclude the idea of knowledge, but they place less weight on the acquisition of knowledge.

The third trend characteristic of Americans involves heavy references to books and libraries, suggesting that the acquisition of knowledge comes from books, reading and libraries. While the American emphasis shifts from learning to knowledge and from knowledge to learning, across the board the attention paid to knowledge and learning together is always higher from Americans than from the Chinese. Furthermore, books play a much greater role in the American mind than in the Chinese mind.

Also, thinking of education and school, Americans emphasize more the importance and necessity of education, and in doing so they make it clear that they have very practical considerations in mind. They see that education is essential to such practical objectives as having a good job, gaining employment and starting a good career. As the most immediate objective along this purpose, Americans think more about earning degrees and graduation, the steps which have to be taken to reach the broader objectives of career and employment. Some of these goals do occur to the Chinese students as well, but the attention paid to them is less and their other goals are less immediately practical.

Learning, Knowledge -- The Performance Dimension

Not only do Americans think more of knowledge, studying, learning and intelligence in the context of school and education, but in the context of knowledge, study, and intelligence, their response rate is higher, indicating the greater importance and richer content they assign to these factors that affect knowledge and educational objectives. Also, in connection with knowledge, Americans think more of school and of education than the Chinese. They emphasize such qualities as intelligence and smartness as essential to gaining knowledge.

In their view of knowledge, the Chinese are particularly strong in emphasizing the process of learning and studying. Again, in the context of knowledge and educational performance, there is the contrast of American individualism versus the Chinese centrally-controlled concept. The Americans predominantly consider personal objectives, goals and advantages. The Chinese think more of common, collective objectives. They speak much more of culture and society as beneficiaries of knowledge. In connection with the subject emphasized, the PRC group thinks more intensively of subjects which bear on national development, development of economy and progress in general. The same is true of the meaning of study, which for the Chinese group involves problems, advancement and development. Study and knowledge are the only contexts in which the Chinese make more references to books than the Americans. In all other contexts, books and libraries are more central to the American way of thinking than to the Chinese. Similarly, intelligence is a more emphatic issue to the Americans. They relate it more to knowledge and they speak heavily of the I.Q. as a measure of intelligence. The PRC Chinese pay little attention to I.Q., while the Taiwanese place a great deal of emphasis on I.Q. Generally, the Chinese think more in such terms as clever and smart, stupid and dumb. Most of the Chinese relate these qualities to achievement and consider them congenital. Also, the PRC group relates intelligence with being cultivated and developed.

Student and Teacher -- the Personal Dimension

While the personal dimension of education receives relatively little attention from Americans, it is consistently more dominant in the context of most educational themes for the two Chinese samples. In the context of education and school and college, the Chinese think more of students and more of teachers. The student/teacher relationship appears to be a dominant dimension of all their thinking related to education.

While the Americans emphasize more books and educational technologies, the personal dimension is much more prominent in the minds of both Chinese samples. This dominance is apparent not only in the context of education and school, but the same trend can be observed in the context teacher and student as well. Teacher and student as stimulus words receive higher recognition from the Chinese, and they relate them more specifically and directly to school and school experiences. The Chinese identify themselves more as students and pay greater attention to the student role. While they see teachers and students in close relationship, their image of teachers and students is also somewhat more distinct and differential. The PRC students are particularly inclined to view their teachers in an idealized role endowed with a great deal of authority, esteem, and respect. They show a strong awareness of age differences, and at the same time characterize their teachers as dear and good friends. These characterizations are true both for the Taiwanese and the PRC students. On the other hand, the PRC image of students includes such characterizations as naive, simple, simple and pure, moral character. These views reflect trends of stereotypical idealization and simplified duality, whereby students are seen as innocent and needing instruction, contrasted with the knowledge and authority of the teacher as mentor and role model.

As a clear difference, the Americans relate the teacher more narrowly to school and classroom, emphasizing their role in education and transmission of knowledge as instructor or professor. The teacher image by the Americans includes little relationship to students, and, similarly, the student image does not include any reference to teachers. While in the Chinese case the student role also conveys a distinct amount of awareness and status, in the American context, the student role is characterized by references to learning and to intellectual qualities of smartness, and by many references to parties, friends, and social involvement.

Schooling Versus Proper Conduct

In the context of practically all educational themes examined, Americans have shown a consistent trend to focus primarily on schools, institutions of formal learning. Education, knowledge, school, college, teacher, intelligence, study and student all show a heavy American concentration of attention on school and knowledge. In contrast, both Chinese populations score lower on school and on the relationship of school and knowledge, while they pay more attention to other social and interpersonal dimensions of education such as proper conduct, behavior, morality, and character. Chinese society has high hopes for students and expects them to live up to certain criteria and norms in society.

The Taiwanese responses show that for them education in a broader sense includes also the shaping of moral values, character and personality of the youth. For the Taiwanese, education goes beyond transmission of knowledge and encompasses also the forming of conscience and character, the development of discipline and motivation as part of their meaning of study, teacher, and student as well. Similarly, the Mainlanders place more emphasis on the societal, cultural, and developmental implications of education. To both of these Chinese groups education means more than attending schools but a broader, more encompassing process of upbringing.

The emphasis by the two Chinese groups on behavioral and moral dimensions of education consistently shown by the results can be traced to the Great Sage. Confucius is seen as the ultimate source, and the absorption of his value system is a major part of education. Many sayings of Confucius deal with education and have permeated Chinese consciousness for more than twenty-four centuries. He is known for having taught four things: literature, conduct, loyalty, and reliability. Although he was famous for his knowledge and love of learning, the instilling of proper attitudes and behavior were far more important to him than transmitting mere knowledge and understanding.

Learning Guides Versus Role Models

Americans who view education as a process of accumulation of knowledge through attending schools and learning think of teachers as guides to learning. Responses indicate respect toward teachers. Key responses to teachers are knowledge, understanding, reflecting that their authority is based on their knowledge or competence. They do not mention intelligence to the extent that Chinese students do, nor do they mention respect much. Boredom, discipline, and teacher's pets are mentioned with some frequency. Also, according to their understanding of study, school, teacher, education, intelligence, and college, Americans place less emphasis upon teachers, compared to the Chinese.

Teachers are mentioned much more frequently by both groups of the Chinese, in comparison to Americans, in the contexts of education, students, and college. Mainland students describe teachers as dear, kind, lovable, selfless, dear person, and other similar responses. The Taiwanese say that the teacher solves confidential problems; the Mainlanders mention solving difficult questions. Respect and esteem are other important responses to the teacher.

The response trends observed indicate that the Chinese groups place not only more emphasis on the role of the teacher in the field of education but that they see this role rather differently than the American student. Although they appreciate the knowledge and technical competence of their teachers, they view teacher in a broader more personal role than a mediator or transmitter of technical information. They place much more emphasis on the human, personal qualities of teachers, all of which suggest, more than a depository of information, an idealized role model, a resource for solving all types of human problems, and a model for lifestyle as well.

From the American perspective, teachers are likely to develop a more detached and impersonal relationship with their students, also because they see them only sporadically, once they are past about the sixth grade. In great contrast to the Chinese situation, it is rare in American public schools for a teacher to maintain contact with a particular student for more than three or four years - in school or out.

According to the Area Handbook for Communist China, "Traditionally, teachers occupied an important position in Chinese society and were held in high esteem. . . Many

Chinese still look upon teachers with particular respect." This situation has persisted for centuries probably because of the high caliber of the persons who became teachers, because of the personal qualities of wisdom, warmth, and concern shown by teachers, and because teachers were the keepers of the keys to advancement and influence. In both Chinese settings the relationship between students and teacher is modelled on the traditional master-disciple bond, with one-on-one mutual obligations and, at times, the establishing of lifelong ties of concern and affection.

Chinese attitudes toward teachers have ramifications not only in other aspects of education but in virtually all human relations where a younger, and less knowledgeable, person interacts with an older and wiser person in authority. This is a deep cultural element, and the responses of the Taiwanese and the Mainland Chinese show still considerable similarity.

The affective tone of the Chinese reactions -- dear, kind, lovable -- reflects individualized personal ties that are close and warm, indicating again that they do not relegate their teachers to the role of occasional technical expertise, but relate to their teachers through more personal, multidimensional and lasting ties. These are naturally reminiscent of the Confucian disciple-master relationship that is one of the basic tenets of the Confucian moral philosophy. It may be noted that the Taiwanese students do make explicit references to Confucius, indicating that they show some awareness of the historic roots of their educational views. What may appear particularly paradoxical is that the Mainland students, who show in their views even strong affinities to the Confucian principles, did not make any reference to the Great Sage.

Individual Needs and Interests Versus Collective, National Goals

Americans look at education and educational issues with a strong focus on subjective, personal interests. Their views are dominated by perceptions of what education offers or promises at a very practical level for personal advantage and benefits. In almost all educational contexts Americans mention such things as jobs, career, profession or success. They also frequently mention obtaining degrees, much more frequently than the Chinese groups. They describe knowledge as important, useful, and necessary. Grades are another related concern of Americans, much more so than for either of the Chinese groups. In their role as students, Americans focus strongly on self, in contrast to the Chinese focus on classmates.

Americans think of being prepared for their career by the process of learning or education rather than by mastering specific subjects or accumulating a specific type or amount of knowledge. This process, according to American responses is to be guided by the expertise and wisdom of teachers. They tend to stay focused on their goal: a diploma or degree, as well as good grades, all of which are seen as necessary for success in job or career. In other words, Americans are preoccupied with the very subjective, individually relevant utility of education.

The Chinese meanings of knowledge, education,and intelligence were found to show a strong preoccupation with development, progress, and national achievement. These reactions reflect concern with broad national objectives that are characteristic of third-world countries mobilizing their resources to promote life conditions, economic welfare, and national development. This trend, which was also observed to be present in the results of our research on south Korea, Iran, Colombia, and Mexico, is less pronounced among the Taiwanese, but it is very strong with the Mainlanders.

The collectivistic trends present in China's culture for millennia, and emphasized by Confucius, has been apparently further reinforced by Communist ideology. As the Mainlanders responses indicate, these remain a lasting contribution to the Chinese world view. The PRC government has also made use of, and reinforced, China's nationalistic fervor (including a persistent xenophobia) by promoting an intensive campaign of glorification of China's historic greatness. As DeBary (1964) observes:

If we were to characterize in one word the Chinese way of life for the last two thousand years, the word would be "Confucian." No other individual in Chinese history has so deeply influenced the life and thought of his people, as a transmitter, teacher, and creative interpreter of the ancient culture and literature, and as a molder of Chinese mind and character....Many Chinese have professed themselves to be Taoists, Buddhists, even Christians, but seldom have they ceased at the same time to be Confucianists. For Confucianism since the time of its general acceptance has been more than a creed to be professed or rejected; it has become an inseparable part of the society and thought of the nation as a whole, of what it means to be Chinese, as the Confucian classics are not the canon of a particular sect but the literary heritage of a whole people.

At various times since 1949 the PRC government has tried to denigrate or minimize the influence of Confucius -- especially during the decade-long rampages of the Cultural Revolution. More often, however, it has attempted to make use of Confucian ideas, attitudes, or discipline for its own purposes. This influence is so pervasive that even Communist officials will compliment one another on being "real Confucianists," implying integrity, sense of duty, and selflessness. Since about 1978 Confucius has been in a kind of limbo, being neither acknowledged nor condemned officially. But much of Chinese behavior, and many of the PRC's educational norms, are implicitly Confucian, without being acknowledged as such. Rules of conduct in both the home and the classroom are overwhelmingly Confucian. The Confucian tenets have long been so deep-rooted in the minds of the Chinese people, that they cannot be easily eradicated. In other words, the Communist attempts to minimize the influence of Confucius have been to no avail.

REFERENCES

Apter, D.E. (1966). "System, Process, and the Politics of Economic Development," <u>Political Development and Social Change</u>. New York: John Wiley and Sons.

Alvy, K.T., Harrison, D.S., Rosen, L.D., Fuentes, E.G. (1982). <u>Black Parenting: An Empirical Study with Implications for Parent Trainers and Therapists</u>. Studio City, CA: Center for the Improvement of Child Caring.

Chaffee, F.H., et al. (1967). <u>Area Handbook for Communist China</u>. Washington, D.C.: G.P.O.

Ching, J. (1990). <u>Probing China's Soul: Religion, Politics, and Protest in the People's Republic</u>. New York: Harper & Row.

De Bary, W.T. et al. (1964). <u>Sources of Chinese Tradition</u>. New York: Columbia University Press.

Diaz-Guerrero, R. & Szalay, L.B. (1991). <u>Understanding Mexicans and Americans: A Mexican-U.S. Communication Lexicon of Images, Meanings and Cultural Frames of Reference</u>. New York: Plenum Press.

Emerson, R. (1966). "Nationalism and Political Development," <u>Political Development and Social Change</u>. New York: John Wiley and Sons. (Finkle and Gable, eds.)

Foster, R.J. (1969). <u>Dimensions of Training for Overseas Assignment</u>. Washington, D.C.: HumRRO, The George Washington University (Technical Report 69-11).

Frey, F.W. (1967). Statement before the Subcommittee on International Organizations and Movements. <u>Modern Communications and Foreign Policy</u>. February 9, 1967.

Hall, E.T. (1959). <u>The Silent Language</u>. Garden City, New York: Doubleday & Company.

Hall, E.T. (1966). <u>The Hidden Dimension</u>. Garden City, New York: Doubleday & Company.

Hsu, F.L.K. (1977). "Whither American Family? A New Perspective," adapted from a paper presented at the Smithsonian's Sixth International Symposium "The Peopling of America," June 1977.

Hsu, F.L.K. and Chu, G. (1979). <u>Moving A Mountain: Real Cultural Change in China</u>. Honolulu: University of Hawaii Press.

Hsu, F.L.K. (1981). <u>Americans and Chinese: Passage to Differences</u>. Honolulu: University of Hawaii Press.

Mead, M. (1951). Soviet Attitudes Toward Authority. New York: McGraw-Hill.

Mosher, S.W. (1983). Broken Earth: The Rural Chinese. New York: MacMillan (Free Press).

Pye, L., ed. (1963). Communications and Political Development. Princeton, New Jersey: Princeton University Press.

Pye, L.W. (1972). China: An Introduction. Boston: Little,Brown.

Shils, E. (1966). "Alternative Course of Political Development," Political Development and Social Change. New York: John Wiley and Sons.

Szalay, L.B., Lysne, D. & Bryson, J.A. (1972). "Designing and Testing Cogent Communications," Journal of Cross-Cultural Psychology, III, 247-258.

Szalay, L.B. & Maday, B.C. (1973). "Verbal Associations in the Analysis of Subjective Culture," Current Anthropology, XIV, 151-1713.

Szalay, L.B. & Bryson, J.A. (1974). "Psychological Meaning: Comparative Analyses and Theoretical Implications," Journal of Personality and Social Psychology, XXX (1974), 860-870.

Szalay, L.B. (1981). "Intercultural Communication: A Process Model," International Journal of Intercultural Relations, Vol. V, No. 2.

Szalay, L.B. (1982). "How Much We Share, How Much We Differ Culturally," Contemporary Perceptions of Language: Interdisciplinary Dimensions. Washington, D.C.: Georgetown University Round Table, 1982. (H. Byrnes, ed.)

Szalay, L.B. & Maday, B.C. (1983). "Implicit Culture and Psychocultural Distance," American Anthropologist, Vol. 85, No. 1.

Szalay, L.B., Strohl, J.A., Vilov, S.K., Inn, A., Chow, I., Sun, MingHe & Liu Fu, 1986. American and Chinese Public Perceptions and Belief Systems. Bethesda, MD: I.C.S.

THE ASSOCIATIVE GROUP ANALYSIS (AGA) METHOD

DATA COLLECTION, ANALYSES, AND MAIN CATEGORIES OF INFERENCES

The Associative Group Analysis (AGA) is a method of in-depth analysis of perceptions and attitudes, of dominant psychological dispositions that affect people's thought and behavior. The main units of analysis are subjective images and meanings, the main elements of cognition, or systems of mental representation.

AGA is an unstructured, open-ended approach. Rather than asking direct questions, AGA works by reconstructing a group's psychological dispositions based on the distribution of hundreds of thousands of free associations to strategically selected stimulus themes. Through extensive computer-assisted analyses, AGA is used to map systems of mental representation and to identify behavioral dispositions evasive to the more direct and structured methods of assessment.

As the examples below illustrate, AGA offers in-depth insights not available from other sources. For instance, an analysis of how Chinese students from the PRC, Taiwan, and Hong Kong vary in their views of ancestors, can be used to trace the effects of nationalism, communist ideology, evolutionary theory, and Confucianism. As other examples demonstrate, AGA can be used to assess how the subjective culture of black students compares to whites by reconstructing their priorities, measuring distances in views, or mapping their cognitive organization.

The AGA approach has its roots in two main lines of development. One is represented by Charles Osgood (Osgood, Suci, & Tannenbaum, 1957) and Harry Triandis (1964) who performed ground-breaking work in approaching subjective culture through the empirical study of subjective meaning. The work of Clyde Noble (1952) and James Deese (1962) is also relevant because it initiated a reorientation in the interpretation of free associations by recognizing the role of subjective meaning. A summary of the AGA method is offered in the monograph by Szalay and Deese (1978), as well as numerous articles in various journals of the social and behavioral sciences (see attached list of publications).

DATA COLLECTION, TEST ADMINISTRATION

The standard AGA testing conditions of group testing, written form of administration, and working with little time pressure help promote more spontaneous, meaning-mediated responses. Individual subjects remain anonymous (demographic data being obtained by a brief questionnaire that carries the same code number as the subject's test slips); assurance of this helps to reduce the likelihood of bias in the form of acquiescence, considerations of social desirability, etc.; it also opens up a variety of emotion-laden issues to objective inquiry.

The subjects are asked to write free verbal associations to each of the stimulus words presented on randomly sequenced cards. They receive the following instructions, as well as the test material, in their native language:

> This experiment is part of a study in verbal behavior, and this particular task involves word associations. They are group experiments, and your responses will not be evaluated individually but collectively for your group. Your responses are completely anonymous, and you are free to give your associations concerning any subject. There are no bad or wrong answers, so do not select your responses but put them down spontaneously in the order that they occur to you.
>
> The task is easy and simple. You will find a word printed on each slip of paper. Reading this stimulus word will make you think of other associated words (objects, ideas, issues, etc.). You are asked to write as many separate responses as you can think of in the time allotted. Try to think of one-word responses and avoid long phrases or sentences.
>
> It is important that in giving your responses you always take the given stimulus word into consideration. For example, if the stimulus word was *table* and your answer was *writing*, in giving the subsequent responses you must refer back to *table* and avoid "chain" responses (i.e., *writing, pen, ink, blue, ocean, sail...*).
>
> Please work without hurrying, but do your best to give us as many answers as possible. One minute will be given for each word. At the end of each minute I will ask you to go on to the next word. Do not work longer than one minute on any word and do not read ahead or return to others later.

DATA ORGANIZATION: SCORING RESPONSES, COMPILING GROUP RESPONSE LISTS

A logical assumption is that earlier responses are more meaningful than later ones, that the first response has more salience to the subject than the last. This assumption is supported by empirical evidence. The stability of responses obtained at different rank places was studied by comparing the responses obtained from the same group in two separate sessions one month apart (Szalay and Brent, 1967). The responses obtained at higher rank places in the first test showed higher stability in the second test than did the responses first obtained at lower rank places. The coefficients of stability obtained in the comparative study provide the weights for the various rank places. The weights, beginning with the first response, are 6, 5, 4, 3, 3, 3, 3, 2, 2, 1, 1, 1.

The cards are organized by stimulus words, and the individual responses from all the subjects are tallied into group response lists (see Figure 1). Certain responses (e.g., *school* to **educated**) will occur to many members of the group; other responses may be given by only one or two members. In order to focus on the shared meaning for a particular group, the responses given by only one person are excluded from analysis. Dropping the idiosyncratic responses helps us to concentrate on the more stable, shared responses and implifies the data processing and analysis.

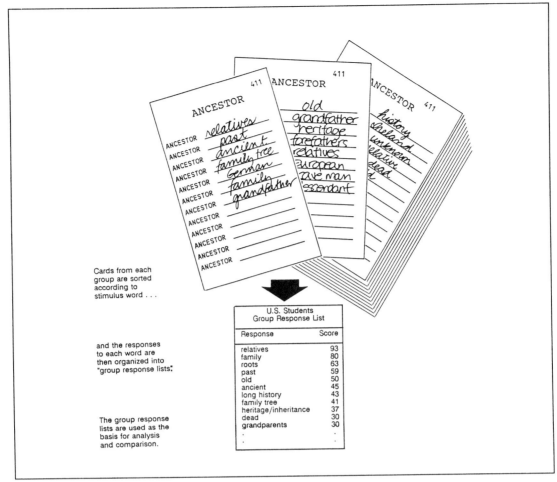

Figure 1. Formation of Group Response Lists

If we look at associations produced by members of our own culture group, they appear to be just plain common sense. We tend to feel that everybody would produce similar responses and that the responses do not tell us anything new. This impression is probably the major reason that the potential information value of associative response distribution has not been clearly recognized in the past. The systematic exploitation of associations as an important information source is the central objective of the AGA method. The feeling that everybody would produce similar responses is a culture-bound impression. This becomes apparent if we compare associations obtained from groups with different cultural backgrounds.

A comparison of American, PRC Chinese and Hong Kong Chinese responses to the stimulus **ANCESTORS**, for instance, shows that the most frequent U.S. responses *relatives* and *family* do not even appear on the list of most frequent responses for the PRC and Hong Kong Chinese (see Table 1). These lists contain numerous responses which have high scores or salience for one culture group and low or no salience at all for the other group. A quick glance at the most frequent responses readily reveals that they are not accidental, but deeply rooted in the cultural background, religious-moral philosophy, life conditions, and contemporary experiences of the respective groups.

Table 1

ANCESTORS

Comparison of Most Frequent Associations from Three Culture Groups

UNITED STATES Response	Score	P.R.C. Response	Score	HONG KONG Response	Score
relatives	93	ape,s	89	respect, pay respect	186
family	80	great	63	Ching Ming Holiday	97
roots	63	industrious	49	death	62
past	59	developed,-ment	40	tablet, upright, wood	50
old	50	culture	35	tomb	42
ancient	45	hard working	35	history	42
long history	43	motherland	34	pray to god	40
family tree	41	civilization	31	temple	40
heritage/inheritance	37	generation, former	31	sweep a grave	39
dead	30	emperor	26	Chinese	35
grandparents	30	primitive man	25	grandfather	29
Mayflower	27	brave	23	graves	29
forefather	27	forefather	23	time, antiquity	29
grandfather	25	generation, older	23	ancient	28
Europe	23	four ancient inventions	23	visit tomb	27
descendant,s	23	China (old name)	22	motherland	25
people, old	21	labor	22	countryside	25
German	17	clever	21	graveyard	25
before	15	yellow river	19	homeland, hometown	25

As illustrated by the group response lists, it is already apparent from the top few responses that the meaning of ancestors is quite different for the groups compared. The American meaning involves predominantly relatives, family members, ethnic heritage and history. The PRC Chinese think of the creators of the ancient Chinese civilizations who they remember with considerable national pride; they also think of apes and primitive man along the evolutionary theory. The Hong Kong group thinks of ancestors in terms of respect and religious practices which are part of the Confucian principles of veneration and worship.

The lengthy response lists provide an exhaustive inventory of the mosaic elements which make up each group's image of a particular theme. Each group response list represents a rich information source reflecting the group's characteristic understanding of the stimulus word, including perceptual and affective details which are frequently unverbalizable and below their level of awareness. Actually, a systematic examination of such response lists has shown that every response contains a piece of valid information about the group's characteristic understanding and evaluation of the stimulus word. Responses with a sizable score value (10 to 15) are rarely accidental. Using conservative estimates, score differences of 18 can be considered significant at the .05 level, score differences of 24 at the .01 level. The wealth of information provided by the group response list is impressive, since even small score differences can have significant implications for communication and behavior (Szalay, Lysne, & Bryson, 1972).

The treatment of the responses is consistent with the conceptualization of subjective meaning as a composite of several main perceptual and evaluative components. It reflects enterprise to reconstruct this composite meaning through a reproduction of its main components by their context, and in their actual salience. In the framework of our analysis, the subjective salience of specific perceptual and evaluative elements is inferred from the response scores. The more people give a particular response, like evacuation, the greater is the salience of this of this mosaic element, for instance in the subjective meaning of ANCESTORS. In our effort to achieve a faithful proportionate reconstruction of the group's subjective meaning we rely on all of the shared responses given by the members of a group to a particular issue or theme. The salience of each mosaic element revealed by a particular shared response is revealed by the response score which is a function of how many people gave this response and with what subjective weight. Along this rationale of proportionate representation the relative salience of a specific response or of a particular response cluster is not only a function of the absolute score value but depends also on the relationship of the responses to the total score accumulated by all shared responses given to that particular stimulus theme. The same score value shows less salience in the context of a group which produces many responses, than in the context of another group which produces fewer responses.

In the following treatment of the data the requirements following from this principle of proportionate representation are consistently maintained. It is particularly important to keep this distinction in mind to understand certain basic differences between the AGA and the survey results. In the case of surveys, the number of those who took a favorable stand and those who chose a negative position on a particular question represent absolute numbers reflecting positive vs. negative choices. In comparison, the response scores used by AGA convey relative salience. To maintain consistency with this rationale of relative salience in the processing of the AGA data, as necessary, various types of score adjustments are made to maintain comparability. The following two examples may be indicative.

In the comparative study of Chinese and U.S. cultural meanings, we found that in responding to 120 themes in over 15 domains, the PRC Chinese group gave fewer responses than the U.S. and that the Hong Kong Chinese gave even fewer than both the U.S. and PRC groups. These differences were largely due to the influence of the Chinese alphabet, which requires more time to write. To account for this discrepancy, unrelated to the subjective meanings, adjustment scores were calculated and applied to make the scores comparable (PRC scores were used as a reference point and were not adjusted; U.S. scores were reduced by 18%; H.K. scores increased by 33%). To maintain comparability, samples of 100 respondents are generally used. In a few instances where we have to compare smaller groups, like 75 adults with 100 students, we adjust the scores of the smaller group (in this case by 33%) to maintain direct comparability.

For the identification of various psychocultural characteristics, several analytical procedures have been developed, relying on the group response lists as the main data base.

GROUP PERCEPTIONS, IMAGES, AND MEANINGS

The group response lists contain a rich variety of responses, each reflecting a different mosaic element of the total psychological meaning. Grouping responses with similar content together helps to identify the main components of meaning and their characteristic salience. This content analysis is performed by two or more independent judges whose background and frame of reference is by and large similar to that of the group tested. If Korean and American groups are to be tested, the coders would be a Korean and an American. Each judge receives a list of all responses to a particular stimulus word (the Korean responses translated into English). They choose eight to sixteen categories which they feel subsume all the responses in meaningful groupings relevant to the stimulus word, and then assign the responses to these categories. The categories may be of low or high generality, concrete or abstract; but they should be simple, not very abstract, and at the same level of generality. It is important to chose clearly different, well-delimited categories that do not overlap. It is necessary to choose between alternative possible categories: some will fit into the total system of categories better than others; some will communicate better than others. Responses that do not seem to fit into any of the categories are put into a miscellaneous category. Responses that may be assigned with equal justification to two or more categories are recorded for further discussion. The coders then meet with a senior researcher to discuss their agreements and disagreements. Where there are discrepant categories, three solutions are possible: new alternative categories, category combinations at a higher level of abstraction, or complementary categories. The final categories are selected to highlight the most characteristic aspects of the groups' responses to the stimulus word. This method maintains comparability of results in the analysis of the responses from the different cultural population samples. Once the categorization is finalized, a final check is required to make sure that all the responses are included and that they have their proper response scores.

Each category is described by a score and by a label to indicate its content. The category score is the sum of the scores of each subsumed response and expresses the importance of the category for a particular group. If a category yields a high score for a group, it may be said that the category constitutes an important meaning component of that theme for that group. The categories and category scores present a logical set of data from which the central meaning of the stimulus word may be deduced, either directly or through advisors or background literature on the culture.

Using this procedure to analyze the stimulus theme **ANCESTOR**, for example, we find that the Americans' references to foreign countries reflect a strong awareness of their cultural heritage and foreign ancestry. (See Figure 2 for examples of selected clusters) This category of responses does not even occur to the two Chinese groups. The PRC Chinese strongly describe ancestors as great, industrious, hardworking, brave, all of which point to an intensive national pride in regard to ancient Chinese civilization. Almost all of the responses in the sizable cluster dealing with respect, worship, rites and veneration come from the Hong Kong Chinese. A modest familiarity with the cultural background of the Hong Kong Chinese makes it obvious that this component reflects the traditional Confucian ancestor worship and shows how salient this cultural element is in the minds of contemporary H.K. Chinese citizens.

ANCESTORS

Selected Main Clusters of Responses

Main Components and Responses	US	PRC	HK
FOREIGN, ETHNIC ORIGIN	145	3	0
foreign	7	-	-
Europe	23	-	-
old country	7	-	-
English	11	-	-
England	9	-	-
Ireland	5	-	-
Irish	14	-	-
Italy	11	-	-
Scotland	5	-	-
Jewish	3	-	-
German	17	-	-
Spain	7	-	-
Africa	7	-	-
Africans	5	-	-
Indians	7	-	-
Israel	7	-	-
world	-	3	-

Main Components and Responses	US	PRC	HK
GOOD, KIND, LOVING	57	249	32
great	9	63	-
industrious	-	49	-
hard working	-	35	-
brave	-	24	-
proud	-	18	-
do pioneering work	-	11	-
sacrifice	-	-	16
clever	-	21	-
mysterious	-	-	16
interesting	11	-	-
hardship	-	5	-
hero	-	6	-
pride	4	-	-
strength	4	-	-
struggle	7	-	-
wise	6	-	-
wisdom	-	9	-
different	4	-	-
kind-hearted	-	3	-
famous	7	-	-
love, -able	5	5	-

Main Components and Responses	US	PRC	HK
RESPECT, WORSHIP	16	26	382
respect, pay respect	-	13	186
respectable	-	13	-
pray to god	-	-	40
religion	11	-	-
sweep a grave	-	-	39
temple	-	-	40
visit tomb	-	-	27
worship	-	-	9
faith	5	-	12
believe blindly	-	-	8
commemorate	-	-	9
conservation	-	-	12

Figure 2

In the case of the responses to ancestors the judges used twelve categories to identify the most salient components of the groups' contemporary meanings of ancestors (see Table 2). The scores the various components accumulated in this process reflect the subjective salience of each component for the cultural groups compared. The main content categories obtained by this analysis describe the total subjective meaning of the theme in terms of the main components characteristic of each group's understanding. Because there is usually a difference between the two groups in their level of responding, the category scores are converted to percentages of the respective total scores in order to make them directly comparable.

Table 2

ANCESTORS

Content Analysis Revealing Main Components of Perceptions and Evaluations

Main Components	Percentage of Total Score		
	US	PRC	HK
FOREFATHERS	10	5	13
RESPECT, WORSHIP	1	2	27
DEATH, GRAVE, TOMB	4	2	23
GREAT, INDUSTRIOUS, BRAVE	4	21	2
TIME: PAST, OLD	15	9	8
RELATIVES, FAMILY TREE	35	7	7
FOREIGN, ETHNIC ORIGIN	11	0	0
MOTHERLAND, COUNTRY	1	12	10
HISTORY,CULTURE,TRADITION	9	9	5
PREHISTORIC MAN, APE	8	19	3
DEVELOPMENT, CIVILIZATION	0	14	1
MISCELLANEOUS	1	1	1
Total Adjusted Scores	1318	1197	1390

The reliability of the content analytic method was tested by comparing the performance of five judges working independently from each other. The interjudge reliability measured by product-moment correlation across 76 categories was .7. The validity of such inferences on particular single meaning components cannot be directly assessed because simple criterion measures are not available. There are, however, findings which show, for instance, that the salience of these meaning components provides valid predictions on the meaningfulness of messages in intercultural communications. Communication material that capitalized on salient components of cultural meanings was judged by members of this culture as relatively more meaningful than comparable communication material produced by cultural experts (Szalay et al., 1972).

Another way to present the results of content analysis is the semantograph (see Figure 3). It shows the main categories of group meaning by using radially arranged bar graphs. The solid dark bars represent the main components of Chinese interpretations and the outlined bars show the main components of U.S. interpretations. Where the bars are similar in length, substantial agreement exists between U.S. and Chinese responses. The bars are arranged so that those on the left of the semantograph show meaning components especially strong (salient) for the U.S. group and those on the right show meaning components especially strong for the Chinese group. This presentation is designed to help the reader to recognize components on which his own group and the other culture group are in agreement or disagreement.

258

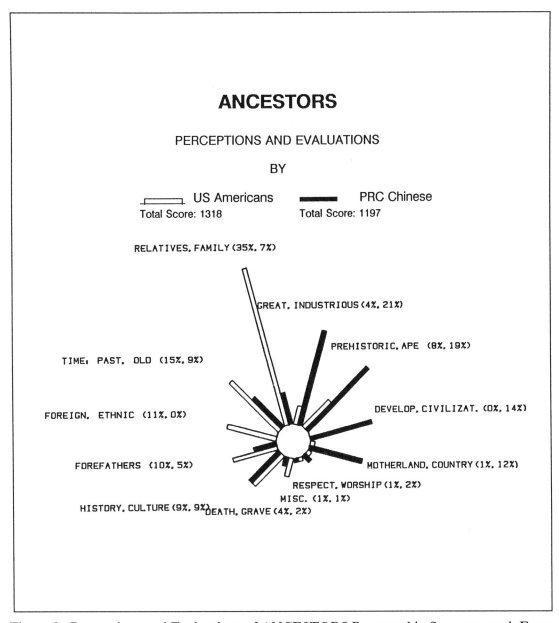

ANCESTORS

PERCEPTIONS AND EVALUATIONS

BY

US Americans   PRC Chinese
Total Score: 1318   Total Score: 1197

RELATIVES. FAMILY (35%. 7%)

GREAT. INDUSTRIOUS (4%. 21%)

PREHISTORIC. APE (8%. 19%)

TIME: PAST. OLD (15%. 9%)

DEVELOP. CIVILIZAT. (0%. 14%)

FOREIGN. ETHNIC (11%. 0%)

FOREFATHERS (10%. 5%)

MOTHERLAND. COUNTRY (1%. 12%)

RESPECT. WORSHIP (1%. 2%)

MISC. (1%. 1%)

HISTORY. CULTURE (9%. 9%) DEATH. GRAVE (4%. 2%)

Figure 3. Perceptions and Evaluations of ANCESTORS Presented in Semantograph Form

The analysis of single concepts such as **ANCESTORS** reveals deep insights which can be traced to the religious-moral philosophy, history, life conditions, and contemporary experiences of the respective culture groups. The PRC Chinese students have abandoned Confucian beliefs and view ancestors with a mix of national pride, industry, tradition, and evolution. The Hong Kong Chinese, in contrast to their very modern, industrial environment, view ancestors predominantly in terms Confucian ethics and practices. The Americans show a great deal of cultural diversity and pluralism. These trends of cultural interpretations are not limited to single concepts; rather, they reflect general cultural experiences, life conditions, and philosophies characteristic of the groups compared.

SUBJECTIVE PRIORITIES OR IMPORTANCE

THE DOMINANCE SCORE

Every group has its own set of priorities: Americans are said to be preoccupied with material comfort, technical details, and scientific progress, while Hispanics are said to focus on family traditions, personal friendships, and spiritual values. The psychological priorities characteristic of a particular group can be inferred from dominance scores. How important a certain subject, theme, idea, or issue is to a particular group can be inferred from the number of responses they give to it as a stimulus word. The dominance score, simply the sum of the scores of all responses elicited by a particular theme or domain, is used to measure subjective importance. It is a modified version of Noble's (1952) "meaningfulness" measure.* The priorities of different social or cultural groups can be compared by looking at their dominance scores on the same concepts. Dominance scores reveal group-specific priorities not only on single issues but also for larger domains, as shown in Table 4 below. These results come from a study of Black and White blue-collar workers who were compared on the relative importance they assigned to 60 selected themes in 15 domains. The table indicates that the Black group was more concerned with social problems and needs, while the White group placed more emphasis on political isms and nationalism.

Table 4
DOMINANCE SCORES OF BLACK AND WHITE GROUPS

Domain and Theme	White	Black	Domain and Theme	White	Black
-ISMS			SOCIAL PROBLEMS		
democracy	636	449	society (U.S.)	316	342
socialism	396	280	social class	402	475
capitalism	362	298	social justice	376	378
communism	733	502	social progress	260	334
mean	532	382	mean	338	382
NATION			NEEDS		
nation	661	591	goal	514	581
United States	887	765	expectation	236	298
patriotism	508	222	desire	621	701
Americans	605	648	valuable	832	876
mean	663	556	mean	551	614

The group-based dominance scores have been found to be highly culture- specific (Szalay, Moon, Lysne, and Bryson, 1971a) and have a reliability of .93 calculated from a test-retest comparison of 40 themes. More information on the dominance scores can be found in Communication Lexicon on Three South Korean Audiences (Szalay, Moon, and Bryson, 1971b).

---

*Noble (1952) first demonstrated that the number of associations given by a person in a continued association task of one minute provides a measure of "meaningfulness" that is highly correlated with the person's familiarity with the word and its meaning.

THE SIMILARITY COEFFICIENT AND INTRAGROUP HOMOGENEITY MEASURE

Without considering the actual <u>nature</u> of differences one may ask generally to what extent do two groups differ in their understanding of a particular theme. Free verbal associations offer an empirical answer to this question based on the principle that the closer the agreement between the associations of two groups on a particular theme, the more similar their meanings are. To measure the extent to which two groups agree in their perception and understanding of a particular theme, idea, or issue, the coefficient of similarity is used.

Similarity in subjective meaning is inferred from the similarity of response distributions measured by Pearson's product-moment correlation. Close similarity (high coefficient) means that the high frequency responses produced by one group are also high frequency responses for the other group; similarly, the low frequency responses produced by one group will generally be the same as those produced by the other group. The scores for the same (translation equivalent) responses from two groups represent the pairs of observations (x, y) used in this calculation. $\underline{N}$ represents the number of pairs of observations, that is, the number of word responses used in the calculation of a particular coefficient. The coefficients provide a global measure of the level of similarities and differences without elaborating on the semantic components on which they are based.

In the example below the problem areas or domains are presented in descending order of agreement (see Table 5). The reactions of the Black and White groups were most similar in the areas of education and family. The problem areas showing least agreement, social problems and needs, are the same areas in which the dominance scores reflected more concern from the Black group.

Table 5
INTERGROUP SIMILARITY BETWEEN BLACK AND WHITE GROUPS

Domain and Theme	r	Domain and Theme	r
EDUCATION		NEEDS	
school	.90	goal	.38
knowledge	.88	expectation	- .47
educated	.92	desire	.76
to learn	.79	valuable	.90
mean	.88	mean	.53
FAMILY		SOCIAL PROBLEMS	
father	.80	society (U.S.)	.38
mother	.92	social class	.50
family	.84	social justice	.15
home	.79	social progress	- .04
mean	.84	mean	.25

The reliability of the coefficient of similarity measure was tested by comparing two groups obtained by splitting a larger group randomly into two halves; the coefficients produced on a sample of themes were then averaged. In a comparison of two split-half groups on 26 themes, a correlation of .73 was obtained. An earlier comparison resulted in an r of .82, calculated over 40 themes. The coefficient depends a great deal on the particular theme under consideration. Themes that are specific and concrete produce steep response distributions characterized by a few widely shared responses, or meaning elements. The theme **family**, for example, is specific and concrete, and for everybody if means to a certain extent father and mother. The themes **concern** and **anxiety** are less definite, and instead of everybody agreeing on a few particularly salient responses, people produce a broad diversity of responses. In this situation, low correlation does not necessarily indicate low reliability of the measure but may be a consequence of the indeterminate nature of the theme. In such a situation the stability of the measure may better estimated by considering how stable a coefficient is within particular themes rather than across all themes. To assess this stability, the coefficients obtained on the same themes for the two split-half groups were correlated over the 26 themes and produced an r of .89.

Certain Limitations of This Measure. Calculation of the similarity coefficient requires literal agreement; it does not take into account semantically closely related responses such as home and homely or synonyms such as house and home. Consequently, this measure is bound to underestimate the actual level of similarity. These biases are likely to increase the more the groups differ in their vocabularies. One could argue naturally that differences in vocabularies are not accidental and they themselves are likely to reflect on psychocultural distance. Nonetheless, as some of these differences in the words used do not correspond to similar differences in perceptions, they are likely to give a somewhat inflated estimate of the actual perceptual differences. These biases are usually not significant and they are in general randomly distributed; in other words, the bias is likely to be the same regardless of the words used. This should not interfere with the utility of the coefficient to provide a valid estimate of the relative level of semantic differences.

In other words, the coefficient of similarity cannot overestimate similarity but it may overestimate the degree of differences in the perceptions of two groups. This problem can be offset through the use of one of the other analytic techniques developed with the AGA method. Once the similarity coefficient has been used to identify themes where the greatest differences are, it is desirable to take a closer look by categorizing the semantically related responses into clusters. In the content analysis the total score of the response cluster (synonyms, partial synonyms), rather than the individual response scores, represents the main source of information by revealing the salience of the main components of perception and evaluation. Thus, for instance, the nature and intensity of emotional ties projected into people's relationships by a particular group emerges from the total score accumulated by such responses as *love*, *affection*, and *friendship*. In this analysis the scores of single responses (e.g., synonyms) are inconsequential. The differences between groups may then be identified by a comparison of the scores showing the salience of the main attitudinal and perceptual components.

While the similarity coefficient is useful in measuring overall similarity or distance, the content analysis may be used to identify more specific cultural dispositions such as the Puerto Ricans' tendency to see personal relations within the framework of family in contrast the disposition of Americans to see people as individuals independent of family.

262

<u>Intragroup Homogeneity.</u> A comparison of split-half groups shows how much agreement exists within a particular group on a particular stimulus theme. This intragroup agreement is affected by several factors.

One factor influencing the value of the coefficient is the size of the group. Based on 32 themes in the domains of family and health, mean coefficients were calculated using sample sizes of 13, 26, 52, 78, 104, and 156. They showed a distinct increase with the size of the groups compared. The rate of the increase is fast if we increase the size of small samples. For instance, an increase in sample size from 13 to 26 produced an increase of 27 points in the coefficient, while an increase from 52 to 104 produced an increase of only 9 points. Thus, there is a distinct decline in the growth rate in the case of large samples, and the coefficients come close to their plateau with a sample size of 200. Correlations do not generally increase just because the base of their calculation is extended. An explanation is likely to be found in the nature of mechanics of the calculation; the relatively large number of 0 scores obtained with a small sample decreases the correlation value.

Other important factors influencing the homogeneity coefficient relate to the nature and characteristics of individual themes under consideration. The variations are apparently explicable by the fact that some themes and domains are more concrete, definite, tangible (e.g., car, money), while others are more indeterminate, unobservable, abstract (equality, expectation).

These variations may be illustrated by calculating coefficients of homogeneity on 16 themes in the family domain (family, mother, father, home, etc.) using three different sample sizes: 13, 52, and 156. In contrast to the wide range of variation (-.12 to .70) observed at the level of the smallest sample, in the case of the largest sample the range was narrower (.72 to .96). Furthermore, the mean coefficient based on a sample size of 156 was .90, in strong contrast to the mean of .35 obtained with a sample size of 13. As a tentative explanation the phenomenon of "cultural sharing" (D'Andrade, 1972) seems appropriate. It follows from the rationale of this sharing phenomenon that larger groups, which provide a broader basis for observations, can be more completely described than smaller ones. These data underscore the importance of working with a sample size of at least 50.

ATTITUDES AND EVALUATIONS

THE EVALUATIVE DOMINANCE INDEX (EDI) AND THE CONNOTATION SCORE

How people evaluate ideas and events---ERA, arms embargo, human rights, legalization of marijuana---can be assessed without asking them directly. Attitudinal inferences are derived from the distribution of associative responses with positive, negative, and neutral connotation. Based on empirical evidence that the evaluative content of associative responses is a valid indicator of the evaluative content of the stimulus word (Staats and Staats, 1959), a simple attitude index was developed to express the relative dominance of responses with positive or negative connotations (Szalay, Windle, & Lysne, 1970). First, the proportions of positive and negative categories are assessed by two independent judges who place the associative responses into positive, negative, and neutral groups. (In previous experiments this grouping task was performed with an interjudge agreement of .93 measured by product-moment correlation across categories.) Next, using the total response score for each of the three groupings, an index of evaluative dominance is calculated by the following formula:

$$\text{EDI} = \frac{\text{scores of positive responses} - \text{scores of negative responses}}{\text{scores of all responses}} \times 100$$

Based on this formula, group indices are obtained on each stimulus for each group. The distance between groups in their evaluations is measured by comparing EDI scores using Pearson's r coefficient.

A higher index implies more intense group evaluation, in either a positive or negative direction. The example below shows that Koreans are more negative in their evaluation of political systems, particularly communism. Their less negative evaluation of poverty and beggars may indicate more familiarity with or tolerance of these problems.

Table 6

EVALUATIVE DOMINANCE INDICES FOR U.S. AND KOREAN GROUPS

Theme	U.S. Group	Korean Group
family	25	22
proud	12	28
educated	51	51
knowledge	50	44
offense	-27	-53
capitalism	10	- 4
communism	-14	-32
equality	19	20
poor	-58	-28
beggar	-63	-42

The EDI measure is described in A Study of American and Korean Attitudes and Values Through Associative Group Analysis (Szalay, Lysne, and Brent, 1970).

A direct method of assessing attitudes can also be used. It involves asking the respondents to give a general evaluation of each stimulus word after performing the verbal association task. To express whether the words mean something positive, negative, or neutral, they use the following scale:

+ 3 - strongly positive, favorable connotation   - 1 - slightly negative connotation
+ 2 - quite positive, favorable connotation   - 2 - quite negative connotation
+ 1 - slightly positive connotation   - 3 - strongly negative connotation
.....0 - neutral (neither positive nor negative conn.)

A mean group attitude score is obtained for each stimulus word. Distance in evaluations is then measured by Pearson's r coefficient comparing two groups across stimulus words.

RELATEDNESS OF THEMES, CONCEPTS

THE AFFINITY INDEX

Measures of meaning similarity have considerable potential to assess how particular groups organize and interrelate elements of their environment. The associative affinity index measure indicates which words are related by a group to which other words and to what extent. The degree of relationship among these elements of a group's subjective world view is an important dimension of their cognitive organization. It is defined as the shared associative meaning of stimulus words as measured by the number of associations produced in common to these words (Szalay & Brent, 1965). Similar concepts based on various theoretical positions are: overlap coefficient (Deese, 1962); verbal relatedness (Garskof and Houston, 1963); mutual frequency (Cofer, 1957); co-occurrence measure (Flavell & Flavell, 1959); and measure of stimulus equivalence (Bousfield, Whitmarsh, and Danick, 1958). These concepts, however, use single-word associative responses rather than continued associations. The associative affinity index, a modified relatedness measure similar to those reviewed by Marshall and Cofer (1963), was developed for use with continued associations.

The index of interword affinity (IIA) measure the relationship of one theme (A) to another (B) for a particular group based on the responses in common to the two themes. The formula for the affinity of them A to B is as follows:

$$\frac{\text{score for responses} + \text{score for direct elicitation}}{\text{total score A}} \underset{(A\text{------}>B)}{\text{in common}} \times 1000 = \begin{array}{l}\text{index of interword}\\ \text{associative affinity}\\ (A\text{------}>B)\end{array}$$

The formula for the affinity of theme B to theme A is:

$$\frac{\text{score for responses} + \text{score for direct elicitation}}{\text{total score B}} \underset{(B\text{------}>A)}{\text{in common}} \times 1000 = \begin{array}{l}\text{index of interword}\\ \text{associative affinity}\\ (B\text{------}>A)\end{array}$$

In the two lists in the table below *beggar* and *poverty* were responses to the two stimulus words under consideration. The lower score of the response in common (e.g., 38 for *beggar*) is used in the calculation because that is the portion that is common to both. (Although *hunger* and *hungry* are very similar as well as *poor* and *poverty*, they are treated as separate responses here.) Also, in the calculation is the score of the response to one stimulus word that is identical to the other stimulus word (e.g., the stimulus **HUNGRY** eliciting the response *poor*). They are said to elicit each other directly; hence, what is here measured is called direct elicitation.

Table 6

INDEX OF INTERWORD ASSOCIATIVE AFFINITY

Stimulus A: HUNGRY		Stimulus B: POOR	
Response	Score (Colombian Group)	Response	Score (Colombian Group)
meal	107	hungry	77
food	73	money	71
hunger	65	poverty	44
poor	59	beggar	38
beggar	43	necessity	30
poverty	38	house	28
Total Score A	385	Total Score B	288

The score of the responses in common to HUNGRY (76) plus the score of the directly elicited response (59) indicates the total degree of shared meaning. The score representing the shared portion of the total meaning reaction cannot be taken by itself or it would be merely a function of the length of the response lists. Therefore, it is divided by the total score of all responses (e.g., to HUNGRY, 385). The score representing the shared portion of the total meaning reaction is thus expressed as a fraction of the total score representing the total meaning reaction. This fraction is multiplied by 1000 in order to make it an integral number. The resulting number is called the interword affinity index, here calculated for HUNGRY to POOR:

$$\frac{76 + 59}{385} \times 1000 = 351 = \text{index of interword associative affinity, HUNGRY to POOR}$$

If the relationship of POOR to HUNGRY is being considered, the index would be different: the score representing shared meaning plus the score for the direct elicitation of *hungry* (77) would be divided by the total score for POOR (288), giving an index of 531.

The following matrix shows the relationship of eight themes from the motivational and economic domains. The generally higher indexes for the Black group suggest a stronger relationship between motivational themes and economic matters. On the relationship of single themes, the table shows that the Black group sees a relationship between expectation and unemployment, which does not emerge from the White group's responses.

Table 7

AFFINITY RELATIONSHIP OF MOTIVATIONAL AND ECONOMIC THEMES FOR BLACK (B) AMD WHITE SAMPLES

STIMULUS WORD A	GROUP	STIMULUS WORD B AND DIRECTION OF RELATIONSHIP															
		Goal		Expectation		Desire		Valuable		The rich		The poor		Unemployment		Prosperity	
		A-B	B-A	A-B	B-A	A-B	B-A	A-B	B-A	A-B	B-A	A-B	B-A	A-B	B-A	A-B	B-A
Prosperity	W	163	216	182	111	134	214	167	358	259	531	133	252	96	162		
	B	190	361	243	237	151	346	139	398	202	521	157	365	131	263		
Unemployent	W	27	21	0	0	53	50	60	76	158	160	156	204				
	B	117	110	181	88	82	94	87	124	179	210	227	313				
The poor	W	66	46	25	8	146	123	97	110	397	291						
	B	128	105	319	97	156	154	122	151	270	253						
The rich	W	82	63	59	21	103	96	257	323								
	B	134	108	193	80	200	194	308	375								
Valuable	W	136	84	76	22	211	157										
	B	198	131	158	54	254	203										
Desire	W	220	182	330	113												
	B	132	110	205	87												
Expectation	W	89	237														
	B	97	224														

Indexes on single word pairs provide empirical data on single relationships; index averages calculated on the affinity of one word with a set of words representing a particular domain have more generality. Indexes calculated between domains may be expected to gauge cognitive organization at an even higher level of generality by revealing how closely interrelated are such areas for a particular group.

The reliability of this index in split-half comparisons was in the range of .90 (Szalay and Windle, 1968). The validity of this measure was estimated in a comparative study based on correlations of this measure with other independent measures: similarity judgment .73; judgment of relationship .77; grouping task .84. (The calculations were based on 66 index pairs.) (Szalay and Bryson, 1972).

More information on the affinity measure can be obtained in Communication Lexicon on Three South Korean Audiences (Szalay et al., 1971b) and in "Psychological Meaning: Comparative Analyses and Theoretical Implications", Journal of Personality and Social Psychology (Szalay and Bryson, 1974).

RELIABILITY AND VALIDITY OF ASSOCIATIVE RESPONSES

The continued verbal association task used in the Associative Group Analysis method produces extensive response distributions characterized by contrasts of high and low response frequencies. Even though conclusions are never based on a single response, the specific responses are the fundamental mosaic elements of information obtained in the association tasks and thus it is necessary to determine how their reliability. The answer to this question depends naturally on the number of people who gave the particular response and on the score the response accumulated based on its rank places of emission. The use of continued associations required the development of a weighting procedure to account for the differences in information value between first responses and the responses produced later at lower rankings. An empirically founded weighting system was derived based on the differential stability of responses observed in test-retest results. The following reliability scores were obtained as a function of the rank place.

Table 8

STABILITY OF RESPONSES DEPENDING ON THEIR RANK PLACE

Stability and	Rank of Response									
Weights	1st	2nd	3rd	4th	5th	6th	7th	8th	9th	10th
Stability, percent of recurrence in retest	.60	.48	.42	.34	.32	.30	.25	.20	.15	.11
Weighting score based on the stability	6	5	4	3	3	3	3	2	2	1

This suggests that the average stability of a single response in continued association tasks is .32. This mean value represents the stability of an average response for an average person. The mean stability substantially increases when calculated on group basis. The increase becomes explicable by the observation that while a particular person may fail in retest to give the same response he gave in the first test, it frequently happens that other subjects will use the word as a response in the retest although they may not have given it in the first test. Thus, particularly the common responses substantially increase this stability on group basis.

As the Associative Group Analysis method draws inferences on groups rather than on individuals, the stability of responses on group basis requires particular attention. The group response lists representing response frequencies weighted by their individual rank places serve as the data base for such inferences. With focus on the shared responses of the group, responses given by only one person are disregarded as idiosyncratic. To assess the stability of group responses, split-half comparisons were made of a group of 100 subjects split randomly. Comparing the group response lists of the two groups of 50 subjects, an average stability of .61 was obtained. Interestingly, this stability increased gradually when split-half groups of larger sizes were compared (N = 100, N = 200). This phenomenon bears apparently on the cultural sharing phenomenon which has been described by D'Andrade (1972), but its implications go beyond our present concern with stability.

In connection with the problem of stability of response lists and the average stability of particular responses, it should be pointed out that this stability is also affected by the stimulus words considered. Certain stimulus words are specific and produce steep response distributions focusing on a definite set of responses. Others are less definite and produce responses with great intragroup variations. This definiteness depends partially on the characteristics of the stimulus theme such as its concreteness and specificity; it also depends on the homogeneity of the group's experiences in respect to the stimulus.

These different variables cause considerable variations in the stability of responses. Thus, the average response stability value reported above is a rough estimate. When more precise data are needed, as in the case of the evaluation of changes, learning and training effects, it is desirable to obtain stability data on the relevant themes in separate split-half stability tests. The stability of specific responses as a function of the size of responses is discussed in the relation to the problem of statistical significance.

Although the Associative Group Analysis method is used to derive information on diverse categories of variables, the inferences are usually based on entire response distributions or clusters of responses rather than on single individual responses. Thus, although the measures are based on responses, the problem of validity can be examined more meaningfully in the context of the particular measures rather than single responses.

REFERENCES

Bousfield, W.A., Whitmarsh, G.A., & Danick, J.J. (1958). Partial response identities in verbal generalization. *Psychological Reports, 4,* 703-713.

Cofer, C.N. (1957). Associative commonality and ranked similarity of certain words from Haagen's list. *Psychological Reports, 3,* 603-606.

D'Andrade, R.G., Quinn, N., Nerlove, S.B., & Romney, A.K. Categories of disease in American-English and Mexican-Spanish. In A.K. Romney, R. Shepard, & S.B. Nerlove (Eds.), *Theory and applications in the behavioral sciences.* New York: Academic Press.

Deese, J. (1962). Form-class and the determinants of association. *Journal of Verbal Learning and Verbal Behavior, 1,* 79-84.

Flavell, J.H. & Flavell, E.R. (1959). One determinant of judged semantic and associative connection between words. *Journal of Experimental Psychology, 63,* 159-165.

Garskof, B.E. & Houston, J.P. (1963). Measurement of verbal relatedness: An idiographic approach. *Psychological Review, 70,* 277-88.

Marshall, G.R. & Cofer, C.N. (1963). Associative indices as measures of word-relatedness: A summary and comparison of ten methods. *Journal of Verbal Learning and Verbal Behavior, 1,* 408-21.

Noble, C. (1952). An analysis of meaning. *Psychology Review, 54,* 421-440.

Osgood, C.E., Suci, G.J., & Tannenbaum, P.H. (1957). *The measurement of meaning.* Urbana: University of Illinois Press.

Staats, A.W. & Staats, C.K. (1959). Meaning and m: Correlated but separate. *Psychological Review, 66,* 136-44.

Szalay, L.B. & Brent, J. (1965). *Cultural meanings and values: A method of empirical assessment.* Washington, D. C.: The American University.

Szalay, L.B. & Brent (1967). The analysis of cultural meanings through free verbal associations. *Journal of Social Psychology, 72,* 161-187.

Szalay, L.B. & Bryson, J.A. (1972). *Measurement of meaning through verbal association and other empirical methods.* Kensington, Md.: American Institutes for Research.

Szalay, L.B. & Bryson, J.A. (1973). Measurement of psychocultural distance: A comparison of American blacks and whites. *Journal of Personality and Social Psychology, 26,* 166-177.

Salay, L.B. & Bryson, J.A. (1974). Psychological meaning: Comparative analyses and theoretical implications. *Journal of Personality and Social Psychology, 30,* 860-870.

Szalay, L.B. & Deese, J. (1978). *Subjective meaning and culture: An assessment through word associations.* Hillsdale, N.J.: Lawrence Erlbaum/Wiley & Sons.

Szalay, L.B., Lysne, D.A., & Brent, J.E. (1970). *A study of American and Korean attitudes and values through Associative Group Analysis.* Kensington, Md.: Center for Research in Social Systems, American Institutes for Research.

Szalay, L.B., Lysne, D.A., & Bryson, J.A. (1972). Designing and testing cogent communication. *Journal of Cross-Cultural Psychology, 3,* 247-258.

Szalay, L.B., Moon, W.T., & Bryson, J.A. (1971a). *A lexicon of selected U.S.-Korean Communication Themes.* Kensington, MD: American Institutes for Research, Center for Research in Social Systems.

Szalay, L.B., Moon, W.T., & Bryson, J.A. (1971b). *Communication lexicon on three South Korean audiences: Social, national, and motivational domains.* Kensington, Md.: American Institutes for Research.

Szalay, L.B. & Windle, C. (1968). Relative influence of linguistic versus cultural factors on free verbal associations. *Psychological Reports, 12,* 43-51.

Szalay, Windle, C., & Lysne, D.A. (1970). Attitude measurement by free verbal associations. *Journal of Social Psychology, 82,* 43-55.

Triandis, H.C. (1964). Cultural influences upon cognitive processes. In L. Berkowitz (Ed.), *Advances in experimental social psychology, 1.* New York: Academic Press.